Lady Anne Clifford

The Great Picture, the centre panel of the Appleby Triptych, 1646/8 (Reproduced by courtesy of Abbot Hall Art Gallery, Kendal)

LADY ANNE CLIFFORD

Countess of Pembroke,

Dorset and Montgomery

(1590–1676)

Richard T. Spence

SUTTON PUBLISHING

First published in 1997 by
Sutton Publishing Limited · Phoenix Mill
Thrupp · Stroud · Gloucestershire · GL5 2BU

British Library Cataloguing in Publication Data
A catalogue record for this book is available from the British Library

ISBN 0 7509 1311 8

Title page illustration: *Lady Anne's Sackville-Clifford arms and crests, Book of Coats
of Arms (Cumbria County Record Office, Kendal, WD/Hoth/A988/14. Photo: the
author)*

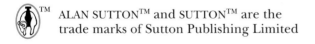 ALAN SUTTON™ and SUTTON™ are the
trade marks of Sutton Publishing Limited

Typeset in 10/12 New Baskerville.
Typesetting and origination by
Sutton Publishing Limited.
Printed in Great Britain by
Butler & Tanner, Frome, Somerset.

Contents

For Graham and Margaret

List of Illustrations

GENEALOGICAL TABLES

TABLES

MAPS

Acknowledgements

I am particularly grateful to the owners of the four principal collections of records relating to Lady Anne Clifford for giving me full access to them in preparing this study and making available illustrations: to Lord Hothfield for the Hothfield MSS deposited with the Cumbria County Record Office, Kendal; Hugh T. Fattorini Esq. for the Skipton MSS deposited with the Yorkshire Archaeological Society; Lord Sackville and the Trustees of the Knole Second Trust for the Sackville MSS now at the Centre for Kentish Studies, Maidstone; and the Duke of Devonshire and the Trustees of the Chatsworth Settlement for the Clifford and Burlington papers at Chatsworth.

I am also indebted to the following for permission to examine and use the documents in their possession and for providing illustrations: the Duke of Northumberland for the Syon MSS at Alnwick Castle; the Marquess of Salisbury for the Hatfield MSS; the Marquess of Northampton for the Compton Family Papers at Castle Ashby; the Earl of Pembroke and the Trustees of the Wilton House Trust for the Wilton House Records at the Wiltshire County Record Office, Trowbridge; the Earl of Lonsdale for the Lowther MSS in the Cumbria County Record Office, Carlisle; Lord de Clifford; His Grace the Archbishop of Canterbury and the Trustees of Lambeth Palace for the Lambeth Palace archives; Robert Hasell-McCosh for the Dalemain Collection; Mrs Natalie Hodgson; the Treasurer and the Masters of the Bench of Lincoln's Inn for the Hale MSS; and the Master of Queen's College, Oxford, for access to the college library archives.

My warm thanks are due to archivists and others who facilitated my researches or enabled me to obtain illustrations, notably Peter Day, Keeper of Collections, Michael Pearman and Thomas Askey at Chatsworth; Robin Harcourt-Williams at Hatfield House; Dr Colin Shrimpton at Alnwick Castle; Peter Mackay at Castle Ashby; Ray Stedman at Wilton House; Miss Lavinia Wellicome at Woburn Abbey; Jim Grisenthwaite and Richard Hall at the Cumbria County Record Offices; Christian Barnes at Abbot Hall Art Gallery, Kendal; Mrs Sylvia Thomas of the West Yorkshire Archives Service; Simon D. Hobbs at the Wiltshire County Record Office; and the staff of the Centre for Kentish Studies, Maidstone, and the Greater London Record Office.

For my understanding of the portraits of Lady Anne and her relations, I owe much to Dr Helen C. Gladstone, Dr Anne Laurence, Miss V.J.H. Slowe and Miss Santina M. Levey. The Courtauld Institute, University of London, the Rijksmuseum, Amsterdam, and the RKD, the Netherlands Institute for Art

History, The Hague, generously allowed me to examine their extensive archive collections. D.J.H. Clifford kindly made available to me the prints he owns and John Higgs provided the print of North Hall.

I have acknowledged in the Notes the help of a number of scholars with whom I have exchanged information to our mutual benefit, in particular the late Revd John Breay whose researches into Westmorland history overlapped mine. The interpretation of documentary and published sources and the views expressed on Lady Anne in this study, in many respects markedly different from those of previous writers, are my own.

Abbreviations

Accounts Lady Anne's Westmorland accounts, 1665–8 (KRO, WD/Hoth/A988/17) and 1668–75 (KRO, JAC 495/7)

BL British Library

Bolton MSS Chatsworth, Bolton MSS

Books Lady Anne's Great Books of Record (KRO, WD/Hoth/A988/10/1, 2, 3)

Catalogue S.J. MacPherson and V.A.J. Slowe, 'Proud Northern Lady': *Lady Anne Clifford 1590–1676*, Exhibition Catalogue, Kendal, Abbot Hall Art Gallery, 1990

CKS Centre for Kentish Studies, Kent County Record Office, Maidstone

Clay J.W. Clay, 'The Clifford Family', *YAJ*, xviii, 1905

Clifford Hugh Clifford, *The House of Clifford*, Chichester, Phillimore, 1987

CPR *Calendar of Patent Rolls*

CRO Cumbria County Record Office, Carlisle

CSPD *Calendar of State Papers, Domestic*

Currey Chatsworth, Currey Papers

Diaries *The Diaries of Lady Anne Clifford*, ed. D.J.H. Clifford, Stroud, Alan Sutton Publishing, 1990

DNB *Dictionary of National Biography*

GEC *The Complete Peerage*, ed. G.E. Cokayne, 1910–59

Gilson J.P. Gilson, *Lives of Lady Anne Clifford, Countess of Dorset, Pembroke and Montgomery (1590–1676) and of Her Parents*, Roxburghe Club, 1916

HMC Historical Manuscripts Commission

Holmes Martin Holmes, *Proud Northern Lady. Lady Anne Clifford 1590–1676*, Chichester, Phillimore, reprint, 1984

KRO Cumbria County Record Office, Kendal

Lismore Chatsworth, Lismore Papers

MSS Manuscripts

N&B J. Nicolson and R. Burn, *The History and Antiquities of the Counties of Westmorland and Cumberland*, 2 vols, 1777

PRO Public Record Office, London

Rainbow *A Sermon preached at Appleby, April 14, 1676 at the Funeral of the Rt Hon Anne Clifford, Countess of Pembroke, Dorset & Montgomery*, by Edward Rainbow, Bishop of Carlisle (1839)

Sedgewick George Sedgewick's MS, in N&B, I, 294–304

Spence R.T. Spence, *The Privateering Earl: George Clifford, 3rd Earl of Cumberland, 1558–1605*, Stroud, Alan Sutton Publishing, 1995

Spence 'Earls' R.T. Spence, 'The Cliffords, Earls of Cumberland, 1579–1646: a study of their fortunes based on their household and estate accounts' (unpub. Ph.D. thesis, London University, 1959)

STC A.W.Pollard & G.R. Redgrave, *A Short-Title Catalogue 1475–1640*, 2nd edn, 3 vols, The Bibliographical Society, 1976–91

VCH *Victoria County History*

WD/Hoth KRO, Hothfield MSS

Whitaker T.D. Whitaker, *The History and Antiquities of the Deanery of Craven in the County of York*, 3rd edn, ed. A.W. Morant, reprint, Skipton, 1973

Williamson G.C. Williamson, *Lady Anne Clifford, Countess of Dorset, Pembroke & Montgomery. 1590–1676. Her Life, Letters and Work*, Kendal, 1922.

YAJ *Yorkshire Archaeological Journal*

YAS Yorkshire Archaeological Society

YAS, DD121 Skipton MSS

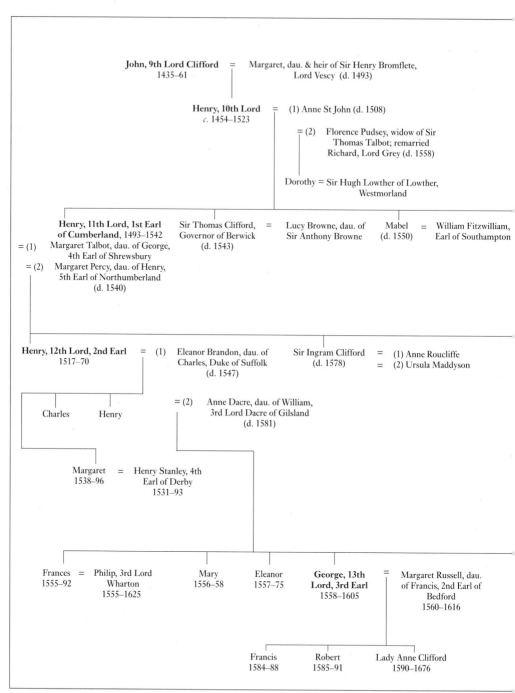

John, 9th Lord Clifford = Margaret, dau. & heir of Sir Henry Bromflete,
1435–61 Lord Vescy (d. 1493)

Henry, 10th Lord = (1) Anne St John (d. 1508)
c. 1454–1523
= (2) Florence Pudsey, widow of Sir
Thomas Talbot; remarried
Richard, Lord Grey (d. 1558)

Dorothy = Sir Hugh Lowther of Lowther,
Westmorland

Henry, 11th Lord, 1st Earl Sir Thomas Clifford, = Lucy Browne, dau. of Mabel = William Fitzwilliam,
of Cumberland, 1493–1542 Governor of Berwick Sir Anthony Browne (d. 1550) Earl of Southampton
= (1) Margaret Talbot, dau. of George, (d. 1543)
4th Earl of Shrewsbury
= (2) Margaret Percy, dau. of Henry,
5th Earl of Northumberland
(d. 1540)

Henry, 12th Lord, 2nd Earl = (1) Eleanor Brandon, dau. of Sir Ingram Clifford = (1) Anne Roucliffe
1517–70 Charles, Duke of Suffolk (d. 1578) = (2) Ursula Maddyson
(d. 1547)

= (2) Anne Dacre, dau. of William,
Charles Henry 3rd Lord Dacre of Gilsland
(d. 1581)

Margaret = Henry Stanley, 4th
1538–96 Earl of Derby
1531–93

Frances = Philip, 3rd Lord Mary Eleanor **George, 13th** = Margaret Russell, dau.
1555–92 Wharton 1556–58 1557–75 **Lord, 3rd Earl** of Francis, 2nd Earl of
1555–1625 **1558–1605** Bedford
1560–1616

Francis Robert Lady Anne Clifford
1584–88 1585–91 1590–1676

The earls of Cumberland

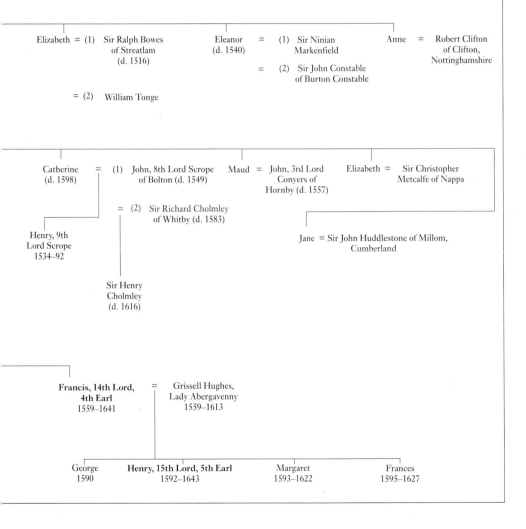

Elizabeth = (1) Sir Ralph Bowes
                 of Streatlam
                 (d. 1516)

Eleanor = (1) Sir Ninian
(d. 1540)   Markenfield

         = (2) Sir John Constable
                 of Burton Constable

Anne = Robert Clifton
         of Clifton,
         Nottinghamshire

= (2) William Tonge

Catherine = (1) John, 8th Lord Scrope
(d. 1598)   of Bolton (d. 1549)

Maud = John, 3rd Lord
         Conyers of
         Hornby (d. 1557)

Elizabeth = Sir Christopher
              Metcalfe of Nappa

           = (2) Sir Richard Cholmley
                   of Whitby (d. 1583)

Henry, 9th
Lord Scrope
1534–92

Jane = Sir John Huddlestone of Millom,
                 Cumberland

Sir Henry
Cholmley
(d. 1616)

Francis, 14th Lord, = Grissell Hughes,
     4th Earl   Lady Abergavenny
     1559–1641   1559–1613

George   Henry, 15th Lord, 5th Earl   Margaret   Frances
1590   1592–1643   1593–1622   1595–1627

Lady Anne Clifford: Upbringing and Maternal Influences

1590–1609

Lady Anne Clifford was conceived on 1 May 1589 in her uncle Philip, 3rd Lord Wharton's house in Cannon Row, Westminster, born at her father's great castle at Skipton in Craven in the West Riding of Yorkshire on 30 January 1590 and baptized three weeks later at Holy Trinity parish church. By ancestry, birth and upbringing she was destined for high noble rank. Her father George, 3rd Earl of Cumberland, was descended from the Cliffords, barons Clifford and earls of Cumberland, one of the oldest noble families in the realm, whose roots could be traced back to before the Conquest. Her mother, Countess Margaret, was the youngest daughter of Francis Russell, 2nd Earl of Bedford, a great landowner who enjoyed royal favour as one of Queen Elizabeth I's privy councillors. Marriage with noblemen of comparable standing, in 1609 to Richard Sackville, 3rd Earl of Dorset, and in 1630 to Philip Herbert, 4th Earl of Pembroke, assured Anne's exalted status in Stuart society for the rest of her long life.

Even so, she might have passed virtually unnoticed into history, like so many of her near-anonymous noble contemporaries. High rank, even when allied to intelligence, learning and strength of character, did not guarantee prominence in early modern England, let alone the acclaim of posterity. Enduring fame has had to be earned by achievement or notoriety. Lady Anne's particular distinction is at the same time intensely private and exemplary. It has little to do with the conduct of national and public affairs under the Stuarts. She stands out because of her spirited response to the adverse circumstances which beset her from an early age and, contrasting, her dominant role in later life as a dowager countess with baronial titles and great estates held in her own right in the north of England. Altogether, hers is rightly considered a unique and illuminating contribution to life and manners in the seventeenth century, a judgement which this study will endorse and amplify.

Lady Anne became a potential heiress as a very young child. Earl George's elder son, Lord Francis, had died aged six on 11 December 1589, a few weeks before she was born. His other boy, Lord Robert, also six, died on 24 May 1591, when Anne was fifteen months old. From this time, because there were no more children, Anne was the earl's only direct heir. To her and through her would legitimately descend the centuries-old Clifford noble line. As comprehension of this slowly dawned on the girl during the next few years, she was also made aware that her father intended to exclude her from the inheritance in favour of his brother

1. George Clifford, 3rd Earl of Cumberland (1558–1605), artist unknown (Reproduced by permission of the Duke of Devonshire and the Trustees of the Chatsworth Settlement. Photo: the author)

Francis. In his will made early in 1598 prior to leaving on his great Puerto Rican enterprise, the earl generously provided for Anne in case of his death, though only as his daughter, not as his heir. It was Francis who stood to get George's big estates in Westmorland and Craven in the West Riding of Yorkshire which, with his own gentry properties in the East Riding, would support his standing as 4th Earl of Cumberland.[1]

Hereon, guided and prompted by her mother, Anne gradually focused her hopes and ambitions on attaining her father's baronial titles and landed inheritance. This objective she tenaciously pursued whatever the obstruction or opposition until her dying day, 22 March 1676, at the age of eighty-six. The manifold facets of her life-long struggle will be the central theme of this study, as indeed they were in reality for her. The biographical content, however, will be much wider in scope and will reveal far more than is currently understood about her attitudes, actions, behaviour and personality, presenting a more rounded picture of her complex character than available hitherto. New light will be thrown on her relations with her mother, her husbands Dorset and Pembroke and her daughters' families. Particular emphasis will be placed in the later chapters on her life as dowager countess on her northern estates and on the rich legacy of artistic patronage and building for which she is revered in Westmorland and Craven to this day.

The parental influences on Anne's upbringing were decidedly unequal. This was not unusual. Noblemen gave far more attention to their sons, their wives more to the daughters. Moreover, Earl George was frequently away for long periods preparing and commanding his privateering fleets and attending the queen at Court, especially in public celebrations, performing in his role as Champion. Had their marriage been happier the earl and countess would perhaps have spent more time together at their London homes, the Charterhouse 1593/5 and the mansion in nearby Clerkenwell 1595–1605. Instead, they often lived apart, with little mutual warmth and only occasional reconciliation. Countess Margaret was offended by her husband's profligacy and mounting debts, his long-standing affair with a 'lady of quality' and, after Lord Robert's death in 1591, his effective designation of Francis as his heir instead of Anne.

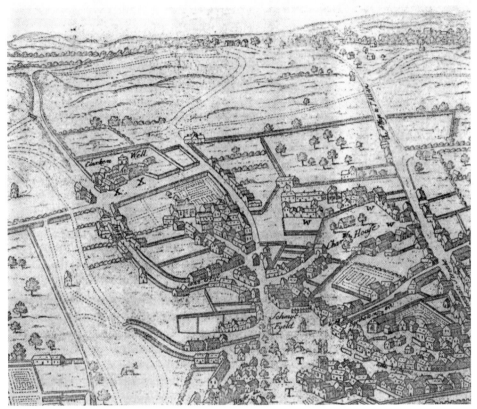

2. Clerkenwell Green and the Charterhouse, from the Agas map, 1633 (Corporation of London. The Greater London Record Office (Maps and Prints. FA 6603))

Consequently, she frequently resided in the countryside with her Russell relatives, either at their family home Chenies in Buckinghamshire or at North Hall in Hertfordshire, home of her sister Anne, Countess of Warwick, or sometimes with her other sister Elizabeth, Countess of Bath, but also with her aunt Mrs Alice Elmers at Lilford, Northamptonshire, who had tended her until she was eight years old. Living with relatives would be to Anne's benefit as an only child because she had companionship within those households and friendships with children of her own age. Their stays at Lilford, Anne comments, caused both her mother and herself ever after 'to love a country life the better, they being there better seasoned with the grounds of goodness and religion'.[2]

Earl George probably saw little of his daughter when she was very young. Nevertheless, Dr Whitaker's judgement on him as a negligent and thoughtless parent is harsh and unjustified. The earl regarded 'Nan', as he called her, with paternal affection. In the late summer of 1596, when she was only six, he sent his coach and horses for her to join him at Court until Michaelmas. She would be present with her parents at social gatherings until their formal separation in 1601. After that, the earl may have met Anne rarely until James I's accession when, as she recalled, he sometimes visited them at Clerkenwell. Anne

3. Chenies, the Russell family's manor house in Buckinghamshire (Lt-Col. A. MacLeod Matthews. Photo: the author)

4. North Hall (Northaw), the Warwicks' mansion in Hertfordshire, c. 1700 (John Higgs)

accompanied her mother in Queen Anne's train and was present at the Coronation, which her parents attended in their robes, and at the earl's Grafton House in Northamptonshire where he twice entertained the king, queen and Court. Anne recorded in her diary that at Grafton in June 1603 her parents' dislike of each other was obvious, though when they happened to meet her father acknowledged her and spoke to her, if only briefly.[3]

The least happy instance of Earl George's influence on his daughter is his refusal to let her learn a foreign language so that, like her mother, she read only in translation throughout her life. This may have been an expression of his dislike of foreigners during a dangerous war in which his fleets participated by plundering not just enemy ships but often so-called neutrals too. But it could have had deeper origins in the xenophobia of the circle of Puritan and anti-Spanish overseas expansionists among whom he spent his formative years. George's guardian, his future father-in-law the earl of Bedford, was one of the leading Puritan noblemen and it would be no coincidence that a book warning against association with foreigners was dedicated to his young successor in 1592. This was *Epistola de peregrinatione Italia* by Justus Lipsius, a distinguished Latinist from the University of Leyden, translated by Sir John Stradling. Ignorance of languages acted as a barrier to association with foreigners both in the flesh and through the wealth of their literature. There is a marked strand of insularity, which elevated Englishness and English history and traditions and rejected foreign influences, discernible in writers with whom both Earl George and Countess Margaret were connected during the last decades of the Elizabethan era.[4]

A much more favourable view of Earl George as father is given by Anne herself after she had stayed with him pleasantly on her own at Grafton in August 1605. By then she had reached marriageable age and the young gallants at Court had an eye on her. Though he saw her infrequently, the earl intended to exercise his parental right over the choice of her husband. He and Francis had visited the Countess of Shrewsbury, Bess of Hardwick, in July and discussed the possibility of a double marriage, Anne with Lord Cavendish's son William and her cousin Henry (Francis's son) with Cavendish's daughter. This would have been a very suitable match in terms of equal social status, not to mention kinship with the formidable Bess who was on good terms with Countess Margaret. But, as Anne told her mother, the earl would not impose his wishes on them. He had discussed the marriage a great deal with her and 'hath promised me that there shall nothing pass for any match whatsoever, but that your consent should be asked as a chief matter'. After the earl's death, the proposal went no further. William Cavendish was to succeed in 1626 as 2nd Earl of Devonshire. It is one of the little ironies of history that his descendants were to obtain by marriage Bolton Abbey, Barden Tower and other Clifford estates in Craven which Anne and her mother so coveted after Earl George's death.[5]

Both the earl and countess would be sensitive about forcing Anne to marry against her will because of their own memories of being wed contrary to their desires. In pondering Anne's marriage, the earl displays not only consideration for her well-being but a fond attachment to her, a far cry from the 'thoughtless' image usually portrayed. His last letter to his wife included a homily which ruefully reflected on his own past shortcomings. In 'the nearest love of my heart', he wrote,

'I desire thee, to take great care that sweet Nan, whom God bless, may be carefully brought up in the fear of God, not to delight in worldly vanities, which I too well know be but baits to draw her out of the heavenly kingdom'. No doubt the words were meant for Anne's eyes because Countess Margaret had never wavered from those sentiments. Anne carefully kept the letter and endorsed it. Even better, as will be seen, she took those precepts to heart, pulling herself up sharp when, a decade later, she found herself sliding into the gambling and carelessness with money which had contributed so greatly to her father's financial ruin.[6]

Much will be hinted at in this study about Anne's remembrance of her father. His treatment of her over the inheritance, it is sometimes argued, made her reluctant until later in life to laud him and his renowned activities. This view is mistaken. There is no doubting her pride in his high rank, his maritime deeds, his jousting prowess as Elizabeth I's Champion and his Garter knighthood. During her married years she had little opportunity to do his memory justice, but her desire to do so is evident from her middle twenties. If there is any sign of reserve in her regard for him it is that although she often referred to his birth in Brougham Castle she never mentioned the anniversary of his death at which she and her mother were present and only once the anniversary of his funeral at Skipton, which they did not attend, possibly to her regret.[7] It may be that the pain of bereavement was too intense for her in recollecting his death, following as it did so quickly her happy visit to him at Grafton; or perhaps she could not forgive the hurt she felt when the dispositions in his will became known. Judging by the feelings he expressed in his last letter, it was likely to be the former rather than the latter.

The course of Earl George's eventful career is too well known to comment on except where it is relevant to this discussion of his daughter's life. However, it is worth reiterating his reasons for setting aside Anne and bequeathing his lands to his brother. If the practical dominated, there was an ethical imperative. He had accumulated enormous debts mainly because of his privateering losses. To help reduce them, he raised big sums from his estates by sales and leases which permanently diminished the value of the Clifford inheritance. Yet he still owed a great deal when he died. He was convinced that in his brother lay the only hope of clearing the debts and that could be done only if Francis had the income from all his properties, those in Craven immediately and the Westmorland lordships, Countess Margaret's jointure estate, as soon as she died.

Honouring the debts was for George a moral commitment, a matter of conscience. But he also had a personal obligation to safeguard his sureties, those friends and officers whose own lands would otherwise be exposed to litigation by his creditors. Francis, as his successor in the earldom, willingly took over all those responsibilities. How onerous the task proved for him and his son Earl Henry is shown by the fact that the slate was not finally cleared (and even then with much defaulting by him and foregoing by the creditors) until more than sixty years after George's death. Anne herself, like her mother and both her husbands, was spared the importuning of her father's creditors and the anxieties over payment of the debts which so weighed down her uncle and cousin for the rest of their lives. Anne stressed her father left his lands to Francis because of his love for his brother and for the advancement of the heirs male, but never mentions the matter of debts and the obligations which went with them.[8]

Countess Margaret has tended to be a shadowy figure, visible more by reflection from the grand images of her husband and daughter than as a person of substance in her own right. In fact, she merits a thoughtful assessment. There is not space here to do her justice, but an outline will indicate how varied her interests were and more will be noticed in later chapters. She was from the outset Anne's mentor and exemplar and if either of them is enhanced by a comparison it is more likely the mother than the daughter. Indeed, only by considering the countess's attitudes and policies can Anne's be fully appreciated. Anne captured the essence of her mother in the word pictures she has left of her. Portraits attest the accuracy of her description of the countess as having 'a very well favoured face with sweete and quick gray eyes and a comely personage'. Her behaviour was 'graceful' and she was civil and courteous to all manner of people. Like all the Russell girls she was intelligent and well-educated. In Anne's words, she 'had a sharp natural wit' and was extremely knowledgeable. There were few books of worth translated into English that she did not read. By these 'that excellent mind of hers was much enriched, which even by nature was endowed with the seeds of the four moral virtues, Prudence, Justice, Fortitude, and Temperance'. Anne might well have been describing herself, so close is the parallel between them. How strong the maternal influences were on Anne this study will make clear.[9]

The countess's associations with noted Elizabethan writers such as Edmund Spenser, Henry Constable, Samuel Daniel and Fulke Greville have been well publicized and further comment would be superfluous. What has not before been stressed is that in all her interests the countess reveals a practical bent, not just a contemplative mind. Her own literary efforts have been neglected. She was, if not a diarist in her daughter's mould, at least a summarizer of her own life, perhaps the inspiration for Anne in this as in much else. Her letter to Dr Layfield is the best source for understanding her emotions, especially towards her husband and his risky and profligate lifestyle. Unfortunately, it has survived incomplete, so that it is Anne and not the countess who tells of her passionate affection for her husband and the heartbreak when he parted from her.[10]

Far more important, the countess has not been accorded

5. *Margaret Russell, Countess of Cumberland (1560–1616), after George Gower (H.T. Fattorini Esq.)*

her due for the immensely valuable historical research she undertook in person, with professional help, during the lawsuits over her daughter's inheritance. She even missed the birth of her granddaughter Margaret on 2 July 1614 because, delving into the records at the Tower of London, she was locked inside when the building was prematurely closed. She employed a genealogist and antiquary, Mr St Loe Kniveton, to compile for her not only accurate family trees of the Cliffords but legally sound precedents and arguments which would give substance to her case in the litigation with Earl Francis.[11] Much more will be said about this research in Chapters 3 and 9.

The countess's foremost intellectual pursuit was the study and practice of alchemy, which had magical and mystical connotations. She distilled waters and other chemical extractions because, Anne writes, she had some knowledge of most kinds of minerals, herbs, flowers and plants. By this means she found 'excellent medicines' which did much good to many people. Distilling was a useful hobby for titled ladies, which appealed particularly to those of godly and pious outlook. A manuscript volume of alchemical works is shown above the countess's head in the Appleby Triptych, which will be discussed in Chapter 10. She was a close friend of Dr John Dee, mathematician, astrologer and alchemist with the most fertile scientific mind of the Elizabethan age, who frequently lodged with Earl George. Dee noted in his private diary on 25 October 1593 his surprise that her preacher Mr Gray wrangled with him and denied and despised 'alchemical philosophers'. When Dee's daughter Margarite was baptised on 27 August 1595 the countess was one of her godparents.[12]

Anne does not mention her mother's entrepreneurial concerns, her investments in lead-mining in Craven and experiments in smelting iron-ore with coal, which were in part extensions of her alchemical studies, and in commercial developments. The countess lived long enough to put money into both the East India Company's first voyage in 1601 (Earl George being a founder-governor of the company) and the Virginia Company in 1612. Few noblemen, let alone noble ladies, could boast her breadth of scientific interest and support of industry and commerce at the forefront of England's expanding economic horizons. Anne is not known to have emulated her mother in this respect. She may even have disapproved of her employing risk capital, however small-scale, because she asserts that the countess eschewed wealth and profit for their own sake. Anne might deliberately have suppressed this aspect of the countess's interests because she thought it reflected ill on her reputation for piety and frugality. If so, she was wrong.[13]

Like all the Russell family, Countess Margaret was brought up a Puritan, that 'hotter' sort of Protestant who put great faith in the scriptures. Anne encapsulates this when she writes that her mother 'was truly religious, devout and conscientious' from childhood. She spent much time reading the scriptures and other good books and 'in heavenly meditations and in prayers, fastings and deeds of charity'. The death of her sons, Anne judges, afflicted her so much 'that ever after the booke of Jobe was her dayly companion'. After her separation from the earl she sought solace in her devotions. Her stoical outlook, with its professed indifference to pain and pleasures, the natural philosophical stance for Puritans, was her other protective shield against life's adversities and temptations. In the Appleby Triptych Anne depicts her mother with the four books which sum up the guiding influences on her life – in her hand a book of Psalms, on the shelf above her the Bible, the works of the stoic philosopher Seneca and her manuscript collection of 'Alchemical Extractions, of Distillations and Excellent Medicines'.[14] If Anne's object in picking out those volumes was to emphasize the countess's inclination towards the ascetic, cloistered life it is misleading, as has already been made clear. Moreover, as will be explained in Chapter 10, her literary tastes were far more wide-ranging and eclectic.

The countess attracted dedications particularly from Puritan writers but also commissioned translations from the Latin for her own use, getting access to otherwise unreachable treasures of thought and experience from the ancient world. Ten books and sermons are listed in the *Short Title Catalogue* and Dr Williamson describes some. One typical dedication was by William Perkins who in 1597 published *A Graine of Musterd-Seede*, calling her 'the exceedingly pious lady' and wishing her 'Grace and Peace'. No doubt she had heard Perkins preach and her keenness to support and obtain good preachers is plain in her correspondence with her husband. Other dedications included Richard Venner's *The Right Way to Heaven* (1602) and Samuel Hieron's *The Sermons* (1615). Thomas Tymme, author of a work on devotion, translated Dudley Fenner's 'Sacred Divinitie' from the Latin for her in 1590, the work with its inscription known to Williamson. Another rare survivor from 'the mouldering domestic Evidences' Dawson examined in Skipton Castle during the 1880s is a manuscript translation dedicated to the countess on 1 January 1584 by Thomas Ryther of extracts from 'Boetius: his Philosophical Comfort'. The long dedication makes plain the countess was used to accepting translations from him and would welcome this work 'of a grave writer, the woordes I saye of a right noble, wyse, lernyd, and religius man'.[15]

Characteristically there was a practical side to the countess's piety, expressed in charitable provision for which by 1589 she was highly regarded in Craven. James Ryther gent. of Harewood, one of her household officers, informed Lord Burghley from Barden Tower on 26 September:

> This vertuus Lady, as mayny other of Gods favors to this comonwealth, is placed here I trust for her Maiesties good, for her actions in this ebbe of her estate, in releevinge the poore, in setting the idell to woork upon her owen cost, & that which is princypall, in spreddinge good doctryne by her life & preaches as not unwoorthie to be left in remembrance to all posteritie.[16]

The countess's links with Puritan preachers such as Christopher Shute at Giggleswick and Robert Moore at Guiseley and with the Puritan Lord President at York, the earl of Huntingdon, have been remarked on in *The Privateering Earl*. Her outstanding charitable work, post dating Ryther's comments, was founding a hospital or almshouse for a Mother and twelve Sisters – poor widows – at Beamsley near Skipton. The preamble to the letters patent obtained on 16 March 1593 explains that she had been saddened by the sight of so many poor women in the town. George Clapham Esq. provided a suitable site, three roods of land called Rackmyre alias Roe Park on his Beamsley demesnes on the north side of the main road four miles east of Skipton. Included were the rights to obtain turves and other fuel for the Sisters and get stones for building and repairs. She did not buy the site, and bound Clapham, his son Gresham and grandson George in quadrennial agreements to keep to their terms. She drew up the rules, or 'Orders', for the almswomen that year.

However, she was able to provide accommodation only for the Mother and six Sisters. Her intention of financing the building and securing the hospital with a permanent endowment by purchasing James Ryther's closes called East Stockton Fields at Harewood was stymied by his imprisonment in the Fleet Prison for debt, then his death and the sale of his estate. Not until 18 March 1605 did her agents, William Constable gent. of Drax and John Loskey gent. of Linton-upon-Wharfe, obtain Ryther's former lands from Albany Butler, a Lancashire gentleman, and they did not assign them to her until 1611. The project was incomplete when she died in 1616. In her will, she requested Anne to finish the building.

The countess's hospital is of unusual circular construction, about 30 feet in diameter, with the chapel in the centre (15 feet in diameter) reflecting her sense of primacy to prayer and services. Its lantern shape echoes the round Romanesque churches, such as the fifth-century Sant' Angelo in Perugia, or the eleventh-century Crusader churches in Cambridge and Northampton which she would have known, all inspired and named after the Church of the Holy Sepulchre in Jerusalem. The central windows light up the chapel. The rooms for the Sisters radiate around the chapel and can be reached only through the chapel. The Mother had two 'handsome rooms' and a garden, every Sister one room and a garden. A Reader (a local clergyman) was paid to hold services and take other responsibilities. The regulations, or 'Orders', which she issued in 1593 remained essentially the same under all her successors (Table 3).

What is not usually stressed is that the hospital was founded with Earl George's approval and the patent was obtained by them jointly and no doubt through his agency. This was essential because, by the common law doctrine of coverture, a married woman could not sign a contract or take legal action without her husband's collaboration. The patent gave the earl and countess authority to hold annual visitations with disciplinary powers to ensure affairs were conducted with propriety. They chose the first Mother and Sisters; thereafter, being a corporate body, the Sisters chose the replacements, although they had to obtain approval.[17] The earl's and countess's dual involvement was marked by their separate escutcheons in stone erected probably by Anne during the 1650s after she had taken over the Craven estates.

Not previously appreciated is Countess Margaret's support for education. It looks as if there was a school, in the church perhaps, at Kildwick in Craven because John Collyn gent., one of the grooms of Queen Elizabeth's chamber, had been taught there. Efforts were made by the vicar and leading parishioners in 1580 to obtain a royal licence to found what would have been called the Queen Elizabeth's grammar school. They made no progress and may, therefore, have approached the countess for her help. In October 1595 she was licensed through the signet office to establish a free grammar school and provide the land and all other requirements up to a cost of £30. Nothing else is known of the scheme, which may have run up against obstacles. Yet, because of the flimsy nature of the evidence for schools in the early modern era, it is conceivable that

6. *The Round Building, Beamsley Hospital, built by Countess Margaret, c. 1593 (The Landmark Trust. Photo: the author)*

she did aid the existing teaching, conducted probably by the vicar, as was often the practice. Kildwick, within the Skipton Fee, had always been under Clifford influence, and Christ Church, Oxford, held the right of advowson and the tithes. The parish, which included the big township of Silsden, was populous and could have supported its own grammar school, Ermysted's at Skipton being a good ride away.[18]

An intriguing fusion of Countess Margaret's literary and religious sentiments is her befriending and conversion of Aemilia Lanyer whom Georgiana Blakiston has called 'the unfortunate, ambitious, dissatisfied and promiscuous wife of a court musician', Alfonso Lanyer. Dr Rowse identifies Aemilia with Shakespeare's 'Dark Lady of the Sonnets'. Her conversion happened when she and the countess were staying with the immensely scholarly and Puritan Lady Margaret Hoby (Lady Russell by her second marriage) at Cookham in Berkshire. Lanyer had penned verses which penetrated the chink in the moral armour of any noblewoman of stoic, Puritan persuasion, such as the countess and Lady Russell, and of Anne herself:

Though being rich, no riches dost respect,
Nor dost thou care for any outward show,
The proud that do fair virtue's rules neglect
Desiring place, thou sittest them below.

11

After her conversion, Lanyer expressed her new-found spirituality in her poetry, which she published in 1611. Her long religious poem *Salve Deus Rex Judaeorum* has dedicatory verses to 'that excellent Lady', the countess, and is interspersed with others directed to her, whom Aemilia calls 'the wonder of our wanton age'. One of the poems she dedicated to Anne because

> For your faire mind I hold the fittest place,
> Where virtue should be setled & protected.

Anne records that her mother had many 'honorable and rich offers of matches made to her' but rejected them because her mind was 'too much sett of an heavenly devotion to marry again'.[19]

Anne's own intellectual and practical passions were to emulate her mother's, with a bent towards religion, literature, history and good works. Her education would be directed by her mother though nothing is known about its course until Samuel Daniel became her tutor. Daughters of titled families were usually taught privately because there were no schools for them to attend and in any case that would not have been proper. Earl George's sisters had been tutored by their father's gentry officers and Anne's early instruction would also have been done within the household. By her ninth birthday she had clearly mastered both reading and writing, the calligraphy in the dutiful letter written to her father in January 1599 being confident and distinctive, with the touching decoration of 'NN's in the corners for her father's diminutive 'Nan' (Pl. 7).

When Mrs Anne Taylor became her governess is not clear. She was probably connected with the Cliffords by marriage because she was the daughter of Mr Cholmley, a merchant who lived in the Old Bailey in London, possibly one of the Yorkshire branch of that name who were related to the earl. Two other Taylors, Stephen and John, were among his most trusted officers. Anne describes Mrs Taylor as 'a Religious and good Woman'. Her portrait in the triptych shows her wearing a black gown with falling linen collar and black cap tied under her chin and somewhat severe in demeanour (Pl. 74). Anne's comment on her confirms that she shared the countess's beliefs and her strict approach to discipline, which doubly qualified her to be governess.[20]

Very early, Anne's precocious abilities called for a tutor of Samuel Daniel's stature (Pl. 73). He was a poet and historian, an intimate of leading Elizabethan scholars and an experienced teacher, having been tutor in the Pembroke household at Wilton where Countess Mary, Sir Philip Sidney's sister, had encouraged his writing. His philosophical outlook was attuned to Countess Margaret's. His patent sympathy with her marital plight, expressed in compelling literary form, has been commented on in *The Privateering Earl*. Chagrin at English backwardness compared with Continental nations spurred him in his historical writing. His works on English history show familiarity with a long span of the nation's past and he was remarkable, comments Dr Rowse, 'in refusing to acknowledge anything other than historical evidence beginning with Caesar and Strabo'. This is apposite considering how much weight both the countess and Anne were to give to documentary proof, as will be demonstrated in particular in Chapter 9. Anne spent some of her most impressionable years with Daniel. The warmth of her lasting regard for him may have been more than respect for his intellectual gifts and diligent tuition; as a surrogate father-figure perhaps.

Daniel helped develop Anne's enthusiasm for the best of English prose, poetry and history and it has been argued that he also introduced her to philosophical works in translation which, as a corpus, would have given her an education not just equalling but superior to that her male contemporaries received at university. Private tutors could construct a curriculum tailor-made for their pupils with greater flexibility than, for instance, even Dean Whitgift's for Earl George and his fellows at Trinity, Cambridge, during the 1570s. The books displayed in the left-hand panel of the triptych are taken to be indicative of what Anne studied under Daniel (Table 5). Undoubtedly they point to what

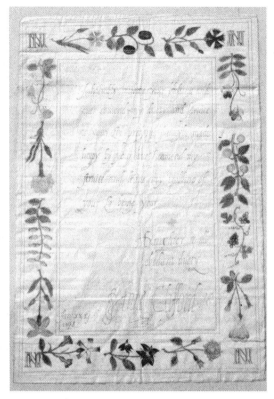

7. *Lady Anne's letter to her father, 31 January 1599, the day after her ninth birthday (Private collection. Photo: the author)*

she recalled in her later fifties and instructed the painter to place prominently so as to catch viewers' eyes and commendation. She would indeed have studied those publications at some stage in her early life; however, not necessarily under Daniel's supervision.[21]

Daniel, it has to be remembered, was her tutor for only three years, from the age of nine to twelve. Of the volumes shown in the triptych the Bible, Chaucer, Spenser's *The Faerie Queene*, Camden's *Britannia*, Sidney's *Arcadia*, Ovid's *Metamorphoses*, Castiglione's *The Courtier*, and Tasso's romance of the First Crusade *Godfrey of Bulloigne*, would all have been suitable intellectual fare for a girl of Anne's mental development by the age of twelve. *Arcadia* offered romantic escapism, which appealed especially to women, its central characters indulging in amorous and martial activities in 'a plot designed to exhibit personal virtue through a variety of testing circumstances'. It was Chaucer, *Arcadia*, *The Faerie Queene*, Montaigne's *Essays* (translated by Daniel's brother-in-law John Florio) and most of all the Bible which were to be her mainstays during her tormented twenties; mostly read to her, as Daniel himself might have done.[22] It is doubtful, however, if the critical, speculative and philosophical publications, mainly by foreign authors, shown in the triptych would have been within even Anne's compass at twelve. To benefit from such demanding works would require a maturer mind. It will be posited in Chapter 10 that most had belonged to her mother. Indeed, the countess was just as well fitted as Daniel to continue her daughter's education after the tutor had left or (since cash was short) perhaps been dispensed with.

Anne was precocious enough to be in part autodidactic but the Russell ladies and their officers would have been eager to give her the benefit of their own extensive scholarship and skills. Her introduction to Elizabeth I's Court was undertaken by her aunt Warwick, the queen's favourite Lady of the Bed-chamber, who died in 1604. Anne's officer George Sedgewick stated in his memoirs that her 'chief breeding' had been under Lady Warwick. These early experiences, recorded in her 1603 diary, prepared her for the far greater intimacy she came to enjoy, at first under her mother's guidance, with James I's Queen Anne and then Charles I's Queen Henrietta Maria, as will be described in later chapters.[23]

What is not gainsaid is that Anne developed a stoical and enquiring cast of mind with a breadth and depth of understanding of current philosophical and religious arguments and familiarity with the most widely studied works of her time. As a result, she could hold her own in conversation on any topic with the best minds of her age; as Dr Donne testified, from slea-silk to predestination.[24] Without precise evidence, it is perhaps invidious to apportion the credit. The countess, her relatives and friends, Daniel and Mrs Taylor would count for much; the rest would be Anne, with a true scholar's appetite for knowledge and understanding. As Daniel makes plain in his verse epistle to Anne in 1603, for the countess as for himself her education had primarily a moral purpose:

> With so great care doth she, that hathe brought forth
> That comely body, labour to adorne
> That better part, the mansion of your minde,
> With all the richest furniture of worth;
> To make y'as highly good as highly borne,
> And set your vertues equall to your kinde.[25]

The last two years of Daniel's tutoring coincide with the surviving fragment of presumably Mrs Taylor's accounts for Anne from August 1600 to August 1602. But he stands at her shoulder, because Whitaker identified his handwriting in a prayer and verse at the beginning. 'O Lord, increase o'r fayth, and make us evermore attentyve hearers, true conceivers, and diligent fulfillers, of thy heavenly will!', followed by

> To wish and will it is my part,
> To yow, good lady, from my hart,
> The yeares of Nestor God yow send,
> W'th hapynes to your life's end!

Another obvious link is the purchase of a book for Anne to write her catechism. Otherwise, the accounts throw light on her clothes and entertainment. Lawn, slea-silk, two pairs of Jersey stockings and one of green worsted, two pairs of Spanish leather shoes and one of calves leather, and Holland cloth for smocks and handkerchiefs give some notions of her ordinary wear, the farthingale for her formal dress no doubt. The coif and forked cloth bought bring to mind Mrs Taylor's costume in the triptych. The ring and jewel and basket pendants of gold and pearl were suitable trinkets for a countess's daughter. Having Anne's portrait drawn on canvas for only three shillings does not suggest a large painting nor a Court artist.

The Cliffords were patrons of music and drama, and the accounts and Anne's 1603 diary tell something of the young lady's training and entertainment, mainly in the Russell houses. A servant, Stephens, spent a whole month teaching her to dance. A vizard was bought for her to wear at a masque held in her honour, or for her to take the lead in, and musicians were hired to play in it and later at her door; a birthday celebration perhaps. Virginal wires were purchased. At North Hall, sometime after Michaelmas 1603, she was taught how to sing and to play on Jack Jenkins's base viol. She learnt the more housewifely accomplishments of stitching and making cushions and preserves such as marmalade. Like a true daughter of the Renaissance, Anne was educated in the practical as well as the scholastic.[26]

It has not been remarked how nostalgic in tone is the left panel of the triptych, the objects shown all reminiscent of Anne's happy youthful years, even though some are of later date (Pl. 8). The fifteen-year-old girl depicted has her left hand on music with a lute (of the type popular after 1630) leaning against the table. On the table stand her embroidery and an hour-glass, symbolic of time's passing – the accounts record one purchased for her. The lozenge bearing her arms denotes her unmarried status. Her sea-green and silver satin dress dates from perhaps a decade later. On the shelves are the books Anne studied and above them, prominent, are Daniel's and Mrs Taylor's portraits. Innocence, culture, the pleasurable bookishness of a burgeoning mind under the gaze of her honoured tutor and governess pervade this tableau, a six years' spell encapsulated in the one scene.

There was one great lacuna in Anne's upbringing. She was entirely cut off from her northern roots until she was seventeen. She never experienced the grand life in her ancestral homes and the emotional impact of their immense size and ornate splendour, their rich furnishings and stained glass embellished with the Clifford and Cumberland coats of arms and emblems and the shields of the great families with whom they had intermarried. She was denied the chance to absorb the history lessons explicit in such an environment. It is all the more remarkable, therefore, that she, of all the Cliffords, became in later life so inspired by their traditions and achievements. It is tempting to suggest Daniel had some part in rousing his pupil's curiosity. His poetic imagination had been inspired by Henry II's mistress, the beautiful Fair Rosamund Clifford. Anne's interest, however, would came in stages, as will be noted in subsequent chapters, though Daniel's may be regarded as the first. His concluding couplet in his epistle to her reads:

> Since nothing cheeres the heart of greatnesse more
> Then th'Ancestors faire glory gone before.

Until Earl George's death, his wife and daughter had got most contentment in the company of their Russell relatives and in their houses. Thereafter, it was the Cliffords' traditions, history and descent and the Westmorland estates to

8. *Left hand panel of the Appleby Triptych, depicting Lady Anne, c. 1605, artist unknown, 1646/8 (Reproduced by courtesy of Abbot Hall Art Gallery, Kendal)*

which they gave their attention. If Anne had felt a Russell and southerner in her upbringing, she was to be a Clifford and aspiring northerner henceforward. Earl George had worried that if his inheritance came to Anne it would be to a Russell in mentality who would take it out of the family. Yet it was to be fought over by two Cliffords, his daughter and his brother. Only in a general sense perhaps had Anne's education prepared her for this. The vital spark came from her circumstances following her mother's death when her emotions were in turmoil, as will be explained in Chapter 4. This apart, the tutoring and maternal influences produced in Anne firm support for the established Church but with a distinct Puritan leaning; faith in the scriptures and the predestined course of her life; a love of literature and intellectual dispute, and a sense of status and self-belief, all of which will be illustrated during the course of this study. They reinforced the innate talents and strength of will for which she is renowned. That 'wilfulness' was a trait already evident to Daniel when she was aged but thirteen and was to be remarked on throughout her life. He took it upon himself to warn her in his epistle that 'in our strongest parts we are but weake' and of the danger of judgement being betrayed

> when our selves be come t'applaud
> Our owne abilitie and our owne parts.

How far 'wilfulness' and self-approval affected Anne's behaviour needs bearing in mind as her actions are considered. Daniel's respect and affection for his charge shine throughout the epistle. They remained close until his death. Suffering, it is thought, from a slow, wasting disease, he recurrently anticipated his early demise. When dedicating his history of the Wars of the Roses to her in 1607 he appears also to nominate her as his literary executor and supervisor of his will.[27]

Socially, Anne entered into her own during her early teens, enjoying the varied activities of a crowded young life in the company of people of similar status, accompanying her mother in Queen Anne's train, staying in the magnificent royal palaces and visiting with her the houses of the nobility so that she became well acquainted with that exclusive and close-knit social group around the Court and in the home counties. She mentions four friends in particular: her cousins Lady Frances Bourchier, daughter of her aunt the Countess of Bath, to whom she became very attached, and Lord Francis Russell, on whom she was to lean heavily in later life; Mary Carey; and Bess of Hardwick's unfortunate granddaughter Lady Arabella Stuart who was to die in the Tower of London. She met her Clifford cousin Henry for the first time at Althorp in 1603, treating him (at least in her recollection) with some reserve because he would eventually become her rival for the inheritance.

There is no hint in Anne's diary, though much in her mother's letters and petitions to King James, that they were woefully short of cash in the years after the separation. Earl George had promised the countess £1,000 a year to maintain them. With empty coffers and huge debts he could hardly support himself let alone his family. He did allow them sole use of his Clerkenwell mansion, though four years elapsed before he could provide the essential linen and tableware. To keep an establishment at the house would be beyond the countess's means for most of the time. Staying with her relatives was cheaper although she paid her way in household expenses, much of it by borrowing as she explained in her will.[28]

One bystander familiar with the countess and her daughter sketched perceptively how their condition and characters appeared to him – Archbishop Matthew Hutton in his rather irreverent and affectionate view of the 'companie of the fairest ladies that ever I sawe'. He invited the Court ladies to try their fortunes in his 'Lotterie' and 'yf any light upon an unfortunate lott, lett her thinke that Fortune dothe but mocke with her in these trifles, and meanes to do her a pleasure in a greater matter'. For the countess he drew in his mind's eye 'A Falling Bande' with the comment,

> Fortune would have you rise, but guides your hande
> From other lotts, to take this falling bande.

Anne's lot was 'A Lace',

> Geve her the lace that loves to be strate laced,
> Soe Fortune's litle gifte is aptlie placed.

This couplet is almost a simile for Anne's demeanour in one of her earliest portraits (Pl. 9). She is composed, with a touch of primness in her self-assured look which the archbishop would have known. Yet her square-cut, reddish-brown costume is slightly risqué, lower at the left shoulder to reveal her flesh from neck to breasts, as might be expected of a young lady at Court with suitors in the offing. Her renowned long hair is held decorously in place by a pearl-encrusted wire, with a large pendant pearl. At her forehead is a brooch, perhaps with a wyvern inset. Her famous pearl necklace and ear-rings have been handed down through the female line (Pl. 95). At North Hall in the autumn of 1603 Anne wore her hair 'color'd velvet every day'.[29]

Most of Countess Margaret's financial problems ended with her husband's death on 30 October 1605. She now entered her large jointure estate, the whole of the Cliffords' Westmorland properties and big dower castles at Brougham and Appleby. The income was a financial godsend even though, as will be explained in Chapter 2, she had to struggle to collect all the moneys due. For the first time she had cash to spare and this enabled her to hire the best lawyers in her litigation on her daughter's behalf. It was the difficulties she was having in

9. Lady Anne, aged fifteen, attrib. to Sir Peter Lely (Private collection)

Westmorland as well as the lawsuits over the Clifford inheritance which led her to visit the north-west with Anne in July 1607. They resided in her castles and visited Lord William Howard at Naworth near the Scottish border. On the return journey through Craven they found the entrance to Skipton Castle barred against them by Earl Francis's servants, who regarded them disdainfully. They stayed with George Clapham (the younger) at Beamsley Hall so that they could inspect the almshouses, Anne for the first time, the countess for the last. The next day, 14 October, the countess made one of her quadrennial agreements with Clapham, covenanting in turn to enclose the whole site with a 3-feet-high wall. Anne had not been to her birthplace since she was seven weeks old and she was not to come again for forty-two years. Yet she now had a sharp image of the great houses and properties she claimed as her own, which later visits to Westmorland helped reinforce.[30]

Anne's own situation was equally transformed by her father's death. He had made provision in his will for her to receive £15,000 as a marriage portion, in instalments: £3,000 within two years of his death, £3,000 a year later, £4,000 a year after that, and the final £5,000 in two sums the year following her twenty-first birthday. She was to be supported for the first two years with £200 annual allowance. The snag was that the payments were conditional on her not commencing suit against Earl Francis for the inheritance, and that is what she and her mother did. Nevertheless, Anne was on the marriage market either with a tempting £15,000 dowry or as potentially a great heiress in Westmorland and Craven.[31]

Anne had reached both the age of consent and her majority (twelve and fourteen respectively for a girl) but by the canons of 1603 she would need a guardian's consent to marry before twenty-one. It looks as if she was quite prepared to stand on her own two feet, because she explains that it was her mother who 'out of her affectionate care for my good, caused me to chuse her my her guardian', formally no doubt to the Earl of Salisbury who was both Master of the Court of Wards and George's executor. This was sensible because Anne was entirely dependent on her mother for income, unless she accepted her father's will. The guardianship gave the countess legal charge of Anne's affairs. It was she who initiated in Anne's name the lawsuits over the Clifford titles and estates and made the decisions about her marriage.

Despite the well-known obstacles to Anne's cash or landed fortune, there was no lack of suitors. The countess made plain in her letter to Salisbury on 3 March 1606 that neither she nor Anne had consented to her marriage with William Cavendish and had not begun negotiations for it. In 1608 he was married off forcibly to Christiana Bruce, daughter of the Master of the Rolls Lord Kinloss.[32] There were two other serious approaches for Anne. First, Lord Treasurer Buckhurst, whom James I made Earl of Dorset, asked Sir George Moore in April 1607 to use his good offices with the countess to arrange a match with Anne for his grandson Richard Sackville. Why nothing came of this immediately is nowhere made clear because Anne and Richard were often in each other's company. In her poem to Anne, Aemilia Lanyer lifts the veil on how they and 'noble Dorset' spent time together, linked by friendship and literature,

But specially the love of that faire tree,
That first and last you did vouchsafe to see:
In which it pleas'd you oft to take the ayre,
With noble Dorset, then a virgin faire;
Where many a learned Booke was read and skaned
To this faire tree, taking me by the hand.[33]

Anne's next suitor was the Scottish courtier Robert Carr who in December 1608 was granted Sir Walter Raleigh's forfeited lands by James I and was then 'in speech' to marry her. He was socially much less desirable as the third son of a border laird, Kerr of Ferniehurst, but he promised great political sway over the king as the rising favourite. James was keen on Anglo-Scottish marriages and no doubt would have ennobled Carr. How Anne and her quest for the Clifford estates would have fared as Carr's wife is a fascinating question. Nothing, however, came of the proposal. Much later, Carr's notorious marriage with Lady Essex brought a relationship with Anne. Their daughter Anne Carr married her cousin Francis Russell's son William, who succeeded him as 5th Earl and was created 1st Duke of Bedford.[34]

All this while, Anne was in the throng of the high life of the Jacobean Court, taking part in the elaborate ceremonials and extended entertainments put on by Queen Anne and her ladies. On Sunday 14 January 1608, now all but eighteen, she was one of the queen's attendants received on land by the river god in the second *Masque of Beauty* presented by Ben Jonson in Whitehall. Her colours would have been sea-green and silver. A year later, Shrovetide 1609, she played Berenice in the *Masque of Queens*, a part chosen for her and in a costume designed for her by Inigo Jones because she, like Berenice, was famed for the beauty of her hair.

This she tells us, 'was Browne and verie thick and so long as that it reached the Calfe of my Legges when I stood upright'. In the masque, Berenice's hair is sacrificed as a votive offering, so Jones designed the fantastic head-dress of the costume to hide the 'mutilated' hair (Pl. 10). In Isaac Oliver's miniature of about the same time, Anne wears her hair long and loose beneath a coronet (Pl. 11). This may be another masque dress, almost certainly a Court dress because it is rich and lavishly trimmed with lace. Gone is the earlier primness, even if there is some reserve captured by the limner. She has more of an eager, almost windswept look as if she has just come indoors after cavorting in the gardens with Aemilia Lanyer and Richard Sackville. She was now aged nineteen, or near to it, and marriage was much closer than she could have expected.[35]

Anne was patently in age, looks, noble birth, potential fortune and royal favour one of the most eligible of the young ladies close to the queen. Less than a fortnight after Jones's masque she was married to Richard Sackville (now Lord Buckhurst) in Countess Margaret's house in Austin Friars, London, on 25 February 1609. Their wedding was solemnized in unseemly haste and without banns, an 'irregular marriage' for which letters of absolution had to be obtained afterwards. The reason was that Richard's father, Robert, 2nd Earl of Dorset, was on his death-bed. Richard, nineteen and so under age, would if unmarried become a royal ward and predatory courtiers could not wait to importune James I for his guardianship. It was rumoured that Ludovic Stuart, Earl of Lennox, was in the hunt and as the king's relative he was certain to win.

If Richard became his ward, the Crown and Lennox between them would control a large part of his huge estates in Kent and Sussex and, even more alarming, give Lennox the vital decision about his marriage.

At Richard's behest, his friend Henry, Prince of Wales, wrote to the king for the wardship to prevent other suitors getting it. But Earl Robert was too ill to await the outcome. To be safe Richard had to marry and Anne was the obvious bride. Within two days Earl Robert was dead, Richard succeeded him and Anne, Lady Buckhurst, became Countess of Dorset. That shrewd observer John Chamberlain commented that however much Earl Richard had 'don a true part, and pleased himself, yet the matter might have ben better handled, and he eased himself of a burthen he may peradventure feele hereafter'.[36]

The same might with equal truth have been said about Anne. Her alliance with Dorset was at times far from happy and she had the mortification of witnessing her interests in the Clifford inheritance eventually sub-ordinated to his. But in 1609 there was an immediate advantage for the countess and her daughter. Dorset was one of the great nobility with politically powerful friends and relatives who would be sympathetic to their cause. This was even true of the Howards who, as Catholics, had always hated the Puritan Russells. Increasingly the dominant faction in the Privy Council and at Court, they were a counter to Salisbury who still held the king's ear and, though strictly impartial during the course of the lawsuits between Anne and her uncle, nevertheless remained Earl Francis's close friend. Moreover, a husband of Dorset's standing gave Anne security and ended anxiety about what would happen to her should the countess die leaving her unmarried.

In view of the circumstances of her own marriage, it ill became Anne to denounce her cousin Henry's match with Salisbury's daughter Lady Frances Cecil in July 1610 as merely a device to enlist his aid for her uncle's cause. In fact, it cemented a long friendship between the families.

10. *Inigo Jones's design for Lady Anne's masque costume as Berenice of Egypt in the 'Masque of Queens', 1609 (Reproduced by permission of the Duke of Devonshire and the Trustees of the Chatsworth Settlement)*

It was not Henry's marriage but Anne's which had much the greater effect on the course of the inheritance dispute by elevating it into the realm of Court politics and making Dorset arbiter of her fortunes, as will be explained in Chapter 3. The Cecil marriage, indeed, saved the Bolton Abbey estate for the Cliffords (and after them the Burlingtons and Devonshires) because it was Lady Frances's £6,000 portion which enabled Earl Francis to redeem it from his late brother's creditors.[37]

For Anne, the die was cast. This study will seek to unravel the tangled skein of her problems and relationships which have become more familiar, though no better understood, since the publication of her *Diaries*. It is worth considering here a contrary view to what happened to her in reality. The alternative course so vehemently argued by the countess and Anne has never been scrutinized for its likely consequences. To do so is to offer a salutary touchstone for Anne's actual experiences. If on his death-bed in 1605 Earl George had changed his mind and made his daughter his heir, the potential difficulties for her and the Clifford inheritance would have been legion. Countess Margaret would have entered the Westmorland lordships as her jointure estate and faced the difficulties which will be described in the next chapter. Most of the Craven lands had been assigned to pay George's legacies and debts. On the fifteen-year-old girl would have fallen the responsibility not just for their management but for coping with her father's clamorous creditors.

Enormous complications would have followed. If the city merchants and other big creditors had decided to foreclose on the mortgages and begin legal action for repayment of the other loans, then the inheritance might have disappeared before Anne's very eyes. Moreover, Earl George's sureties, such as his brother and his gentry officers and friends, would have been compelled to join in the legal action to safeguard their own estates. Most of all, Earl Francis would in 1606 have challenged with his claim to the Clifford inheritance and baronial titles, the subsequent dispute quite as damaging as that which in fact occurred. He would have done so from strength, as an earl and able to dispose relatively large resources from his East Riding and other properties and leases and, especially, the £2,000 a year income from his cloth licence.[38]

11. Lady Anne, miniature attrib. to Isaac Oliver, c. 1608/9 (Private collection)

Speculation on what might have been in history is often fruitless. In this instance it serves as a reminder that, however hurtful Anne's situation and experiences at times were as Dorset's wife, denied what she held most dear, all might have turned out best for her, as she was wont to reflect when looking back as an elderly dowager countess on the course her life had taken.

CHAPTER 2

Countess Margaret and her Westmorland Jointure Estates

The conflict with Earl Francis over the inheritance was one of the two paramount issues in Countess Margaret's affairs after her husband's death and it was this which came to dominate Lady Anne's life. Just as immediate, however, was the countess's need to establish herself on her Westmorland jointure estates (Map 1). To do so was as vital for her daughter as for herself. The estate revenues would provide the badly needed cash to support them and their household in Brougham and Appleby Castles when they visited the north but more especially, and at first unavoidably, in costly residence in the vicinity of James I's Court and the Westminster lawcourts. Moreover, the best London lawyers had to be hired to present Anne's case against her uncle and they did not come cheap. An ample and regular flow of cash from Westmorland would finance the expert legal advice, the submissions to the courts and the private research the countess herself so impressively conducted. The successful management of her northern estates was, therefore, inseparable from the pursuit of the Clifford inheritance. However, the two were interlinked in the contrary direction. Doubts about who was entitled even to her jointure estates were exploited to the countess's discomfit in Westmorland itself, by Earl Francis and even more by her own tenants there.

She also had to contend with the legitimate presence on her estates of Francis's officers. He had varied interests in the county. He owned the tithes of the parish of Kirkbythure and was perpetual lessee of the Dean and Chapter of Carlisle's tithes in Skattergate, one of the countess's jointure manors next to Appleby. In the borough itself, he leased from their brother-in-law Philip, Lord Wharton, the lands of St Nicholas. At Brougham, he owned the mills as part of his Carleton property. He had extensive patronage with which to reward his supporters. As sheriff, it was his appointed deputy who dealt with the collection of Crown dues, the serving of writs sent from the Westminster lawcourts, the empanelling of juries, the management of elections to the House of Commons and of the annual assizes, which he moved to Kendal because Appleby Castle was in the countess's hands. The sheriff's bailiffs operated in every ward, collecting moneys and rounding up and selling waifs and strays, the sheep and cattle which escaped from fenced pastures.[1]

The earl's prestigious role as one of James I's commissioners on the Borders entailed frequent residence at Carlisle and gave him solid support from most of the Cumbrian gentry of note. It was his political standing in the north-west

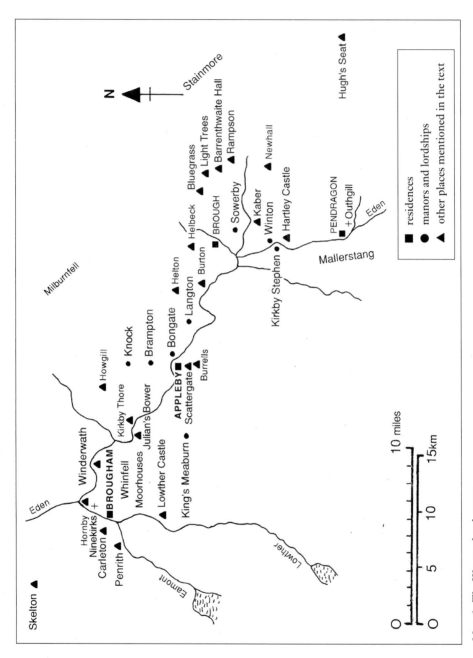

Map 1: The Westmorland estates

12. Brougham Castle, Cumbria, from the north-west, from a drawing by Samuel and Nathaniel Buck, 1739 (Photo: Cumbria County Library)

which was to give him the edge over the countess and later Lady Anne and Dorset in affairs concerning Westmorland. There is no evidence that he openly embarrassed the countess except in one respect, which will be described, yet the mere presence of his officers would be annoying. After her death Francis was to be even more relieved that it was he who exercised the sheriffwick, not his opponents.[2]

Earl George had been essentially a rentier landlord in Westmorland. He had kept in his hands very little of the extensive arable and pasture demesnes at Brougham, Appleby and Brough, the notable exceptions being Whinfell Forest deer and timber reserves and the large Southfield at Appleby. The rest had been let on short leases ranging from one to twenty-one years or, if distant from the castles, split up among the tenants. The demesne lessees, especially the more substantial men around Appleby and Brougham, were not likely to cause problems for the countess because of the competition for the premium quality land of those holdings.

Far more numerous and much less amenable to their landlords were the customary tenants who held most of the farms and other holdings on the lordships by warrants for the life of the lord and the tenant. On the death of the lord, all holdings fell in for his successor to re-grant, usually to the sitting tenant or one of his family, as Earl George had done in 1582. The incoming tenants on those occasions paid gressums (that is, entry fines) in theory at an arbitrary rate determined by the lord, in practice at a level negotiated formally by the lord's estate commissioners and juries of tenants drawn from each lordship. On the death of a tenant or when a tenant disposed of a part or whole of his holding, then a 'dropping fine' was paid by the incoming tenant, again with offers from the prospective tenant followed by bargaining between him and the commissioners. Under Earl George, at a time of high and fluctuating inflation, the gressum varied between a $3d$ and $7d$ fine on descent – that is, three to seven years' ancient rent of the holding – to as high as a $20d$ fine on alienation to another tenant. The bulk of these customary tenants were independent-minded, stock-rearing farmers on the southern lordships, including the small townships of Brough and Kirkby Stephen. The latter was part-owned by Lord Wharton. Appleby borough had never been a Clifford property, though always dominated by them and their great castle.

In 1606 Countess Margaret faced the problems of any new landlord, compounded by the fact that she was a woman and a southerner resident in London, who had last visited Westmorland in the early 1580s. She took over her jointure lands at a difficult time. As was explained in *The Privateering Earl*, the farmers on the Cliffords' lordships had just experienced the heavy-handedness of Earl George's special commissioners after enjoying two decades of light rein by local men while he was away pursuing his maritime career. Nor could the region have fully recovered from the strains of the 1590s, the four successive years of harsh weather, poor harvests and subsequent visitations of the plague with their debilitating social consequences.[3]

Incoming Clifford lords had often experienced problems in asserting their authority over these pastoral farmers of the lower Eden Valley. Moreover, memories there were long and ambitions perennial. One of their grievances expressed in the Pilgrimage of Grace in 1536 had been the high gressums paid to the lord on entering a tenement, which they had demanded should be abolished. In Henry VIII's bloody suppression of the uprising thirty-one of the fifty-three rebels hanged had been Clifford tenants, mostly from their southern lordships. Since then, better educational provision, higher literacy and a cannier appreciation of what could be achieved by litigation and political pressure locally and nationally had made the tenants far more resilient opponents. With the muskets and calivers paraded at musters they were better armed than the bowmen and billmen of 1536, but they had learnt their lesson. Litigation, not brute force, was the weapon for the Jacobean era.[4]

The aspirations and perceptions of the tenants came into focus on Countess Margaret's entry into her jointure lands. To them she was an unknown quantity but, as a woman, perhaps expected to be a soft target. They quickly found out she had no intention of being a neglectful, absentee landlord like her late husband. That would have been enough to ensure she would have for several years a rough rather than a tranquil tenure of her dower estates. However, the unique factor of the split in the family over the inheritance intruded and to the countess's disadvantage. It proved a boon to her refractory tenants and they were quick to take advantage of it. They proved doughty opponents. The better-off farmers individually and the tenants of any one lordship collectively had the wealth and the will to retain solicitors and match the countess by hiring London counsel. Lawyers raised and practising in the county who were familiar with tenurial customs were available to both sides, such as Thomas Hutton, opposing his brother, Richard, Earl Francis's chief legal adviser. The countess's disputes with her tenants were to be settled by local argument, legal action and the due enforcement of law; though, for her part, she would not have eschewed the use of force had it been permissible.

At first sight, the eleven commissioners Countess Margaret appointed in 1606 were a disparate group partly culled from friendships mainly made in the north. Yet she chose shrewdly, with local men to maintain continuity and outsiders of higher status than her late husband's officers to give them backbone. Of Earl George's men, she retained Henry Blenkinsop, a Roman Catholic; Thomas Salkeld; the attorney Thomas Braithwaite, and her old friend Robert Leigh, despite his misdemeanours while the earl had been absent. Thomas Hilton, the greater miscreant, she employed with sensible caution in a lesser post than he had previously held. The other two local men she took into her service were Edmund Dudley Esq. of Yanwath and Francis Southaike Esq. of Skelton. Both were gentry of note, the former having been sheriff of Cumberland in 1602. Southaike's father Robert had bought George's property in Skelton and Unthanke in 1582.[5]

The weightier commissioners in social standing and experience were all outsiders. The senior was Sir Robert Stapleton of Wighill, Yorkshire, once wealthy and a favourite of Queen Elizabeth until his courtier career was ruined by Archbishop Sandys's Star Chamber case against him. He was to die later that year. Sir Edward Yorke of Ripon had captained the *Edward Bonaventure* on Earl George's 1593 voyage. Sir George Freville of Sedgefield, County Durham, was keeper of Raby Castle and constable of Brancepeth and had sat for Appleby in the 1572 Parliament. The other two commissioners had close links with the Countess. Will Constable gent. of Drax had acted for her over Beamsley Hospital and Richard Burton MA was the rector of Linton-in-Craven.[6] The commissioners apart, the countess had much patronage to dispense in appointing her estate and household officers and, as usually happened with a new lord, she was importuned by those who wanted to serve her, which would bring her a degree of support within the county, though much less so than Earl Francis enjoyed.

The size and composition of her commission should have warned the tenants that their new mistress meant business. Now that she had come into her own in Westmorland, a noblewoman, a Russell, devoutly Puritan and long-suffering as George's wife, Countess Margaret proved tough, resolute and lordly until she had full command of her lands and rights. Then she showed she could be forgiving and generous, as befitted her religious persuasion. Her actions over her dower lordships reveal a facet of her personality not touched on in the assessment of her in the previous chapter. In Craven during George's long absences she had been, according to James Ryther, too easy-going over deer-hunters.[7] Like her husband, she had learnt her lesson in the intervening years; adversity is a great teacher and necessity an incentive to action.

What is worth emphasizing here, because it is relevant to what Lady Anne achieved, is that in managing her dower estates the countess held herself up as a model to be admired and followed. Anne appreciated at the time that the struggle with the tenants was as much in her interest as her mother's and integral to the much greater conflict over the Clifford inheritance. As will be seen in Chapter 8, when faced with similar opposition after taking possession of the Westmorland estates in 1649 she knew precisely what had to be done to win control. There is, moreover, a continuity of theme and litigation spanning the interval of four decades between their respective ownerships of the Westmorland properties. Anne's actions after 1649 are explicable only in the context of the earlier phase.

Uncertainty about whether Earl Henry or Anne was entitled to the Westmorland estates was the reason – or pretext – put forward by many of the tenants for refusing to pay their rents to Countess Margaret early in 1606. Her commissioners let some of her demesnes at an increased rent but other lessees withheld theirs because of the earl of Salisbury's executorship, whilst the customary tenants could not be persuaded on any security to pay their Candlemas rents. Moreover, there were already signs of the deep rift which was to develop between the more substantial tenants on the one hand and both the countess and her rival Earl Francis on the other. These wealthier farmers pursued devious tactics. The countess's commissioners explained that 'the better sorte of them it seemeth wilbe willing them selves [to pay their rents] and draw the rest to preferre a bill in Chancerie against my Lord and my ladie both'. The interlinked issues were tenures and gressums. As usually happened, the tenants with the connivance of the bailiffs had got hold of the manorial court rolls and refused to hand them over to the commissioners. A few relevant folios were torn from the 1604 survey. Perhaps other estate documents were lost for ever at this time.[8]

The opposition to the countess was mainly in the southern block of the estates, in Stainmore, Mallerstang, Brough and Kirkby Stephen, but also in the northerly manor of King's Meaburn, an echo here of the 1536 troubles. The leaders, as the loyal bailiff Michael Brunskill reported, were the wealthier farmers such as Michael Ewbanke of Barrenthwaite, Arthur Shipde [or Shepheard] of Rampson and Simon Nicholson of Light Trees in furthest East Stainmore. Altogether as many as two-thirds of the farmers on the Countess's estates were in dispute with her. They refused to take new tenures from her or pay entry fines or hand over the evidences they had seized. These actions would have been consonant with their claim that they had taken new warrants and paid gressums to Earl George not long before his death and so should not be required to buy new tenures. The circumstances have been explained in *The Privateering Earl.*

However, the tenants made two additional demands which were aggressive towards the Cliffords' seigniorial position whoever was lord. The first was the claim to hold 'by an ancyent Custome of tenant right time without memorie' which in their view created estates of inheritance tantamount to freehold. The second demand was that juries of homage selected in the lordships should decide titles according to common law. By this they argued that when titles were disputed the plaintiffs should have the right to obtain an injunction from the Council in the North at York for juries to determine the matter. This was the practice on the Wharton manor of Ravenstonedale and it was undoubtedly known and envied by the Cliffords' tenants. With these demands they were mounting a challenge to the Cliffords' traditional authority and aiming to set themselves free to manage their own affairs according to local custom and the common law.[9]

With her attorneys' advice, Countess Margaret rejected the demand for juries of homage as unfounded on the Clifford estates. Writing to Henry Blenkinsop on 4 April 1607 from Sutton in Kent, she reiterated her resolution to defend her right. She threatened that if the tenants did not 'the more spedilie conforme themselves', she would, God willing, 'take that course as shall make them thorrowlie feele both what their offence and my authoritie is'. She wished to know from Blenkinsop what additional powers she could give him, mindful that with the union of the Crowns she could not appoint armed stewards.[10] Her principal action was to enter bills of complaint against groups of her tenants in Chancery, a court of equity whose jurisdiction included landlord–tenant issues. The litigation, as usual in big cases of this kind, was to be protracted.

As it happened, the climate of political opinion was unfavourable to the defendants. James I's accession had transformed the national scene, outmoding the custom of 'border service' which was the granting of tenancies in the marcher counties at low rents and almost in perpetuity with the proviso that the men were always well armed and readily available to fight against the Scots. In the hearings Lord Chancellor Ellesmere repeated James I's pronouncement that 'the said costome of Tennant Righte by the happie union of both kingdomes' was dissolved. This negated the tenants' argument based on border service. But Ellesmere gave greatest weight to the nature of the tenures on the Clifford estates and the evidence of the granting of warrants. He declared that 'the saide grauntes and warrantes . . . could make no such estates of inheritance' as the tenants pretended. He ordered them to submit and pay such entry fines to the countess as were fitting. Countess Margaret obtained writs for the execution of the order.

Her tenants, however, had the conviction to continue their argument. Through their solicitors such as Thomas Hutton they reiterated before the court their claim to tenant-right and reasonable fines on the death of the lord and tenant. The court referred the case against one group for trial at Westmorland assizes in 1609, where it was heard by the circuit judge Sir Edward Phelips. He ordered arbitration by Earl Francis's lawyer Sergeant Hutton and Countess Margaret's Thomas Braithwaite, but this too failed. The countess offered to make new grants upon reasonable fines and this was also rejected by the defendants. Consequently, she procured a subpoena against them and the case again came before the Lord Chancellor.

Because Ellesmere had already given his judgment, the issue now concerned the size of the fines the tenants should pay. Following the practice of the court for the last two decades, he ruled that this was to be two years' value of their holdings and the basis of the valuation would be 20 nobles (a noble being 3s 4d) for every 20 shillings yearly rent they paid. Two years' value, therefore, would be 20 marks (a mark being 13s 4d) for every 20 shillings' rent, that is, £6 13s 4d per pound rent. Whatever fine a tenant actually paid, and that would depend on his annual rent, he would pay in two equal portions, at Pentecost and Martinmas 1610. But on grounds of equity Ellesmere made an exception in the case of King's Meaburn because only there were heriots paid to the lord in the form of the best beast or goods whenever a tenant died. To ensure equal demands on all the tenants throughout the Clifford estates, he freed the king's Meaburn farmers from the burden of paying heriots. This would not please either the countess or Francis.

One factor which worked against the tenants in this dispute – and the same applies to Anne's lawsuits in the 1650s – was that there were such large numbers (well over 800) living in so many discrete communities that Countess Margaret had to enter a bill of complaint against each group, which meant a number of separate suits. Because of the courts' procedures – annual hearings in Westminster aided by local assize hearings in summer if need be – the earliest cases were being concluded whereas the latest had barely started. Consequently, some groups of tenants had already agreed to pay fines at the rate laid down by Ellesmere whilst others were disputing the method of valuation. In these later cases, the countess's solicitors continued to seek her advantage by submitting that farms of 20s rent could be let for £8 a year whereas the tenants' counsel averred that they could not be let above £5 annually. Ellesmere settled this difference by imposing the valuation he had set in the earlier cases, which was in reality a compromise between the two assessments.

Neither judgments nor decrees made much impression on large numbers of the tenants who continued to trouble Ellesmere 'with theyre Clamerous peticions'. An outstanding and meticulous Lord Chancellor, he at last became impatient with them, saying he had spent enough time on their case and given his judgment. He now referred it for further action to his subordinates Sir John Tyndal and Henry Thoresby, two of the Masters in Chancery. They called for, and the countess's officer Ralph Coniston gent. provided, a list of the names of the tenants, 101 in all, who had broken the court's decree. Then they informed Ellesmere that this further trouble 'grewe more oute of the turbolent spirrits' of four of the defendants, Robert Jackson, Christopher Dickinson, Francis Ewbanke and Nicholas Crakew, and that the rest were prepared to accept his judgment. Ellesmere consequently confirmed on 14 May 1610 his earlier decree against them. Yet the resistance did not end. A year later, Michael Ewbanke, Edward Guy and several other tenants were ordered to appear in court during the next term in October 1611. This order marks the virtual conclusion of the litigation begun in 1607. The decrees, writs, subpoenas and proclamations, the pressure of Countess Margaret's solicitors and estate officers and the cost in time and legal fees and of travelling to hearings in Westminster eventually forced even the most recalcitrant into acquiescence.

Ellesmere's decrees added one more strand to the intricacies of the Clifford family quarrels and administration in Westmorland. Attachments made by the court, for instance on 8 April 1610 against thirteen tenants who had broken the decrees, were directed to the sheriff of Westmorland, that is, Earl Francis. Consequently, through his deputy the earl carried out the directions of the court to his sister-in-law's benefit with whom otherwise he was in contention both in the Court of Wards and in Chancery and who had objected to his exercise of the sheriffwick. In this instance, he would privately have welcomed her assertion of authority in the long-term interest of the Clifford inheritance. She had fought the legal battles for herself and Anne but, because of Francis's reversionary interest in the Westmorland lordships, just as much for him and his successors, provided of course he prevailed in his struggle for the inheritance.[11]

Although most tenants had given in to *force majeure* they had not conceded the principle, as a new dispute in 1611 makes clear. Countess Margaret began a suit on behalf of her officer John Birkbeck, yeoman, and his son Geoffrey against Thomas Skayfe, Henry Shaw and other Mallerstang men. Their quarrel was over occupation of a messuage. The accusation made against Skayfe and his friends was the serious matter of 'dangerous combination' and forcible entry, hence the recourse in this instance to the Court of Star Chamber which dealt with questions of public disorder. The messuage in dispute, rent 7s 6d, had changed hands regularly. Henry Birkdale had been admitted to it by Earl George in 1582 and had later assigned it to Barnaby Skayfe who was formally admitted in 1592. It escheated (reverted) to Earl George when Skayfe died without issue. The earl then granted it to one of his estate officers, Henry Blencarne, on a warrant as recompense for his pains in writing the 1582 Book of Dimissions, though Skayfe's widow retained the moiety she was entitled to and was still living there in 1604.

John Birkbeck, a member of an able, ambitious and rising family, paid Blencarne £46 13s 4d for both the tenement and, he also believed, the tenant-right. He was mistaken in that, because of the nature of the earl's grant to Blencarne and because he held by warrant. Birkbeck then illegally built a firehouse on the waste and enclosed a rood and a half of ground for his own use, without permission. For these infringements, he was forced to compound by the tough commissioners Earl George appointed in 1604. Afterwards, he assigned the tenement to his son Geoffrey, who also received a warrant from George and on the latter's death dutifully paid his entry fine to the countess so that he now held on a warrant from her.

The contention possibly started on the death of the widow Skayfe. Thomas Skayfe, brother of Barnaby, and his supporters gave it out that Barnaby had held it in fee simple, that is, he owned it. They removed the Birkbecks' livestock from the messuage and commenced suit for trespass against them in the Court of Common Pleas in Easter Term 1611. In the depositions taken in January 1612 Henry Shaw, yeoman, aged seventy-two, and his fellows asserted that they held by tenant-right and warrants. If decrees and orders against tenant-right in favour of the countess had been made in Chancery then they must refer to some other parts of her estates, certainly not to those which they were claiming. The Birkbecks were ultimately restored to the tenement. This case shows that Ellesmere's decrees had made no impact on the Mallerstang farmers' belief in their tenant-right. Their attitude on this occasion makes all the more explicable the strength of the opposition Anne was to face forty years later.[12]

Countess Margaret had won only a partial victory over her customary tenants by her litigation. The Lord Chancellor had decreed in her favour over tenancies, yet lowered her officers' valuation of the holdings and relieved the King's Meaburn tenants of heriots. His interpretation of the customs of the Clifford lordships was correct and scrupulously fair. The tenancies were leaseholds and the estate officers had never regarded them as anything but that. The previous practices had been mutually advantageous, successive earls being content that their tenants trafficked in holdings with an element of freedom, always provided that they paid their due rents and gressums. But, especially under Earl George's lax management, the habit of easy trafficking had become ingrained. The tenants had come to believe in their ownership of estates of inheritance, which they could freely buy and sell. It was this conviction, bolstering their ambition to hold freely, their eagerness to exploit Countess Margaret's apparently weak position because of the dispute over the inheritance and, finally, their desire (at least of the better informed) to share whatever practices on other landlords' manors appeared more advantageous to them, which brought on themselves Ellesmere's rigorous definition of their tenures in a Chancery judgment which created a precedent for any subsequent conflicts.

The issues in Countess Margaret's litigation were not parochial, indeed could not be so in the climate created by James I's pronouncements on border service and tenant-right, let alone the farmers' awareness of practices elsewhere in their region. It was because of the special circumstances following Earl George's death that the issues came to the fore and were resolved earlier on the Cliffords' Westmorland estates than anywhere else. Ellesmere's judgment was to have wide repercussions throughout the north as the first legal decision in the fraught question of tenant-right and was interpreted and quickly exploited as a victory for the landlords, most notably on the Percy and Howard estates.

Roger Delaval, the earl of Northumberland's agent, informed him on 13 June 1609 that he had acquainted the Percy tenants in Northumberland 'with the laett order in Chansarye sensured against the Ladye of Comberlands tennents that noe Coppye houlder, Lyable to a fyne at the death of Lord and tennent, can have any state of Inherytance at All'. This had put them in such fear, he added, that they were ready to take twenty-one years' leases and pay a double rent for every farm. He told Northumberland his intention was to convert all the copyhold and tenant-right tenures to leasehold. Delaval was far too sanguine. Long conflicts on the Percy estates and throughout the northern counties were for the next two decades to embitter landlord–tenant relations. Lord William Howard, Dorset's uncle, similarly seized on the Chancery judgment, attempting in 1610 to convert the customary tenures in Gilsland into estates for lives by warrants. The Gilsland men resisted *en masse* and took action against him in the various equity courts, the strife only being settled, here as elsewhere, by a cash composition in the 1620s for which the Cliffords' settlements were a precedent.[13]

One almost neutral participant affected by Countess Margaret's policies was the unfortunate John Corney, the vicar of Orton in Westmorland who admitted, in the Star Chamber suit against him at the time of the royal Kendal barony tenant-right case in the 1620s, that he was the author of the 'libel' on tenant-right which argued, contrary to King James's views then, that it was not dependent on border service. In fact, he had written the piece at the request of Countess Margaret about 1608 and delivered a copy to one of the judges in Westminster when that argument was both acceptable to the King and germane to her litigation. By 1625, when the judges in Star Chamber gave their decisions over the Kendal barony dispute, legal opinion had moved on apace and they found that the customary tenures there were essentially copyholds of inheritance.[14] But those issues had seemingly been settled on the Clifford lordships by the King's Award of 1617 which terminated the inheritance dispute, as will be explained in Chapter 3.

The degree to which the great controversy over who was entitled to the Clifford properties impinged on Countess Margaret's tenure of her jointure estates will now be clear. Only with determined action had she established herself in Westmorland and levered from reluctant tenants the cash in rents and gressums she and Anne must have if they were to fund their suits against Earl Francis. To this end, the Countess, in contrast with her late husband, aimed to maximize income from her estates, making the best use of whatever resources were available. The quickest to convert into ready money were the timber resources, always a favourite with hard-up landowners. Trees were easily felled and sawn and there was an eager demand for all manner of wood which was scarce outside the enclosed parks of the nobility and gentry. Great timber for building was in shortest supply but chopwood for fuel and lats for fencing were just as marketable.

However, the countess ran into difficulties with the courts over her exploitation of her timber resources, this time as defendant. Earl Francis, following reports from his friends in Appleby that she was felling wood, challenged in Chancery her right to both the standing trees (worth by her admission at least £1,000) and the windfalls, on the grounds that she had only a life interest in them. The earl's officer Plantagenet Ireland hindered the carrying away of timber in March 1607. When the countess complained, his colleagues on the Border Commission intervened on Ireland's behalf with the justices of assize at Lancaster. The countess protested to the Privy Council on 15 August that she had taken only enough oaks to repair her houses and enough birches for local people to do the same, which they badly needed. She reacted vehemently to her brother-in-law's charges of spoil of woods by making public proclamations in the churches that she would now not only make weekly sales but defend them against anybody who tried to interfere.

It was again up to Chancery to settle the issue. With nobility quarrelling over estates which were very much in contention, Baron Altham of the Exchequer Court joined the judges to add his stature to their deliberations. They concluded that the countess had the right to timber for the usual purposes of building, fencing and reparations of her castles and grounds, but limited her use to only what was necessary. In this they were affirming the custom on many manors that a widow should not sell, make waste, or destroy any wood on the estate, merely take what was needful for repairing houses and husbandry gear. To secure compliance, the court appointed a commission (taking the place of the sheriff who was a litigant) to decide how much the countess needed, then to sell the surplus windfalls and return the proceeds to the court, which would decide what to do with the moneys. The commission did its job. The windfalls certified in 1610 were four score oaks and thirteen birches. The court's decision implemented effectively by the commission meant that Earl Francis had won the substantive case. The dowager countess was restricted in what she could use, denied profitable sales and prevented from wholesale felling of the valuable timber reserves, which would come intact after her death to him or his son or conceivably to Anne.[15]

However, the earl's skirmishing did not end with this satisfactory outcome, indeed it could not if he was to maintain credibility among not only his supporters in Westmorland but also his opponents. The countess's 'spoil' of woods did not stop and she would obey no court order. So he brought further actions of waste against her in the Common Pleas in 1613 both over the timber and such matters as repairs to Brougham Castle. In the trial, although the earl was sustained in only four of his listed complaints, the other fourteen being found for the countess, he had another victory because the coroners of the county (again substitutes for the sheriff) were commanded to allow no wasting. Thereafter, he renewed his actions against his sister-in-law on the grounds that her people had continued to do some damage since the court's writs were published.[16] These incessant irritations of the countess and her officers were the stuff of rivalries in the localities and essential if the earl was to gratify his gentry supporters and estate officers on whom he depended. She appears not to have taken them amiss, judging them the usual cut and thrust of landowners duelling over valuable assets and the needling obstruction which was part and parcel of the greater issue of the inheritance. Prosecuting Plantagenet Ireland, Simon Musgrave and other of Francis's gentry supporters in the Star Chamber for poaching her deer in Whinfell was one satisfying way in which she hit back.[17]

As a landed proprietor, Countess Margaret was highly successful. Even without income from wood sales, her revenues were appreciably higher than Earl George's. By 1611 they totalled £1,070 16s 9¼d (Table 1). The Stainmore coal-mines were much more profitable under her direction than her husband's. At the conclusion of the suits against her customary tenants she would have received at least £2,400 in gressums. Thereafter for entry and dropping fines she usually collected a two years' rent, occasionally as much as four. However, mindful of how George had behaved towards her tenants, she worried that, now well into her fifties, the new warrants she granted might not last long. In the will she first drew up on 18 May 1613, revised later and in its final draft signed on 27 April 1616, she abated the third part of any fines paid her within the two years prior to her death.[18] This concern was entirely consistent with her religious and moral outlook, which was commented on in the previous chapter.

Not even Anne writes with adequate appreciation of the importance of the countess's tenure of the Westmorland lordships. She ensured with the help of diligent officers, who often endured unpleasant confrontations with her tenants and Earl Francis's servants, that her properties were far better managed than in her husband's lifetime. Furthermore, she periodically lived in Brougham and Appleby Castles with her small household and spent the last two years of her life at Brougham, the first landlord to reside there for so long perhaps since the 1330s. In the final decade of her life and by her own efforts she came to enjoy a large and regular income, higher than that of most northern gentry. This compensated to some degree for the penury following her separation. Anne, with filial affection, wrote that her mother so wisely and prudently managed her estates that 'she lived both very honorably of it, and did many charitable deeds therewith', notwithstanding the great costs of her lawsuits with Earl Francis.[19]

However, Anne tactfully forbore to mention that the crucial contest on which the countess's later affluence was built and the Cliffords' position as landlords perpetuated was her struggles against her tenants. Yet to draw a veil over her lawsuits does her no favour. There was an ethical drive in them because the end was to achieve her daughter's rights as well as her own. Raising cash had a good purpose, but no less was obtaining what was her landlord's due, otherwise her tenants would get away with injustice, undermining the moral order of society. Without Countess Margaret's tenacity and full-blooded reaction to the

TABLE 1 *The value of the lands belonging to Countess Margaret's jointure estate in Westmorland, 1611*

1 *Woodside and Moorehouses*

	£	s	d
Free rents, viz Thomas Birkbeck in Hornby	6	0	0
Rents of customary tenants per annum	10	3	0
Cliburn Ling 23s 4d			
Peatmoss silver 6s 8d			
Farm rents, viz.	2	0	0
Turves called woodside moss 10s			
Custom rents Castle silver 40s			
Boon silver 8d	2	0	8
Sum total	20	3	8

2 *King's Meaburn*

	£	s	d
Rent of customary tenants	19	4	1¾
Farm rents, viz. Geiste silver	5	0	0
Custom rents, viz. mill farm	3	0	0
Demesne rents with the mill and Mill Croft	2	15	11
Sum total	30	0	¾

3 *Knock*

	£	s	d
Rent of customary tenants	8	8	0
Farm rents Fence field £10	16	0	0
The Pike and Maske £6			
Custom rents Boon silver 7s	0	11	0
Cowsley scape 2s			
Escape at Troutbeckfoote 2s			
Sum total	24	19	0

4 *Brampton*

	£	s	d
Free rents	0	1	9¼
Rents of customary tenants	5	4	3½
Farm rents viz for Flakebridge fryth	2	0	4
Custom rents Multure farm 2s	0	7	3
Boon silver 5s 3d			
Moveable rents, viz. the price of three hens per annum	0	0	6
Sum total	7	14	1¾

5 *Bongate*

	£	s	d
Free rents	1	6	1
Rents of customary tenants	14	9	3
Farm rents Sandford mire 10s	1	14	0
Fell rent 20s			
Ayston flatt 4s			

		£	s	d
Demesne rents	The watermill £3 6s 8d	3	13	4
	Langton watermill 6s 8d			
	Sum total	21	2	8

6 *Scattergate*

	£	s	d
Free rents	0	11	4
Rents of customary tenants	19	4	4½
Farm rents, viz. Minscoe Manor	2	0	0
Burgage rents	1	1	10
Sum total	22	17	6½

7 *Brough*

		£	s	d
Free rents		1	8	10½
Rents of customary tenants		31	2	8
Farm rents	Barton garth 3s	2	13	0
	The Fair £2 10s			.
Custom rents	Constable silver 6s	1	18	0
	Borough money £1 4s 6d			
	Gatelaw 7s			
	Search silver 6d			
	Sum total	37	2	6½

8 *Sowerby*

	£	s	d
Free rents	0	0	7
Rents of customary tenants	21	13	2¼
Watermill	2	6	·8
Sum total	24	0	5¼

9 *Stainmore*

	£	s	d
Rents of customary tenants	142	2	½

10 *Winton*

	£	s	d
Free rents	0	6	7
Rents of customary tenants	27	0	10½
Custom rents, viz. mill farm	5	6	8
Sum total	32	14	1½

11 *Kirkby Stephen*

	£	s	d
Free rents	1	6	0
Rents of customary tenants	24	2	8½
Farm rents, viz. for Stankredge	0	6	0
Custom rents, viz. for dry multure	3	0	0
Sum total	28	14	8½

12 *Mallerstang*

		£	s	d
Rents of customary tenants		36	1	3
Farm rents, viz. for Geiste silver		1	13	4
Custom rents, viz. for Running Gressum		2	10	2
	Sum total	40	4	9

13 *The Three Wards*

				£	s	d
Cornage, viz. in the	East Ward	£18	6s 8d	34	13	1
	Middle Ward	11	11s 5d			
	West Ward	4	15s 0d			
Free rents	East Ward	0	8s 7d	1	15	10
	Middle Ward	1	7s 3d			
Custom rents	East Ward	3	8s 5d	3	15	1
	Middle Ward	0	6s 8d			
Sergeant food	East Ward	7	7s 0d	13	6	8
	Middle Ward	4	14s 7d			
	West Ward	1	5s 1d			
Suit of county	East Ward	1	14s 8d	3	2	8
	Middle Ward	1	0s 8d			
	West Ward	0	7s 4d			

637 hens at 3*d* the hen		£ 7 19s 3d	33	12	9
513bz 2 pecks oats at		£25 13s 6d			
12*d* the bushell					
Sum total			90	6	1

14 *Demesne rents, yearly*

	£	s	d			
Appleby	160	2	1	547	15	10
Brougham & Whinfell	289	16	11			
Brough & Stainmore	90	16	0			
Kirkby Stephen	3	0	0			
Mallerstang	4	0	0			

Of which:	£	s	d
Free rents	47	10	1¾
Customary rents	359	15	9½
Farm rents	33	6	8
Custom rents	38	18	2
Burgage rents	1	1	10
Moveable rents	33	13	3
Demesne rents	556	10	11

SUM TOTAL OF THE RENTS AND REVENUES	£1,070 16s 9¼d

Source: Alnwick Castle, Syon MSS, X/II/3, Box 7, bundle h

challenge from the Westmorland farmers, neither Earl Francis nor Anne herself would have surmounted in quite the same way the opposition they in turn encountered to their seigniorial authority.

The Westmorland estates were the fulcrum of the great dispute over the inheritance. The countess's continuing presence there until her death in May 1616 held at bay the rival claimants Earl Francis and Dorset, as will be made plain in Chapter 3. How in her great noblewoman's life-style and piety she influenced local opinion is not recorded. Her bequests throw some light on her personal belongings in Brougham Castle, even though she lived frugally. Silver tableware, rings, pearls, diamonds, garnets, cloth of gold and silver, a satin bed canopy and stool were left to various members of the Russell family, the Shrewsburys, other titled friends and her faithful officers, including Dr Layfield and Sir Edward Yorke and his wife. She made gifts of a religious nature, apart from the obligatory moneys to the parish poor. The lands she had bought in Warwickshire and lands and woods near Kendal (proof of her affluence) she wanted to be sold 'to the best benefitt' to help provide the legacies. From her extensive library, which will be discussed in Chapter 10, she gave Plessis Du Mornay's book on the sacrament to Lady Herbert and a Bible to Christopher Shute, the Puritan Giggleswick vicar whose sermons had comforted her during her young married life. The rest of her belongings she gave to Anne and her granddaughter Lady Margaret. She made Anne responsible for completing Beamsley Hospital and her executors were to oversee the lands in its endowment.

The countess bade farewell to the world as befitted a Puritan 'with assurance to meete with God's electe in that greate Cittye, in the presence of the Lambe, by whose victorye wee are delivered, and by whose merittes wee are redemed and addopted coheires with hym of lyfe everlastinge'. Her stated wish was that she be buried at Alnwick, Northumberland, beside her brother who was murdered in 1585 on the Scottish Borders. On hearing of her mother's death, Anne asked Sir William Selby of Ightham Mote, Kent (a Northumbrian and one of her father's former associates on the Borders), about the possibility. Then she learnt of her mother's death-bed change of mind, leaving the decision to her. Anne's emotional preference was for her mother's coffin to lie alongside her father's in the Clifford vault in Holy Trinity, Skipton.[20] But Earl Francis's control there ruled it out. With Alnwick so remote, St Lawrence's Church, Appleby, was the practical alternative. This enforced choice had implications for Anne's commemoration of her parents which, as will be seen, was separated in time and location. It is, however, a commentary on her filial sentiment towards both parents that had it been in her power they would have been buried together and she could then have planned a joint memorial to them.

The splendid alabaster monument which she erected to her mother in St Lawrence's in 1617 was in every sense, the social as well as religious, highly appropriate (Pl. 13). The countess's recumbent and finely sculpted effigy, life-size and recognizably hers, lies with a metal coronet on its head and a lamb at its feet atop a tomb-chest which bears on its sides symbols of mortality. At one end Anne placed her mother's Russell coat of arms, at the other her father's, their colours adding to the striking attraction of the tomb. The inscription on the north side has the ring of Samuel Daniel:

13. Countess Margaret's monument, erected by Lady Anne, St Lawrence's Church, Appleby-in-Westmorland, by Maximilian Colt, 1617 (Photo: the author)

WHO, FAYTH, LOVE, MERCY, NOBLE CONSTANCIE,
TO GOD, TO VIRTVE, TO DISTRESS, TO RIGHT,
OBSERV'D, EXPRESS'T, SHOW'D, HELD RELIGIOVSLIE,
HATH HERE THE MONVMENT THOV SEEST IN SIGHT.
THE COVER OF HER EARTHLY PART, BUT, PASSENGER,
KNOW, HEAVEN AND FAME CONTAYN THE BEST OF HER.

The tomb's similarity to Queen Elizabeth's in Westminster Abbey by the outstanding monumental sculptor Maximilian Colt indicates that Anne commissioned it from him and with that style in mind. By employing so gifted an artist Anne not only commemorated her mother with suitable grandeur but also brought dignity and the excellent craftsmanship normally associated with the Jacobean Court to a church which then was in one of the culturally remote and dark corners of the realm. Happily the monument escaped damage during the Civil Wars so that it adds lustre to St Lawrence's to this day.[21]

CHAPTER 3

The Great Inheritance Dispute

1606–17

The inheritance suit begun by Countess Margaret on her daughter's behalf was to be a long and costly action, the dominating legal dispute in which the Cliffords were concerned. It embittered relations in the family and the uncertainty it brought over possession of the estates continued long after Lady Anne's death in 1676. There were two issues, separately pursued. The lesser, in the sense that litigation was not involved, was the claim for the titles other than the earldom which passed to Francis Clifford as heir male of Earl George; the greater was the tug of war over all the properties held by George at his death. Yet they were interrelated because for the countess and Anne the same principles were at stake.

Struggles between heirs male and heirs general (which included females) were common and the greater the rank and landed wealth the more was at stake and often the more acrimonious the contention.[1] Few equalled the Cliffords' controversy in its complexities and even more rare was a dispute whose echoes impinge so much on popular as well as scholarly opinion today. Only Francis's wife, Countess Grissell, was to distance herself from the argument and with reason. She was related to the Dorsets as well as the Cliffords. She had been on the fringe of the quarrel over the Abergavenny barony between her stepson Edward Nevill and Lady Mary Fane. Earl George had been one of the noblemen who assisted the Earl Marshal in 1598/9 at the hearings. One aspect of the Abergavenny dispute had bearing on the Cliffords'. The Lord Chief Justices determined that the heir male had no right because common custom favoured the heir general, a decision Earl George and his lawyers would have pondered. James I eventually settled the quarrel by arbitration, giving Nevill the Abergavenny barony and reviving for Lady Mary the barony of Le Despenser.[2]

Neither the countess nor Anne would have been appeased by resurrecting an ancient if honoured title; only Earl George's baronies would satisfy them. Anne's claim for Clifford (1299), Westmorland and Vescy was set out in a petition by her mother to the Court at Whitehall on Sunday 23 November 1606. The supporting submission had been thoroughly researched, as mentioned in Chapter 1, and was impressively argued with evidence from inquisitions, charters and grants, abstracts from wills, pedigrees and analogous cases, including that of Abergavenny. One telling point was that the three baronies had been created by writ and a writ was intended to create an estate of inheritance in new barons 'whiche is in Lawe a fee simple', so not restricted to male heirs.

The wider argument for female inheritance of baronies put forward on Anne's behalf is worth considering because it helps us to understand her later attitudes and actions. If it seemed absurd (the question was posed) that the dignity of baron should be transferred to the heir female when the original creation was for advice and counsel to the King in Parliament (from which women were excluded) then it could be answered that in France and Spain women by custom enjoyed that honour. Even though a woman was better fitted by her very nature to give counsel than to be a warrior, the rhetorical question was posed why shouldn't a woman be a baroness, King's Champion, Countess Marshal, or hold her lands by knight service; this considering that everyone called by writ to parliament was called by the name of 'chevalier', not baron.

The gender obstacle to each aspect of this notion was neatly sidestepped. It was conceded that 'man in his sex be more excellent than woman, yet in quality wee see often women excell men'. So there was no reason to bar them especially when, as in Anne's case, there would be no detriment to the commonwealth. Though a woman physically could not perform knight service, that is, fight for her monarch, she could take a husband to do it for her and in law her son was allowed to perform it. Indeed, many barons who claimed as heirs male did so from females and they were not denied the right to do knight service. The custom of England was that, where a baron had only a daughter or daughters, the eldest son of the eldest daughter would inherit the title. This interpretation of inheritance by and through the heir female the sixteen-year-old Anne latched on to and held to thoughout her long life.

The countess's petition was passed to the Earl Marshal for consideration and he referred it to the commissioners for matters of honour and arms, the senior royal officers the earls of Dorset, Lennox, Suffolk, Worcester and Northampton and Lord Admiral Howard.[3] J.H. Round has pointed out that the proceedings afford, perhaps, the earliest instance of the doctrine of 'attraction' in peerage law. The question was whether all or any of the baronies were, by virtue of the patent of Henry VIII creating the earldom in 1525, entailed upon Earl Francis as belonging to the earldom, or ought to descend to Anne as heir general. Francis was summoned to defend his right.

What the Earl Marshal's commissioners decided is obscure. There was no clear precedent or practice to apply to the case in 1606. In a similar claim ten years later for the barony of Roos the point was sufficiently uncertain for the King to settle that matter also by compromise. Neither Earl Francis nor his son ever conceded any part of their claims to all the Clifford titles and styled themselves barons as well as earls. Their argument seems to have been accepted. Henry was called to the House of Lords in 1628 on the assumption his father held the barony, the occasion and consequences best considered in Chapter 5. For her part, Anne never relinquished her claim to the titles and this view eventually prevailed, though not until after her death. As late as February 1667 Sir Henry Yelverton, writing to Sir William Dugdale, Norroy King of Arms, cited the Cliffords as an instance of baronies going with the earldom. On one aspect both sides were mistaken. The barony of Vescy had become extinct in the fifteenth century because of the limitation, then unique, to the heirs male.[4]

The contention over possession of Earl George's estates was to prove immensely complicated, an entanglement of legal rights, matters of practicality and equity, and emotional and political issues. It was these ramifications which made the Clifford inheritance dispute a classic of its era. The roots of the problem reached back to 1555 when the 2nd Earl's two marriages had produced three daughters but no sons. As explained in *The Privateering Earl*, his anxiety to ensure that the earldom continued led him to execute a special deed of entail. This, suitably amended to give precedence to George and Francis, he incorporated in his 1569 will. By its terms, all his estates were entailed on George; if George left no sons then they were to go to Francis and his male heirs, and if Francis, too, died without sons then successively to other named male Cliffords from related branches of the family.

This entailing of all the Cliffords' properties on George and the designated sequence of inheritance lulled him and his legal advisers, John Pigott and Richard Hutton, into assuming that he had inherited from his father in fee simple. On that assumption, they began in 1591 the standard legal procedure to bar his father's entail, which would leave George with the power to sell, assign or devise his lands as he thought fit. The method was a fine and recovery in the Court of Common Pleas, a fictitious sale and return of the estates in question which usually took a year to complete and was called in the records by the regnal year it was done, in this instance 33 Elizabeth.

This fine and recovery enabled Earl George in 1591 to make a settlement of his estates on his younger and surviving son Lord Robert and at the same time arrange the Westmorland jointure for Countess Margaret. Following Robert's death later that year, he made a new settlement of all his landed possessions on Francis, who from now on was his designated heir. The documents asserted that George 'had an absolute estate' in all his properties, which is what he and his lawyers believed. Nevertheless, there was a legal flaw in all the settlements and deeds on which Francis's claim to inherit was based, although the court actions were well under way before it came to light.[5]

Early in 1606 it looked as if Earl George's death-bed plea to avoid controversy would be heeded. Countess Margaret's reaction to receiving a copy of his will from Salisbury was more than conciliatory because she promised to keep and observe it. She asked for a commission to appraise her husband's goods and chattels so as the better to satisfy his creditors and perform his will. She said she would write to Francis for a speedy answer on this matter. However, she was in two minds about what to do. She informed Salisbury she desired 'more to obeye your lordships directions, than annye other course', but somewhat contrarily looked to him for support 'yf necessitye inforce my alteration of present disposition'. She asked him to show favour towards her and Anne 'in this troubled course'.[6]

Earl Francis had the advantage throughout of occupying all his brother's estates except Westmorland. The onus of seeking to change the status quo by offering proof of her case lay with Anne. Francis had one early success. Both he and Anne claimed the sheriffwick and this forced an immediate political intervention. The Privy Council allowed him to exercise the office because he (rather than a young girl) would maintain the essential administration in the county.[7] He also had the satisfaction of watching the countess from early 1606

14. Francis Clifford, 4th Earl of Cumberland (1559–1641), by Augustine Harrison, 1610 (H.T. Fattorini Esq.)

being embarrassed by opposition to her from her Westmorland tenants who exploited the conflict over ownership, as has been described in Chapter 2.

Because Anne was under her mother's guardianship, the Court of Wards was the proper place for legal action. Countess Margaret's first step when she, Francis and their counsel met Salisbury in his lodging in the court, was to ask for a commission for an inquisition post mortem. The inquisition would ascertain Earl George's estates at his death, their value (if imprecisely), and what dispositions and conveyances he had made. The composition of the commission – the king's officers and for impartiality six men, three named by either party – had been agreed when she changed her mind, as her letter to Salisbury had hinted. She began suit for Anne's claim to all George's estates with a formal submission to the court. What or who persuaded her to this course is not revealed in the written records. She also bombarded the King and councillors with arguments and pleas on her daughter's behalf.[8]

Earl Francis immediately responded, waiving his parliamentary privilege in the hope of satisfying her. The court, following normal procedure, appointed a commission which required Francis to answer interrogatories, a list of searching questions about the estates. The countess rejected the counter-arguments he put to the court and accused him of delay in answering the interrogatories and in supplying the evidences the court requested from him. 'I hear they intend to make it a suite of many years to us', she complained to Salisbury. Later in the year she repeated her charges of unnecessary delay, which drew from the earl an equally vigorous protest. He claimed he had brought all the conveyances asked for and had offered a full view of all in his Skipton Castle muniments. He had answered the interrogatories and his solicitor had been in constant attendance on the court's surveyor whereas none had come from Anne. He thought there was 'neither cause nor colour to tax him with any dilatory intent'.[9] Yet Francis was soon to have good reason for delay and for adopting the defensive in the controversy, an attitude only partly dictated by his occupying the Craven estates.

15. *Sir Robert Cecil, Earl of Salisbury (1563–1612), by John de Critz the Elder (Reproduced by courtesy of the Marquess of Salisbury)*

Historically and legally Earl George's estates comprised three blocks: that is, the Westmorland lordships; the

Honour of Skipton in Craven; and all the rest combined. Anne's claim for them was twofold, a joint argument for Westmorland and Skipton, another for all George's other lands. The Westmorland lordships had been granted by King John in 1203/4 to Robert, 1st Lord Vipont, and had come into the Cliffords' possession by the marriage of Roger Clifford the Younger (d. 1282) with Isabella de Vipont, heiress of Robert, 3rd and last Lord Vipont. The Honour or Fee of Skipton-in-Craven with the castle and its demesnes, the Forest of Barden and the lordships of Silsden, Stirton and Thorlby, had been granted by Edward II in 1311 to Roger's son, Robert, 1st Lord Clifford. Anne's claim for both these parts of her family's inheritance was that they had been granted in tail, and that the reversion of both was still vested in the Crown. A grant in tail meant inheritance by the heirs general. The reversion in the Crown meant that the estates would revert to the Crown when there were no heirs left. In this instance, there was one, Anne.

The third block of George's properties had cohesion in the sense that almost all were in Craven. The two most important elements were the Percy Fee with its lordships and Bolton Abbey. Outside Craven there were just the small residues of three manors in Cumberland and Clifford's Inn in the city of London. In her claim for this block, Anne relied on a daughter's superior right under common law over a brother or nephew, which would be even stronger over a remoter relative such as her uncle.[10] Earl Francis's counter-claim for Craven and Westmorland was that he owned all the properties because he held them in fee simple, George having bequeathed and willed them to him on that assumption.

It was the countess and Kniveton who, by assiduous research, discovered the flaw in Francis's case. When Earl George had taken the precaution (as he thought) of barring the entail by the fine and recovery of 33 Elizabeth, his lawyers had blundered in failing to realize that the reversion had never been taken out of the Crown. By the statute 32 Henry VIII c. 36, when a reversion was still vested in the Crown a fine and recovery were inoperative.[11] The settlement of the estates on Francis was, therefore, invalid and Anne, it appeared, was entitled to inherit as George's surviving heir general.

During the 1650s, Anne's lawyer Sir Matthew Hale explained how the blunder had happened. Earl George, 'as is the use of great persons of plentiful estates', he wrote, had looked no further back than his father's will, while the learned Sir Richard Hutton and his other counsel had never suspected that the reversion was still vested in the Crown. It has to be said that besides George's legal advisors his father's were equally at fault and, by including George, Hale was unfairly spreading the blame to some degree. Earl Francis's counsel at once recognized the doubtful validity of his case. 'Taking the alarme, and thinking to mend his condition', Hale continued, Francis petitioned James I to allow him to compound for the 'manors castles etc whereof his Majesty has not only a remainder but a pretence of title in respect of some imperfections in his grant being since made to his ancestors'; the wording couched to minimize the legal disaster it conceded.[12] The King was agreeable. The grant, in June 1607, comprised the Honour of Skipton-in-Craven, the Westmorland manors and the sheriffwick, and cost Francis £500. It took the reversion out of the Crown, but too late to affect the dispute.[13]

Though this action explicitly conceded the strength of Anne's claims to the original Clifford and Vipont lordships, there was no guarantee she would win because the test at law had still to come. Nor, in the cut and thrust of the duel over rights and possession, did Francis scruple to use his new grant to embarrass the countess in Westmorland. Writing to the Privy Council from Appleby on 15 August, she complained that he had made it known there that his brother's estates, being forfeited to the Crown, were now his by reason of the grant. She took this report 'as a device to bring her title into discredit and to terrify the country from dealing with her'.[14]

The countess's suits in the Court of Wards proceeded on the lines of the county-based system of legal administration. The Westminster lawcourts dealt with cases shire by shire and relied on the sheriffs to carry out much of the local work for them such as serving writs and empanelling juries of enquiry, as was seen in the previous chapter. The Cliffords' properties fell neatly into either Yorkshire or Westmorland. Consequently, to prosecute her daughter's case at law and dislodge Francis, the countess pursued two separate processes in the Wards, one for Westmorland, the other for Craven. The hearings did not coincide but that was no hindrance because, as it happened, the argument for Anne's right to the Westmorland properties took a different course from that for Craven, so that the court was dealing with two quite distinct issues. That for Westmorland will be described first.

The commission appointed by the court in Westmorland comprised gentlemen employed by the earl – the two escheators for the county, Sir William

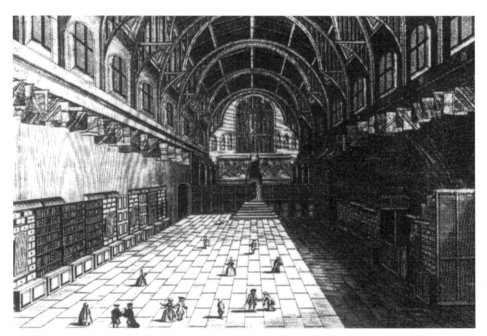

16. *Interior of Westminster Hall: the courts sat in the partitioned areas at the end and side of the hall (British Museum)*

Hutton and Thomas Carleton Esq., and Thomas Birkbeck Esq. of Hornby Castle – yet they acted scrupulously. Their inquisition at Kendal on 20 December 1608 traced the conveyances of the Westmorland lordships from the jointure made by the 2nd Earl Henry to his countess, Anne Dacre, in 1554, to Countess Margaret's jointure and finally George's will. They found that George on his death held in chief by knight service of King James; that is, directly from the Crown without any intermediary. The case came before the court in Easter Term 1609. When nobility were at loggerheads in such an important matter it was usual for three senior judges to sit – here Sir Thomas Fleming the Chief Justice, Sir Edward Coke the Chief Justice of the Common Pleas, and Chief Baron Sir Lawrence Tanfield. At the hearing, they decided that the inquisition had been properly conducted and that the reversion of the Westmorland properties on Earl George's death had been vested in the Crown, so they were subject to the Henrician statutes governing estates held in chief. Despite the objections of Francis's counsel, this is what they decreed. The finding favoured Anne's claim to the Westmorland lordships as the direct descendant of the Viponts though, again, that was not conclusive.[15]

The argument over the Yorkshire properties proved much more difficult to resolve. The examination of Francis and his senior officers by a commission appointed by the court began at York on 23 November 1607. In the following April, 1608, there was 'great pleading' in the court. The inquisition for George's lands was taken at York Castle on 24 April 1609. This rehearsed the original grant of Skipton by Edward II and affirmed in addition that Henry VI had granted the reversion of those lands to Thomas, 8th Lord, before 1443/4.[16] It was these two matters which most exercised Judges Fleming, Coke and Tanfield when the case was argued in Michaelmas Term 1609, now with the added authority of Salisbury presiding as Master of the Court.

The judges came to the first vital conclusion in the whole dispute. They accepted that all George's Yorkshire lands, except for the Honour of Skipton, were held in fee simple and properly settled on Francis and his heirs male. The 33 Elizabeth fine and recovery in this instance was given precedence over Anne's rights as a daughter under common law. Francis had thus won possession of all his family's lands apart from Westmorland and the Honour of Skipton. Anne's comprehensive claim to all her father's properties had been rejected.

What now remained to be settled, therefore, was ownership of the Honour of Skipton and the manors named in Edward II's 1311 grant. The crucial point was the validity of Henry VI's supposed patent to Thomas, 8th Lord, because, if accepted, this would make the 33 Elizabeth fine and recovery effective for the Honour of Skipton too. Anne's lawyers objected to the clause in the inquisition asserting, in Hale's words, that it had been 'shuffled' into the inquisition by Francis's lawyers 'without any coller of evidence'. He was writing long after the event. What caused the judges to give it close attention was that it was the attorney of the Court of Wards, no less, who vouched for the patent.

The problem over the clause brought a new dimension to the case because it lifted the legal argument on to a higher plane altogether. The judges had to assess what effect accepting the validity of Henry VI's supposed patent would have on the Crown's interest, an overriding consideration. As Coke remarked in his *Reports*, whatever was most beneficial to the King would in many cases take precedence. The issue in this instance was the Crown's right to regain the properties should the Clifford line die out. The judges declared that it would be greatly 'mischievous' to divest the King of part of his inheritance unless the grounds for doing so, that is, Henry VI's patent, were proven. However, they thought their court was not the place to reach a decision of that kind. They advised the attorney of the Wards to grant Anne the right for a special livery – a much more meticulous enquiry than an inquisition – to be done without prejudice to the title of either party, so that Francis could try his right and title by an action at common law rather than continue the argument in the Wards. The livery, completed three years later in 1612 at a cost to Francis of £116 13s 4d, ended the first phase of the dispute.[17]

The achievement in legal terms by 1612 was, first, that the courts had restricted Anne's claim to just Westmorland and the 1311 Honour of Skipton. Second, the arguments about them had been clarified. Further action could continue on that basis in the Court of Common Pleas. However, the nature of the dispute had changed because the Crown's interest now had to be considered. Moreover, personal relations between the contesting parties, which had already tinged the controversy, began to overshadow the legal aspects. For these reasons, the later phases in the dispute became far more fractured.

The new dimension was the legitimate intrusion of the Earl of Dorset following his return from his year-long grand tour of France and the Low Countries. Now of age, he supplanted Anne because under the doctrine of coverture a married woman had no legal identity, held no property in her own right and lost the right to 'moveables', which included her jewellery and other chattels. The £15,000 portion which went with Anne had become Dorset's on marriage and so, too, her claims to the Clifford estates. The documents often refer to 'Dorset's portion', as indeed it was.[18] He now legitimately replaced his mother-in-law. The Common Pleas suits were conducted in his name and Anne's. His manipulation of the opportunities which fell to him was predictable and not just because of his character and the dominance of husbands over wives which both contemporary social philosophy and judicial practice accepted.

For the most part, Dorset behaved correctly towards his wife. From 1609 he had supported her financially, meeting her living costs with an allowance, and he continued to do so. When able, he granted her a jointure. All this was in the expectation that he would receive either the portion by Earl George's will or, better still, the Cliffords' large estates. His subsequent behaviour and treatment of his wife, however reprehensible they may seem, are understandable in view of the frustration of his financial expectations. He had to wait ten years for his due. In the meantime his own income was restricted by the jointure lands held by his stepmother and the annuity his grandmother took in lieu of a jointure. Moreover, his mother-in-law occupied the Westmorland lordships which he coveted and to which through his wife he had a claim.[19]

The potential for discord increased because for Anne her father's estates were an intensely emotional as well as a legal issue. Indeed, she and her mother shared with Earl Francis and his son the common bond of Clifford sentiment.

17. Richard Sackville, 3rd Earl of Dorset (1589–1624), by William Larkin, c. *1613 (English Heritage: Ranger's House, Blackheath)*

Not so Dorset, who wanted his £15,000 and a bigger sum if he could get it, or the Craven and Westmorland estates; indeed, both cash and lands should the chance occur. He pursued these objectives consistently throughout, as the legal decisions and the changing situation allowed, yet always for the maximum gain. At varying times he was at loggerheads with his wife, his mother-in-law, Earl Francis and Lord Clifford. In the end, after litigation and political intrigue had failed him, he bowed to the king's will. His attitude was only what might be expected from a leading Jacobean courtier whose expenditure always exceeded his income. It was Anne who jibbed against the accepted norms, which brought for her periods of isolation and distress as she endured the wrath of her husband and her monarch and disavowal by her friends.

Despite Dorset, it was Countess Margaret who remained the key player. Francis regarded her as such and acted accordingly. Crucially she held Westmorland, on which emotions and ambitions were focused. Anne, lacking the substance, lands and an income of her own to stand up for herself, continued to depend on her mother's judgement, determination and moral support. After the countess's death, she had little to contribute but obstruction and strength of will, neither subtlety nor ingenuity being of any use to combat the dominance of her husband, her relatives and the king. Only occasionally, when Dorset's attitude coincided with her own, did she have an iota of influence over him.

A distinguishing feature of the dispute after Dorset's intrusion was its reach not just upwards into the factions of James I's Court and Privy Council but also downwards into the local politics of the north-west. Salisbury's death in 1612 gave Dorset and his supporters the upper hand over Earl Francis at Court, which they never relinquished. In Westmorland, tensions heightened as their rivalry and jostling for advantage caused divisions in local administration and in the attitudes of their tenants and gentry supporters. In the end the local antagonisms got out of hand and compelled the king's intervention to calm the situation and bring the dispute to a conclusion.

Early in 1613, as a new round of court hearings loomed, both Dorset and Francis favoured arbitration, not by lawyers but by a knight who was not a lawyer. Sir William Wentworth of Wentworth Woodhouse was the most suitable and declined only because he was unable to ride to London without endangering his health. The next stage of litigation was held up by practical difficulties. When Francis's cause came before the Common Pleas on 6 November 1613 only three of the jury appointed in Yorkshire turned up at Westminster Hall. Dorset's counsel requested that a jury of Yorkshiremen with freehold in London should be appointed instead, they being thought more likely to attend. This the court refused, deferring the case until Easter Term 1614.[20]

Heavily in debt and fretting at the delay, Dorset now tried a new tack, a private settlement with Earl Francis but raising the financial stakes much higher. John Taylor in London reported to Francis on 18 January 1614 the rumour that William, 2nd Earl of Salisbury, had offered £25,000 on his behalf to Dorset for an agreed settlement, the cash to be paid within two years. Taylor's opinion, for he had not seen Salisbury to seek confirmation, was that Anne's supporters (Dorset's really) had given 'oute these speches to grace their Tytle'. But there was, in fact, substance to it and Anne, writing from Bolebrooke, promised to let her mother know as soon as any composition was agreed between her husband and uncle.[21] Such a large sum was beyond Francis's means and he did not respond.

A year and a half later, on 16 June 1615, the trial in pursuance of the order granting the livery began at the Common Pleas bar in Westminster Hall. Before the hearing, Dorset approached Lord Clifford and demanded £20,000 for the portion and, in addition, that both the Skipton and Westmorland properties be assured to Anne after the heirs male, that is, if Francis's and Lord Clifford's male line failed. Clifford wrote to his father about this new offer and the crucial statement by Lord Chancellor Ellesmere that Anne could have either the lands or the portion but not both. This was the second definitive decision in the dispute. It had profound implications, setting clear bounds on what Francis stood to lose (no doubt to his relief) but especially on what Dorset and Anne could hope to gain. Both sides accordingly had to modify their tactics.

Replying immediately, Francis rejected Dorset's demands. If, he argued, he were to pay the £15,000 portion, he would expect Anne to release the lands to the heirs male, as in her father's will; but if Dorset wanted more, then he would expect a release to the heirs general, his own and Cliffords' daughters as well as sons. He was certain that Anne and Dorset had no just claim to the lands in Westmorland and he still hoped his own title to Skipton was strong enough. He did not think Dorset would benefit from his attempt to recover Skipton because of the Lord Chancellor's definitive statement.

Francis reminded his son that he had always been prepared to pay the portion and hoped the judges would not increase it since he would have no choice but to raise the money from the estates. 'It must be considered', he added, 'that my Brother dyed greatly indebted which must be payd.' He had written to the judges on this matter. 'I doubt not but they will doe us right with favour', he concluded. However, he hoped that he and Clifford would have no cause to regret that the decision was left to the 'grave and worthy Judges' who, he was certain, did not wish the ruin of the House of Clifford and, he trusted, would not punish them by enlarging the portion. It was their opponents' fault that the portion had not already been paid and now he was in a much worse position to pay because of the expense of the litigation. As to his sister-in-law, he was not prepared to waive the advantage he had over her unless all cause of further suits between them could be prevented. This he doubted, her disposition considered, unless she assigned her jointure over to him for 'a valuable consideration'. For Francis to occupy the Westmorland properties would give him a decisive edge over his opponents.

In the Common Pleas, Dorset's counsel set forth Anne's title to Skipton on the grant in tail to Robert, 1st Lord Clifford. Against this, Sergeant Hutton pleaded the grant of the fee of Skipton Castle and its lands to Thomas, 8th Lord. Yet he could do this only by inference because the patent had been lost (assuming it had ever existed). The court rejected his plea. Arbitration by consent was again attempted and once more failed. A decision could be delayed no further. In their award Lord Chief Justice Sir Henry Hobart and his fellow judges followed the earlier findings in the Court of Wards and Ellesmere's statement and to that extent foreshadowed the terms of the final settlement. To Francis they gave Westmorland and the sheriffwick and, though they upheld Anne's right to Skipton, the earl was to retain it and pay a composition. On two important details, the earl lost. First, the composition was much higher than the original portion; £20,000 should Anne agree, £17,000 if she refused. Second, the inheritance, as Dorset had demanded, was restricted to the heirs male.[22]

It is hard to escape the conclusion that the judges had given less weight to Anne's claims as lineal heir general than to the other important factors. These included Dorset's rights by coverture, the practical necessity of ending discord in Westmorland in the interest of effective local administration, and the appeasing of two of the country's leading earls whose quarrels reached into the Privy Council. Just as Coke had anticipated, the ongoing Crown interest, which under Kings John and Edward II had led to the endowing first of the Viponts and then the Cliffords, now under King James had been given precedence. Grants in chief had always implied obligations and responsibilities owed to the Crown. Earl Francis and Lord Clifford, like Earl George before them, were discharging these in the Middle Shires administration, as governors of Carlisle and sheriffs in Westmorland. They deserved the estates; they needed them to pay the composition; and without them they would be financially ruined and of little use in royal service.

Had it been left to Francis and Dorset, the dispute might now have ended. Instead, it had two more years to run. The problem was to compose the division in Francis's opponents, because the judges referred their award to the consent of all the parties, which was essential if it was to be effective in law. Francis and Dorset did consent, Anne would not. Despite his belief that Countess Margaret, her disposition considered, would not cease suit for the estates, Francis asked Sir John Bowyer in August 1615 to sound her opinion. 'I do proteste', she told Bowyer, 'that, next myselfe, daughter, and sister, I do wish well unto my lord of Cumberland, my lord Clifford, and his lady, and will not think the better of any that shall exasperate me against them.' She seemed, Bowyer reported, much offended with Dorset because of some comments he had made in public. Bowyer formed the opinion that she would incline to peace.[23]

The countess's letters to Anne show that she put a different construction on her meeting with Bowyer. She warned Anne on 8 October of their opponents' 'preaktas with you, to seveur you from me' and thanked God they had not prevailed. She condemned in the passionate language of the righteous Puritan their 'wiket praktis' to try to sever Dorset from herself. Earl Francis's intent, she implied, was to break up their triple alliance. She urged her daughter to stand firm and reminded her of a witty aphorism, 'the feminy ginger is much mor constannt then the marskilin'. The countess may have perceived Dorset as the weak link, far less constant than she and her daughter. She ended her letter with a benediction on Anne, 'the lord of hostes the god of all marcy blies you'.[24]

In November the judges met Dorset and counsel on both sides to try to compose the differences between them. 'Still the delay', wrote John Taylor, 'is on their partes, not ours'. But Dorset was so certain of reaching agreement with Anne that he wanted the earl and Clifford to come up to town at once. Though neither the earl's counsel nor the judges would advise that, Taylor requested that they to be ready to make the journey as soon as word was sent.[25] The caution was justified. Dorset could not persuade Anne to agree to a settlement by composition as the judges thought fit. 'My Lord is still earnest to press me to the finishing of this matter with my uncle of Cumberland', she averred to her mother on 10 November, 'but by the power of God I will continue resolute and constant.' On 6 December, she reported that Dorset's desire was to take the money, surrendering for it her right to the estates. She would do whatever she could to alter his mind 'though I fear me it is impossible'.

This obstinacy exasperated Dorset who complained: 'your land transports you beyond yourself and makes you devoid of reason'. He kept up the pressure on his wife, as she told the countess in January 1616; 'my Lord is more and more earnest with me to make a final end of this business with my uncle of Cumberland, and persists that, if I do not, he will go into France and leave me'. Even Francis Russell wanted her to settle and used all his persuasive powers to that end.[26] During March Earl Francis and Dorset both tried, in different fashion, to overcome her opposition through her mother who, though far away, remained Anne's emotional buttress. Prompted by friends of both parties in London who desired 'a general peace amongst us', Francis instructed Sir Christopher Pickering to approach the countess again in the hope that she would be willing to accept arbitration even if Anne would not. He was so far from spleen or malice, he wrote, that if she were of the same mind he was prepared to refer all matters in dispute to the judges to settle in an award. He stated firmly that he was not suggesting this course out of necessity or distrust of his own right, only as *'knowinge whose wife shee was, for whose sake I must ever honor her, and preferring peace farr before warr'.*[27]

Dorset allowed Anne to journey to Westmorland to confer with her mother, taking with her the copy of the award which the judges required them to sign and seal. The countess signified to Lord William Howard and his colleagues who would have witnessed the documents that they would not sign. Anne returned to Knole early in April after a 'grievous & heavy Parting' from her mother, the last time they were together. More determined than ever not to sign, she intensely annoyed her husband by deliberately leaving the documents at Brougham. She wrote to her mother from Knole on 26 April, 'Be assured that I will stand as constantly to my birthright as is possible for me', but with the cautionary comment that she could do only what was within her means.[28] On 18 May Dorset proposed to the countess through Anne that she allow him to occupy her jointure lands and pay her the yearly value of them, which widows often preferred. His intention is plain. Occupation would be for him possession and he would then do with them as he pleased and most likely settle with Francis over Anne's head.[29]

Countess Margaret's death at Brougham Castle on 24 May 1616 turned an opportunity for peace into the occasion for war. The news reached Earl Francis at Skipton within twenty-four hours, Sir Christopher Pickering, Sir Christopher Lowther and Edward Birkbeck all hastening to let him know. This gave the earl the initiative because Anne did not learn 'the heavy news' of her mother's death until four days later. The earl at once sent John Ecton post haste to London and his Craven steward Stephen Taylor and Richard Hughes to Westmorland to take charge for him. Next day, the 26th, the earl issued a warrant to Birkbeck and his other officers, Henry Brougham, William Grimston and Richard Backhouse, to enter the castles and manors there and to hold them for him in peaceful and quiet possession. Soon after, he sent Lord Clifford with a small party to Appleby to bolster the actions of their officers and gentry friends in the county.

If Francis was quickest off the mark in Westmorland, Dorset and his allies had the influence at Court. The Privy Council on 4 June warned Lord President Sheffield at York, Lord Howard de Walden (Francis's titular fellow-Lieutenant), the deputy lieutenants and justices of the peace in Westmorland of the likelihood of trouble. Hearing reports that the earl's men had used force to enter Appleby Castle, breaking doors and windows, they ordered those officials to take all steps necessary to keep the peace and to safeguard the countess's goods. Francis was swift to defend his action. He explained to the council that he had given instructions for peaceful occupation. Indeed, he had expected no opposition. The Common Pleas award had given him the succession to the Westmorland estates, Dorset had recently affirmed his acceptance of it and they had not only agreed assurances on this but drawn up the documents ready for signing.[30]

For their part, the eight Westmorland justices, including Sir James Bellingham, Sir Christopher and Sir John Lowther and Pickering, reported to the council that at Clifford's request an enquiry had been made into the use of violence and that none had been proved. The late countess's goods at Appleby, of little value since she had not resided there for two years, had been inventoried by her own and the earl's servants together. Her officers were still in possession of Brougham Castle and Pickering had charge of its contents. The justices had clearly acted with propriety, yet their report was not well received by King James, now more attuned to Dorset's viewpoint than Francis's.[31]

The dispute had, in fact, entered a new phase. This became apparent first at Court following a complete reversal in Dorset's attitude upon realizing the possibilities of his situation. Since the Common Pleas award, he had been willing to cooperate with Francis in hope of a speedy settlement and cash payment. Now the vacated Westmorland estates were within his grasp. It was a position he could not fail to exploit. Early in June he sent a letter to the late countess's servants and tenants to keep possession for him and Anne, which greatly pleased her because she feared her uncle had too easily taken over the properties. On 20 June Anne at last gave in to his persuasion and, before Lord Hobart, passed a fine to her husband of her Westmorland inheritance, though with the proviso that she had no heirs of her body. With this authority to act, Dorset straightaway wrote letters to Lord William Howard and sent them with Anne's attendant Edward Marsh to take possession of Brougham Castle, where the countess's body still lay. By the end of June he and Anne were great friends again and she returned most of her jointure lands to him with the promise of a new jointure in Michaelmas Term of the full third of his estates, which were now much bigger because of his grandmother's decease the previous year.[32]

In the first week of July word reached Francis from London that there was now no hope of agreement and that Dorset was not only shrinking from the terms of the award but seeking every means to begin suit again. This news put him on his guard. He was not willing to yield the initiative. He heard that Anne, on her way north attended by twelve servants, had in fact reached Boroughbridge, and that Dorset would shortly follow her. He feared she might attempt at Appleby to deprive him of possession. He was confident of the care and discretion of his officers there but again sent Richard Hughes in haste to add purpose to their authority. He gave orders to Hughes to get in twelve loads of hay from the Southfield, have some beer brewed and make it known that he himself intended to travel there soon, 'for so it is very lyke'. He was heartened by the assurance of Sergeant Hutton who offered to wager his whole estate at Goldsborough that all was clear on their side if they could but hold on to what they had got.[33]

Anne arrived in Westmorland in the second week of July. On the 11th, having obtained permission from the Appleby borough authorities, she carried her mother's body with much ceremony from Brougham for burial in St Lawrence's parish church at midnight. Her presence in the county heightened local political tensions because Lord William Howard's faction gave her overt support against their Clifford opponents. On 17 July Anne rode into Whinfell Park and told the tenants, who were hay-making, to withhold payment of their rents. On the 25th she signed a warrant for the killing of a stag on Stainmore. This direct challenge to her uncle and cousin led to a serious disturbance on 29 July when two of the earl's men, who interrupted her people hay-making in the park, were hurt. They complained to the assize judges on circuit in Carlisle. Those judges, who two days before had sequestered Brougham Castle to preserve the peace, ordered the culprits to appear before them when they held the assizes at Kendal.

August saw the divided loyalties and political antagonisms grow into a confrontation. Anne was joined at Brougham on the 22nd by both Dorset and Howard with a big company, having carried all their beds and furnishings from the south. Clifford took up residence in Appleby Castle on the 26th though, to Anne's satisfaction, with a much smaller train.[34] To preserve the peace, the Privy Council had empowered a commission of eight Westmorland justices on 12 August to take possession of all the disputed manors, but not the two castles, Clifford being allowed Appleby and Anne Brougham. However, the split in county allegiances obstructed the efforts of Lord Sheffield to ensure this was done in the proper and equitable fashion the Privy Council had ordered. The justices could not agree among themselves, dividing five for Francis, three for Dorset. So, on the 20th they delivered separate certificates to Sheffield.[35] That same day Dorset and Anne challenged Francis's claim to the sheriffwick by issuing a patent to an under-sheriff nominated by them.[36] On 27 August there was another serious disturbance, this time in Penrith. As Anne recorded, 'our Folks being all at [Penrith] there passed some ill words between Matthew, one of [Clifford's] Keepers & William Durin, whereupon they fell to blows, & Grosvenor, Grey Dick, Thos. Todd & Edwards [the groom] drawing their Swords made a great Uproar in the Town, & 3 or 4 were hurt, & the Men [who] went to ring the [church] Bell fell from a ladder and was sore hurt'.[37]

Three weeks later, both parties appeared at York before the Lord President to plead their causes. It was a great social gathering, Clifford's company comprising twenty-four knights and gentlemen and twenty-eight serving men and waiters. On 17 September they dined with Sheffield at the King's manor and ate supper at Mr Fawcett's.[38] At the hearing on 19 and 20 September, no reconciliation was achieved. But in a letter to Sheffield on 27 September Francis repeated his wish for a peaceful settlement and for the first time offered lands as well as cash to Dorset and Anne provided he could be certain the dispute would then end.[39] There was no response to this conciliatory gesture.

Anne continued to live at Brougham until 9 December, when she set out for London to join her husband. The in-fighting continued after the main protagonists had left, Howard's gentry clique against those who supported Clifford. The dispute had shifted from London to Westmorland and York; then inevitably south again to London. Almost upon arrival, Dorset and Clifford, both accomplished jousters, threatened to put their rivalry to the private test of skill in arms. The king, hearing of it, ordered them to 'forebeare one another, and try out theyre controversies by warres in Westminster Hall'.[40] But a return to legal sparring, of which there had been a surfeit in the past ten years, was no means of assuaging quick tempers primed now by constant cause for provocation and legitimate discontent. No course was left but for the contestants, Dorset and Francis, jointly to approach the king. James intimated that he would be pleased 'to take into our Princely consideration the hearings endinge and finall determination' of all the suits and controversies between them.

Once again Anne proved the stumbling-block to an agreed settlement. On 8 January 1617 she and Dorset fell out anew over the question of her lands. On the 18th they were taken by the king's favourite, George Villiers, Earl of Buckingham, into James's Drawing Chamber in Whitehall Palace and left alone with him. As they knelt before him side by side he tried to persuade them both to peace and to put the whole matter into his hands. Dorset consented, but Anne 'beseech'd His Majesty to pardon me for that I would never part from Westmoreland while I lived upon any condition whatsoever'. Two days later she and Dorset, Francis and Clifford with their lawyers, the judges and privy councillors were assembled before the king when Anne again defied him, at which he 'grew into a great chuff'. James, however, was not prepared to let Anne delay the ending of a controversy which had caused so much dissension among his courtiers and in the north-west counties and in which the Crown had a vested interest. He gave his decision, the 'King's Award', on 14 March 1617. That same day Francis and Clifford came to Dorset House where they signed and sealed the writings, doing as Anne lamented 'what they could to cut me off from my right'. Next day James set off on his progress towards Scotland, on the return journey being entertained by Earl Francis at Carlisle and Brougham Castles.[41]

The King's Award confirmed the earlier findings of the courts and in particular the Common Pleas award of 1615. Although it acknowledged Anne's claim to the original Clifford estates of Skipton, Westmorland and the sheriffwick, it recognized that the dispositions her father had made were an equitable as well as a practicable arrangement. There is a continuity clearly discernible from the 33 Elizabeth fine and recovery and George's subsequent settlements, through his wills of 1598 and 1605, and the 1609 and 1615 judgments in the Wards and Common Pleas, to the King's Award. With the status quo as its basis, Earl Francis retained the estates and was to give £20,000 compensation to the Dorsets, the larger sum already mooted. He was to pay £17,000 within two years, a huge increase over George's unconditional £10,000 portion which is not fully explained by the rise in prices since 1605. Payment of the final £3,000 again depended on Anne's acceptance of the award.

The King's Award was a comprehensive document which regulated the present tenure and future inheritance of the estates, the payment of the compensation and the means allowed Francis to raise that money from the estates. George's dispositions were affirmed in the succession to the estates. Skipton and Westmorland with the sheriffwick were to be held by Francis during his life, then descend to Clifford and his heirs male, and in default to the heirs male of the earl. If the male line failed, they would pass to Anne and her right heirs, male first, then female, and in default to Clifford's daughters, and finally Earl Francis's daughters. Francis had, therefore, been forced to climb down over release to the heirs general for the larger sum, a concession not quite matched by the condition attached to his payment of the extra £3,000. All the other properties inherited by Francis from his brother were to pass to his right heirs, as the Court of Wards had decreed in 1609.

The award was more favourable to Anne's inheriting than she at first thought. The same applied to tenures in the Honour of Skipton which might some day belong to her or her heirs. The earl was restricted in the leases he could make. He was forbidden to grant terms longer than 99 years or three lives, except in Silsden. Because of George's great sales and leasing in 1602/5 Francis would have difficulty in raising the £17,000 compensation. The award, therefore, permitted him to collect £2,000 by granting leases for any number of years to tenants in Silsden to a maximum rental value of £20 a year. The remaining £15,000 was to be raised from the Westmorland lordships by confirming the tenures of those who held, or claimed to hold, by custom of tenant-right at rates to be agreed between them and the earl. The final, conditional £3,000 would also come from Westmorland. The Westmorland tenants had mixed feelings over these terms. Only five years after being beaten by Countess Margaret in the lawcourts they had got what they wanted, the overthrow of Ellesmere's 1609 decrees, though at the huge collective cost of at least £15,000. Their resistance to paying this cash will be commented on in the next chapter.

James I took cognizance of the likelihood of Anne's refusal to accept the award. To safeguard Francis after he had paid the compensation, Dorset was to assure him manors worth £25,000 which he could lawfully sell to recover his money if, after Dorset's death, Anne should again commence suit. Finally, any ambiguity in the award or dispute over interpretation were to be referred to James himself.[42]

The subsequent events were to reveal how futile Francis's hopes had been of settling the differences by mutual consent. The terms of even this final decision were put into effect by compulsion. Anne would not, and never did, accept the award. Moreover, she did her utmost to undermine her uncle's takeover of the

Westmorland lordships to which, as her mother's jointure lands and where her father was born and her mother died, she had the deepest attachment. Her intrigues will be described in the next chapter and the consequences of her refusal to accept the award in Chapters 7, 8 and 12.

For their part, Francis, Clifford and Dorset strictly observed its terms. Dorset made the necessary assurance of lands for the earl's protection. In a deed he conveyed to the earl's officers Pickering and Ecton his Sussex manors of Michelham, Parkgate, Milton, Lullington, Swanborough, Sticcles, Hangleton and Houndean. The new jointure Dorset made Anne in 1623 included most of those manors. If this proved a check on her attempts to win back her estates, it was done for lack of alternative choices, not by design, as will be explained in Chapter 5.

Francis gave security for the £20,000 to Dorset and paid the first £17,000 on the due dates so that at last Dorset got the cash he had chafed for since his marriage.[43] To his discomfiture, his stepmother saw her chance and sued out her thirds in May 1617, which were now more profitable to her than her jointure lands, and this only increased his troubles and the discontent which he focused on Anne.[44] Francis also refrained from granting leases in the Skipton manors for periods longer than the award stipulated, although he badly needed to do this to diminish his debts. He introduced a private bill in parliament for confirmation of the estates of the Westmorland tenants, which he was obliged to do if Anne refused to accept the award.[45] In this instance only is there a semblance of a breach of good faith. The bill was not enacted because of the dissolution of the 1621 Parliament, but the earl may not have been unhappy because enactment would have meant having to pay the final £3,000 to Dorset. The economic condition of his Westmorland tenants, not to mention his own finances, would probably have made that impossible.

Indeed, for Francis, the King's Award was a Pyrrhic victory. Although he got the estates, he was forced to borrow the £17,000 to pay the instalments to Dorset because it would take years to raise all that cash from his tenants; in reality, as long as eight. These new loans re-created the huge indebtedness he had inherited from his brother and took twenty years to clear, by which time other debts had accumulated. For the rest of their lives, he and his son faced another uphill battle which leached away their landed wealth except for the Skipton and Westmorland manors which the award protected, as it turned out, to Anne's future benefit.[46]

CHAPTER 4

Anne, Countess of Dorset

1609–24

So far in this study, Lady Anne has only intermittently appeared centre-stage. The associates of her younger days, her parents, tutors, uncle, husband and King James, have been the main *dramatis personae* as the themes of inheritance, titles and estates, which came to dominate her life, have been considered. The spotlight now falls on Anne herself as a countess, married for fifteen years to Richard, Earl of Dorset. So much is known from her *Diaries* about Anne's relationship with Dorset that to dwell on the minutiae of the events and emotions they reveal would be needless repetition. What is offered here is a different perspective of their married life. In one sense it is a continuation on a broader scale of the appraisal of Dorset's behaviour which was offered in the previous chapter. In another, it draws attention to aspects and phases of Anne's life which neither her *Diaries* nor her biographers adequately cover. Her views of marriage as a sacrament and for procreation were conventional and will not be explored. But her perception of marriage in a secular sense did alter as the years passed and this will be looked at both here and in Chapter 6.

A major obstacle to any assessment of the Dorset marriage is that virtually everything known about it comes from Anne herself. Moreover, she presents a reader with three tangentially different views of her attitude towards Dorset and the nature of their relationship, as if seen through a prism. One facet is chronologically detached, her recollection of him set down much later in life. There is no doubting Anne's love and admiration for Dorset, which never really dimmed even when his actions were most hurtful. This may colour her memory of him as 'of a just mind, of a sweet disposition and very valiant in his own person'. Similarly, her testimony on the marriage, that she 'was happy in many respects being his wife', has a rosier tinge than might be judged from her *Diaries'* entries, yet it does concede that in some respects she was unhappy.

The second facet is contemporary and there is a case for giving it the greatest weight. Anne defended her husband in letters to her mother when Countess Margaret was most critical of him. On 20 November 1615 she stressed that Dorset was 'a very kind, loving, and dear father' to their daughter Margaret. She continued: 'in everything will I commend him, saving this business of my land, wherein I think some evil spirit works, for in this he is as violent as is possible'. She was even more vehement on 26 April 1616, after her return from Westmorland. The countess had been bitter about her son-in-law's demand that she and Anne sign and seal acceptance of the judges' award, so much so that Anne had not the courage to speak up for him. Now she could open her mind;

'whatsoever you may think of my Lord,' she wrote, 'I have found him, do find him, and think I shall find him, the best, and most worthy man that ever breathed'.

It is these heartfelt words, close in sentiment to her later memories, which must be borne in mind when the third facet, the perspective of her *Diaries*, is cited as laying bare Anne's relationship with him. There are grounds for regarding the *Diaries* as a partial, even prejudiced, source which has to be assessed cautiously and critically like any historical document. More will be made clear on this point in later chapters. Granted that limitation, the *Diaries* are a rich quarry for details of Anne's life and the following discussion will draw heavily on them, as have the previous chapters in this study.

It is partly because of the *Diaries* that Dorset has suffered so much adverse comment by Anne's biographers. He had shortcomings aplenty, shown in his extravagance, gambling, infidelity and wasting of his huge landed inheritance in a manner recalling Earl George's, though without the latter's redeeming feature of outstanding service to the realm. Anne was all too conscious of the parallel and her reaction to it is reminiscent of her mother's, as will be seen. There was another side to Dorset. He was certainly as valiant in life as in her memory, courageous in his personal dealings and in jousting and hunting, though he was never put to the test in warfare. There were times when he went out of his way to be kind, considerate and generous to Anne and he always was to their children. His other good qualities may have been less visible in his relations with her than with his friends, for obvious reasons. Her love for him apart, Anne would have counted it her good fortune to have as a spouse a nobleman high in the king's esteem, popular with his fellows, endowed with a fine physique and presence, accomplished in field sports and impressively wealthy. She let speak for itself the manly appeal which would have made her the envy of many a lady at the Jacobean Court, Aemilia Lanyer, for instance, calling him 'beauteous'. Unhappily for her, several ladies openly usurped it.

On Dorset's weaknesses, John Aubrey is the best gossipy source. The earl lived, he wrote, 'in the greatest splendor of any nobleman in England. Among other pleasures that he enjoyed, Venus was not the least.' His mistresses included Elizabeth Broughton, 'a most exquisite beautie', whose 'price was very deare'; the 'wondrous wanton' wife of Dean Overall; and Lady Venetia Stanley, by whom he had one or more children and on whom he settled £500 a year (though Venetia's lover may have been his brother Edward). Anne herself mentions in her *Diaries* the affair her husband had with Lady Penistone, though not the two children he had by her.[1]

Dorset had been a scholar of repute at Oxford, encouraged by his 'wise grandfather' Lord Treasurer Buckhurst. Throughout his life he patronized men of learning. Had his own bent been rather different, leaning more towards intellectual matters than to the excitements of Court life and outdoor pursuits, Anne might have found in him an ideal husband with a questing mind attuned to her own. However, theirs had been an arranged match for the advantage of both parties. John Chamberlain had foreseen the likely pitfalls. Dorset was placed in the unfortunate position of having to strive to obtain his portion, whereas his friends had immediate access to theirs. Anne, for her part, needed a protector and, if possible, a champion for her cause. The two ends were all but incompatible granted Earl Francis's entrenched position and the complications of the inheritance issue.

Moreover, to judge from Anne's own writings she and Dorset appear not to have had much in common in their tastes, the one being more intellectual, literary and country-loving at heart, the other reckless and flamboyant, with the wealth to indulge a courtier's wastrel instincts. This impression is misleading. The obvious appeal of the Elizabethan and Jacobean Court to Anne herself in her younger days cannot be ignored. She had been brought up there or on its verges, and its gaiety had almost the same magnetic attraction for her as for Dorset. The exuberant cultural pleasures, the masques, plays, dances and feasting and the sumptuous dresses she wore of the highest quality and latest fashion were enough to turn the head of any young noble lady. Before her marriage she had taken part in some of the best entertainments and this continued as Dorset's Countess. For the celebrations which accompanied Prince Henry's creation as Prince of Wales in June 1610, her old tutor Samuel Daniel devised the masque *Tethys' Festival*, in which the Court ladies represented the river nymphs of England. He aptly cast Anne as the nymph of Aire, the river

which flows past her birthplace, Skipton Castle. Dorset was one of the tilters who performed on the last day of the celebrations.[2]

It would not have been fitting for Anne to stay in London unescorted while Dorset was abroad in 1611/12 and she says she remained at Knole. A few entries in the account of George Wood, steward of the house, for the year starting 1 October 1611 mention Anne's activities there. In January 1612 when William Hall, the baker, injured his hand, Anne sent for a London surgeon, Mr Allen, to examine it and Hall was also given medicine. It was to no avail; he died and was buried in Sevenoaks church. That same month a close seat was made at Anne's request and oiled and coloured by the painter 'that it may endure the weather'. In February she had wicker screens made for her use. Then on Dorset's return, they took communion together with

18. The Great Staircase, 1605/8, Knole House, the Dorsets' seat in Kent: the pillars Lady Anne recalled with emotion (Photo: Country Life *Picture Library)*

others of his household. During August, pens were bought for her use, a lock made for her closet door, and she had eight tables and twenty-four joined stools made and other things done about the house, Dorset providing the material.[3]

During 1612 they were frequently at court, residing at Little Dorset House. There were great occasions, such as Prince Henry's impressive funeral on 7 December, when the attendance of all the noblemen and their ladies was obligatory. In the procession Dorset was one of the twelve earls who carried the train of Elector Palatine, Count Frederick, and Clifford carried the banner of the prince's dukedom of Cornwall. Mourning could not last long because of the marriage of Princess Elizabeth and Prince Frederick on St Valentine's Day 1613. Dorset took the eye as the most richly attired man among the great number of nobility present and Anne, who was with him at the ceremony in the King's Chapel in Whitehall, assuredly matched him in her own attire. Dorset was an imposing tilter at the ring when he and also Clifford performed in the great entertainment on the King's Day, 24 March.[4] Princess Elizabeth, the unfortunate Queen of Bohemia, was a good friend of Anne and wrote affectionate letters to her.[5]

Anne, as one of the premier earls' wives, would often have been drawn into Queen Anne's entourage on great court occasions. She probably sat with the queen's party at Thomas Campion's *The Lords' Maske* at the royal wedding. She was certainly one of the leading ladies who accompanied the queen on her progress in great state to Bath and Bristol, leaving Hampton Court at the end of April 1613 and returning to Windsor late in June. The Lord Chancellor and various noblemen escorted them, Dorset included. He was one of the performers who entertained the royal party with revels and in Thomas Campion's masque at Caversham.[6] Anne would have found particular pleasure and companionship in the queen's entourage. Both Samuel Daniel and John Florio were grooms of the queen's privy chamber with £60 and £100 fees respectively. There was hardly a hiatus in Anne's links with Daniel up to his death in 1619.[7]

Dorset performed again in another Campion masque given in the Banqueting Hall of Whitehall Palace on St Stephen's Night, 26 December, as part of the festivities for the marriage of Robert Carr, now Earl of Somerset, and Lady Frances Howard. On New Year's Day he and nineteen others tilted in Whitehall and thereafter he always took part along with the earls of Pembroke and Montgomery (the latter Anne's future second husband) on special occasions such as the King's Day in 1614. Anne would have been in duty bound to be present at the Somerset wedding, Carr being the king's current favourite. However, having become pregnant in October she may then have cut down her social activities until after Lady Margaret's birth on 2 July 1614 at Little Dorset House. Although her mother missed the event because of her researches in the Tower, she was present at the christening a few weeks later in the private chapel of Great Dorset House.[8]

Anne's letters indicate there was no change in the Dorsets' life-style just yet. They had great feastings of their own at Christmas in Knole. Dorset had a huge household and followed the usual noble establishment pattern of formal, hierarchical seating at mealtimes, with his and Anne's table set apart for them, their children and a few favoured senior officers. On festive occasions, however, when many friends and relatives joined them, the gatherings would be jovial, in a relaxed, even bucolic conviviality. They returned to Little Dorset House for the whole of the January-to-March law term 1615. Then in April Anne, staying at Bolebrooke, visited Bath and the next month thought she might be pregnant again.[9]

However, in June 1615 Anne's pattern of life and her relationship with her husband began to change. The reason, the great issue of the inheritance dispute, is clear from her letters to her mother. Countess Margaret had now retired to Brougham Castle and did not visit the capital any more. When the Common Pleas hearing began on 16 June Dorset refused to let Anne journey to Westmorland until the business was settled. Although the evidence is scanty, it looks as if she spent most of the summer with her daughter at Bolebrooke. In September, however, she was with Queen Anne on her progress to Bath. It was Anne's servant who guided the queen from Oatlands to Horsley and thence back again on the 9th, receiving £3 6s in reward for his pains.[10] When Dorset and the whole household moved to London on 29 October his hopes were high that he could persuade Anne to accept the judges' award and he wanted Earl Francis to come up to Westminster. Dorset's chance of a settlement petered out as the law term drew to its close and his wife still resolutely refused to agree. She told her mother on 20 November:

> I must either do it next term, or else break friendship and love with him. God look upon me and deliver me, for this last term I have lived in fear and terror daily, with griefs and terrors daily, which have made my eyes sore as I dare not write much, but I must be sparing of them for a while.

With the term over, Dorset decided to return with her to Knole, which suited her purposes admirably.

For a while, she does not appear to have accompanied him to the great Court gatherings, even though Knole was within easy ride of Whitehall Palace and Dorset House was on its doorstep. Her diary shows her making visits, though not frequently and for quite brief stays. New Year was almost a mandatory appearance. On Twelfth Day 1616 she sat with the Countess of Arundel in her box to watch Ben Jonson's masque *The Golden Age Restored* at its second performance. She also visited Chenies that month, which she omits to mention in the diary. Much of the first half of February was spent in London and Anne was lobbied heavily to try to persuade her to accept the award.

Her version is well worth relating because it is at variance with the standard interpretation. She twice records in her *Diaries*, both at the time and sixty years later in retrospect, how on the afternoon of the 17th in the best gallery of Great Dorset House Archbishop Abbot of Canterbury, Lord William Howard, Lord Roos, her cousin Francis Russell, her brother-in-law Edward Sackville and 'a great company of men' did their utmost by terrifying her and also by flattery to get her to sign acceptance of the judges' award. She stood up to them all, asserting to 'his Lordship that I would do nothing till my Lady & I had conferred together'. They concluded that she should have leave to visit her mother and send answer by 22 March whether they would agree to the award or not. The next day, she writes, 'was a marvellous day to me through the mercy of God, for it was generally thought that I must either have sealed to the Argument or else have parted with my Lord'.[11]

What occurred instead was the happiest episode Anne recorded in her *Diaries*, not, however, in its chronological place (which would have ruined the impression of a beleaguered lady) but one she recalled with special pleasure almost at the very end of her life. Dorset set off with her towards Westmorland with the judges' documents, which he expected she and the countess would sign. They left Little Dorset House on the 21st for what was a sight-seeing journey together; a pointer to what their relationship might have been in different circumstances. Anne rode with her husband; not, as her contemporary entry might suggest, by herself, in the 'little coach lined in crimson velvet' which Dorset's stepmother Cicely Baker had recently bequeathed her.[12] They travelled without haste, stopping at inns, passing near Grafton House, visiting Anne's cousin Thomas Elmers at Lilford, looking round two of the country's great old castles at Warwick, with the church there, and Kenilworth. They stayed two nights in Lichfield so that on Sunday 25th they could go morning and afternoon to the sermon and service in the cathedral and 'afterwards into other of the most remarkable places in that towne'.

After visiting the Curzon house at Croxall in Derbyshire (Dorset's sister-in-law Mary's family home), they parted company, Dorset returning to Lichfield for a few days for a great foot-race, Anne proceeding towards Brougham with ten persons and thirteen horses in her party. *En route*, she continued to go out of her way to see the outstanding places of interest. On the 27th, she looked round the earl of Devonshire's houses at Hardwick – the old Hall and Robert Smythson's modern glass palace – which would have been hers had she married into the family. The next day she called at the earl of Shrewsbury's strong manor house Sheffield Castle and passed the night at Rotherham. Riding over the Pennine moors she did not stand on ceremony, putting up at a poor parson's house in Penistone and a Manchester inn. She passed near to her Stanley relatives' great Lathom House (destroyed in the Civil War) but it was obscured by mist. At Chorley, she spent the night in a cottage, in fact a poor ale-house and not to her taste, and the next night at a Preston inn. At Lancaster, where she put up at another poor inn, she entered what remained of the old castle and walked on the leads with their fine panorama of the Pennines, Morecambe Bay and the Lakeland mountains.

Her viewing continued later in her mother's company. From Naworth Castle, where they spent a few days with Lord William Howard and his wife Lady Elizabeth Dacre, her father's cousin-german, they went to Carlisle. How Earl Francis reacted when he heard they had looked over the castle where he was governor is not known. Anne mentions that they entered the chamber where Anne Dacre, Countess of Arundel, was born. She went to the cathedral where her great-grandfather William, Lord Dacre, was buried, but she would have also noticed the fine organ her Cumberland grandfather had donated in 1542, bearing his own Clifford coat of arms and that of his countess, Eleanor Brandon.[13]

This tour, which had begun so happily, ended acrimoniously. No sooner had Anne and Dorset left London than Samuel Daniel wrote at length to Countess Margaret, warning her that Dorset with 'Resolution & Wilfullness' intended to take the portion and sacrifice Anne's inheritance as the judges' award allowed. In phrases reminiscent of the advice the countess received during the 1590s, he warned her against showing anger towards Dorset and counselled that Anne, likewise, should 'endure the Storms that may come from an angry husband with Patience & sufferance' instead of responding in kind, because reconciliation might come in time. They should leave the business wholly to the protection of Almighty God.

Daniel wrote as the spokesman for their friends in London and this almost certainly included Queen Anne and her intimates. Here again, as in the 1590s, there is in Daniel's intervention a 'whiff' of oppositionism, from a faction embracing the countess, her daughter and friends and the queen's circle. Their sympathy had a firm ethical base in Anne's legal title, another echo of the 1590s. The queen's household at Somerset (Denmark) House was a separate court from the king's and in some senses its rival. This was one of the disparate elements in the cross-currents of sentiment, self-interest and politicking which bedevilled the later stages of the great dispute. In the event, as related earlier, the countess refused to sign the documents and Anne deliberately left them in Westmorland, to Dorset's annoyance. But afterwards she defended him against her mother's strictures. How far she thereafter took Daniel's advice to heart may be judged from her subsequent behaviour.[14]

Nothing makes plainer the Dorsets' ambivalent marriage relations than the troubles over the inheritance following the countess's death in May 1616. Anne had to call on all her stoicism to survive her deepest personal crisis in the months that followed. She found herself isolated, impotent, and almost friendless and under intense pressure from the court; a rare glimpse of the lobbying power which could be mustered, here against the obduracy of a young countess. The Archbishop of Canterbury, her mother's confidant Dr Layfield, Francis Russell and many more urged her to accept the judges' award and settle. Only Queen Anne, who talked to her in her withdrawing chamber at Whitehall Court, and Lady Wotton (her cousin and Earl Francis's niece) consistently stood by her.

Dorset's treatment of Anne see-sawed, from apparent fondness to hostility according to whether or not his ambitions coincided with hers. He had little option but to employ harsh tactics to force her acquiescence. Without Anne's agreement to the award, he could not get his long overdue portion. What upset Anne the most was his taking custody of Lady Margaret and withdrawing her jointure, her financial safety net if she were widowed. Dorset was underhand over the latter, cancelling it when she was with the countess in Westmorland in the spring of 1616 and not letting her know until a year later, after the King's Award. It has to be said in his defence that a jointure was a wife's quid pro quo for the portion she brought to her husband. Until he got the cash Dorset was not obliged to make provision for her, yet he had done so. What he had given he could just as well take away until he got his portion. It was his wife's own fault, he could argue; all she had to do was settle.[15]

Anne's greatest ordeal came in February 1617, escorted twice into the king's presence and bravely defying him. On both occasions, Dorset proved far kinder than she had expected. He was anxious that the king should not disgrace her publicly. With his help, she came through the nerve-racking encounters far better than anyone expected; miraculously she said, with God's providence and by trusting her welfare to the 'worth & nobleness of my Lord's Disposition'. Over the next weeks as Dorset's agreements with her uncle were being drafted, she had several more chances to accept them. When she still adamantly refused she was 'condemned' by public opinion. Finally, she refused to sign and seal the King's Award, justifying herself on the grounds of the promise made to her mother and the world at large that she would not do so. She was even more downcast when she received and studied a copy of the award on 9 July, its terms being, she thought, worse than she had reckoned.

Emotionally drained in these months, Anne was reduced to frequent 'blubbering'. She found consolation in her favourite reading but that was not enough to stave off periods of deep depression. The sense of betrayal and failure took its toll. She was often sad and melancholy, with bouts of weeping. It is not surprising that for over a year royal palace life lost much of its appeal. Her visits were more to keep up appearances and attend the masques and plays of Inigo Jones, Ben Jonson and Thomas Campion, all shot through with contemporary philosophical and political concepts and classical allusions which teased scholarly minds like hers. Anne had become much more home-living, even perhaps home-loving. She had never approved of some of her husband's diversions, the gambling, hunting and gaming. When Dorset visited Knole, he preferred not to stay long, setting off quickly for his house at Buckhurst or to Penshurst and Arundel, hunting all the way.

Furthermore, when at Court Anne was probably embarrassed and offended by the presence of her husband's mistress, Lady Penistone. Theirs was a public affair, conducted at her mother's house in the Strand, and brought them eventually two daughters to Anne's solitary child. Whether Lady Penistone was the cause or consequence of Anne's partial withdrawal from Court is a moot point. If the diary records all the occasions Dorset slept with his wife at Knole, his sexual diversions for three or four years were almost entirely with this mistress, not with her.

Anne's reaction to this personal affront was not unlike her mother's during the 1590s, though at a much younger age, Daniel's advice perhaps deep in her mind too. In other words, she fell back at Knole on her own interests and resources, the kind of living which in her later years she much preferred. She stitched cushions, played card games, glecko and tables with her attendants and, most of all, took pleasure in being read to from Spenser, Montaigne and the Bible. After her mother's death she added the countess's library to her own and fell on this new stock of books with relish.[16]

This was a period when Anne began to develop and express her maturing artistic sensibilities. She had been familiar from her earliest years with the monuments in the Bedford family chapel in St Michael's Church, Chenies, and the magnificent royal tombs in Westminster Abbey. Lady Arundel took her, Dorset and others to see the famous collection of pictures and classical statues at Arundel House. Anne admired the 'fine delicate things' in the upper rooms of Queen Anne's residence, Somerset House. She viewed with Dorset the ornate tombs in the Beauchamp chapel in St Mary's, Warwick, on her journey to Westmorland in 1616.[17] However, the creative direction of her cultural interests, erecting monuments, could have been inspired by Countess Margaret's memorial to Richard Cavendish, her associate in Craven lead-mining, which she had set up in Hornsey Church, Middlesex, in 1601.[18]

Anne's object, to laud and perpetuate the memory of relatives and friends who had passed away, was particularly apposite to her first choices, her cousin and childhood friend Frances Bourchier and then Countess Margaret. Frances had died on 30 August 1612 at the countess's house at Sutton in Kent. Anne appropriately placed the monument where her cousin was buried, in the Russell mausoleum at Chenies (Pl. 19). It is a simple tomb of classical design, with four white Tuscan columns supporting a black marble table slab. Superimposed on its black marble base slab are the coats of arms of Lady Frances and her parents, carved in relief in white marble. Round the edge of the tomb is an identifying inscription. Anne saw it on her visit in January 1616. Her splendid monument to her mother in St Lawrence's, Appleby, completed in 1617, was described in Chapter 2.

What is regarded as a more surprising commission was the monument to Edmund Spenser which the noted mason Nicholas Stone made in freestone for her in 1620. As he recorded in his notebook: 'I also mad a monement for

19. *Lady Frances Bourchier's monument, erected by Lady Anne in the Bedford Chapel, St Michael's Church, Chenies, c. 1615 (Photo: Dr H.C. Gladstone)*

20. *Edmund Spenser's monument, Westminster Abbey, erected by Lady Anne, by Nicholas Stone 1620, restored 1778 (The Dean and Chapter of Westminster)*

Mr Spencer the pouett and set it up at Westmenster [Abbey] for which the Contes of Dorsett payed me 40£.' Certainly, it was entirely in keeping with Anne's emotional state in these years because the inclusion of Chaucer in the inscription combined tributes to those favourite poets who continued to give pleasure as well as solace during her worst years of tribulation.

However, Anne's action has been misunderstood. A monument to Spenser had been erected before January 1600 when it was described in a little Latin treatise by William Camden, printed under the auspices of Gabriel Goodman, Dean of Westminster. Camden may have been the author of the monument's brief eulogy to Spenser inscribed in Latin which ended with a verse linking him with Chaucer, who had already been lauded in a monument in the Abbey. Camden included an epitaph to Spenser in his *Remaines Concerning Britain*. This first commemoration of Spenser may have decayed or been a simple slab not dignified enough for Anne. She replaced it with a standing monument, appropriate to someone above Spenser's station in life but not in her esteem (Pl. 20). Stone copied the earlier inscription and added an English translation, though Spenser's dates were wrongly given. Anne did not, as has been asserted, create Poets' Corner in the Abbey, but she did refurbish and perpetuate it. Her own monument was recorded as old and defaced in 1708, its Latin inscription wholly lost. It was so much decayed in 1778 that it was restored in marble, though only with the English section of the original inscription.[19]

This artistic patronage was one means by which Anne expressed her individuality and cultural enthusiasms while living in Dorset's shadow. It helped offset the drawbacks to living in a great house like Knole run by officers with clearly defined duties in day-to-day charge and at her own Bolebrooke with but a few women to attend her. The worst was boredom, since she often had too little to occupy her or stimulate her thoughts and rarely a scholar such as Dr Donne, then vicar of Sevenoaks, to converse with. She was also under strain. She remarks in her diary on the languor which at times sent her to bed at eight in the evening to rise at eight in the morning. On 31 July 1617 her diary entry reads, 'I sat thinking the time to be very tedious.' Indeed, away from Court Anne developed a different persona. She fell into the habit of dressing herself more for comfort than display, a style better captured for posterity by a Dutch genre painter like Jan Steen than the decorative pomp of her surviving portraits by Larkin and van Somer.

When Anne was criticized for wearing her yellow taffeta waistcoat and green flannel gown she riposted by putting on her black grogram mourning gown, a coarse cloth of silk and mohair. Her inclination throughout her life, following her mother, was to clad herself in black. There is no doubting the quality of her black silk grogram gown or black taffeta night gown, both suitable for a lady of her quality. It was the colour which jarred on her well-wishers. Her inclination towards Puritanism, again her mother's influence, might help explain the preference for black. But she was flouting the convention that when a lord was away the lady as acting head of the household should uphold his dignity with the dress and deportment to match her status and impress servants and visitors. This was the least Dorset could have expected of his countess.[20]

Anne's dowdiness did her no favours in comparison with Lady Penistone and other feminine temptresses in the royal palaces. Like her mother during the 1590s, she gives a distinct impression of deliberately declining to take head-on the challenge to Dorset's affections posed by his rather more fashion-conscious mistress. Yet, as the portraits show, when she was so minded or persuaded by the artist, costume finery and coiffure enhanced her good looks, enviable hair and the shapely figure of which she was so proud. Anne's strict adherence to mourning cannot be all the answer. The frumpish garments she chose to wear at Knole might have been a studied reaction to the competition of her husband's mistress, even a form of rebellion against and a distancing from Dorset as much for his attitude towards her inheritance as for his infidelity and profligate life-style of which she so disapproved.

However, a change is discernible in Anne from the summer of 1617, as will be commented on below, and not altogether attributable to her coming out of mourning. This was marked by her purchase in May of a superb gown, damask embroidered with gold, made by Lord St John's tailor, and alterations to her seawater-green dress. But her outlay raises the question of how she could afford these and her other indulgences. The strictures on Dorset have implied that, so spendthrift himself, he kept his wife short of cash. Nothing could be further from the truth. She was usually well supplied with an allowance, and Lady Margaret also, even though Dorset did not receive any part of the award's compensation until the end of September 1617. The period when Anne was less affluent was early 1615 when, as she explained to her mother, because of Dorset's mounting debts 'money is not as plentiful with me as it hath been'.[21]

As a noblewoman, Anne would have been expected to meet her own and her serving women's necessary expenses. Her diary entries of money spent give some idea of the amounts available and her priorities. Gifts and rewards were expected of nobility, such as the 'bow'd Angel' she sent to Mrs Hartley and gloves to Sir John Lowther's lady in Westmorland and the £10 to Mr Bean who had returned from Jerusalem and told her the news of Rome, Naples and other places. Her richest present was to Queen Anne on 2 November 1617. The skirts of a white satin gown 'all pearl and embroidered with colours' cost her £80 besides the satin. New Year's gifts to the queen were obligatory, about £18 the usual value. In 1617 Anne gave her a sweet bag (and a standish to Mrs Hanns), in 1619 a cloth-of-silver cushion embroidered richly with the King of Denmark's arms, a thoughtful choice which reflects her own growing interest in her forebears and their emblazons.[22]

The monuments would have been Anne's most substantial individual outlays. Spenser's cost £40, Frances Bourchier's would have been at least that, with extra payments for their erection. By far the biggest expense would be for her mother's memorial, £100 or even twice that, not including the cost of digging the vault. Dorset cannot have cavilled at this form of extravagance and was probably dismissive of Anne's debts from gambling at glecko and tables. Though minuscule compared with his, her losses of, for instance, £18 and later £27 to Ladies Gray and Carr at Court in 1616 mounted up and then they pricked her conscience. She was determined not to follow her father's and husband's awful examples. When she had 'such ill luck' playing glecko at Knole with the steward Edward Legg and gentleman of the horse Peter Basket on 2 November 1619, she forswore play for the next six months.[23]

Although Anne did become far more outgoing from the summer of 1617 she was never again compliant towards Dorset and their often amicable relations were interspersed with angry scenes. What has not been remarked is that Dorset's attitude to his wife was also permanently altered by the traumas of 1615/17. His annoyance with her over Westmorland did not abate. He was just as unforgiving as she over the issue and subjected her to bouts of temper. On 15 December 1619, for instance, he told her if ever she got her land he would insist she assured it in the way he wanted, which as a husband he could rightfully demand.

One explanation for his attitude is that the overwhelming courtier and noble support for Dorset during 1615 and 1616 began to evaporate. Indeed, Anne had much to be thankful for because of the King's Award. Public opinion divided when its terms were known and a sizeable minority concluded she had been right to resist. Lady Arundel was particularly attentive. Even King James, whom she met again on 4 November 1617 after his great progress to Scotland, 'used me very graciously and bid me go to his Attorney who would inform him more of my desires'. She became much more outgoing, with longer spells at Court, and enjoyed a fuller social life. Friends rallied to her and came to stay at Knole. She deliberately cultivated her Sackville relatives, having learnt the drawbacks of near-isolation. All this had its effect on her husband. When she confronted him at the end of May 1619 with behaving kindly towards others but unkindly to her over her jointure (the compensation from Earl Francis having been mostly paid) he relented and promised to assure her a jointure with a generous income, £4,000 a year, which was greater than many noblemen received, let alone their widows.

Furthermore, Dorset faced far more public disapproval of his activities during 1619 than ever before. His dalliance with Lady Penistone was the cause. She spent the summer months taking the waters at Tunbridge Wells where she would be close to him. On 24 August she came with her husband and Sir Maximilian and Lady Dallison to Knole for the day, 'there being great Entertainment & much stir about them,' Anne writes with glee and perhaps a little malice in her diary, her ladies no doubt repeating to her the snide comments and ribaldry of the household servants. As she says, Lady Penistone's coming to Tunbridge 'was much talked of abroad and my Lord was condemned for it'. This may have brought the affair to an end; at least, from 29 November Dorset ceased visiting Lady Penistone at her mother's lodgings.[24] It has not been remarked what good friends Dorset and Penistone were, the latter often acting for him in assignments and other estate matters.[25]

The most positive aspect of Anne's life was the sense of purpose which came back gradually but permanently. In one respect she began to revert to her roots. She had continued to read her earlier diary which her attendant Mr Marsh was writing up and the two Books of the Cliffords sent her by Kniveton. She was also absorbing the books, letters, records and alchemical works in the great trunk which had been carried from Brougham after her mother's death. The breadth of her reading is shown by her 1619 diary entries, which reveal a deep religious phase. In February, it was St Augustine's *Of the City of God*. In March she finished both Sarracol's *Supplication of the Saints*, which her husband had thoughtfully given her, and Harrington's manuscript 'In Praise of a Solitary Life,' which has survived in the Hothfield MSS. Harrington drew heavily on the ancient philosophers including Seneca, whom he cites. Its final folio would have appealed to Anne as much as to her mother:

> Let everie one labor to have true wishes, and interteyne himselfe with vertuous qualities: I mean those, that are eternall: for so shall worldly wishes, honor, and earthly pompe, be lightly regarded.

At the end of May, her cousin Mary finished reading to her the Jesuit Father Robert Parsons' *A Resolution of Religion . . .* (1601). In December, she studied a manuscript copy of another pro-Catholic work (then thought to have been one of Parsons's writings), the scurrilous anti-Puritan tract 'Leicester's Commonwealth', published in 1584 on the Continent and distributed surreptitiously. Its author's purpose had been to defame Robert Dudley, Earl of Leicester, Queen Elizabeth's favourite and the leader of the Puritan cause, in his private as well as his public life. Yet there was much in it about her family which would have intrigued Anne. Leicester had engineered the betrothal of Anne's parents. The royal connections of Countess Eleanor, the 2nd Earl and Lady Derby were commented on and Earl George mentioned. Indeed, this could well have been his copy which Countess Margaret kept. What really appealed to Anne, however, was reading about Mary, Queen of Scots.[26]

Anne's new-found interest in the Cliffords was then at the peak of its first inspirational stage. For this she had to thank Sir John Taylor who visited her on 19 November 1617, spending two hours with her in London and telling her about the 'ancient times of my Father and the North.'[27] To hear her father's life and doings described by a man who knew and respected him must have been a revelation for Anne. Hitherto she had been under her mother's shadow, browbeaten almost by the countess's animus towards the earl and repeatedly reminded of 'the wrong you had by your father'.[28] Now Anne began to learn for herself and from impartial sources about her father's achievements. One result was that she became stirred by his voyages. At the close of December she instructed Richard Jones to look into them and commissioned their writing up into an illustrated volume which is still extant. Sir Francis Slingsby, a relative and one of Earl George's most capable sea-captains with unique experiences of his expeditions, stayed with her in November 1619 to reminisce and read to her from the 'Sea-Papers' which had been collected for that volume.[29]

This growing fascination with her family's past was laudable and students of the Cliffords are thankful for what it produced. However, what Anne badly needed to restore her peace of mind in 1617 was a psychological uplift and this she got from the opportunities to undermine her uncle's and cousin's position in Westmorland. Her negative, obstructive attitude was transformed and she began to take an active, participating role. For Earl Francis the boot was on the other foot compared with 1606. Then, he had chivvied the tenants to oppose Countess Margaret. Now, Anne took the offensive, interfering in his Westmorland estate affairs to her advantage. Francis was vulnerable. He had been forced to borrow all the £17,000 in order to pay Dorset on the due days. To clear these huge debts and pay the £1,700 yearly interest he had to persuade the Westmorland tenants to agree to big fines to assure their tenancies by the terms of the award.

As in 1606, they resisted *en masse*. Anne sent letters of encouragement to their leaders and cash to help pay for their defence in the lawsuits Francis initiated, knowing that she was not in any way jeopardizing the payments to her husband. In this she had Dorset's support. Together they discussed a copy of Francis's bill in Chancery which the tenants' solicitor, their own lawyer John Davies of the Inner Temple, brought them. She met the two leading defendants and on parting gave them gold and silver for their expenses. Not surprisingly, Earl Francis was hardest on the countess's former estate officers Mr Hilton and Michael Brunskill. On 28 November 1619 Anne noted with sadness that things were going ill for them, as indeed they were. Like Countess Margaret, Francis succeeded by legal means in enforcing his tenants' submission and the payments due to him. But Anne had the gratification of having done her best to spite him.

Moreover she, or her legal advisers, had by now perceived the great flaw in the award, which Sir John Lowther had been quick to note in his private journal. Two of Francis's Stainmore tenants, John Shaw and Robert Wasdale, propounded it in their defence in his 1619 lawsuit against them. In brief, because Anne had not accepted the award it lacked validity in law. Lowther, in addition, believed that because she had a remainder, a reversionary interest, in the estates, Parliament would never sanction the tenures the award permitted Francis to grant.[30] Lowther's interpretation of the law was not put to the test because, as stated in Chapter 3, the proposed private Act of Parliament could not be proceded with. This left a situation in which neither the award nor the tenures granted in conformity with it were secure. Anne understood this and drew strength from the fact that she had consistently refused to acknowledge the award. All her future actions, to the end of a very long life, were based on the premise that if she kept pressing her claims she would in the end succeed.

Compared with the countess's time, there was now an extra dimension to Westmorland affairs and that was political conflicts between the local factions which Dorset and Anne had stirred up during their 1616 visit, as described in the previous chapter. Although Dorset was now on good terms with Clifford and enjoyed friendly jousting competitions with him at Westminster, the factional strife in the north-west continued unabated and his wife dabbled in it. Lord William Howard was striving to impose his influence and oust Clifford from county administration, coveting the sheriffwick. The discord between them reached into the Privy Council where the Howards were powerful and this posed problems for the king and his senior ministers. Anne noted in February 1619 that the factional conflict in Westmorland was good for her; the cost was the harm it caused to local government and social tranquillity. In the end the Privy Council had to take sides and it was Clifford, supported by most of the local gentry, who won the day.[31]

There is no question that Anne became more worldly wise as a result of grappling with legal matters, the King's Award, local politics and her husband's temperament. They brought her out of herself and gave her sharper awareness of how Court society and government operated. Having at last to stand up for herself instead of always looking to her mother she lost if not her innocence then her naivety. Something of this greater maturity and poise is caught in two original portraits of her. The first, attributed by Sir Roy Strong to William Larkin, she may have sat for in the summer of 1618, as her diary suggests (Pl. 21). Her dress is heavily decorated and lavishly trimmed at the *décolletage* with fine lace. The ruff is steeply tilted, starched into honeycomb configuration and supported, at a flattering angle, by a wire frame. Her hair is crimped and brushed up and back from the forehead and temples, and fluffed out round the cheeks, with the back hair coiled into a flat bun at the occiput. A baroque pearl is suspended from the ear-string threaded through Anne's left ear. Her face rather belies the richness of her costume. It has a set, determined, somewhat withdrawn and hurt look, with a tightening of the mouth which Vita Sackville-West believed became a permanent feature, the consequence of enduring her troubles with fortitude.[32]

A rare, full-length portrait attributed to Paul van Somer depicts Anne in 1619, her thirtieth year, when she may have been pregnant again (Pl. 22). Her dress has a gathered skirt worn without farthingale or bum roll and a transparent apron. Her embroidered shoes are lavishly decorated with shoe roses. Ear-strings were then in vogue. She holds in her right hand a large locket, a picture-box for a portrait miniature of her husband or one of her parents. Her left hand relaxes over the back of a chair. Two head-and-shoulder portraits derived from the van Somer date from within the next two years, the painters unknown. In the first Anne's dress features an acorn design and she wears pearl ear rings instead of the ear-strings and a pendant pearl headdress (Pl. 23). The second, slightly later portrait is closer to the van Somer with its vine scroll design and its falling-standing ruff, falling at the front only (Pl. 24).[33]

In all four portraits there is the stubbornness about the mouth and chin

21. Lady Anne, Countess of Dorset, by William Larkin, c. 1618/19 (Private collection)

which Vita Sackville-West espied. This may help explain the independent streak Anne now showed, which at times could almost be termed eccentric. One notable instance is her behaviour at the formal repast given in honour of the new French ambassador, the Marquess de Cadenet, on 8 January 1621. He had been conducted to his first audience with King James on New Year's Day by

22. *Lady Anne, Countess of Dorset, attrib. to Paul van Somer, c. 1619 (Private collection)*

23. Lady Anne, Countess of Dorset, c. 1619/20, artist unknown (Private collection)

Buckingham, Dorset, Warwick and others. Ben Jonson's masque *News from the New World* was played to the Court with the ambassador present on Twelfth Night. Two days later Dorset had the distinction in the tilting to run against Prince Charles as the first pair, both breaking their staves successfully.

That evening the whole party was invited to a costly supper by James Hay, Viscount Doncaster. The king, Prince Charles and the ambassador sat at a table placed crossways on a low dais at the end of the room. The rest of the distinguished company were seated either side of a long table lengthways down the room, ladies and lords alternating. Anne was placed honourably near the top, on the opposite side to, but below, the ambassador's lady. But she declined to sit there, because of a dislike of someone near her or, as was then thought, because she refused to sit below the '*ambassadrice*'. Another possible explanation is a touch of xenophobia after reading about French criticism of her father's maritime activities. Instead she moved further down, sitting between two ladies inferior to her in rank, which offended convention and was a snub to the marquess's lady and conceivably to the king and prince. Her behaviour would do neither her husband nor herself any credit.[34]

Courtiers were used to the ebbs and flows of royal favour and Dorset from 1617 had his share. Strangely, he had never accompanied the king on one of his summer progresses, preferring his own residences and estates and hunting with his friends. His failure to travel with James on his great Scottish progress in 1617 slightly eclipsed him for a while because Earl Francis and Clifford had a triumph in entertaining the king, his favourite Buckingham and many of the high courtiers at Carlisle Castle and the famous Brougham Feast in August. Twice over the coming months Clifford, in London on family business, was appointed to escort foreign ambassadors, on one occasion using the king's own coach. Then early in 1618 Dorset came into the reckoning again.

There were two great occasions in 1619 when Dorset and Anne were present together. As usual, they attended the masque, Jonson's *Pleasure Reconciled to Virtue*, presented to the king on Twelfth Night. On 13 May at the funeral of Queen Anne in Henry VII's Chapel, Westminster, Dorset was in the procession of the nobility, Anne walked as one of the 'Countesses Assistantes' and Clifford

24. Lady Anne, Countess of Dorset, 1620, after van Somer (H.T. Fattorini Esq.)

had the honour of bearing the Banner of Denmark. During the next two years Dorset continued to be in favour; for example, escorting the new Spanish ambassador Count Gondomar from Gravesend in March 1620 and, as has been seen, the French ambassador in the following New Year.[35] Then during 1621 his career began to take a downturn. He had frittered away much of his vast wealth and his debts had grown enormously. His 1614 sales have already been mentioned, when he disposed of lands worth £1,035 in rents for £22,850, Anne being associated (as wives usually were) in at least some of his transactions. The £17,000 from Earl Francis tided him over for a year or two. Then, in February

1620, he sacrificed another four manors with a yearly rental of £952 for £14,350. By the end of his life he had raised £74,300 by land sales alone.[36] In his latter years, no longer able to afford lavish expenditure, he found his credit at Court fell and his popularity naturally suffered.

Then he wrongfooted himself politically, rousing the ire of Buckingham and the king himself. When parliament met, he and Salisbury acted as leaders of thirty-three peers who petitioned the king in protest at the claims to precedence over old-established English noblemen by newly created Irish and Scottish peers and, by implication, the inflation of honours and the selling of new titles by Buckingham. If the favourite was the immediate target, King James could not be absolved and he was furious with them. In contrast, Sir Edward Sackville was a firm adherent of Buckingham, so at a time when Dorset's influence was fading and his health beginning to be troublesome his likely successor to the earldom was politically in the ascendant.[37]

Although there was a spell when Dorset appears to have neglected Anne sexually for Lady Penistone he wanted a male heir. She is known to have been pregnant in 1617 and 1619. Three sons died young or in infancy, the longest-lived Thomas, Lord Buckhurst, born on 2 February 1620, surviving until 26 July following. Anne's pregnancy in 1622 again brought out his affection for her. 'Sweet Liffe', he wrote to her from Dorset House on 13 May, 'God blesse you and my Lady Margarett, and the Little sweete thing in thy belly be it a Richard or an Isabella. Farewell Your very loveing husband R. Dorset.' He also told Anne he had sent Margaret's half-year's allowance and her own £100 by his receiver-general, Lindsey. It was an Isabella who was born on 6 October 1622; her pre-chosen name of immense emotional significance for Anne because it was from Isabella de Vipont that the Westmorland titles, lands and sheriffwick she claimed descended to her.[38]

Dorset's neglect of Anne had redounded on him. He did not procure a son who might inherit. She did not make life easier by acting as godmother to Sir Edward's younger son at the christening at Great Dorset House on 23 January 1624. Two days later, after returning to Knole, she and Dorset had 'a great falling out' at dinner, though whether for that reason

25. Lady Margaret Sackville (1614–76), aged four, attrib. to Paul van Somer (Private collection)

or another she did not record.[39] His health was now troublesome. Ash Wednesday, 9 February, was the last time Anne saw him. He kissed her and their daughters before leaving for Great Dorset House and the meeting of parliament. On 28 March at the age of thirty-four he came to a premature end, worn out, Williamson writes, 'by reckless living, extravagance and carelessness', though in fact dying of 'a bloody flux'. During his last illness, Lady Margaret and Anne were unable to visit him because they were both ill with smallpox. They survived, though Anne's face was permanently scarred. In his last letter to her, written shortly before he died, Dorset concluded; 'So, with my love to you, and God's blessing and mine to both my children, I commend you to God's protection.' As recently as July 1623, when he was very sick, he had executed the deeds for her jointure, ensuring her financial support during her widowhood.[40]

Edward Sackville, 4th Earl, and his countess easily stepped into the shoes of Earl Richard and Countess Anne, the noble and courtier succession all the more natural to them because of Buckingham's patronage. Edward already had the greater merit in his service to the Crown, whereas Richard had been no more than a rich play-boy whatever Anne's regard for him. Edward's career blossomed under Charles I and he continued to make an impact on national affairs up to and during the Civil Wars. His prominence in royal service was to have an influence on Anne's decisions over the next decade, which will be one of the themes considered in the following chapter.[41]

CHAPTER 5

Dowager Countess of Dorset

1624–30

Dorset's death was a watershed in Lady Anne's life. For the first time, aged thirty-four, she enjoyed financial independence and also freedom from an overpowering husband. This was the happy lot which befell many a titled widow, coverture no longer applying. Moreover, she was in a much more ebullient frame of mind because the recent misfortunes of her Clifford relatives had sent her hopes for her inheritance steepling and given new impetus to her life. Anne, obsessed with her own cause, had in the past all but willed troubles on her relatives, eagerly seeking news of her uncle Francis's poor health in 1615 and showing relief at the early death in July 1619 of her cousin Clifford's son who would have been the male heir to exclude her from the inheritance. Francis's severe illness in 1623 had brought him to death's door and he never properly recovered his strength. Clifford now assumed full control over the family's concerns which he had largely managed since 1616. He thus became Anne's principal adversary over the titles and estates.

However, the balance of hope and despair had swung against him. The death of his only surviving son, Henry, on 30 August 1622 left him grief-stricken not just at his bereavement but, even more, because the male line looked like ending with him. Another daughter, Frances, was born in 1626 but she was not to reach adulthood.[1] The odds from 1622 were that, provided Anne outlived Clifford, she would get her estates. Although she aspired to all her father's lands, the award would guarantee her heart's desire, Westmorland with Brougham Castle and the Honour of Skipton. From now on she concentrated on that objective, on her titles, and on the welfare of Lady Margaret and Lady Isabella whom she intended would succeed her.

Her wealth was the key to her activities during her widowhood. Clarendon correctly asserted that Dorset had consumed almost all the great fortune which had come to him, leaving little but his title to Earl Edward. Granted his circumstances, Dorset was generous in his provision for Anne and their daughters, a fair return for the £17,000 compensation he had received. His jointure settlement was in two parts. She was to have Bolebrooke Place in Sussex as her dower house and its associated manors, a big property. On her death that and other specified manors were to pass to Margaret and Isabella and then to their right heirs, so they would be lost to the main line of the Sackville family. The other part, comprising fifteen manors with other properties in Sussex, reserved rents from three more in Essex, with the advowsons of the vicarages in seven of the Sussex townships and two in Essex, was to be Anne's for life and then revert to Earl Edward and his descendants (Tables 2, 7). Initially, then,

Anne held properties worth £2,000 a year or more, revenues which placed her near the apex of the Sussex landed elite. However, the properties were varied in character and would require diligent management by her officers. For instance, the moiety of Meeching included half the demesnes, the lodge and its lands, downs with the game of coneys (and the tithe of coneys), saltmarshes on the east side of the river or haven called New Haven and her part of a messuage commonly called the Shipp, and of two ferries called Meeching ferry and Stake ferry.

Thoughtfully, too, Dorset provided his widow with a London home with its coachhouse, stable and garden in Dorset Court, formerly Salisbury Court, which Lord Treasurer Dorset had enlarged 'with stately buildings'. It was then occupied by Sir John Suckling, Controller of the king's household, so Anne became landlady of a high royal official, father of the noted

26. *Edward Sackville, 4th Earl of Dorset (1590–1652), by William Larkin, c. 1613 (English Heritage: Ranger's House, Blackheath)*

poet. The trustees appointed to oversee her jointure estate were men of weight in the capital and in Sussex. Two were her relatives, the rising lawyer Oliver St John of Bletsoe and Francis, Lord Russell of Thornhaugh (as he now was). Two were leading Sussex gentry, Sir Henry Compton of Brambletie and Sir Francis Stidolfe, tenant of her Michelham jointure mansion. The others were lawyers, the Prince of Wales's attorney Sir John Walter and her own John Davies.[2]

Anne would need all the support she could get. Earl Edward's enmity is understandable considering the size of her jointure estate. There was also Dorset's legacy of huge debts and importuning creditors whom Lord William Howard, Sir George Rivers and Richard Amherst, sergeant-at-law, as trustees had to try to satisfy from a badly depleted inheritance. This problem was made almost intractable for decades by Dorset's failure to make adequate financial provision to maintain Sackville College, East Grinstead, the fine residential home for twenty poor men and ten poor women under a warden which he, in association with Anne, founded in accordance with his father's will. The inscription in the college's hall, 'I pray God bless my Lord of Dorset, and my

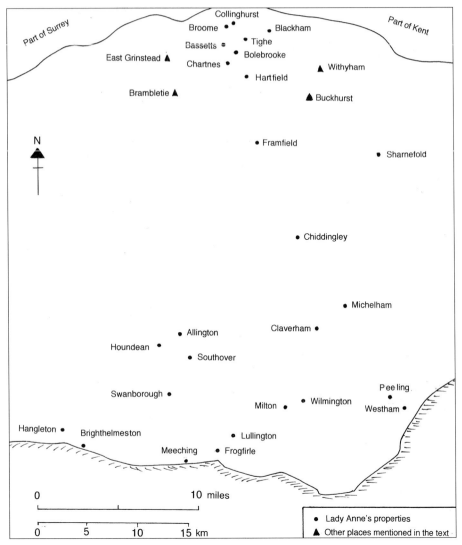

Map 2: Lady Anne's jointure manors in Sussex, 1624

Ladie, and all their posteritie. Ano. do. 1619', was to ring hollow for the inmates over the coming decades.

Dorset had assigned a rent charge of £300 a year from his Buckhurst manors to support the college, but died before he could secure that revenue by an Act of Parliament. Consequently, the warden and the poor struggled to win even a bare minimum income by constant litigation against Amherst and his fellow trustees and also Anne and her daughters over the manors they occupied. Soon after Dorset's death, Anne joined Earl Edward in a lawsuit to safeguard the college's lands against local intruders.[3] But it was her manipulation of her jointure estates

TABLE 2 *Lady Anne's jointure estate in Sussex and Essex, and her daughters' inheritance, 1625*

1. *Jointure manors held on a life interest, reversion to the earls of Dorset*
SUSSEX
Manors of:

Allington	Framfield	Park gate
Blackham	Hangleton	Southover
Broome	Holwith	Swanborough
Chiddingley	Lullington	Brighthelmeston (½)
Claverham	Michelham	Meeching (½)
Collinghurst	Milton	Houndean (¼)

Advowsons of: Chiddingley, Framfield, Hangleton, Hartfield, Meeching, Wilmington

ESSEX
Manors of: Mountbaries, with the advowson
Sackville
Westbergholt, with the advowson

2. *Jointure manors held on a life interest, reversion to Lady Margaret Sackville, with value, c. 1625*

	£	s	d
The lordship of Bolebrooke, with the capital house and park	164	12	6½
The manor of Bassetts	100	4	6
The manor of Tighe	69	7	0
The manor of Chartnes cum Golbins	94	1	8
Sum total of the clear yearly value	428	5	8½

Besides the value of the park of Bolebrooke worth 100 marks yearly and the lease of Houndean worth 200 marks yearly and the lands in Yorkshire [?Essex] worth £60 per annum, and the possibility of the lands of the earl of Cumberland and the portion of the money of £6,000.

3. *Jointure manors held on a life interest, reversion to Lady Isabella Sackville, with value, c. 1625*

	£	s	d
The lordship of Wilmington, with the capital house and Wilmington wood	183	4	0
The Manor of Frogfirle	26	16	4
The manor of Sharnefold	104	1	5¾
The manor and rectory of Peeling and Westham	80	3	0
Sum total of the clear yearly value	394	4	9¾

Sources: CKS, U269/T.70/10; Castle Ashby Papers, 833

27. Sackville College, East Grinstead, Sussex, the court and well (Photo: the author)

to her own and then, even more, her daughters' advantage which created difficulties for all parties concerned, as will be related below and in Chapter 12.

By Dorset's will, completed the morning he died, Anne received the rings and jewels she had owned on their marriage and also the rock ruby ring he had given her. His other bequests to her were no more than any nobleman's widow would have expected to uphold her status in her dower house: sixty silver pieces and two silver basins and ewers for her table, six silver candlesticks, half his household linen and £500 in cash for her better maintenance. She would travel in style, in his splendid carriage upholstered in green cloth edged with green and black silk lace and drawn by his six bay geldings. He left £200 in old gold jointly to his daughters. Lady Margaret kept her share and bequeathed it on her death in 1676. He also instructed his executors to sell more land to raise marriage portions, £6,000 for Margaret, £4,000 for Isabella, a kindly thought but impossible to implement. Mementoes of Dorset which, through Anne, eventually came into Lady Margaret's possession were a miniature of her father, head to foot, two pedigrees of the Sackvilles and Sackville-Howards on vellum and eight books covered with red velvet and marked with his initials 'R.E.D'.[4]

Granted Dorset's care for his family's financial well-being and Anne's expressed love and admiration for him, it was somewhat discourteous of her to refuse to be included in the expensive memorial which he instructed his executors to erect in Withyham Church. She protested forcibly at the proposal, saying she intended to be buried on her northern estates. This is a graphic instance of how far she had veered away from him in recent years. She did not commemorate their sons, calling them 'his sons', whereas their daughters were 'her' daughters. It was on the girls that she focused her ambitions and through them that she intended her inheritance would descend. Her Dorset marriage in practice became almost a closed episode hereafter and she tended not to treat the Sackville family with much solicitude, as will be shown in Chapter 12.[5]

In the longer perspective there was a conjunction of events between 1622 and 1624 – Dorset's death being the last – which marked a turning point in Anne's affairs comparable with that of 1612. One parallel she would not have missed, although its irony she did not comment on. The situation of the 3rd and 4th Earls of Dorset repeated that of the 3rd and 4th Earls of Cumberland – heavy debts, run-down estates, no direct male heir, a younger brother who succeeded and a widow who occupied jointure properties which the new earl begrudged. Earl Edward was to be mortified at his sister-in-law's longevity which denied him her dower lands. So too was his successor, because Anne was to occupy them for the inordinate length of fifty-two years; compensation indeed for the desolate moments of her marriage. Earl Edward she regarded as her sworn enemy; his countess remained her good friend.

With assured revenues, authority and responsibilities, Anne became forthright and energetic. As early as 13 November 1624 she purchased for £15 the walled site of Beamsley Hospital, which Clapham conveyed with the almshouse and liberty to erect more buildings to her lawyer Davies and servant Christopher Marsh. Her most positive action was to purchase from the Crown the right to her daughters' wardship and marriage for the hefty sum of £1,333 6s 8d. The obligations she entered into with the Court of Wards on 29 June 1625 required her to pay £333 6s 8d immediately in ready money, followed by three instalments of £200, the first on 10 December following, then 10 June and 10 December 1626 and the final £400 on 10 June 1627, so that she cleared the debt in two years. There is no evidence that she had to borrow and, indeed, her ample means would have made that unnecessary.

It was Earl Edward whose finances were harder hit because his brother was succeeded by two daughters who were under-age. The Crown was entitled to occupy a third of Earl Richard's former properties during Margaret's and Isabella's minorities or until they married. The Court of Wards, therefore, took £186 6s 8d annually in rent for each of them, a total of £372 13s 4d. These sums did not come from Anne's jointure estate, which was fully protected, but from the other manors Richard had held at his death. The difficulties the court had over this because of the assignments of manors to pay his debts will be commented on later. Anne and her daughters benefited because the court granted them the customary exhibitions for minors' maintenance and education, in their case £50 each per annum. The court also notionally apportioned the girls' lands between them as fairly as was possible at that moment. Margaret's share was the manors of Bolebrooke with its house and park, Bassetts, Tighe and Chartnes, with a clear yearly value of £428. Isabel received Wilmington (with its residence), Frogfirle, Sharnefold and Peeling with its rectory, valued at £394 (Table 2). Anne thus achieved her immediate aim of keeping her daughters with her, which enabled her to oversee their upbringing, and, just as Countess Margaret had done for her, make the substantive decisions when it came to the question of their marriages.[6]

28. *Bolebrooke House, Hartfield, Sussex, engraved by Letitia Byrne from a drawing by P. Amsink, 1809 (D.J.H. Clifford's collection)*

With her new-found wealth, Anne was generous to her friends in need. Sedgewick, who relates this, mentions one 'strange and unexampled piece of charity she did, which few ladies would have done'. She raised Dorset's two natural daughters by Lady Penistone. One died, but for the other she found a good husband, John Belgrave, who had gained his BA at Trinity College, Oxford, in 1622 and was ordained in 1624 and 1632. He was licensed to marry Faith Flute on 15 October 1632. With her second husband, Pembroke, Anne placed Belgrave in the rectory of Hangleton in November 1636, worth £140 a year, the advowson included in her Dorset jointure estate. Anne also aided Dorset's former chaplain, Dr Henry King, by settling a rent charge of £40 a year on him from her Sussex lands. Later he became Bishop of Chichester. She was to give the same to Pembroke's chaplain Dr George Morley, who was her godson and became Bishop of Winchester. When these clergy fled abroad during the Civil War she supported them in their subsistence, in all to the tune of £1,000.[7]

Biographers of Lady Anne have too readily accepted the impression her writings give that after Dorset's death she led a fairly sedate, mainly rural life with her young children. She tells us that when Lady Margaret had recovered from smallpox in June 1624, she removed to Chenies, a return to the environment of her younger days, and subsequently spent much time there and also at Bolebrooke, from where she could oversee her Sussex manors. She had gone to Bolebrooke to receive her May Day rents in person and take the accounts when an attempt was made on 6 May 1626 to steal them, for which she blamed Earl Edward. Happily, it was foiled. She visited Woburn once with Lady Margaret, staying a few nights. Her cursory mention of London residences is the clue to how often during her widowhood she lived in close proximity to the Court. She rented a house in Totehill Street near Westminster Abbey with an outlook over St James's Park and green fields and also two others in the palace itself (Pl. 29).[8] She thus continued alternating sojourns in the home counties with Court life, a pattern which she had known with Dorset. She must have been almost as familiar a figure at the palace as when she was married. There

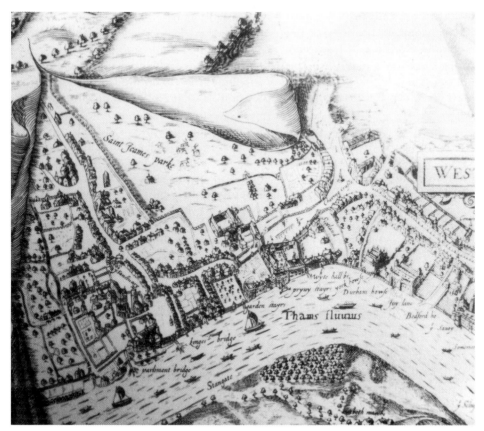

29. *Westminster, showing Totehill Street running beside the abbey, Whitehall Palace and the Cockpit, 1600 (John Norden, 1600. London Topographical Society. Photo: the author)*

would have been some constraints, lacking a consort, and fewer occasions when she could attend the great Court events as long as the widowed King James occupied the throne. These, however, multiplied once Henrietta Maria became settled as Charles I's queen. There was an open invitation for ladies lodging nearby to join those in her entourage, all adding to the gaiety of palace society under its young and lively queen.

Anne, noble and well-off, attracted suitors and this may have been an intention of her Westminster residence. One whose name is known, Sir Thomas Wentworth, had much to commend him as a gifted and politically prominent scion of one of the wealthiest gentry families in Yorkshire. His wife Lady Margaret Clifford, Earl Francis's elder daughter and so Anne's cousin, had died about July 1622. He was a suitor first for the younger daughter of Sir William Craven, the wealthy Wharfedale-born London merchant, then for Lady Diana Cecil, daughter of Thomas, 2nd Lord Burghley, now Earl of Exeter, and so related to Lord Clifford's lady. Anne came third. The matter was not pursued far, partly because she was held to be 'of that age which did not give any great hope of childrene' but equally perhaps because Wentworth was too close in loyalty to her Clifford 'enemies'. In the end, he married Arabella Holles, one of the outstanding beauties of her era just as Earl George's youthful heartache, Gertrude Holles, had been of hers.[9] Anne had to wait until 1630 for her own remarriage. She may have regarded this as secondary to showing off Lady Margaret as a highly suitable match for some nobleman, the Court being by far the best milieu for attracting such attention. If so, it paid off handsomely, as will be seen.

Before that happened, however, Anne for the first time had to grapple with the issue of the Clifford titles. This came to the fore because of her cousin Henry's role as effective head of his family and his work in northern administration. He was not a nobleman in his own right, merely Sir Henry, Knight of the Bath, 'Lord Clifford' being his courtesy title as an earl's son. Meriting better recognition, he was called to the House of Lords by writ on 17 February 1628 on the assumption (erroneous it later proved) that the ancient barony of Clifford (1299) was vested in his father. On his previous visit to London Henry had sought the help of the antiquary Sir Robert Cotton about the first creation of Lord Clifford. He now wrote to Cotton from Londesborough on 24 February because he put more reliance on 'youre grounded iudgement and knoledge' than the heralds', which was often in his opinion conjectural. In return, he had searched for a little manuscript to give Cotton, an ancient rarity, presumably from the Londesborough muniments.

30. *Henry, Lord Clifford, 5th Earl of Cumberland (1592–1643), shown wearing his uncle Earl George's famous Greenwich armour, attrib. to Daniel Mytens, 1631 (Reproduced by permission of the Duke of Devonshire and the Trustees of the Chatsworth Settlement)*

Henry, Lord Clifford, was brought to the House on 6 May when, in the accustomed manner, he delivered his writ kneeling in his parliamentary robes before the Lord Keeper. He was then placed with the precedence of the older barony above Lord Abergavenny whose title dated from 1392. Anne's faithful cousin Francis, now 4th Earl of Bedford, at once questioned Clifford's right to the barony on her behalf. As a result of his motion Clifford was ranked 'in the place pretended to be due to the ancient Barony of Clifford', without prejudice to Anne or to the right and title of Abergavenny or any other lord. In her own petition to Charles I and the House on 16 May to enjoy the titles her father had held Anne repeated the 1606 claim that, by common law, dignities conferred by writ of summons to parliament descended to females where there was a sole heir. She again cited the Abergavenny case as proof. The petition would have been considered by the committee of privileges in the next session had the king not dissolved parliament. No other chance occurred for Anne to pursue the matter for many years. Clifford's place in the Lords, however, was quite proper. The writ in error had the effect of creating a second barony, that of Clifford (1628), the title to the ancient barony being still unresolved.[10]

Clifford's elevation to the Lords spurred Anne to renew her claims to the estates. After taking legal advice, she instructed Robert Scawen gent. on 20 July to make formal entries into the Skipton demesnes, the pastures at Tarn Moor, Snaygill and Holme. Entries were made in Westmorland on 14 August; for instance, the corn fields at Winton, the gatehouse of Brough Castle and the iron forge Earl Francis had erected on a parcel of Brougham demesnes. More entries in the Craven manors on the 25th included several holdings of Peter Jennings gent. of Silsden, such as John Armor's house which he had bought, a barn lately built by him, and a piece of waste ground he had recently enclosed at Holden Park gate. In London, Clifford's Inn dining hall and gardens were entered.[11] By this initiative Anne proclaimed to the world at large that her claim to the estates as well as the Clifford dignities was still a live issue.

Nevertheless, the 1628 events made Anne appreciate far more the handicaps of being a dowager countess, reckoned in the nobility's pecking order as of least account even when youngish, with a good dower income and prospects of great landed wealth. She had no husband to lobby on her behalf. Bedford worked hard for her, yet as a mere cousin he could not be really effective as her torch-bearer. Her 'powerfull enemy' Earl Edward was a Knight of the Garter and Lord Chamberlain to Queen Henrietta Maria. Her cousin Clifford was in the Lords where he could stand up for his family's interests. Clifford's political patronage at Appleby and Carlisle boroughs and for the shire seats in Westmorland

31. Francis Russell, 4th Earl of Bedford (1593–1641), engraving by J. Cochran from a portrait by Sir Anthony van Dyck (D.J.H. Clifford's collection)

assured him of friends in the House of Commons. He and his father had legitimate and secure possession of the estates. Anne now sought a protector, weighing the dangers to herself and her daughters against the material support she could expect.[12]

First, however, she had to look to her elder daughter's welfare. In negotiating Lady Margaret's marriage with John, Lord Tufton, she had the influential backing of her cousin Russell and of the earls of Rutland and Wimbledon. Tufton was the heir of Nicholas, 2nd Earl of Thanet, and the marriage terms drawn up on 17 April 1629 make plain why Anne gave Margaret priority. The girl was still only fourteen, Tufton five years older. They were to marry on or before 25 June, a week before her fifteenth birthday. The earl of Thanet agreed to settle lands worth £5,000 a year on her as a jointure, with £400 a year rents arising from them to support her necessary expenditure throughout the marriage. After the wedding, he was to keep them with 'fatherly Curtesie' as long as they wanted. Anne promised to surrendered her wardship rights over Margaret to Tufton.

All this was standard and straightforward yet there were some extremely tricky matters to settle. It was up to Anne to provide her with a suitable portion. For this, in the first place she conveyed to the young couple Bolebrooke Place with its park, demesnes and associated manors worth £419 19s 3d a year in rent and their reversion in tail. These properties were to be assured to Lady Margaret by a deed of trust as Thanet thought fit. Dorset had also bequeathed £6,000 to Margaret as her portion by the codicil to his will. Anne agreed to petition the Court of Wards for this money to be delivered in land, which she said had been Dorset's intention. However, because of his debts, it was extremely unlikely that Margaret would receive anything from that source. So, instead, Anne used part of her own jointure estate, opting for the manors of Framfield, Allington, Claverham and Holwith and the moieties of Meeching and Brighthelmeston, in which she enjoyed a life interest and were then worth at least £335 5s per annum (Table 2). These were to be conveyed to Tufton and Margaret, and would pass to whichever of the two survived the other. Moreover, she promised to give Margaret gold, jewels, plate, apparel and other things to the value of £1,000, provided no further claim was made on her, and all the household stuff in Bolebrooke Place which was also hers on a life interest.[13]

Granted Anne's circumstances, all this was quite lavish provision for her daughter, though essential in view of her marriage into an earl's family, the really valuable part being Bolebrooke. These grants and gifts reveal how much wealth in land and chattels Anne then had at her disposal. Overshadowing the matter of land, however, was the entanglement of problems caused by Dorset's debts, the assignments to pay them and the demands of the Court of Wards for its third of his revenues. Furthermore, there was impending litigation in the court against George Strode Esq., who occupied the assigned lands and owed the court a full year's revenues on its wardship account, that is, £372 13s 4d, and, in addition, over half a year's which had accumulated up to Margaret's marriage. After the marriage Tufton himself owed the court £137 13s 9d because to him fell the responsibility of paying Margaret's livery fine, set at half a year's income, a prerequisite before taking over her lands. All these matters were considered by the judges who, in a sensible decree imposed in 1633, acknowledged that the money owed by Strode could not be collected. Accordingly, they cleared the slate for him but required Tufton, now 2nd Earl of Thanet, to pay the livery fine.[14]

Not only Anne but the Thanets would have deemed it imperative to complete this delicate balancing of advantages to all sides before she put her lands and personal belongings within the grasp of a second husband. Lady Margaret's wedding took place speedily after the marriage terms had been agreed, on 21 April 1629, at St Bartholomew the Great, Smithfield, the Earl of Bedford giving her away. Anne had been living with her daughters in the Priory House and it would be there that she feasted the big gathering of Russell and Tufton relatives and the many other noble friends who attended. If the cost of the celebrations fell entirely on her, as it should have done and she would have wished, getting her elder daughter off her hands made a big dent in her cash resources and future income.[15]

Anne could now contemplate her own future. Having transferred so much of her jointure estate away from the clutches of a new spouse, she may have felt the need for a rich husband's outlay on herself and Isabella. She was now financially more at risk. Dorset's debts had still not been cleared, all the lands assigned to pay them had been sold and Amherst, the only surviving assignee, reported in 1630 that Anne's jointure estate was all that was left. He had offered that property to Dorset's creditors in the hope they would accept it, even though it meant waiting for her decease. In the meantime, he sought from Charles I another year's protection against the creditors.[16] In retrospect, the expectation of Anne's early demise has its amusing side but Amherst's negotiations with the creditors would have been very unsettling for her and Isabella.

Yet there was far more than financial concern in Anne's shrewdly calculated choice of a second husband. In terms of standing and authority it could not have been bettered. Philip Herbert, Earl of Montgomery, was Charles I's Lord Chamberlain and so one of the great men in Caroline England. She had known him – and his reputation – from youth. He and his elder brother William, 3rd Earl of Pembroke, Lord Steward of the king's household, were prominent patrons of the arts, the 'incomparable' brethren to whom the first folio edition of Shakespeare's plays in 1623 had been dedicated. The Pembrokes had a fine library at Wilton and a magnificent collection of paintings. Samuel Daniel had been Earl William's tutor before he became Anne's. After Philip's Countess Susan died in February 1629, he sought another wife of comparable social status to himself, young enough to have children and not over-encumbered, a noblewoman who would accompany and support him at Court.

Anne's availability would have been common knowledge and Montgomery lost little time in pursuing her. John, Lord Paulet, passed on the news as early as 1 May 1629 that the Lord Chamberlain was to marry the Countess of Dorset.[17] It was well over a year before that happened, possibly from strict adherence to mourning, Anne being a stickler for etiquette. A portrait of her attributed to Gerard Honthorst shows her in mourning. Her large ruff, oval from side to side, was in fashion. Her high-necked bodice denotes she was a widow, married women wearing it low-cut. Her hair is dressed in the new style, with a

32. Philip Herbert, 4th Earl of Pembroke and Montgomery, KG (1584–1650), by Daniel Mytens, c. 1628/9 (Reproduced by courtesy of the Marquess of Salisbury)

straight forehead fringe, the side hair frizzed out and hanging from partings to the neck. The back hair is coiled into a flat bun and left uncovered, though trimmed here with her usual pearls. The black bows and trimmings would be *de rigueur* in mourning. In three later copies the bows and trimmings are scarlet, giving a celebratory, even festive aura appropriate for attendance on the queen (Pl. 33).[18]

33. Lady Anne, Dowager Countess of Dorset, attrib. to Gerard Honthorst, c. 1629 (Private collection)

Quadrepartite articles, the marriage settlement, were signed on 20 May 1630. Two high court officers were parties to the agreement for Philip – Sir Benjamin Rudyard, Surveyor of the Court of Wards and one of his protégés, and Sir James Palmer, Gentleman Usher of the King's Privy Chamber. Shortly before the wedding on 3 June 1630 in the Russell family church at Chenies Philip inherited the earldom of Pembroke from his deceased brother. Anne therefore became a triple countess, of Pembroke, Dorset and Montgomery. The entry in the Chenies parish register has her stamp on it: 'Phillip Herbert Earle of Pembrooke and Mountgomery Lord Chamberlayne to the Kings Maiesty was maried this thirde day of June 1630 to the Ladye Anne Countesse Dowager of Dorset, which Ladye was daughter, and sole heire, to George Clifford late Earle of Cumberland by his wife Margaret Russell daughter to ffrancis Russell late Earle of Bedford.'[19]

She makes no bones about her motives. This second marriage, she writes, 'was wonderfullie brought to pass by the Providence of God for the Crossing and disappoynting, the envie, malice and sinister practices of my Enemyes'. The Old Testament fervour to smite her Clifford and Dorset opponents wells up here as nowhere else in her writings and cracks the genteel façade of her popular persona. She had harnessed one of the 'greatest subjects in the Kingdom' to her cause. She fully appreciated she would again be a 'feme covert' and surrender her legal status and right to the Clifford properties to her second husband. It looks as if, by the marriage settlement, she held on to her Dorset jointure lands, which would save Pembroke making her an allowance. The other terms are clear. Pembroke wanted to be able to dispose of his great estates as he chose, without any claim from Anne, so he agreed to make her an allowance from his lands of £1,200 a year in lieu of her dower and her thirds. Moreover, if she happened to inherit her father's properties, she was to have £800 yearly from them for her own benefit.[20]

34. Lady Isabella Sackville (1622–61), aged about eight, artist unknown (Private collection)

Pembroke, it has often been said, was the antithesis of Anne, almost illiterate, a man of violent temper, foul language and dubious morals. She herself called him 'choleric', which his testing work as Lord Chamberlain made worse. To stress this, however, misses the point. Anne was no stranger to his behaviour. What needs to be appreciated is just how great a subject and royal favourite Pembroke was. The Lord Chamberlain was the most prestigious officer of state and Pembroke during the 1630s was also head of the king's whole household. He had charge of the Chamber with its thirteen departments whose officers served the sovereign in a strict hierarchy of familiarity from his most private rooms, the bedchamber and privy chamber, to his public appearances in audience and in the splendour of state occasions. This called for a profound understanding of the workings of the household and of protocol, perceptive management, sensitivity to the king's needs and a good relationship with the Queen's chamberlain, Dorset. They and their respective vice-chamberlains regularly cooperated over Court functions. Courtiers were well advised to keep in Pembroke's good books because the Lord Chamberlain's responsibilities (as noted in the previous chapter) included approving noblemen to meet and attend foreign ambassadors when they arrived in England or were escorted to audiences with the king. Access to the reigning monarch was the greatest privilege for anyone with aspirations and Pembroke had priority over everybody else.[21]

Moreover, he was efficient. Sir John Finet, Master of Ceremonies, describes how things were 'excellently ordered' by him. Aubrey tells us, too, that he had 'a wonderful sagacity of the understanding of men', being able to espy their real motives. Because of the nature of his duties none of his residences was really private. All had to be at the disposal of the dignitaries he was dealing with, the king most of all. This was especially the case with his chambers in Whitehall Palace, the nearby Cockpit and, for Charles and Henrietta Maria, Wilton too. Pembroke, for instance, entertained the Russian ambassador in his own house in 1629. The queen's half-brother, the Duke de Vendôme, visited him in November 1631. Baron Oxenstierna of Sweden was entertained on 16 February 1633. On 8 April 1634 a comedy was staged at the Cockpit. The Lord Chamberlain had to be most solicitous of the king. On 30 November 1630 Charles rested in Pembroke's lodgings before going into the Council chamber to meet the assembled ambassadors. Pembroke's own household servants prepared the repasts and he bore the expense, his then income from his various offices of over £5,000 a year comfortably meeting all his official outlays. His total revenues, according to Aubrey, had reached £30,000 at his death.[22]

Power, great wealth, royal favour, the Court, Westminster and Wilton were what Lady Anne opted for in 1630. They do not fit into the received notions of her preference for rural quietude which she as much as anyone insinuates. Yet, apart from her depressed years from 1615 to 1618, it was in the throbbing heart of the realm, peopled with her noble and courtier relatives and friends, that she had been most at home since her early teens. Lady Margaret had shared and Lady Isabella was to continue sharing that experience with her. As a triple countess, the Lord Chamberlain's consort, stepmother to his five sons and a daughter and intimate of the royal family, Anne achieved the pinnacle of her social standing and esteem, a position envied by all but a handful of the great noble ladies of her generation.

CHAPTER 6

Countess of Pembroke, Dorset and Montgomery

1630–50

Immediately after their wedding Lady Anne took her rightful place at Court beside Pembroke who lived 'in a noble and splendid manner' in his Whitehall residence where his household numbered eighty, his Wilton establishment being double that number. Her first royal occasion as his consort was the christening of the baby Prince Charles on Sunday 27 June 1630. In the great ceremonial procession, Anne was one of the second pair of countesses, walking alongside Elizabeth Hume, Countess of Suffolk, wife of her relative Earl Theophilus Howard. Her cousin Bedford carried the great gilded covered basin to the font. There was to be similar ceremonial at James, Duke of York's baptism on 24 November 1633.

Anne would be presented to distinguished foreigners in Pembroke's residences as well as at Court. When the ambassador extraordinary from the King of Poland arrived in September 1631, he was given a 'very honourable reception' in the Banqueting House of Whitehall Palace, 'the lane through which he passed being built of pensioners on the king's side, and of the beauties of the court on the queen's'. Regularly throughout the year the Court ladies served the queen, at the masques and dancing they jointly put on; filling the many coaches which, for example, accompanied the Duchess de Trémouille on her departure from London; at the Lord Mayor's reception with its crowded running buffet, and at the sumptuous banquet when the Inns of Court performed Shirley's masque *The Triumph of Peace* on 4 February 1634 in the Banqueting House, whose ceiling Rubens painted in magnificent colour on that theme, lauding King James.[1]

For Anne there would be personal honour when Charles and Henrietta Maria visited Wilton almost annually. Pembroke's Wiltshire home was the king's favourite place. He was exhilarated by the hunting there and took interest in Isaac de Caus's refashioning of the old Tudor building and its gardens. Art was the king's great passion and Pembroke was almost his equal as a patron of fashionable Court painters. Myten's group depiction of the king, the queen and the 'brethren' (William posthumously), inside Wilton it is thought, is testimony to the intimacy between the royal couple and the Pembrokes. At Wilton, Anne would have been hostess in her own right and all the more welcome to Charles as the attractive and cultured widow of his old tilting partner. Bishop Rainbow, with whom Anne often discussed her life and times, was to remark that she had

35. Wilton House, the Pembrokes' seat in Wiltshire, showing the centre of the east front, the only surviving part of the Tudor building that Lady Anne would have known (Photo: the author)

known greatness at Court, under 'three Great Princes, who (reigning in Peace) had as much magnificence and glory as any that swayed the Scepter of this Land'. In the past Anne had attended Elizabeth I's Court with her parents and James I's in Dorset's company or in Queen Anne's entourage. As Pembroke's consort, she actually lived inside the Court with a degree of intimacy with the royal family never attained by any other Clifford lady.

Anne bore Pembroke two prematurely born children who died in infancy. Though their marriage might not be termed happy, perhaps short of contented if she is to be believed, yet it suited her purpose. She again attained the married status which gave her superiority over single and widowed noblewomen and precedence over most wives as the Lord Chamberlain's consort. She would have lived in opulence. Inigo Jones she had long known and she would have become familiar with the great court painters such as Rubens, Mytens and most of all van Dyck. Pembroke was eventually to assemble the greatest collection of his paintings in England, even more than Charles I.[2]

Moreover, in the essential matter of her estate business Pembroke gave her the weighty authority her wifely status lacked. They jointly appointed commissioners to make further entries into the Westmorland and Craven estates in August 1632.[3] Much the most striking instance of their cooperation was Anne's completion of Beamsley Hospital, carrying out her mother's death-bed request. By 1631 she was in the process of erecting, perhaps had completed, chambers for the additional six Sisters in a row set back from the main Skipton road, at her entire cost (Pl. 36). An archway revealed and gave access to the original circular building. Anne provided superior accommodation, with two 'handsome rooms' and a garden for each Sister. Within the perimeter walls were pleasant walks for all the Sisters to take exercise, shaded by willow trees.

With six new Sisters to support, Anne and Pembroke increased the income from the closes in Countess Margaret's endowment and also added to it. On 13 May 1631 they granted a ninety-nine years' lease of the closes for a rent of £50 a year to Ralph and Lancelot Coniston, faithful servants of the countess and her daughter, the money to be paid to the Sisters in the chapel at four yearly feasts. Soon after, they bought Ireton's farm near Duffield in Derbyshire and conveyed it to the Sisters for their upkeep. Their associates in this conveyance included Charles Herbert Esq. (possibly Pembroke's heir), Sir James Palmer and two influential office-holders in the central administration who reflected Pembroke's high standing and gave the endowment permanency. Sir Robert Pye was Auditor of the Receipt. Sir Benjamin Rudyard, who had acted over their marriage agreement, was especially close because the bespoke wife of Pembroke's son Charles was a ward of court – Mary Villiers, the richly endowed daughter of the murdered royal favourite Buckingham.

Pembroke and Anne found a reliable tenant for the Duffield property. They

36. *Beamsley Hospital, Lady Anne's building, c. 1632, with her plaque and parents' coats of arms, c. 1653 (The Landmark Trust. Photo: the author)*

leased it on 22 May 1639 to Sir Edward Leech, one of the masters in Chancery, for three lives and £40 a year rent, which gave the hospital altogether £90 annual income. This was apportioned £8 to the Reader, £8 to the Mother and £6 to each Sister, with £2 surplus for the Mother to use on repairs to the buildings. Otherwise, the Sisters managed their finances. However, moral oversight in accord with her mother's Orders, which she now reissued, was Anne's province (Table 3). When Widow Ramsden was accused of committing a 'foulle' crime in 1634, Thomas, Lord Fairfax, of Denton in Wharfedale sent her details of his examination. She replied to him on 14 May from Whitehall telling him she would not meddle, but leave it to God in Heaven, the justices on earth and Fairfax in his wisdom to punish the Sister if she was proved guilty, or if innocent acquit her.[4]

All appeared to be going well for Anne and her private concerns as Pembroke's countess. With Lady Isabella in her thirteenth year and reaching an age for betrothal if not a wedding, they agreed marriage provision for her on 4 December 1634 in a document signed by the Lord Privy Seal, the Earl of Manchester, Pembroke, Bedford and Anne herself. It was generous to Anne. Should she inherit the Westmorland lordships, she was to have them all for life in lieu of the £800 per annum agreed in 1630. Pembroke was to occupy the Skipton properties, which were of 'farre greater value'. He had first-hand knowledge of them now. He had attended the wedding of Clifford's daughter Elizabeth to Richard Boyle, Lord Dungarvan, son of the great Earl of Cork, in Skipton Castle on 3 June, probably as the king's representative. He agreed to raise £5,000 towards Isabella's marriage portion from Craven and not take any income himself until the entire sum was paid. The money so collected was to be deposited with Manchester and Sir William Savile, acting for Pembroke, and Bedford and Philip, Lord Wharton, representing Anne. His readiness to sign these terms was partly due to his eagerness for Isabella to marry one of his younger sons.[5]

Then, only two weeks later, on 18 December, because of 'some discontent' Anne calls it, she 'went from Liveing at the Court at Whitehall' to reside on her own at Pembroke's great house Baynard's Castle on Thames-side, where his son-in-law Robert Dormer, Earl of Carnavon, often lodged. This was just before Christmas when Charles and Henrietta Maria were planning dancing in the great hall for the Court and other festivities; an awkward time for anything to happen to upset Pembroke. Anne is disingenuous about what must have been a frightful quarrel. Whatever caused it – her lands, or Lady Isabella's match or the demands on her at Court – she does not deign to mention. Sedgewick who, as Pembroke's secretary from 1640 and Anne's officer from 1652, should have known the reason, explained that it was because Pembroke was 'much given to women, which caused a separation between him and his virtuous lady'. Even this hardly seems sufficient for a breach of such magnitude. It is almost as if, having got the concessions she wanted, Anne provoked his anger. Pembroke's dignity was damaged. He was left virtually widowed a second time and for the rest of his life, a Lord Chamberlain lacking both consort and hostess in his palace chambers and at Wilton.

Anne draws a veil over their parting. In fact Pembroke booted her out of

TABLE 3 *Beamsley Hospital Orders, issued by Lady Anne, 1631*[1]

Orders made by the right Honorable Anne Countess of Pembroke hereafter still to be observed in the Almshouse at Beamsley in Craven which was founded by her dear & blessed Mother Margaret Russel Countess of Cumberland in the year 1593.

First, That Prayers be duly and every Morning read between Eleven and Twelve o'Clock in the Chapel of the said Almshouse by M[r] Thomas Holmes now Reader there, or who shall succeed him in that place and the Mother and all the twelve Sisters give their Constant Attendance at the said Prayers and none of them be Absent at any time unless in Case of Sickness, or other urgent Occasions.

Second, That none of the twelve Sisters be out of the House without the leave of the Reader which prays with them or the Mother of the said Almshouse.

Third, That none of their Children or Grandchildren nor any other shall be with any of the Sisters in the said Almshouse without the leave of the Reader and the Mother which leave shall not be granted but in case of Sickness or some other reasonable Occasion.

Fourth, That the outer Doors of the Almshouse may be constantly locked up every Night at nine o'Clock in the Summer and eight o'Clock in the Winter and to be opened at seven o'Clock in the Winter and six in the Summer.

Fifth, That none of the Sisters do run an Score in the Town because they have their Allowance Quarterly and Constantly.

Sixth, That the Almshouse Court be swept once every Week the Runnels and water courses scoured and kept very clean.

Seventh, That the Mother hereof be carefull to observe these Orders.

Eighth, That the Mother and Sisters do all of them endeavour to Live peacefully and quietly amongst themselves.

Ninth, that if any differences shall arise amongst any of the Sisters or Mother and Sisters that the Business be determined amongst the major part of themselves and the aforesaid Mother & in case they cannot end it then to be refered to the Earl of Thanet whilst he lives and after his death such differences to be refered to the owner of Skipton Castle.

Tenth, That if the Mother or any of the Sisters do break any of these Orders, for the 1st Fault they shall forfeit a fortnight's Allowance to be paid out of the next money they are to receive to be divided equally the one half to the Informer & the other to the poor of the Town for the second fault to be expelled out of the house.

Eleventh, That when any others shall succeed they may submit themselves to the Said Orders or else they shall not be admitted.

Sackville Tufton

NOTE

1. As reissued by Sackville Tufton, 7th Earl of Thanet, *c.* 1730

Source: YAS, MD240

Whitehall. This she acknowledged four years later in her letter of 14 January 1638 when she wrote from Ramsbury in Wiltshire to the Earl of Bedford that although she wanted to come up to London, to stay in either Baynard's Castle or the Cockpit, she dare not do so without her husband's express leave 'lest he take that occasion to turn me out of his house, as he did out of Whitehall, and then I shall not know where to put my head'.[6]

Indeed, it was far worse than that. Anne was, in effect, banished not just from London but from Charles I's Court. She was isolated as never before. She would get no sympathy from other courtiers and their ladies and worst of all would become a *persona non grata* to the king and queen. It was a catastrophic collapse in her status and her cause. She had thrown away the protection and high regard which she had enjoyed for four years. She was now far more vulnerable than at any time in her life. Her friends were closer to her enemies than they were to her. When it came to a choice, they would shrink from offending the Lord Chamberlain, let alone the king, by taking her side. Her enemy Dorset was on excellent terms with Charles and Henrietta Maria and at times was given charge with his wife of the royal children. Her cousin Clifford and his son-in-law Richard Boyle, Lord Dungarvan, were happy to receive instructions from Pembroke because royal and ministerial beneficence was essential for their own interests.[7]

What is surprising, therefore, is the degree to which Pembroke was still prepared to do his duty by Anne and also help her. It is a side to their relationship she plays down. Pembroke incorporated the terms of the 1634 agreement in a formal settlement on 5 June 1635 and, furthermore, made over to Anne as a jointure estate the same five manors in north-east Kent he had assigned to his first wife. They comprised Queenborough and Shurland on the Isle of Sheppey, Milton, Colehill and Northwood on the mainland, all of which James I had granted him when creating him earl of Montgomery. The document reiterated Anne's claim to Barden and its two parks. Three of the men who acted for her were her relatives, Bedford, Wharton and Sir Gervase Clifton of Clifton, Nottinghamshire, and the fourth was Sir John Danvers of Chelsea, a prominent Wiltshire gentleman and stepfather to the poet George Herbert, Pembroke's relative and one of Anne's friends. That same day, Pembroke and Anne reached agreement over the Westmorland estates with Earl Francis. Her jointure from Pembroke was confirmed on the 16th in the presence of two high legal officers, Sir John Finch, Chief Justice of the Court of Common Pleas, and Sir Walter Pye, Attorney of the Court of Wards. In August 1637 Pembroke joined Anne in another formal entry into the Westmorland and Craven estates, thereby publicizing his own reversionary interest as well as Anne's and Isabella's.[8]

He even found a place for his errant wife in the monumental portrait group by Sir Anthony van Dyck, 'Philip, 4th Earl of Pembroke, and His Family', which now dominates the double-cubed room at Wilton House (Pl. 37). He commissioned it to celebrate the wedding on 18 January 1636 of his heir Charles, Lord Herbert, and the rich heiress Lady Mary Villiers, towards whom he gestures in her white dress on the lower steps. With its vast canvas, 330 x 510cm (128½ x 199 in.), Titianesque composition and family historical theme, it

37. 'Philip, 4th Earl of Pembroke, and His Family', by Sir Anthony van Dyck, 1636 (Collection of the Earl of Pembroke, Wilton House, Salisbury)

has been called 'a uniquely vainglorious picture'. Pembroke would have specified the positioning of the figures and Anne is depicted in her correct countess's place on his left. Their chairs are level, but Anne's small stature is enhanced by her long gown. She is slightly obscured, as if set back, by Pembroke's arm caressing his staff and his elder daughter Anne Sophia, Countess of Carnavon, standing to the right. Anne, in a sombre black dress, static in pose and looking withdrawn, almost as if she had been blubbering, is the detached element in a richly colourful, baroque composition (Pl. 38). She was, indeed, divorced from the family group, and van Dyck must have sketched her in Baynard's on her own and then squeezed her into the place left vacant beside her husband. They are conjoined in the sense that both are shown wearing black, a sombre centre in the expansive canvas where the rich costumes of his children's generation most catch the eye.[9]

Van Dyck's depiction of Anne might be regarded as a metaphor for her condition at that moment. No doubt she felt an outcast from Pembroke's large and vibrant family. That would certainly accord with the sketchy view she has left of her life after 1634 with Isabella and a few servants at Pembroke's Wiltshire houses, Wilton and Ramsbury, occasionally visiting Baynard's Castle, and mainly devoting herself in her usual fashion to good books and virtuous thoughts. Ramsbury manor, her favourite home, was described by John Evelyn as 'that exceedingly beautiful seate . . . on the ascent of an hill, flank'd with Woods & reguarding the river'. Its stables were possibly built by Isaac de Caus (Pl. 39).[10] She would have been content there.

But, as has been seen, Anne could call on Pembroke's aid when that was necessary. Moreover, she had the company in his houses of her sister-in-law Mary Talbot, countess dowager of Pembroke, and some of his children. There was the cultural appeal at Wilton of a great library and magnificent collection of paintings. She was also far more active than she implies. When her first grandchild Nicholas was born at Bolebrooke on 7 August 1631 she had been at Wilton, and at Ramsbury on 4 September 1634 when her first, short-lived granddaughter Anne was born. Away from Pembroke thereafter, she took the chance to be present at the birth and christening as godmother of Margaret at Hothfield House in Kent on 13 July 1636 and of her favourite grandson John at Wiston House in Sussex on 7 August 1638. She was in Baynard's Castle when Richard was born at Thanet House in the city of London on 30 March 1640. She could not be with Lady Margaret when she gave birth to Frances on 23 March 1642, also at Thanet House, because she had rented

38. *Detail showing Lady Anne, 'Philip, 4th Earl of Pembroke, and his Family', by Sir Anthony van Dyck, 1636 (Collection of the Earl of Pembroke, Wilton House, Salisbury. Photo: the author)*

accommodation at the widow Mrs Gayes's house in Bath. Altogether, she and Isabella were far more mobile than her own writings might suggest and spent much time with the rapidly growing Thanet family in their various residences.[11]

Anne was at Ramsbury on 28 January 1641 when Earl Francis died, aged eighty-two, and her cousin inherited. This brought her a step closer to obtaining her estates and called for action to publicize her claims once more. She and Pembroke introduced a private bill in Parliament, with Earl Henry's approval, to preserve her right title to the estates without prejudice to the livery to be sued by him. This was realistic because chance would have to play its part and the future was imponderable. If Henry outlived Anne, neither she nor Pembroke would get the lands; instead, they would go to the heiresses on either side. Yet, assuming Henry would die first, Pembroke had to assert his own title to the Skipton manors and hope also that Isabella would become a bride for one of his sons. As Sir Simonds D'Ewes noted in his journal, the passage of the bill from the Lords to the Commons took over a year.[12]

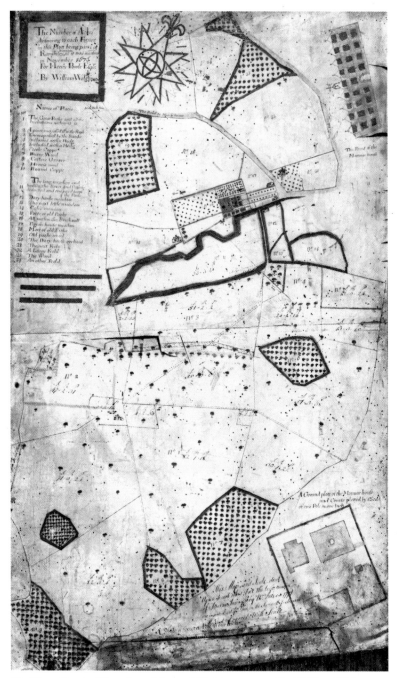

39. Plan of part of Ramsbury Manor, Wiltshire, surveyed by William Walgrave for Henry Powle Esq. in November 1676, amended by William Reeves, 1771. Top centre is the manor house and garden with the avenue and drive from the Marlborough road. Top right is an elevation of the manor house (Lady Burdett-Coutts)

The outbreak of the Great Civil War prevented the further entries into the estates which Anne would undoubtedly now have made. The uncertainties and dangers of the conflict brought her and Pembroke together again, if briefly, in mutual dependence. She was a Royalist whereas he threw in his lot with the parliament, having been dismissed by the king in 1641 for opposing him. He called her to London on 13 October 1642 after hostilities had broken out. At his request she took up residence in Baynard's. There she and Isabella would be far safer than anywhere else and at the same time in his expected long absences could protect the house which was full of riches – his furnishings, paintings, silverware and the like – much perhaps carted there from the Court and the Cockpit and also Wilton, which could not be defended. Looting by either side was one of the worst afflictions of war and to be avoided at all cost. He moved his irreplaceable manorial and estate records from Wilton in November 1643 for safe keeping to Carisbrooke Castle on the Isle of Wight where he was governor. He again helped Anne during 1644 by presenting a petition to parliament with her on Lady Isabella's behalf complaining at the waste committed at Bolebrooke by her son-in-law John, Earl of Thanet.[13]

What is worth emphasizing is Anne's assertion that she remained incarcerated in Baynard's for the next six years and nine months, confining herself from choice, not setting foot outside even to ride to Lady Isabella's wedding in July 1647 at nearby Clerkenwell. Baynard's, since 1446 a royal castle, had been rebuilt by Henry VII. According to Stow, it was not embattled nor strongly fortified but had become 'far more beautiful and commodious for the entertainment of any prince or great estate'. It had a square court and adjoining to the west a large walled garden, so plenty of space for Anne and Isabella to take exercise in privacy. Within the court was an octagonal tower and there were two more at the front. The windows were in pairs, one above the other. Beneath was a bridge and stairs down to the river (Pl. 40). Obviously a fine residence, it was for Anne 'a place of refuge for mee to hide myself in till these troubles were over-passed'.[14]

Relations between Anne and her cousin's family had thawed by now, with her succession inevitable. When Earl Henry's daughter Elizabeth, Lady Dungarvan, gave birth to a daughter, Elizabeth, in the Piazza in Covent Garden on Sunday, 22 January 1643, Anne was one of the godparents, along with the Dowager Countess of Devonshire and the Earl of Salisbury. She may have attended the ceremony in person.[15] Eleven months later she at long last inherited her Clifford lands. Earl Henry, who in 1642 fortified Skipton Castle for the king and acted as a Royalist commander in Yorkshire, died on 11 December 1643 of a fever at York. He was buried in Holy Trinity, Skipton, on the 31st, with the titles of Earl of Cumberland, Lord of Westmorland, Lord Vipont, Vescy, Atton and Bromflete and Lord of the Honour of Skipton in Craven. The King's Award immediately took effect and Anne and Pembroke became owners of the Westmorland and Skipton estates respectively. One of Henry's servants was quickly despatched from York to bring her the news, Ferdinando, Lord Fairfax, the Parliamentarian leader in the county, granting him a safe-conduct.[16] Soon after, Anne had a new pedigree drawn up for a renewed claim for the titles, though what progress she could have made, the war being fought in earnest, is not certain.[17]

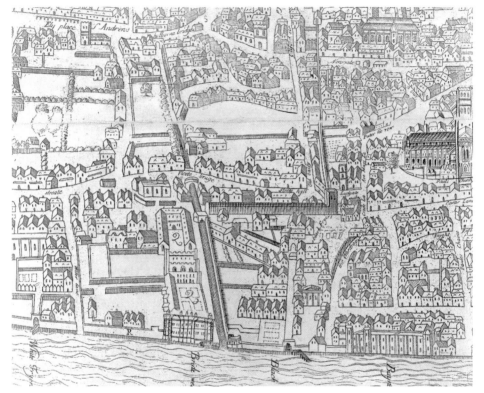

40. Baynard's Castle with, to the left, Salisbury Court, from the Agas Map, 1633 (Corporation of London. The Greater London Record Office (Maps and Prints, FA 6603))

Henry's death, in which Anne spied the hand of God, gave a curious twist to the inheritance dispute and the settlement by the award. She got the estates which she would have received in the natural course of events under her father's will as heir general, albeit after forty years' wait. In the interim, Dorset (and to an extent Anne herself) had benefited by the receipt of £17,000 into his coffers. In contrast, and as Sir John Lowther had perceived, Earl Francis had purchased merely life tenures for himself and his son at a price which cannot be measured only in terms of the huge sum he paid to Dorset. This had brought them close to the financial ruin that Earl George had considered could be avoided only by cutting his daughter out of the Clifford inheritance.

Anne's life and outlook were transformed by her cousin's death from a near-outcast to a noble landowner in her own right. Her sense of purpose and direction and her desire for achievement blossomed, ending another decade in which they had been suppressed or frustrated. She had to wait a further six years before she could physically enter her estates because of the continuing hostilities during the Civil Wars. The two sieges of Skipton Castle in 1645, the Parliamentarian garrisons there and at Appleby and the Royalist uprising in the north during 1648 made it far too risky for her to remove with her belongings until the summer of 1649.

Nevertheless, straightaway in February 1644, even though the Civil Wars in her own words were 'very hot', Anne took up the reins from Baynard's. Her ambition was to resuscitate the Clifford patrimony as her father's sole and rightful heir, discounting whatever Pembroke might have in mind. What action she took over her own Westmorland properties will be considered in Chapter 8. The Skipton estates, however, were properly her husband's by the 1635 agreement, Anne having only a reversionary interest, which meant they would fall to her only if he predeceased her. As will be seen shortly, she was not prepared to wait for that to happen.

For over six years Pembroke and Anne were necessarily absentee landowners. Pembroke's political and private affairs kept him in the south but he was immediately consulted, in January 1644, by Lord Fairfax about Skipton Castle which Colonel Sir John Mallory was holding for the king. His reply is not known, but obviously military considerations came first. The Skipton estates were controlled by the castle's garrison until late in 1645 and their rents quite properly used to maintain it. However, the change in ownership was noted at the manorial courts for Stirton and Thorlby from October 1644 which were called by Mallory in the name of Anne, Countess of Pembroke, as heir to her father Earl George. From May 1646, when the Parliamentarians controlled the estates, the military courts were held at the castle in the names of Pembroke and his countess.[18]

Anne and her husband had to bide their time as long as Mallory held out. Indeed, for the two years following Earl Henry's death it was his only surviving daughter Elizabeth, Lady Dungarvan, now Countess of Cork, who dealt with matters on both her own and the Pembrokes' Craven lordships. For example, she granted leases in Stirton and Thorlby and authorized the tenants to collect peat and turves for fuel as they always had. She wrote to Anne from York in May 1645, when a close siege of Skipton was imminent, telling her that the estate records they jointly owned were still safe in the castle's treasury even though the garrison was not free from disorder. Lord Fairfax had described to her 'woful experiences' of what could happen and she asked Anne to give serious thought to employing two men to examine them. After the castle fell in December, it was to Lady Cork and her officers that the Skipton people looked for protection against the Parliamentarian authorities. All this was good landlordship by her to the benefit of Anne and Pembroke, though it may be doubted whether they appreciated what she did for them.[19]

Commendably, Pembroke's prime concern in 1646 was fulfilling his contract to raise the £5,000 for Isabella's portion. He appointed Henry Currer gent. of Skipton, recently a Royalist captain, as receiver for his Craven revenues. Anne, ignoring her husband's rights, adopted a blatant proprietorial and interventionist role. However, her first concern was quite proper. Mallory had been anxious that the records in the castle belonging to the two ladies and the hangings and other contents belonging to Anne should be safeguarded. Clauses in the surrender terms ensured the evidences were kept secure and Colonel Thornton, for the Parliament, held them under lock and key. Anne's belongings were regarded differently. They were to be priced with all the other contents and not to be sold until she was appraised of them. It was not only the valuable hangings which the wording of the clause put in jeopardy. Her father's superb jousting armours were in the castle. Yet nothing was disposed of; Pembroke, a Parliamentarian grandee, possibly again intervening for his wife. Nowhere is it mentioned how the hangings and armours were cared for until she rode north three years later.

Anne agreed with Lady Cork jointly to authorize the antiquarians Roger Dodsworth and Charles Fairfax Esq. of Steeton Hall near York to sort out the records in the castle on the same lines as the division in the estates. They set to admirably but not without upsetting Henry Thompson, lessee of the Corks' sequestered estates, and other local supporters whom they excluded from the muniment room. Fairfax, brother of Lord Ferdinando and uncle of the general Sir Thomas, held colonel's rank and was a justice of the peace for the West Riding. He busied himself at Skipton early in 1646 on judicial affairs and it was through him that Anne obtained on 19 November Mr Waterton's surveys of both the castle and Barden Tower, neither of which, unfortunately, has survived.[20] Dodsworth's labouring in the castle muniments was especially productive not just for Anne's current concerns but for all historians of the Clifford family and their estates, as will be made clear in Chapters 9 and 10.

Fairfax wrote to Anne for a list of Lady Cork's lands, which he considered he and his fellows ought not to meddle with, and for a copy of the King's Award. Anne's uncompromising reply, as he reported to his brother, was that she had 'never consented unto it, nor would be bound by it, but is now to demand her whole inheritance as rightful heir to her father, both by the laws of God and of the kingdom'. This is the key to Anne's actions both before and after she came north in June 1649. She strove to obtain all her father's properties, the Corks' as well as her own. Her great success was Barden, which she seized as soon as the Roundhead forces overran Wharfedale in 1645. The Corks' names on its court rolls for 2 October 1644 were crossed out and Anne's inserted, as daughter and heir to Earl George.[21]

Barden and its extensive woods were essential for the Pembrokes if Isabella's portion was to be collected. This was Anne's chief concern as much as her husband's and she was not willing to leave the task to him. In effect, she set up her own parallel, even rival, estate administration in Craven. In June 1646, by her appointment, Lord Wharton and Sir John Danvers authorized Benjamin Kent of Fetter Lane, London, in whom she had confidence, to receive the Craven rents on Isabella's behalf. To raise £5,000 would not be easy. The Skipton area had been trampled by the Parliamentarian armies in the two sieges of the castle in the previous year, crops had been ruined, walls and fences thrown down, and the meadows and pastures fouled by the cavalry. There had been much damage to buildings besides the castle, church and Barden Tower, which had all suffered heavily.

Fairfax's letters testify to the administrative dislocation around Skipton, not helped by the retention of a garrison in the castle. Heavy Parliamentarian taxation prolonged the dire economic condition of the populace. Farming, trade and personal wealth were slow to recover from the succession of catastrophes. Lacking close supervision Barden woods, like all the Pembrokes' enclosed parks, suffered depredation. The Royalist uprising in 1648 brought more armies into Craven and the consequent slighting (partial demolition) of the castle. Its cannon were sold, along with the 44 tons of lead stripped from its roofs, much of its good timber and its quality, shaped stone, mostly to local men, many of them Anne's own tenants. Her later animosity towards one Watson of Silsden was said to be because he had purchased timber. Yet she herself is recorded as having bought back £2 10s worth.[22]

It looks as if Pembroke himself visited Skipton in late July 1646, when Lady Cork hoped to meet him there or, if not, at York during August. Over the following months, he became irritated at the slow progress in raising Isabella's portion and began suit in Chancery against Wharton, his fellow Parliamentarian, to speed it up. But at

41. Philip, 4th Baron Wharton (1613–96), etching by Wenceslaus Hollar (National Portrait Gallery Archive Engravings Collection)

the hearing on 22 September 1647 it became plain that the 'great troubles' in the north after Earl Henry's death were the chief reason why Kent had been able to collect so far only £263 16s 6d. In the circumstances, Henry Currer did well to send as much as £1,000 to Kent by the time Pembroke died early in 1650, for which Isabella's husband, the Earl of Northampton, gave receipts. This included at least £351 worth of wood from Barden. Kent himself was active in Craven on Anne's behalf. For instance, he leased demesnes such as Skipton mills to William Kitchen for one year in 1647 for £85 in rent, increasing that to £100 the following year.[23]

Pembroke may well have left his wife to her own devices in Baynard's during the war years, though his officers were often there, lodging in its many chambers. He was busy on the parliament's behalf in his official positions, which included governorship of Windsor Castle. But he must have visited her on occasion, if only to see that all was well with the castle and its precious contents. They would have had recurrent arguments over Isabella, and Anne makes plain that about May 1645 this provoked 'a great cause of Anger & falling out' between them. Pembroke was under the impression that Anne had the power to persuade Isabella to agree to a Herbert marriage. That was correct, though her daughter was now of age. Equally she had the will-power to veto the match, and this she did because of Isabella's aversion to it. But Pembroke also wanted Anne to assign to him Isabella's portion from Craven so that he would get some benefit from his ownership. This she refused to do. She might have reacted with a wry smile to the fact that, although at loggerheads with her husband, she came close through him to becoming a duchess. On 1 December 1645 a parliament grateful for his services voted Pembroke a dukedom.[24]

The Civil War delayed Lady Isabella's marriage for several years because suitable Royalists were engaged fighting far afield from the capital. Anne's planning for it began in 1646, when she requested Sir Thomas Henley, sheriff of Sussex, to make a more precise partition of her daughters' lands than the Court of Wards had done. He completed this on 21 October with the advice of a twelve-man jury.[25] Anne's choice of a husband for Isabella could hardly have been an intended slap in the face for Pembroke, yet that is how he might have regarded it. James Compton, 3rd Earl of Northampton, born in 1622, was an enthusiastic adherent of Charles I, a Fellow of Queens' College, Cambridge from 1637, an active field commander, a gallant Colonel of Horse and then Brigadier in the First Civil War. He succeeded in March 1643 when his father Spencer, 2nd Earl, met a brave death at the Battle of Hopton Heath. His brother William, also a notable Colonel and governor of Banbury, was regarded by Pepys as 'one of the worthiest men . . . in England'.

The Royalist cause being lost, Earl James compounded in April 1646 and was very heavily fined by the parliament, which compelled him to take the oath of allegiance to the Commonwealth. He and Isabella were married on 5 July 1647 in the church at Clerkenwell and took up residence in the Comptons' main house, Castle Ashby. On the 14th, Anne signed an agreement to settle on James the Sussex lands Dorset had bequeathed to Isabella, with a mansion at Wilmington, which she held on her life interest. In the meantime he would enjoy the rents of £542 a year. Granted the circumstances, this was as generous an endowment as could be envisaged.[26] The match had an appealing family link. Dorset's stepmother had formerly been Lady Compton and may also have attended Anne's wedding in 1609, the kind of sentiment which weighed heavily with her.

The manuscript and pictorial legacies of Anne's later years at Baynard's will be discussed in Chapters 9 and 10. She is depicted full-length in the

42. James Compton, 3rd Earl of Northampton (1622–81), by William Dobson, c. 1644/5 (Private collection. Photo: Courtauld Institute of Art)

breathtaking painting from this time, the Appleby triptych, when she was approaching sixty (Pl. 44). A quite separate head-and-shoulders portrait by Peter Lely at about the same age is regarded as a better likeness, although akin that in the triptych (Pl. 45). Both were painted from life, the first authentic portraits since Pembroke's great family portrait nearly a decade and a half earlier. How much Anne had aged in the intervening years is apparent.

Anne quitted London in July 1649. Her bulkiest household belongings would probably have been dispatched north by sea to Hull and by river to York and thence by carrier to Skipton and Appleby Castles. On 3 June she took her last leave of Pembroke at the Cockpit and from there visited the Northamptons at their residence in Islington. Her departure from Baynard's on 11 July would have been ceremonial and symbolic. Both her daughters and their lords and children were there to see her off, friends too whom (in her usual fashion) she would have informed about her quitting London. She pawned a heliotropan cup and a cabinet of silver gilt and crystal to Elizabeth, Countess of Kent, for £100 to cover her travelling expenses.[27]

Pembroke would hardly have been grieved to see her go. She had outmanoeuvred him at every stage both before and during marriage, getting what she wanted for herself and Lady Isabella. He had played fair, yet ended up with neither children by her, nor Isabella as his daughter-in-law, nor a single penny of income from the Craven estates.

He died six months later, on 23 January 1650, at the Cockpit. Anne now legally entered not only Skipton Castle and its properties but also a considerable dower estate in Kent, which Sedgewick suggests brought her £2,000 a year.[28] Wealthy already, she found this transformed her fortunes. She leapt upwards into the ranks of major landowners, with country-wide interests in Kent, Sussex, Essex, Yorkshire, Westmorland and Westminster, the envy of many a nobleman and perhaps uniquely prosperous as a widow. Challenging her 'enemies' over the King's Award or other issues would hold no qualms for her, cushioned as she was by the size of her landed wealth.

Pembroke's bequests to his 'loving wife' were little more than a token gesture – all the chains and jewels she possessed

43. Isabella Compton, Countess of Northampton (1622–61), by Sir Peter Lely (Private collection)

*44. Right hand panel of the Appleby Triptych, 1646/8, artist
unknown (Reproduced by courtesy of Abbot Hall Art Gallery,
Kendal)*

before her marriage and household linen and plate to the value of £500. These goods, a fur cloak and other things were delivered to her in a trunk on 7 October. She had wanted to purchase some of Pembroke's diamond buttons; whether for use, display or sentiment is not explained. The plate is of interest as almost the only clue to the style of living she had enjoyed at Baynard's. The particular items may have meant a great deal to her, with the implication perhaps of a sense of loss in Pembroke's demise which she does not admit to in her writings (Table 11).

Anne still had her Dorset jointure house in Salisbury Court. Surprisingly, on 28 February she expressed interest in buying Baynard's should it come on the

45. *Lady Anne, Countess of Pembroke, Dorset and Montgomery, attrib. to Sir Peter Lely, c. 1649 (Private collection. Photo: the author)*

market because it was the place she would prefer to stay at if she ever came up to London. Even to contemplate such a purchase she must have been confident she could raise the big sum it would command, either in cash or on bonds or even mortgages. At this time she had not emotionally abandoned the Court and the city. Eighteen months later she had. In the settled abode of her three ancient houses, Appleby, Brougham and Skipton, she comments: 'I doe more and more fall in love with the contentments and innocent pleasures of a Country Life.'[29]

A striking feature of Anne's long span as a married noblewoman, from the age of nineteen in 1609 to sixty in 1650, is that she lived with her husbands for less than half that time. Since Dorset's death, she had been on her own as a widow or separated for twenty-two of the twenty-six years. Ahead of her in 1650 was a second widowhood which, though unknown to her then, was to last even longer, so that on her own death in 1676 she had maintained an independent establishment for almost half a century. The next two chapters and also Chapter 11 will consider what kind of a fist the now elderly dowager countess made of taking over, residing on and managing the Cliffords' ancestral estates in the north of England which had been her heart's wish for almost as long as she could remember.

CHAPTER 7

Baroness of Skipton

1643–76

It is hard to imagine the history of Craven or its visual interest without the imprint of Lady Anne's personality on the region. The stone plaques, initials and crests which commemorate her building at Skipton, Barden and Beamsley are tangible evidence of her care and devotion towards her inheritance. Yet the dominance she established, more akin to her medieval forebears than to her immediate predecessors, exacted a price from those dependent on her. Her magnanimity in victory followed the browbeating of her tenants. Moreover, she pursued litigious warfare against some of her neighbours for a decade and a half. To skate over the constant legal skirmishing would be to do her memory a disservice and fail to appreciate how much light her awkward neighbourliness throws on the complex nature of her personality.

For Anne, Craven had an emotional appeal almost as strong as that of Westmorland. She was born at Skipton. Her predecessors since the Dissolution, including her father, were buried in the parish church, where the first Earl Henry had erected a fine tomb for himself and his countess. Barden Tower and Beamsley Hospital were steeped in memories of her mother, though not so much as Brougham Castle and Appleby Church, which gave the latter primacy in her feelings. This distinction explains why in her various agreements with Pembroke she yielded to him occupancy of her Skipton lands on a life-tenure after Earl Henry's death. The estates assigned were those awarded her by James I plus Barden, whose grant in 1607 to Earl Francis she did not recognize. In practice, as was seen in the previous chapter, Anne's officers operated in Craven from early 1646 and there was no hiatus when she took over from Pembroke in 1650.

As baronial mistress of Skipton, Anne was bound to experience some difficulties compared with her predecessors because of the fragmentation of rights and jurisdictions following the division of the estates in 1643. By the King's Award, she was entitled only to the original 1311 estate, less Barden, about a third of Earl Henry's Craven properties at his death, the Corks inheriting the bigger portion. Her Clifford Fee was separated for the first time for over a century from the other great Craven fee, the Percy Fee, which fell to the Corks. Unlike her predecessors, she did not control local administration. The bailiwick, or wapentake, of Staincliffe which comprised most of Craven was held by Cork as successor to Earl Henry. To have this jurisdiction overseen by anyone but herself particularly irked Anne, as will be explained below. Moreover, Cork had also inherited the lease of the Craven tithes held from Christ Church, Oxford, so that he was entitled to the tithe crops from the large parish of Skipton.

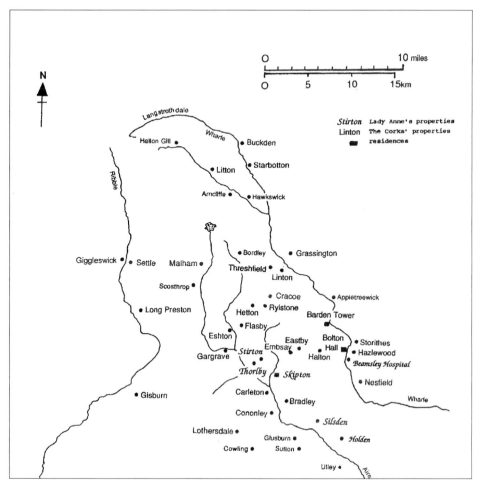

Map 3: The division in the Craven estates, 1643

Anne's position as lord of the barony of Skipton was therefore diminished compared with her father's and this she found hard to accept. Furthermore, the Corks appeared to hold all the aces in their relations with her. They owned the more extensive properties, including the rich Bolton Priory demesnes. The tithes lease gave them an intrusive right. Their officers were entitled to enter Anne's lands, choose every tenth sheaf of the mown corn (the best if they could get away with it) and cart them to their tithe barns for threshing and milling, the work normally being done for them by her tenants. Barden was included in this. But the Corks also, by the terms of the lease, had responsibility for the upkeep of the chancel of Holy Trinity and this, as will be seen, was to have a bearing on its restoration during the 1650s.[1]

In reality, the Corks suffered immense disabilities. Their estates had been sequestered by the Parliament because they as well as Earl Henry had been

46. Richard Boyle, Lord Dungarvan, Baron Clifford of Lanesborough (1644), 2nd Earl of Cork, 1st Earl of Burlington (1612–98), after Sir Anthony Van Dyck (Reproduced by permission of the Duke of Devonshire and the Trustees of the Chatsworth Settlement)

active Royalists. The rents on all their English estates were commandeered and they eventually had to pay a heavy composition to get the properties back. At one stage, they were so penurious they had to pawn their tableware and linen and borrow from their Weighton tenants to scrape enough money to live. Cork's Irish estates were in chaos after recurrent insurrections and warfare. He resided at Bolton Hall during 1650 to deal with his Craven manors but crossed to Ireland in 1651 and remained there for nearly ten years.[2]

Rather than being at a disadvantage, Anne was well placed to exploit the Corks' insecurity. She had taken possession of Barden unopposed. It was she, though this time with Lady Cork's agreement, who in 1654 divided the deer herds which were roaming free over Barden Forest and the Bolton Abbey estate and replaced the paling between them with stone walls for permanent separation. She was equally eager to get Clifford's Inn, Fleet Street, which by the Award had been Earl Francis's property. On 28 February 1650 she instructed her old friend and officer, Christopher Marsh, on what to do, fearing 'My Lady of Cork will cozen me of it, if she can'. Anne misunderstood; the Inn was in fact now quite independent.[3]

Nothing reveals quite so starkly the enigmas in Anne's nature nor her unyielding attitude as her behaviour towards the Corks, her blood relatives, whose daughter Elizabeth was her godchild. It left them more saddened than resentful and friends of both were puzzled by her actions. How she behaved towards them, as will be shown below, can be gleaned only from Cork's own manuscript diary and his officers' correspondence. Anne's *Diaries* and her other voluminous records are largely silent on these matters, which underlines their limitations as sources for studying her life and manners.

Anne began her management of the Craven estates in the most efficient manner by ordering new rentrolls and detailed surveys of the individual holdings, all compiled in 1649/50.[4] She returned to Skipton from Appleby on 13 February 1650 as soon as Pembroke's death gave her full control of Craven. The real work now began. In March she appointed gentry commissioners – her relative Sir Henry Cholmley of Whitby as chairman; Charles Fairfax;

Christopher Clapham gent. of Beamsley, an old friend; Peter Jennings, an elderly Silsden gentleman and former Royalist whose lands had been sequestered; and Robert Hitch, one of her officers. They sat for seven days in the great chamber of the castle's Octagonal Tower, Anne usually with them, compounding with her tenants for the rents due to her, most of which were five years in arrears. Their forceful bargaining based, as the tenants would know, on up-to-date information about themselves, their sub-tenants and holdings, brought the first large sums to help Anne pay £500 of the Northamptons' portion and finance her estate activities. She was over the first hurdle of asserting her seigneurial authority.[5] She also began discussing with her legal advisers in London, Sir Thomas Widdrington, Matthew Hale and John Howell, the settling of her

47. Elizabeth Clifford, Baroness Clifford (1628), Lady Dungarvan, Countess of Cork and Burlington (1613–91), after Sir Peter Lely (Reproduced by permission of the Duke of Devonshire and the Trustees of the Chatsworth Settlement)

Craven and Westmorland estates on her daughters and a £700 per annum allowance on her favourite grandson, John Tufton.[6]

The extensive and valuable Skipton demesne holdings had traditionally been let annually and Anne could build on what Benjamin Kent and her other officers had already achieved by racking the rents to keep them in line with the still rising market levels. Among those who took big holdings were her senior officers Gabriel Vincent (master of works), Thomas Gabetis (auditor), Robert Collings (Craven steward), whose lands had been sequestered, and Christopher and Richard Clapham. Christopher also took Barden Tower with its parks and adjoining lands for £50 a year.[7] This was standard practice by great landowners to reward loyal servants for their endeavours but it gave them a stake in the Skipton estate. Moreover, other demesne tenants could not grumble as long as her officers paid rents at the going rate. The work of Currer and Kent and then Anne herself lifted the annual rental of her Skipton inheritance and Barden from a low of £600 in 1646 to £1,052 in 1652. With the return of stability and prosperity, and with alterations in the leasing the rise continued to £1,752 in 1665.

A more complex task was renewing the many messuage leases which had terminated since the warfare had halted Lady Cork's work in 1645. Here again, raising cash was the immediate purpose. Between 1650 and 1654 twelve tenants in Barden paid £354 10s 8d in entry fines for new leases; in Skipton, twenty-one contributed £914 4s; in Silsden, thirty-three paid £2,185 3s 4d. With a few other grants in Stirton and Thorlby, Skibeden and Crookrise, Anne had raised £4,205 16s 8d from fines by 1654. The biggest single contribution was by Jonathan Mitchell who took the now deceased Peter Jennings's Holden Park for a £900 fine. It looks as if most of the Barden and Skipton tenants were eager to compound with Anne to retain their messuages and farmholds. In Silsden, on the other hand, the bargaining was tougher, as will be seen.

Oddly, whether it was because of this piecemeal beginning or not, Anne did not complete the change to modern economic leasing begun by Earl Francis during the 1630s. He had started to 'modernize' tenures by introducing 'improved' economic rents instead of the traditional low rents with variable entry fines. Under Anne each manor maintained its own traditional tenures interspersed with variations introduced seemingly on an ad hoc basis. In Barden, the demesnes apart, the leases were for three lives, with entry fines and the old, low reserved rents, so no change from the pre-Civil War practice which probably explains the relative smoothness of the transition to the new owner. By contrast, in Silsden most, though far from all, of those tenants who took new leases for three lives had to agree to an economic rent without a fine, the level based on the then current market value. For example, Robert Hamlyn's 'improved' rent was £4 compared with his 7s 4d 'ancient' rent previously. In Skipton twenty-one years remained the standard term. The other properties mostly followed the Barden or Silsden pattern.

Anne did not pick up the threads of her uncle's policy until January 1655. Then she instructed Cholmley and her council in granting new leases to replace fines with an 8 per cent rent increase, though the last fine paid was to be taken into consideration when setting the increase. A similar conservatism is evident in her leasing policies on her Sussex jointure manors. There, she was content to retain fines until Lady Dorset requested her in April 1656 to change to economic renting at full value. 'I know your noble mind', her niece wheedled, 'and that you doe in all thinges indeavour to leave monuments of it to posterity.' Anne eventually complied, because she appreciated that the properties were their inheritance, not her own. An instance is the July 1674 draft lease, signed by her, of her Meeching property to William Lane gent. of Southover.

On the whole, in Craven she respected the existing three-lives' leases granted by her father and uncle. In 1659 sixty-six of Earl George's leases were still in being in Silsden, most depending on one or two surviving lives, but some for the original three because when the leases were agreed in 1602/4 the tenants, where possible, had sensibly opted for young children as the designated lives and not all had yet died. A few similar leases had been granted by Earl Francis, and Anne herself had made nearly forty for three lives at the old rent, fifteen more with economic rents. Far from all of her father's leases fell in even during her lifetime. The longevity of a handful of Silsden people kept about a fifth in being until 1680. For Anne, as for her uncle, George's anticipation of future income from the lordship by collecting fines for three-lives' leases prevented her enjoying its potential value to the full. This in part explains her distinctive treatment of Silsden, which will be discussed below.[8]

Anne's style of management in Craven was not excessively tough; certainly her treatment of her tenants appears no worse than most of her contemporaries. Arbitration may have been the favoured method of resolving minor disagreements, witness Sir Henry Cholmley's honest-brokering with Edward Moorhouse of Skibeden over his rent arrears. However, the tinge of ruthlessness better evidenced in Westmorland is shown by her attitude towards those tenants who were unable to keep up with their rental payments, either from incompetence or personal misfortune. She would then on a first default distrain the tenant's stock or goods for the rent and if he still fell short eject him, reletting to a farmer better placed. This certainly contrasts with the known leniency of Earls Francis and Henry, who stand out as unusually considerate towards their Craven tenantry.[9]

One aspect of Anne's Craven policies is puzzling; that, given her attitude to the King's Award, she did not force the surrender of the Silsden fee farms Earl Francis had been allowed to grant to raise £2,000 towards the compensation to Dorset. She took all the expected preliminary actions for an assault on the fee-farmers by forcing the surrender of some small pieces of land. Then, more important, she ejected by lawsuits Peter Jennings's successor, his elder grandson Edmund, from his fee-farm ownership of Holden Hall; also Edmund's aunt Agnes (the second biggest occupier in the township), and all their unfortunate sub-tenants. In this action Anne was following her usual tactics towards a lordship of concentrating on her most prominent opponents, notwithstanding Jennings's close friendship with Lord Wharton. The Corks' officer Humphrey Hughes was present as an interested observer when Anne won her suits against Jennings at York in January 1656 and he commented that he had never heard a defendant's case so poorly presented. But, he added, he couldn't imagine any other lawyers doing better in the circumstances.

As in several of her quarrels with tenants, Anne's antipathy towards Edmund Jennings before and during the litigation gives the impression of being personal, yet it was mainly due to his prominence because, having won, she relet the property to him for three lives. Continuity of tenancy by a gentry family of note would have been her prime concern in Silsden as elsewhere on her Craven lordships. She believed in upholding rank in society and needed the goodwill of local gentry both to set an example and to manage her properties. As Sir Edmund Jennings, he became influential in county politics and administration. Those who suffered most, Humphrey Hughes informed the Corks on 7 November 1655, were the Jennings under-tenants who had lost all. Anne was careful to let her relatives understand through Hughes that she did not expect trouble to be caused to them by the tenants she had ejected.[10]

The Corks tried to avoid being drawn into the Silsden disputes, but willy-nilly they could not be mere bystanders. In fact they exerted a kind of ameliorating influence, restraining Anne so that she kept to the correct procedures. Humphrey Hughes told her in April 1656 how well the earl had taken it that she had not made new agreements in the lordship until the tenants handed in their old leases. To his surprise, Anne refused to let him see those leases. Then, for once, she let slip what was in her mind and this, carefully reported by Hughes, would have worried the Corks. She explained that if a suit were to arise with them over Silsden she had the evidences. She would have confided more to him but Gabetis, thinking her already indiscreet, warned her to say no more.[11] Anne's general attitude towards the Corks, of which this is an illuminating instance, will be explored later in this chapter.

The impression given by Anne's policies towards Silsden is that, more than anywhere else in Craven, she was an exceptionally disturbing presence there for over a decade and a half. It was not just that bargaining for new leases was more of a struggle for both sides. There was also the litigation to eject the Jennings family and their numerous under-tenants. Most of all, Anne plunged Silsden into turmoil for many years because of her attempt to appropriate the grinding of corn in the lordship. This stems from 1652/3 when she built a new water-driven corn mill on the beck at High Holden. Her target was the existing mill further down in Silsden town operated by the Currers of Kildwick.

Manorial mills, where the tenants were required by clauses in their leases to have their corn ground, were very profitable. Furthermore, in seigneurial terms they were not just symbols of rights in a manor but in practice often the actuality also. Silsden was the most populous Craven township apart from Skipton and its 120 or so tenants were obliged to use the manorial mill even though the Cliffords did not own it or benefit from its profits. Anne, therefore, had the dual incentive of potential revenues and increased authority to invest some of her precious capital in erecting her own mill and then use her baronial authority to divert her tenants from the Currers' mill to her own.

As was often the case in Anne's disputes, precedence supported both sides, though here it was stronger for Hugh Currer gent., the current owner of the mill. Silsden mill was unusual in that it had never belonged to the Cliffords because Cecilia de Romille had granted it in the early days to Bolton Priory and at the Dissolution it was sold separately. When Earl George built (or rebuilt) a windmill at High Holden as deliberate competition John Garforth gent. of Steeton, then the watermill's owner, objected. An agreement between them reached at Lord Wharton's house in Cannon Row, Westminster, in 1584/5 allowed Garforth to pull the windmill down but he had to pay £2 annually in lieu to the earl who reserved the right to build a watermill of his own, though he never did. It was this agreement which Anne took as her precedent, but Hugh Currer was seemingly in the stronger position because a series of lawsuits, the latest in 1641/2, had reaffirmed his mill's monopoly in the lordship.

By the 1650s milling and grinding oats (the main crop) had become much more profitable because, as the Silsden tithe-holders averred, the population of the township had increased, more land had been brought under cultivation, new families had settled in holdings on the moors, and there was more grain grown in Holden Park since Anne had disparked it and taken the deer away. Indeed, they rated Silsden tithe corn as £100 a year higher and the park's had increased by over twenty marks (£13 6s 8d). A landowner as sharp as Anne would have been aware of these demographic and farming changes and the ongoing recovery from the effects of the Civil Wars. The prospect was rising profits if she had a mill of her own and could elbow out Currer.[12]

There was, in addition, a personal, even political, edge to her challenging Currer. He had supported the Parliament in the Civil Wars. His residence, Kildwick Hall, had been a strongpoint whose garrison operated against the Royalists at Skipton Castle. He and Roger Coates Esq. of Kildwick Grange were currently treasurers and collectors of the rents sequestered from Royalists in Craven, with Skipton as one of the meeting places for the sequestrators of the wapentakes of Staincliffe and Ewcross. Currer's activities as an agent of the Cromwellian regime oppressive to people of her sympathies would not endear him to Anne.[13] He was also a local entrepreneur. For instance, he had held with his neighbour Edmond Watson of Farnhill the tithes of Carleton from the Corks. But he was also, with Roger Coates, Edmond Bawden and other prominent local men, a trustee of a charity for the poor of Silsden. In Hugh Currer, Anne was crossing swords with a gentleman of substance occupying a niche in county administration who would not flinch at any action necessary to sustain his rights.[14]

Anne's mill was completed in 1653. Currer's reaction to the intrusion was predictable, though his target was not Anne but John Rushworth and her other tenants who began to take their crops to her mill. He started litigation against them in the Exchequer Court in 1654 and she provided the funds for their defence. Depositions were taken in Hugh Hudson's house in Kildwick in April 1655. One point which emerged was that Currer's mill was on a less well-watered stream than Anne's and often ceased operation during dry summer weather for lack of water. Because most oats were ground in winter that was not over-important. Of greater moment was that Anne's mill, although better sited for the inhabitants on the moors, could not deal with all the grain produced in the manor. The dispute inevitably spread in its ramifications to include investigation of the bounds of the manor, the tithes of Holden Park and the historic rights of the Honour of Skipton.

At the Exchequer Court in 1655 the judges found for Currer. Anne now took over the case in person with counter-claims against him. She tried to assert the precedent of her father's windmill, citing the depositions taken in 1641 in the earlier case. But she was handicapped in presenting her suit, she claimed, by the loss of the court documents with other evidences when the castle was slighted in 1649. If true, this is the only recorded mention of the destruction of Clifford muniments in that way. A technical weakness in her case was given far greater weight by the judges – that it was not Anne but her tenants who had been the defendants in Currer's action. By 1660 she had lost her various counter-suits.

There the matter should have ended but Anne would not give up. She put forward her officer Richard Clapham, a deponent in the 1641 case, who proffered evidence in October 1667 that she, following her father, did have the right of soke in Silsden. Again her quest foundered because the bills and answers for the 1641 case could not be found. The judge terminated the proceedings.[15] It was just as well. For over a decade the Silsden tenants had faced prosecution by one or other of the combatant parties wherever they chose to grind their corn. Many of them, feeling insecure, had come to Bolton Hall on 2 October 1660 to ask Cork for a warranty for the leases granted them by

Earl George, but he refused. By 1663 they had become so sick of the incessant obstruction of their means of livelihood and staple diet that 133 joined in a petition to the court seeking a final and definitive judgment; in effect showing how aggrieved they were that Anne was prolonging the turmoil.[16]

They would have greeted the end of the case with relief. Anne's seigneurial assertiveness had disrupted their lives unnecessarily. She may genuinely have believed that her father's reservation of the right to have a water-powered mill justified her efforts to oust Currer. But the 1642 judgment in the latter's favour should have warned her. Moreover, she could not base her claims on her usual grounds of rejection of the King's Award. For these reasons and, even more, because of her bad landlordship, with its studied indifference to the suffering endured by so many of her tenants, she deserved to lose. On 30 June 1668 she paid £95 5s 4d to Currer, the costs of the last suit which he had recovered from her by an Exchequer decree.[17]

If what has been described so far were the sum of Anne's estate management then little further comment would be called for. It had the hallmark of a new owner stamping her authority on neglected properties, overstepping the bounds in Silsden's case. The surveying, bargaining, leasing and receiving were the humdrum, often taxing, stock-in-trade of estate officers in their profitable by-employments away from their own homes. What distinguishes Anne's overlordship is her calculated and often subtle campaign again the Earl and Countess of Cork which was unlike any pursued by her forebears, even the often belligerent Shepherd Lord. Rivals and litigants often wined and dined each other, the conventions of friendship or neighbourliness binding them more than property or manorial rights divided them. In Anne's dealings with the Corks the dichotomy is more pronounced, her blood relationship and noble protocol jostling with the religious depth of her conviction that she was entitled to the Corks' large Craven estates quite as much as to her own.

Her decision to take legal action must have come like a bolt from the blue to the earl. He had returned from exile in France and during 1650 was in residence at Bolton Hall doing exactly the same as Anne, leasing the holdings on his own extensive properties though without the abrasiveness she at times showed. He called on her socially at Skipton Castle on 11 November where she treated him with 'great civility and kindnesse'. Then, on the evening of the 27th, she sent word by his minister at Bolton Chapel, Mr Brown, that she must commence suit against him for possession of his holdings in Skipton. Lady Cork had inherited from her father about a quarter of the houses, shops, cottages and farms in the town, all of which had been bought by Earls George and Francis. There were other properties there which had never belonged to any of the Clifford lords and were bequeathed, assigned and bought and sold freely. Anne certainly claimed the Corks' holdings (her estate officers noting in the 1650 Skipton rental that they were in dispute) and she may have had an eye on the others. When, on 29 November, Cork went to see her she promised not to demand any rents due to him from his properties until their respective counsels had discussed the matter.[18] This was true only so far as it went because she had another tack in mind which she hid from him.

This was to put pressure on one of his tenants, Captain Henry Goodgion, a former Royalist officer whose family had long held Lambert Hall and other messuages and lands from Earls Francis and Henry. Lambert Hall, alias Winterwell Hall, was a tower house which had once belonged to the Cliffords, been sold in the fifteenth century and been repurchased by Francis in 1606. It had never, therefore, belonged to Earl George, so Anne's claim was based on the longer family perspective. Goodgion and his relatives William, George and Edmond, were already Anne's tenants, having taken new twenty-one years' leases of various cottages they had held from Earl Henry. Moreover, they were the foremost trader-farmers in the town and not easily overawed. By going for so prominent a family Anne had opted for another high profile target, proof that she was deadly serious.

Anne wanted the captain to surrender his current lease granted by Earl Francis and compound for a new one, but he dug in his heels. Cork naturally took his part. When he dined with Anne on 6 December he 'laboured' with her to settle her dispute with Goodgion, arguing his title was as good as any she could make him; as indeed it was. At this meeting Anne surprisingly lifted the veil slightly on her own sense of vulnerability, expressing fears that Lady Cork would assist the Westmorland tenants against her because of the suits she had initiated there; remembering no doubt how she had done exactly that to Francis when he was tussling with the tenants in 1618/19.

Cork again visited Anne on 12 December, pressing her to make her demands known about the disputed Skipton properties and he would do likewise so that their counsel might make an award between them. He stressed he wanted an accord above all else but he was also eager to learn what direction the business would take after he left for Ireland early next year. He was not willing to have his estates molested by her whilst he and his wife were absent. If a storm fell on them, he commented, he wanted it to be before they removed. Anne prevaricated, asking for Lady Cork to return to Yorkshire from her London home so that they could jointly discuss their affairs. Cork, wary of Anne's intentions, pointed out that counsels' advice on their differences was essential and that could be got only in London. Consequently, he entreated Anne to send up some of her tenants to Westminster the next term so that counsel could deal with them. She replied she had not made up her mind yet whether any would go or not. The issue was left in the air. On Cork's next visit Nicholas, Lord Tufton, was present, the atmosphere was friendly and not marred by any further shadow boxing between them. In her *Diaries* Anne airily dismisses the conflict, commenting 'there were divers Differences then on foot betwixt us. Butt we passe them by as Prov. 19.1.' Her chosen biblical text, 'Better is the poor that walketh in his integrity, than he that is perverse in his lips, and is a fool', would not have endeared Cork to her.

The next bout came on 15 January 1651 when Cork dined with Anne and found that, notwithstanding her professions to the contrary, she was 'very willing' to commence suit against him and his wife. The clergyman Dr Du Moulin was with him, possibly to act as witness to the 'fayre offers' he made Anne in order to avoid contention. But she would not make any resolution then and he left the castle rather glumly, fearing that she preferred 'controversy even with her nearest kinswoman before peace'. He took his final leave of her nearly two weeks later, on the 27th. She set out for Westmorland on 18 February. After a quick visit to London, he quitted Craven, having completed his own leasing and other estate business, and began his journey to Ireland on 12 May, not to return to England again (except once briefly to London) until 7 September 1660.[19]

The Corks had hardly set foot in Lismore than what they had feared happened. On 23 July 1651 Anne's officers Collings, Gabetis and Richard Barrow on her instructions entered into the messuage or burgage house in Skipton of George and William Goodgion and took possession in her name of all the houses, gardens, meadows, closes and two oxgangs of arable and other lands belonging to it and 'did discharge them and ther Tennantes from the possession therof'. This burgage was one of those purchased by Earl George.[20] Anne's action initiated a long legal battle to eject her relatives from Skipton. Far away in Ireland, Cork's attitude hardened. In 1652 he informed Humphrey Hughes that he would not now consent to arbitration for either his Craven or his Cumberland estates which Anne also claimed. If she entered any, he would fall on her jointure estate in Sussex 'which is my security for Skipton'. Anne, as ever, maintained she was not breaching the award's terms because her suits were against the tenants, not the owners. This was sophistry. From now on, when Anne made exemplary evictions in Silsden and Westmorland, Cork gave legal notice of his intentions.[21] These and other actions he took and their consequences will be examined later in this study.

Anne's suits and ejectments in Craven were taken with advice regularly sought from John Howell in Westminster. She had been informed, mistakenly he told her on 7 November 1654, that she had to make her claims within five years of taking over, or within five years of Pembroke's death. But, knowing she was straining at the leash, he reiterated that she had to follow set procedures, as by former directions of himself and others of her counsel. When entries into the properties were made, possession had to be demanded. If the tenants refused to deliver, her course was by way of ejectment to void their leases and put them out of possession. Otherwise, they might institute actions of trespass against her for the damages done. This course she appears to have followed carefully in both Craven and Westmorland, however interminable she judged progress to be.[22]

In the Corks' absence, their cousin Humphrey Hughes had charge of all their Yorkshire estates, though he had to divide his time between Craven and Londesborough, his home in North Wales and visits to London to confer with the solicitor Richard Graham, especially during term time. A few surviving letters from Hughes, who regularly reported at length to the Corks, his carefully kept accounts and Anne's own estate papers show something of the personal side which came out in the controversies she provoked. She was herself related to Hughes (Countess Grissell's nephew), obviously respected his abilities and, as has been noted above, confided to him more than she did to Cork, more indeed than perhaps was for her own good and not just because she believed he had influence with his employers. Indeed, through their conversations the private Lady Anne can occasionally be sensed, almost uniquely in terms of reported speech.

Hughes often met Anne during the winter of 1655/6 when she was again in residence at Skipton. He had a long discussion with her early in November about all the differences between her and the Corks which he explained to Graham on the 3rd to alert him about the need to prepare their defences. Sir Henry Cholmley had recently been at the castle and 'preacht peace to her betwixt their honours & her'. He was, in Hughes's opinion, the man who could best effect it, if any man could; in fact, he was related to and employed by the Corks as well as Anne. Other issues which might well end up in the lawcourts had been mentioned to Hughes by Sedgewick; that is, free rents in Bradley and rights in Malhamdale, over Malham Tarn, Eshton and Hawkswick which were thought to belong to the Honour of Skipton. Anne was now suing Captain Catterall of Skipton, who had fought in the Royalist cause, over two tenements in Stirton and Thorlby sold in fee-farm by Earl George. When Hughes produced the inquisition of 7 James I in support of Catterall, to his surprise Anne called for 'a great Booke wherein she hath copied most of the writinges' and found an earlier inquisition, 6 James I. This is the earliest mention of Anne's use of the third of her Great Books as a resource for her land-rights and possible litigation.[23]

Hodge Pichel became an issue at this time. Though superficially Anne's offer to purchase it from the Corks was a normal transaction, in the background was a threat of unilateral action. Hodge Pichel was a four-acre close in Skipton New Park, alias Park George, which despite its name was one of the castle's two great old parks. The close had been bought with a burgage in Skipton on 22 September 1641 for £40 by Earl Henry from the three daughters of the late Laurance Chippendale of Embsay. Anne wanted it, would not exchange land for it but was prepared to buy it from the Corks, and if she could not, she declared, then, she would wall it even at the cost of £80, because 'she cares not a ffart which is her owne expression severall tymes for it'. He was sceptical about all her supposed offers of 'peace'. She makes a pretence, he commented, 'yet persevers in her course as formerly'.[24]

Hughes was intrigued by Anne's building projects, which he duly related to the Corks because of their knowledge of the castle and its chapel, where they had been married in 1634, and their role in Skipton as tithe proprietors. He told them she was much addicted to pious uses in Westmorland, such as repairs of churches, having already rebuilt several. He reveals more than she herself recorded in her *Diaries* – not only that she had rebuilt the steeple of Holy Trinity, but that she had bestowed £200 on her father's tomb in the choir and intended to 'uniforme & beautifie the Church'. She wanted to know if the Corks would contribute anything towards the chancel which they maintained in compliance with their lease from Christ Church, Oxford. It was they who had paid for the new chancel windows in April 1653, the work attested by the churchwardens.

Anne marked her rebuilding of the steeple with an inscription cut in its north-east pinnacle, 'This Church Steeple was repaired by the Lady Anne CLIFFORD, Contess Dowager of Penbrooke Anno Domini 1655'. Four of the five bells taken by the Parliamentarians had been redeemed for £200 by the parishioners and they were reinstalled. By January 1656 Anne had stripped the lead from the chancel roof to recast it but found the wood decayed. To repair in the way she wanted, Hughes estimated, would cost her £20. What the Corks had decided to contribute, if anything, he did not then know. His accounts do not mention any further payments so it is likely that Anne stood all the expense of re-glazing the windows, the quarries with her initials 'A' 'P' in yellow glass and the date 1655 beneath surviving proof of her work (Pl. 48). When Hughes attended the burial of Mr Anthony Walker of Burnsall in April 1656, she called him over and showed him the renovation she had done and the further work she intended. Hughes's comments confirm that her rebuilding was as extensive as her *Diaries'* entry implies.[25]

Anne had not waited to commemorate her father in stone until the rebuilding was under way. She contracted the making of a tomb for him while she was in residence at Skipton during the summer of 1654. Her two agreements with John Ellis, the stone-cutter of Skipton, on 9 October and 29 December for finishing it, the second seemingly superseding or at least enlarging the earlier one, were drawn up after she had moved to Brougham. She ordered the repairs to Holy Trinity and the tomb's erection when she was at Appleby in the summer of 1655. It was clearly *in situ* when Hughes mentions its £200 cost in his 7 November letter, although her work in the chancel was still in progress in the following April. The contracted payments to Ellis, the first for £3 10*s*, the second £20, hardly square with what Hughes obviously was told the tomb cost. However, Anne provided the black marble slabs, from Derbyshire, and the alabaster for the shields, possibly from the large Ledsham deposits Thoresby describes as being used for tombs. George's monument was in style a tomb-chest, its position making a matching pair with his grandfather's (Pl. 49). Their horizontal slabs were the same length, but George's was the broader by half a yard. The polishing of the marble and the carving and colouring

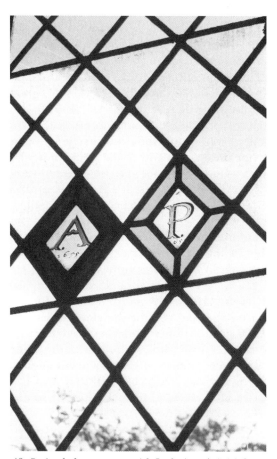

48. *Stained glass quarry, with Lady Anne's initials and date 1655, nave window, Holy Trinity Church, Skipton-in-Craven (Photo: the author)*

49. Earl George's monument, erected by Lady Anne, Holy Trinity Church, Skipton-in-Craven, 1654/5 (Photo: the author)

of the shields were Ellis's responsibility. The epitaph or inscription would not be his work. More will be said about this and the other Holy Trinity monuments in Chapter 10.[26]

Anne had been living with her household in the castle's Octagonal Tower and the Long Gallery which had been repaired in 1650/1. Her pleasure in occupying these fine apartments made for Henry VIII's niece Countess Eleanor would have been marred by the half-demolished complex of medieval drum towers, the partly destroyed outer gatehouse and the rubble of the perimeter walls. Skipton had been one of the great private strongholds in the north, the antiquary William Camden describing it as 'a very proper and strong castle'. Anne's passion for her ancestral possessions called for the re-creation of its medieval and Tudor configuration so far as the authorities would allow. She was not permitted to replace some of its finest features, the massive outer curtain wall with its high towers and the strong, lead-covered roofs which could support cannon and had done so in the Civil War. The splendid, coloured heraldic glass in the Conduit Court and the soaring roofs over the Great Hall and kitchen were lost for ever in the slighting. She began clearing the rubble out of the castle in October 1655 and by November had obtained orders for repairing it in some measure.[27]

To do this she was in part dependent on the Corks. The natural resources in Craven had been about evenly divided as a result of the King's Award, the Corks having the Grassington lead-mines and Bolton and Carleton woods, Anne owning the productive Holden mines, whose coal heated the castle, and timber in the Skipton Parks and Barden. She asked for some lead for the castle's renovation, which she did in fact buy, and also for fifty or sixty trees from Bolton, perhaps having herself over-felled Barden to get the cash for Lady Isabella. She had wanted timber from Bolton the previous year but instead opted for Stubham Park near Ilkley, which had proved too costly in the transporting. Yet, because most of the Bolton woods were 'dire kept & decayed' and the cost of carrying would empty her purse, Hughes offered her whatever she pleased from Carleton Park. She might be at loggerheads with her relatives but commercial considerations dictated she was too good a market for timber to miss. However, her officers did not like the wood available at Carleton. What she eventually purchased is not recorded.[28]

Anne noted in her *Diaries* that whilst at Skipton in June 1654 she took her daughter Isabella to look round the Corks' house at Bolton in their absence but did not mention her second visit about Martinmas 1655 when Hughes also was away. This unannounced arrival worried him because he feared she might make a formal entry or claim on the house without anyone being the wiser except those she took as witnesses. So, at Westminster he conferred with Graham about keeping an eye on the possibility of a summons being entered in the courts which, without vigil, could easily escape their notice. The Corks were still far from secure. They had not yet cleared their debts with the sequestrators. Hughes went to look at the register of sequestrations, agreeing some alterations to gain time for the full payment, a defensive move perhaps though how it might help if Anne started a legal action against them is not apparent.[29]

Anne's success over her Westmorland tenants and Edmund Jennings and his supporters released big sums of cash and with this she set about restoring both Skipton Castle and Barden Tower. She was in residence at the castle from April to October 1657 keeping a watchful eye while Vincent, now her steward, directed repairs of the Great Hall and kitchen and rebuilt the thirteen rooms in the top two storeys of the drum towers which had been demolished. However, she was surprised by opposition to her restoration. A local Parliamentarian, Thomas Heber gent., petitioned the Council of State in Westminster on 11 August 1657 for a stay in the work on the castle until an investigation was made on what Anne intended and a decision reached on whether it was prejudicial to the state. No Council order was made so there was no halt to the rebuilding.

By Michaelmas the castle was finished. The new, lower roofs over the Great Hall and kitchen and inner gatehouse were slated and could not support cannon. The guttering was lead, from Grassington. All the rubbish had been cleared away. In the summer of 1658 Vincent began the rest of the rebuilding, now in Anne's absence. He constructed new perimeter walls, though inevitably lower and thinner than the 1st Lord Robert's had been and lacking towers. The bases of two of the original towers can still be seen. The outer gatehouse was restored and Anne capped it with the Cliffords' motto, now appositely hers, *Desormais*, 'Henceforth', cut in large letters through the north and south sides of the battlements.[30]

Just below, in the hollow of the moulding round its four faces, she commemorated her father with a stone inscription in Latin, in effect a second monument to him, this time placed on high. It is an adaption of the opening of the third ode of Horace and reads in the Revd John Ward's translation:

50. Skipton Castle, Yorkshire, from the Outer Gatehouse, showing, right to left, the Tudor Octagonal Tower and Long Gallery (1535) which were Lady Anne's residence, and the great drum towers (1195–1220). Her 1657 reconstruction of the drum towers is visible in their upper masonry and windows (H.T. Fattorini Esq.)

> George's merit is more enduring than marble, and higher than the royal elevation of pyramids, a merit which the corroding rain and the furious north wind cannot overthrow, nor a countless series of years, nor the flight of time.

This filial tribute has stood the test of rain, wind and pollution, weathered but still legible (Pl. 51). As usual Anne erected a stone plaque at the castle to record her reconstruction.[31]

Anne was pleased with Vincent's work. She judged the castle 'for the most part well finished and better than I expected it could have bin'. The lead rain-water heads in the Conduit Court bearing the Clifford wyvern crest and her initials 'AP' or the date 1659 mark the completion of her restoration (Pl. 52). The famous yew tree in its stone base decorated by heraldic shields was probably planted by her at this time. Pocock described it as old in 1800. Yet the reconstruction could easily have been in vain. As Heber had argued, the castle, though much weaker than in 1642, again became a stronghold which could prove a threat to the regime; indeed, the only one in Yorkshire apart from

51. Skipton Castle, the Outer Gatehouse restored by Lady Anne in 1658 and topped with the Clifford motto 'Desormais' and, immediately beneath, her tribute to her father (Photo: the author)

52. Skipton Castle, a rain-water head in the Conduit Court with the date 1659 and Clifford wyvern crest marking the completion of her rebuilding (Photo: the author)

Clifford's Tower, York. In the crisis of 1659 the Parliament garrisoned it about 4 August with 100 horse and a foot company under Ensign Robert Fennet. In January 40 musketeers were sent for greater security. After the troops were withdrawn, the castle's slighting was ordered. Only General Monck's rapid march south and the collapse of the regime prevented a second destruction, this time with Anne an impotent onlooker.[32]

In the summer of 1657 Anne also gave orders for Barden Tower to be repaired. She is misleading when she avers that the tower had been ruined since her mother stayed there in 1589, with Anne stirring in her belly. In fact, it had been put in good order by Earl Francis, was lived in up to the Civil Wars and, as has been mentioned, the manorial courts were held there until 1644. Then the soldiers stripped its lead roofs and plundered its timbers, and the local people helped themselves to the wood and stone. Anne did more than reconstruct the Shepherd Lord's tower-house, which in Camden's opinion was only 'a little turret'. She enlarged it to suit her own household's requirements. Her contract with Thomas Day and his son Thomas, dated 2 June 1657, like her earlier letting to Christopher Clapham, suggests most of it was still standing. The terms were to pull down the walls of the tower and chapel in the way already agreed, rebuild them, repair windows, arches and other places as necessary and erect a wall above the house a yard high for battlements. For this work she was to pay them £100 and it was to be finished by Michaelmas. There must have been an unforeseen delay because, with Vincent again supervising, it was not completed until 1659, to her 'Great costs and Charges' as she records in her *Diaries*. She took up residence there for the first time on 9 December for a long stay, enjoying the well-wooded vistas of the Wharfe valley until 8 October 1660.

While there, she renewed Hough's mill, the water-driven corn mill which served the lordship. Barden Bridge bears the date 1659 when it was rebuilt either by Anne because it was vital for her tenants as well as travellers and traders or, more likely, at her instance by the West Riding. Certainly she took the lead in August 1675 when it was still unrepaired after floods had carried it away nearly two years earlier. She financed her tenant Thomas Atkinson the younger to solicit the West Riding Quarter Sessions at Pontefract and also York

53. Skipton Castle, the Conduit Court with the yew planted by Lady Anne, c. 1660 (H.T. Fattorini Esq.)

assizes, his costs and those of counsel and witnesses coming to £17 10s.[33] This lobbying succeeded, the work being marked by the inscription:

THIS BRIDGE WAS REPAYRED AT THE CHARGE OF THE WHOLE WEST RIDING 1676

When the Earl of Cork returned to Craven in 1660 Anne was his near neighbour. He dined with her at Barden on 2 October with hardly a change in their relationship since 1651. She treated him very civilly and expressed a desire that their respective counsels should confer about the Skipton houses and other things in controversy between them, but would not refer the matter to arbitration. On 7 October Cork was informed by a Skipton attorney that Anne was detaining from him some land in Stirton and Thorlby which had once belonged to Bolton Priory. The day after, she left Barden for Appleby.

True to form, she waited until Cork was back in London the next year, attending Charles II's coronation on 23 April, before taking further action against him. On 9 April she authorized Richard Clapham and John Miller, her bailiffs of Clifford Fee, and six of their under-bailiffs to enter the manors of Nesfield and Langbar and all the tenements and messuages in Eshton, Malham and Malham Moor and the Skipton houses she claimed. They were to take possession and demand arrears of rent. Five of her officers witnessed this letter of attorney, including Sedgewick and Thomas Strickland. What is revealing about this action is that it is the first indication that Anne had faced facts and now restricted her claim to just these properties which had been her father's, all but acquiescing in the Court of Wards' and King's Award decisions about the Craven estates. The reason for this will be suggested in the final chapter.

As with Currer over Silsden mill, Anne eventually had to give best to her cousins. By 1667 they had legally won possession of the Skipton properties, though Anne never conceded her title. The upset to the Skipton tenants was comparable with, if on a smaller scale, than that in Silsden. The decade and a half in which she put the Corks' tenants to one 'rack' after another left its scars in the town. The houses and shops in question had of necessity been neglected and one of Cork's officers informed him in 1669 that all his properties there were falling down.[34]

In the meantime, a new controversy had arisen between them, by far the widest issue in the sense that shire administration was involved. It concerned Cork's tenure of the bailiwick or wapentake of Staincliffe. This was a liberty from which the sheriff of Yorkshire and his deputies and officers were excluded, all the sheriff's usual responsibilities being exercised by the bailiff. Like the Westmorland sheriffwick it was prized as a source of authority and also profit because the deputy who did the work bought the office and then sometimes sublet it to others. As in Westmorland, the duties included the execution and return of writs and processes to the royal courts and the collection of fees, perquisites, other profits and debts due to the Crown. The bailiff, or his deputy, proclaimed the assizes and quarter sessions at Skipton's market cross.

The bailiff could, and did, make arrests within Skipton town and had the right to enter Skipton Castle courtyard should he need to, the king's writ knowing no bounds. One later instance is recorded of Samuel Wadsworth, a mason, being apprehended whilst he was working in the Earl of Thanet's garden. Anne's immediate predecessors had avoided such indignity by being almost perpetual bailiffs. Earlier still, in Henry VIII's reign, they had held the sub-liberty of Clifford Fee, coterminous with the Honour of Skipton, though that had been rather lost sight of, subsumed in the greater liberty of the wapentake.[35]

Earls Francis and Henry had held a sixty years' lease of the wapentake granted by James I in 1612. After the fall of Skipton Castle, the Clifford Fee was put by the Parliament into the hands of patentees. The parliamentary survey of the wapentake showed the Corks had the right to it as Earl Henry's heirs and they were allowed to take it over, the other consideration being the paramount need after the wartime disorders to stabilize local administration. Because Anne, stranded in Baynard's Castle, had no more than the reversion of her Skipton estates, and that dependent on Pembroke predeceasing her, she was never in contention for the bailiwick and her husband let the appropriate authorities settle the matter.[36]

The question came to the fore again late in 1654 when it was discussed by the Committee of Safety at Worcester House, without any decision being reached. John Howell advised Anne that prescription was likely to be her best title to it. In the event, the Corks won the argument. But their tenure of the bailiwick became an issue in Craven in October 1655 soon after Anne had again moved to Skipton and the Corks had appointed Hugh Currer of Stirton as their deputy.[37] She did not take kindly to either their authority as bailiffs or one of her own tenants acting as their deputy. She sought to wriggle out of this dilemma by championing her claim to serve all writs and processes in Clifford Fee as an independent liberty within the wapentake. One argument she deployed, that the fee pre-dated the wapentake, was specious, but she was on firmer ground with the Tudor precedent.

The conflict was not resolved until after the Restoration, following Cork's return from Ireland, and in his favour. As usual, he made himself fully *au fait* with the history. On 28 November 1661 he perused many books about the Barony of Clifford – the rights of the fee and title to the barony then being interlinked issues with Anne. He had the support of friends at Charles II's Court and at York. Anne's claim for her liberty was of great concern to the High Sheriff in 1662, Sir Edward Osborne, who met Cork on 1 April at York to discuss it. Osborne, Cork, Sir Francis Cobb and other men of substance who served as sheriffs or in other offices collaborated successfully to block her. They were convinced that she should not be permitted to create her own enclave which would split the existing wapentake structure.

This, one may suspect, was not because a separate Clifford Fee posed any administrative inconvenience; rather that she was so notorious for her love of controversy and subtle obstruction that to place the fee in her control would be needlessly to hazard problems. Cork, for his part, could have envisaged endless opportunities for Anne to harass his tenants and meddle with his possessions. The issue was settled, as usual with Anne, after litigation by a judgment in the Court of the Duchy of Lancaster. In Hilary Term 1663 they found for Cork, dismissing 'the pretended Liberty called Cliffords ffee'. However, this was not the end of the matter. Both Anne and her Thanet successors clung to their ambition for an independent Clifford Fee and eventually prevailed, as will be related in Chapter 12.[38]

Anne would not have been overjoyed at how Cork, now Earl of Burlington, was regarded in Yorkshire. On his official visit to York as Lord Lieutenant on 25 April 1667 he was well received and the Lord Mayor reminded him of the interest the Cliffords always had in the city. Sir John Reresby included in his *Memoirs* his report to Lord Chancellor Clarendon six days later, 1 May, on Burlington's success as Lord Lieutenant and the 'perticular respect' for him 'and the memory of the family of the Cliffords, formerly of great interest in this country'. Within the county of broad acres it was Burlington who wore their mantle – a greater landlord in both the West and East Ridings than Anne, also Lord Clifford of Lanesborough in his own right, with a Yorkshire earldom (its name, Bridlington/Burlington, chosen out of admiration for Queen Henrietta who had landed there with arms in the Civil War), and holding high office. As Lieutenant, he represented the Stuart monarchy in Yorkshire, a pillar of the royal establishment and renowned as 'Richard the Rich' because of his great landed wealth in the county and in Ireland. The Duke and Duchess of York, the future James II, visited Londesborough House in August 1665. Lady Anne, Skipton-born, was overshadowed by an Irishman in her native West Riding, which reinforced her love of and preference for her ancestral castles and estates in Westmorland.[39]

The Burlingtons had the edge in their battles with Anne in Craven when their daughter Lady Elizabeth was married on 11 April 1664 to Nicholas, Lord

54. Barden Tower, Yorkshire, rebuilt and enlarged by Lady Anne in 1658 (Photo: the author)

Tufton, heir to the earl and countess of Thanet; Anne's godchild matched with her eldest grandson. In July the Burlingtons first rode to Barden to view her 'reedifying' of the Tower and then, after visiting Carleton Park, saw her other repairs at Skipton church and castle. When Anne made her final visit to Craven in 1667 Hugh Currer was all but assured of his legal victory over Silsden mill. She quit Yorkshire for ever at the end of July.[40] It would be rash to say that tranquillity returned to Craven. Anne was not the only litigious landowner. But she was exceptionally combative and unyielding until the law finally undid her.

Those Craven folk, especially in Skipton and Silsden, who had lived through the Civil Wars and sieges and endured the Parliamentarian occupation deserved better than her continued disruption of their lives. The entanglements of her properties and rights could have been resolved quickly and equitably by the arbitration of perceptive gentry like Cholmley and Richard Graham. All this would have avoided aggravation and saved legal expenses though for Anne it would have been the easy way out and robbed her of the baronial role she had long coveted. Shrewdly calculating and with the pugnacity of a fairground brawler, she had relished her overlordship in Craven. She had suffered bruising and in the end, feeling the infirmities of old age, had thrown in the towel, but what a fight she had put up! Her rough, tough baronial ancestors would have been proud of her.

CHAPTER 8

Baroness of Westmorland

1643–76

Dearest of all to Lady Anne, indeed where her heart lay, was the barony of
Westmorland. This was her family's original property in the north. There was a
continuity of titles, traditions and inheritance through the Viponts and
Cliffords from King John's reign down to her own lifetime. Her deepest
attachment was to Brougham Castle, where her grandfather had died, her
father been born and her mother spent her last years, and to St Lawrence's,
Appleby, where her fine monument commemorated Countess Margaret's
interment. During her most despondent years Anne had clung, above all else,
to her ancestral right to Westmorland. She had lived at Brougham Castle in
1616 and losing it by the King's Award hurt her deeply. The greatest reward for
her faith was on her cousin's death in 1643 to inherit the baronial estate, now
conjoined with its titles to give her a seigneurial standing and authority which
no patriarchal priority diminished because in 1635 Pembroke had yielded it to
her (Map 1). For the sheriffwick she had to await Pembroke's death, because at
Michaelmas 1645 he was granted the office in right of his wife. She entered it
on 23 January 1650.[1]

It is doubtful, however, if at first Anne had any real inkling of the situation on
her Westmorland lordships. Cocooned in Baynard's Castle, she remained
unaware of how disturbed the county became as a result of the Civil War
hostilities and the consequent political and social upheavals. Newsletters sold in
London related the major actions in the north, but ignored the groundswell of
changes in the localities. From the outbreak of the war the north-west had been
deeply divided in its allegiances. Colonel Sir Philip Musgrave of Hartley Castle,
the Royalist commander appointed by Earl Henry, had made Appleby Castle his
headquarters. The borough itself was Royalist but there was widespread
opposition to Musgrave from the Puritan and Parliamentarian dissidents
especially in the southern lordships of the Bottom of Westmorland, the Eden
Valley. He managed to subdue them until the defeat of Prince Rupert at
Marston Moor on 2 July 1644 delivered the north into Parliamentarian control.

Soon afterwards the Scottish army overran the north-west, reducing 'the
Musgravians' to obedience. Many young men were now recruited for the
Parliamentarian forces from the Kirkby Stephen and Stainmore areas and this
gave unprecedented opportunities to Anne's tenants. From the autumn of 1645
the new governor of Appleby Castle, in charge of its garrison, was Captain
Robert Atkinson of Blue Grass in Mallerstang, one element in her later
animosity towards him. Captain Robert Wardell was another tenant with a
Parliamentarian commission. Captain Lancelot Skaife had charge of an

administrative division covering part of her estates. His brother, Captain Robert Skaife, was collector there of the assessments to pay for the army. Henry Shepherd was sergeant to Captain Bates and there were other of Anne's tenants who served in the Parliamentarian forces based on York and in the Appleby detachments which helped besiege Skipton Castle in August 1645. As in other parts of the country, Anne's tenants were mulcted for heavy taxes, efficiently collected by Skaife and his fellows.[2] Many of the gentry, to whom she would ordinarily have looked for support, were in dire straits, excluded from office and their estates sequestered.

However, from 1644 several were able to act for her, notably her cousin Sir John Lowther II and George Hilton gent. of Hilton whom she respected. They were drawn to her service because of their families' earlier associations with the countess and herself and the opportunities a new owner offered for gainful employment and the exercise of authority. Before Marston Moor, Anne gave Lowther a commission to take possession of Brougham Castle for her and he spent money on necessary works and bought corn and fuel for the garrison. After the battle, Musgrave challenged his right to it and set his own guard. Lowther appealed to Prince Rupert, then at Kirkby Lonsdale on his retreat south, who confirmed him in his custody. That ended when the Scots arrived.

Anne's ignorance of the state of Westmorland in 1644 helps explain her unrealistic assumptions when writing to her tenants in April and on several occasions to Lowther, her views perhaps puzzling and certainly handicapping him and his fellows. She expected her tenants to show her goodwill because of her support of them against Earl Francis. It does not seem to have occurred to her that thirty years had elapsed during which they had become attuned to her uncle's style of landlordship and his estate officers managing affairs and granting tenures in compliance with the King's Award. In April, she acted with a mixture of naivety and sensitivity, the Scots then being on the point of besieging York. She informed her 'Good and Lovinge Tennantes in Westmorland', that she intended to be 'a Good Land Lady' to them and told them not to pay rents or fines until further notice because of the troubles. This instruction they were only too ready to comply with. However, she was down to earth about protecting her most vulnerable assets. In June she asked Lowther to repair and keep her castles warm and habitable and made John Hall of Sowerby, 'my deere worthy mothers servant', responsible for her woods. Later, she expressed concern for the preservation of her game. When in the summer of 1645 Anne rescinded her instruction over rents and fines and requested payment, many of her tenants offered her only one year's rent and those in Kirkby Stephen and Stainmore, following tradition, none at all.

Anne would have better understood the situation on her estates and in the north-west following the letter of 3 March 1646 from her receiver, Edmund Pollard gent. of Preston. His endeavours to keep the revenues of Lancashire and the twin counties from 'the mouthes of the greedie soldiers' had prevented him giving the attention he wanted to her affairs. He explained why he had managed to collect no more than £412 of the (near £3,000) rents due to her over the past two years. Only about £40 had come into his hands from Appleby and Brougham demesnes because of the Scots' billeting and 'exceeding great assessments'. He had collected as little as £10 for neatgeld and serjeant oats and, by good advice, had decided not to 'seek the rest by violence'. The Kirkby Stephen tenants would not pay anything except under compulsion, though every other graveship and bailiwick had offered to pay something towards just one year's rent. He had expected a commission to arrive to deal with these matters, but had heard nothing yet.

By October 1646 it was clear that, however diligent Anne's officers were, they could make little headway against the recalcitrant tenants on her southern lordships. She optimistically hoped the example of the good tenants would draw the rest to follow, which had been Countess Margaret's attitude in 1606. But the steel in her character now showed. She wrote:

> Concerning the tenants that are so unwilling to pay me that which is my right from them about Stainmoor and Kirkby-Stephen they will live to see that their scruples and doubts are vain . . .

If they did not respond to gentleness she would have to use 'Ruffe Coursses' – just as her mother had done – though she was reluctant to resort to that because, she told Lowther, 'you know how much I love that country'. She acknowledged the distress armies were causing and was sorry for Westmorland's condition. But, she added, there was now hope of peace, the Scots would then go home and 'the unruly English will also be gone'. In reality, she took the view that all had suffered nationwide so her tenants were no different from elsewhere. Ignorant of the plight inflicted by martial rule, she made no allowance for the extent of the erosion of the rural substance on her own lordships.[3]

Anne was mistaken in believing that the war would end. The Royalist uprising in 1648 caused more disturbance on her Westmorland estates, just as in Craven. Sir Marmaduke Langdale ejected the Parliamentarians from Appleby and Musgrave again took over. On 20 June Langdale requested the commissioners he appointed for the Bottom of Westmorland – Sir Thomas Sandford, John Dalston and Christopher Dudley – to call before them all the men between the ages of sixteen and sixty, except in the five parishes belonging to Musgrave, and recruit 600 for the king's service. On 21 August Musgrave instructed them to collect £200 a month towards the maintenance of his garrison. Only a few weeks later the Royalist occupation ended. The Appleby garrison, swollen by a large force which had retreated there from Cockermouth on the approach of the Roundhead army under Lieutenant-General Ashton, surrendered in October after a four days' siege. Langdale counter-attacked at Kirkby Thore, but then was driven north through Whinfell, the Parliamentarians capturing Brougham Castle *en route*.[4]

Appleby Castle is said to have been made unusable by being de-roofed, although it escaped Skipton's slighting because of intervention by Pembroke or Lord Wharton, who, happily for Anne, was Lord Lieutenant of Westmorland. Whatever damage was done was quickly repaired because Anne stayed there in the main chambers in August 1649. Brougham Castle was in partial ruin because of the fighting. Some repairs were done before she travelled north. Her arrival put an end to the ironworks which Earl Francis had erected in 1619 on the two acres of castle demesne across the Eamont. Lowther had allowed its manager, the ironmaster William Wright, to continue production and in 1647 had sold him timber for the smelting from Lowther Park. Anne would not have relished the noise and fumes of an ironworks almost beneath the windows of her favourite chamber. In fact it was the Corks' officers who wound up the operations. They assessed the goods there in September 1650 as worth £15 and bound Wright to deliver them to Anne for safe keeping. Wright sold his two-thirds of Brougham Hall and its demesnes and continued his career elsewhere.[5]

One consequence of the 1648 campaigns was that by the time Anne journeyed north her tenants owed even larger sums in arrears of rents and fines and, after eight years without firm management, her estates were like Craven in 'extreame disorder'. She may not have learnt until then that many tenants still owed parts of the seven years' fines which fell to Earl Henry by the King's Award on his father's death in 1641 and also arrears of rents which had been difficult to collect before his death because of the war. These largish sums were slowly being gathered for the Corks at the same time as Anne struggled to get in the backlog owed to her. These were hard years for her Eden Valley farmers and townsfolk, which helps explain their widespread resistance to her from 1649. In the summer of 1651 she was to have her own first distasteful experience of military occupation, when Major-General Harrison occupied Appleby Castle and the surrounding area with a Cromwellian cavalry force.[6]

Entering her own did not, therefore, prove for Anne the joyous occasion she had imagined. Expecting loyalty, she was treated just like any other unwelcome incoming lord by many of the tenants of her southern lordships. But the major contentions were very much of her own making. Her efforts to assert her authority and collect arrears of money were from the first subsumed in the greater issue of tenures, just as under her mother. Overarching that in Anne's mind was the cause she had to fight, to which she had been dedicated since 1617. She had dual objectives. The first was to overthrow the King's Award and her uncle's assurances which together had established tenant-right and the 7*d* entry fine on her lordships. By this she would restore the rights her mother had been awarded in 1609 by Lord Chancellor Ellesmere's decree.

In the second she aimed to put the clock back even further, to 1605, by getting possession of all the revenues her father had enjoyed in the north-west at his death. Unlike Craven, she had no territorial ambitions in Westmorland. Beating the manorial bounds from April to June 1651 established what she owned and what her bailiffs and stewards had to account for, a warning to others not to encroach. In her later years she did take legal action against Mrs Bowes of Barnard Castle over the bounds of Stainmore. However, in Cumberland she coveted the minuscule residues of Earl George's 1580s sales. She formally claimed, before the Committee for Compounding in Westminster, the £5 9*s* 4*d* rents of Carleton and Skelton enjoyed by Earls Francis and Henry and since 1643 by the Corks.[7]

Rather rashly, she tried in 1651 as sheriff to obstruct the Corks' resort to what she termed 'my County Court' to recover the arrears of rents and fines still owed them in Westmorland. Anne objected to the Corks getting these on her usual grounds that they originated in the King's Award. Moreover, she worried that if the Corks were successful it would strengthen their case against her over the award. Her lawyer John Howell explained to her the complex legal niceties concerning the different kinds of rent and baldly told her she must not interfere with due legal process in what was clearly not her court. This episode is an insight into Anne's possessive attitude towards the administration of her sheriffdom; akin to that of an overmighty subject of the era of King John or the Wars of the Roses and quite alien to that of her uncle and cousin before her. Had it been possible, she would have trampled underfoot the Corks' legitimate rights in Westmorland and Cumberland as she was already trying to do in Craven. Nevertheless, her bent of mind is evident, and what it led to will be related in Chapter 12.

Anne's principal opponents in Westmorland were not her relatives and neighbours but her own tenants. She left Lowther in no doubt about her intentions. She asked his legal opinion on whether purchasing land near Brough and Pendragon for her accommodation (both castles being derelict) would prejudice her title and right as lady of the manor because, she asserted, 'I do not allowe of that the tennants call Tennant right'. Nor, she added, did other northern landlords such as Algernon Percy, 10th Earl of Northumberland, and Charles Howard, Earl of Carlisle, although they had to acquiesce. These comments forecast the squalls to come.[8]

Once in the north she went headlong into confrontation with her 'tenant-right' tenants. She forced the issue by demanding an 8d entry fine. There were, currently, grounds for this. An 8d rate had become almost standard in the county in recent years and in theory the King's Award had set it, the 7d fine being the practice only because the extra penny related to the last £3,000 due to Dorset which was never raised by Earl Francis. Anne, in fact, was wanting the best of both worlds – refusing to acknowledge the award yet claiming the 8d entry fine it had sanctioned. Most of her tenants, abiding by the award, refused to pay. Consequently, Anne began litigation in Chancery, exhibiting a bill in Hilary Term 1649 against thirteen men including Captain Robert Atkinson, Robert Shaw, George Rudd, John and George Fothergill and John Dent, tradition again asserting itself because their families had defied Countess Margaret. She based her case on Ellesmere's decree and the fact that she had not been a party to the award. She complained that the tenants had got their hands on the court rolls and had confederated; a standard argument put forward by lawyers and frequently true. She argued that if she was not relieved from the opposition of the tenants it would be 'of ill example and dangerous consequence in the Comon wealth.' Furthermore, she asserted, it would be an expensive task to evict them by several discrete actions at law (remembering her mother's difficulties) and 'noe equall tryall could be expected in soe popular a cause'. Both these observations proved correct, the second more so than she anticipated.

Anne requested the court to order her tenants to pay her reasonable duties as well as their arrears of rent. Thirty-six of them, mostly from Brough and Stainmore and led by Captain Thomas Ewbanke, in turn petitioned the Committee of Indemnity on 25 February 1650, complaining that she would make no reasonable allowances and defalcations out of the arrears, that her stewards and agents had distrained their cattle and imprisoned John Wardell, one of her own collectors, because he would not execute what they considered to be 'oppressive and unwarrantable demands'. They stressed the losses they had suffered from the military rule and the fighting over their lands during the past eight years.[9]

Anne's state of mind at this time can be gauged from the message she sent from Appleby Castle on 10 February, via the Countess of Kent, to the great jurist John Selden who was employed as steward on the Kent estates at Wrest in Bedfordshire. 'I pray your Ladyship,' she wrote, 'vouchsafe to remember my love and service to worthy Mr Selden',

> and tell him if I hade nott excellent Chacer's [Chaucer] book heere to comfortt mee I wer in a pitifull case, having so manny trubles as I have, butt when I rede in thatt I scorne and make litte [light] of tham alle, and a little partt of his devine sperett infusses itt selfe in mee.[10]

Anne's pressure did succeed in 1650 around Appleby, where farmers were dependent on her for demesne leases. Twenty-one tenants of Scattergate and Burrells paid 'after the rate of eight years Arbitrary ffynable Rent' for small parcels of ground they surrendered which they had previously bought from Earl Francis. If hardly a precedent, this was the first chink in her tenants' armour. She also acted arbitrarily. William Middleton had been one of her uncle's estate officers. She had his lease of Newhall in Stainmore delivered to her and cancelled it, restricting his income from the place and allowing it only as a gift from her. How resolute she was her favourite officer and personal friend, Christopher Marsh, learnt to his dismay in the letter she wrote to him on 15 July. Far away in the south, he had not been happy about her resort to litigation. Anne replied in a rare display of fury: 'you cut my heart with unkindness, when you do in a manner, in your letter, hit me in the teeth with my suits-in-law, which is not to be avoided by me, except I would let the rights belonging to me in Craven and Westmorland be utterly ruined to me and my posterity.'[11]

Far from all Anne's opponents had been hard-hit financially. Those who became entrenched in local administration were doing well out of confiscated Royalists' estates and proving as difficult to evict by the Parliamentarian authorities as by Anne herself. Robert Wardell, agent for the old Committee for Compounding and formerly a Parliamentarian captain, refused to let the new Committee's agents pasture beasts on the lands confiscated from Sir Philip Musgrave, which were now bringing in £200 a year more than before the war. He was encouraged by Major Arthur Skaife of Winton Hall and his brother Cornet Lancelot Skaife. One of the Major's trumpeters, Thomas Buster, swore at Kirkby Stephen that if any brought horses on to what he called his Major's lands he would run a sword in their guts. The committee, far away in London, proved impotent to curb them and – somewhat risibly – had to initiate lawsuits to try to regain possession of Musgrave's lands. Anne, as sheriff, would have found that highly satisfying.[12]

Any thoughts of visiting London had now gone out of her mind. Better than her father, she understood that to succeed she had to be present on the estates, convinced that her 'worldly fortunes in these northern parts in Craven and Westmorland would slide back to the wonted ill habit again' if she stirred from home. Moreover, unless things went well in the courts her tenants would be 'more insulting than ever', Anne having to endure the kind of disrespectful behaviour her forebears had often known. She busied herself from early 1651 starting the reconstruction of Brougham and Appleby Castles and made plans for St Anne's Hospital, the almshouses she wanted to provide for elderly women in Appleby, all of which will be described below.[13]

Later in the year she suffered a serious setback in the courts. Despite her lawyers' insistence that there were precedents for her request for an 8d fine, which the Commonwealth was itself demanding on former Royalist estates, the Lords Commissioners in Chancery did not agree. They dismissed the bill on 6 November and thereby upheld the customary estates of inheritance and the 7d fine laid down by the King's Award. Anne's reaction recorded in her *Diaries* was 'God send me some good Conclusion for it hath bene both chargeable and troublesome unto mee'. One advantage she did quickly gain, on 21 November, when the Council of State approved her nomination of Thomas Gabetis as her under-sheriff.[14] They were to work in tandem for many years over not just county administrative affairs but specifically her conflicts with her tenants.

Anne was not discouraged even when at the manorial courts held in her name early in 1653 the tenants again proved obstinate and refractory; that is, they appeared but would not answer when called. She had enactments sealed preparatory to a trial against them at common law. On 20 August her cause was heard at Appleby assizes, held in the Moot Hall before Judge Parker. Anne was favoured, as compared with her tenants, because the judges on circuit were accommodated by her in the castle. But what really mattered was the power of the lawyers' argument. As she noted, her cause was dismissed by reason of 'a generall exception taken against most of the Jurie', a sign that Gabetis had followed the all-too prevalent practice of hand-picking local jurors who would favour her cause.[15]

Anne now prepared the 'harshest' measures against her tenants, sealing many leases of ejectment in readiness for the trial at the Common Pleas bar in Westminster Hall. Her suit against Skaife of Stainmore as the defendant appearing on behalf of his fellow tenants was heard on 9 November 1653 before three judges. Once more the outcome was disappointing for her. The jury, as she recorded with some amazement, against all the evidence and the direction of the court and the judgment of all who heard the pleadings found for Skaife. Humphrey Hughes reported to the Countess of Cork on the 28th that Anne had been foiled by Westmorland jurymen even though they were chosen and fetched to Westminster by her.[16]

She and her lawyers continued to be frustrated by the courts. On 12 August 1654, her case again having been referred to Appleby assizes, Judge Newdigate heard it. Although 'itt was conceived I had a reasonable good Suit', she recorded, 'having obtayned a speciall Edict against them', once more she did not win and her tenants persisted in being wilful, refractory and obstinate. She worried at the slow progress of her suits and was dismayed when John Howell told her on 7 November that the trial records for the recent assizes in Westmorland and Northumberland had been lost on their way to Westminster. It was, he pointed out, a misfortune that none could have foreseen or prevented, but nothing more could be done about her suits unless they were found. He counselled patience, and that did not come easy to Anne, fretting away at Brougham.[17]

Despite the succession of legal setbacks Anne – as she is reputed to have informed Oliver Cromwell – still put her faith wholly in the discretion of the law. Her persistence was eventually rewarded. She commenced the 'hardest course' against her tenants in Trinity Term 1656 with suits of ejectment against, for instance, George Shaw for his messuage and lands in East and South Stainmore. Her cause in the Common Pleas was this time heard on 16 May 1656 by four of the chief judges, including her cousin Lord Chief Justice St John and her friend Judge Matthew Hale, one of Pembroke's executors whom she had often employed when he was a sergeant-at-law. In this trial the jury for the first time gave its verdict for her. This was the turning-point. At the second trial on the next day the tenants would not plead and Anne won her second verdict and in addition £250 costs. At the third trial on 12 November James Walker was the defendant. Neither he nor his counsel appeared, so he was non-suited, £100 costs given against him and his land judged to be Anne's. On 12 November, the process was repeated, this time against James Straker appearing as defendant on behalf of another group of her tenants, with the same result, judgment over the land for her and £100 costs.[18]

Straker's land she subsequently let to another person on a twenty-one years' lease, as she did with all the lands the court decided were hers. She describes in her *Diaries* the formality with which she took possession of James Walker's tenement. Neither the manner of the ejection, however legal, nor its timing show her in a good light. On 3 February 1657, in the depth of winter, with a writ directed to him from the court, Gabetis with Mr John Turner, Thomas Carlston, head bailiff for the West Ward, John Darby and Thomas Johnson, 'fairely and gently' dispossessed Walker's wife and family of his house and property. Gabetis then duly delivered it on Anne's behalf to Darby, who was the lessee named in the ejectment, until it could be leased to John Salkeld of Brough for twenty-one years at a yearly rack-rent. Anne's promise to be a 'mild, gentle and good' landlady is not much in evidence here.[19]

In the fourth and final trial at the Common Pleas bar on 23 April 1657 the verdict was once more in Anne's favour and this allowed her to take similar action against her other Westmorland tenants. It had taken seven years to win her battle with them, longer even than her mother's suits in James I's reign. As Sir John Lowther had predicted and Earl Francis's obstructive tenants Wasdale and Shaw asserted in 1619, the 'good securitie' given by Earl Francis, but lacking parliamentary enactment, had not stood the test at common law. The fatal flaw of the King's Award had been exposed – its imposition without Anne's consent as the person in whom the reversion was vested. Like Earl Francis, the tenants now found they had purchased by their huge payments in 1617 little more than a life interest in their messuages.[20]

55. *Lord Chief Justice Sir Oliver St John (c. 1598–1673), Lady Anne's relative and attorney, after P. Nason, 1651 (Lydiard House, Wiltshire. By kind permission of the Borough of Thamesdown. Photo: the author)*

Anne's Common Pleas suits restored the tenures and fines on her lordships to the position her mother had enjoyed. Having won and made the exemplary ejectments, she was to prove generous in her own fashion as a dominating mistress. To her credit, for the remaining twenty years of her life she held to the 8*d* fine she had fought for. On the other hand, she rack-rented her demesnes, mills and other possessions in the usual way. She never had any doubt as to what was at stake in her lawsuits. If she were foiled, she had reiterated to Christopher Marsh in December 1650, 'I and my posterity should have our fortunes in this country in a manner quite overthrown'. She stressed after her victory the service she had done to both her family and her fellow landowners. Her alteration of the tenure on her lands, which was her principal intention, was, she claimed, 'a great Benefitt and advantage to mee and my Posterity, and not only to mee but to all the Landlords and Tennants in that County'.[21]

The defendants would not at first have concurred with this view. Yet in the longer term the practice of a set 8*d* fine on the basis of the 'ancient' rent proved greatly to their advantage compared with an arbitrary fine; less so, it must be said, than a 7*d* fine would have been. The reason is that as prices rose so did the retained margin of profit from farming and ancillary activities. This encouraged the tenants to improve their lands and invest in better housing, which ushered in the era of the 'great rebuilding' and its legacy of fine vernacular architecture in the Eden Valley.[22]

Some of Anne's opponents were to pay a heavier price. Captain Atkinson, whom she regarded with venom as her great 'enemy' for political reasons as much as any other, came to a tragic end in 1664. Fervently anti-Royalist to the last, he was hanged with Captain Robert Waller and other associates for their leading part in the rash Kaber Rigg Plot centred on Kirkby Stephen, that 'nest of all traitors'. His career and those of the other committed Parliamentarians serve as a reminder of the role of religious dissent as well as political opposition and self-seeking which may be discerned in the resistance to Anne's estate policies. As John Breay has shown, the history of espousing new forms of religious nonconformity in the southern region of the Eden Valley was invigorated rather than dampened down by the experiences of the 1650s, Quakerism being the next vociferous phase.[23]

In winning her lawsuits Anne had cemented firm one pillar of the Westmorland baronial edifice she was resurrecting. She now had a secure tenurial footing, manorial control, an assured high income and, at the end, a welcome windfall of arrears of rents and fines. Her second, parallel long-term project, the programme of renovating her castles and churches and other building schemes, was going on apace. Brougham Castle, *pace* Anne, had been in good repair up to the Civil Wars when, Sir Daniel Fleming writes, it 'received great damage'. Anne found it 'verie ruinous' and it took two years to restore it to its original state. At this stage, she made no major alterations. She probably added a third storey to the Great Hall, reroofed the chapel block and other buildings, and inserted new windows and a number of fireplaces and doorways, all of Tudor style. She gave the keep the name Pagan Tower. As with all her reconstructions, Anne marked her work with a monumental inscription recording her titles, which reads:

Brougham Castle was repaired by the Ladie Anne Clifford Countesse Dowager of Pembroke Dorsett and Montgomery, Baronesse Clifford, Westmerland and Veseie, Lady of the Honour of Skipton in Craven and High Sheriffesse by inheritance of the countie of Westmerland, in the yeares 1651 and 1652 after it had layen ruinous ever since about August 1617 when King James lay in it for a time in his journie out of Skotland and towards London until this time. Isa. Chap. 58 Verse 12. God's name be praised.

This, her favourite biblical reference, set out Anne's philosophy of rebuilding:

And they that shall be of thee shall build the old waste places: thou shalt raise up the foundations of many generations; and thou shalt be called, The repairer of the breach, The restorer of paths to dwell in.

Fleming clearly approved of her work, deeming Brougham 'an ancient, strong, and stately castle'. It was finished during 1653 and on 9 December she was able to move in with her household for the first time for thirty-seven years.[24]

Anne began her almshouses in Appleby, St Anne's Hospital, on 23 April 1651, when she laid the foundation stone on the site at the upper end of Boroughgate. She purchased the first land for its endowment on 4 February 1652, a third of the manor of Brougham (quite distinct from the castle's demesnes) from Captain James Browne Esq. at the considerable cost of £2,100.

56. The courtyard, St Anne's Hospital, Appleby-in-Westmorland, completed 1655 (Photo: the author)

She completed the endowment on 29 December 1652 by obtaining the lands of St Nicholas, Appleby, for £900 from William Fielding. Together, they would provide an annual income of £100. The hospital was completed early in 1653. It is constructed of local red sandstone, originally a low, single-storey building, the second floor being added after her death. It is quadrangular in shape, with an archway entrance. The rooms for a Mother and twelve Sisters face inwards onto the courtyard and central fountain, with the chapel in the north-east corner and a common room in the south-east. The frontage on the street is similar in style to that Anne had erected at Beamsley; not vice versa, as is often asserted.

Before the end of March 1653 Anne had put in the Mother, a deceased minister's widow, and all the Sisters, eleven widows and the twelfth a maimed single woman (Table 4). She had been particularly keen on the hospital not just because of some philanthropic imperative but because, unlike Beamsley, it was in part an extension of her household, a retirement home for her women servants in old age. It is a commentary on her outlook that she had given thought to these intimate attendants who, like her, were of advancing years and needed sheltered housing with all the social advantages of community life. Her Orders, the strict rules for the running of the hospital, were those Countess Margaret had devised for Beamsley and were signed by Anne on 18 May and hung in the chapel. Biblical texts adorn the chapel walls (Pl. 84). Following the Restoration, Anne got the king's licence for the hospital under the Great Seal, dated 2 September 1661. More will be said about the hospital in Chapters 10

57. Lady Anne's chapel chest, St Anne's Hospital, Appleby-in-Westmorland, 1655 (Photo: the author)

TABLE 4 *The first almswomen at St Anne's Hospital, Appleby, 1652–4*

Date

1652

24 January	Allas Nelson (Mother)	signs
	Denis Wilson	makes mark
	Barbara Wharton	signs
	Joan Walleys	mark
31 January	Amye Walters	mark
	Francis Wharton	mark
1 February	Grace Brunskill	mark
2 February	Elizabeth Baccus	mark
5 February	Elinor Bainbrigg	mark
	Margaret Fothergill	mark
7 February	Ann Atkinson	signs
	Anne Wetherall	mark
14 February	Julian Browne	mark
Reader:	Anthony Shawe	signs

1653

	Jennet Knewstubbs	mark
	Dorothy Bell	mark
	Em Waller	signs
	Emma Atkinson	mark
	Elizabeth Wawburg	signs
Reader:	Robert Harrison (Shawe is dead)	

1654

August	Joanne Wallas (Mother, see above, Nelson died in July)	
	Grace Jackson (Sister in place of Wallas)	mark
	Frances Salkeld (Sister in place of Wilson who is dead)	

Source: KRO, WDEC/2

and 11. Anne also had to give some attention to Beamsley Hospital's affairs, because in 1657 she obtained from Oliver Cromwell an exemplification of the fine she and Pembroke had originally passed for its Derbyshire lands, but the purpose is not stated.[25]

Anne had started her reparations at Appleby Castle at the same time as the almshouses. She laid the foundation stone for the middle wall in the keep, the Great Tower, on 21 April 1651 and that year also put up the large, quadrangular

58. The keep, Caesar's Tower, Appleby Castle, showing Lady Anne's restoration of its upper storeys and battlements, completed in 1653 (Photo: the author)

59. The stables, Appleby Castle, erected by Lady Anne in 1651 (Photo: the author)

60. A rare surviving window bearing Lady Anne's initials, Appleby Castle (Photo: the author)

stable block and a barn outside the castle walls where there had never been buildings before. She claimed that the keep, which she renamed Caesar's Tower, had been in ruins since 1571. In fact, her uncle had kept it in some form of repair, though it was unusable. What Anne did was to restore its top ten or so courses and, crucially, divide it with the 'middle wall' so that each storey now had two rooms with wooden floors. She inserted 'Gothic'-style fireplaces in them. In July 1653 she witnessed its topping with crenellations, four angle turrets and a lead roof. In the grounds she built a bee-house or private oratory, square in shape with a pyramidal roof, on the foundations of an earlier watch-tower.[26]

By the end of January 1654 Anne had passed her climacteric, her sixty-third year, a time for sober reflection on the past and on the uncertainty of what lay ahead. Perhaps it was this which caused her to devote the year's building to commemoration of her parents, her father's tomb in Skipton as previously described and an unusual yet entirely appropriate monument to her mother near Brougham Castle. While there in the late winter months she oversaw the erection of the Countess's Pillar, a 14-foot structure on the wayside a quarter of a mile south of the castle towards Whinfell, to mark her last, sad parting from her mother on 2 April 1616. The pillar has affinities in shape with northern market crosses. Anne definitively calls it a 'Sun Dyall'. Above its octagonal shaft are a square block, pyramidal capping and a finial. Three faces of the block have painted sundials and the third bears the Clifford and Russell arms, a skull and the date 1654. In her first trust deed for the Appleby almshouses she had directed that £4 should be distributed yearly on that date in perpetuity to the poor of Brougham parish from the stone table at the base of the pillar. A brass tablet on the south facing sundial is inscribed with this. Oddly, Anne did not mention the erection of the pillar in her *Diaries*. The mason she employed has been identified by his mark – John Stainton, who is associated with other masons, Jonathan Gledhill and Daniel Whitfield, in Brough and Appleby Castles. Stainton, a former tenant, was a welcome guest at Brougham in 1671.[27]

During 1654 Anne turned further afield for another charitable memorial which similarly had bearing on her mother and her own Russell roots. By an indenture dated 30 December, she conveyed to William, 5th Earl of Bedford, Richard Crossinge, mayor of Exeter, William Courteney Esq. of Powderham Castle and other local men of standing a 4½-acre close worth £12 a year near to St James's Chapel in the parish of St Sidwell in Exeter which she had bought from Simon Snow. Her intention was charitable provision, mainly for a boy or girl to be apprenticed to an honest trade approved by her, though any surplus was to be divided between the poorest people in the parish. She was to be frustrated. Thomas Shapcote gained possession of the land. Ten years later, Anne appealed to Lord Chancellor Clarendon to intervene with Bedford and the other assignees to abide by the agreement, but

61. Lady Anne's bee-house or oratory, erected on older foundations, Appleby Castle (Photo: the author)

without success. Her charity, it seems, was never established.[28]

It is likely that in this year of commemoration Anne also commissioned her memorial to Samuel Daniel. Not only did she owe him a great deal in terms of education, friendship and moral support; she would have taken seriously his 1607 designation of her as his legatee. A bust, recognizably his, and an epitaph were erected on the wall in Beckington church, Somerset, where he was buried in the chancel (Pl. 65). In Pevsner's words, it was 'the first monument in the county designed in a fully understood classical taste. For not only are there volutes and garlands and an open segmental pediment, but the man represented in the bust in the pediment wears a kind of Roman toga and a wreath.' In the incised epitaph, Anne praised Daniel as an 'Excellent Poet & Historian' who was her tutor and stated that she, now Dowager Countess of Pembroke, Dorset & Montgomery, had erected the monument a long time after his death in gratitude to him. Just as for Edmund Spenser, she had accorded him a monument superior to that his social position merited. But, then, she was a countess.[29]

During 1655 Anne turned her attention to the principal parish churches on

62. The Countess's Pillar, Brougham, Cumbria, erected by Lady Anne, 1654 (Photo: the author)

her northern estates. Her work in Craven was described in the previous chapter, but it was far more extensive in Westmorland. She wrote in her *Diaries* that St Lawrence's, Appleby, was 'very ruinous and in danger of falling of itselfe' and that she caused a great deal of it to be taken down and repaired. As her stated outlay of £600 to £700 suggests, her work was extensive. She completely reshaped the chancel, removing a vestry, opening up the southern aisle to create its present form, and reroofing it. In the process she made a vault for herself in the north-east corner of the church, 9 feet 2 inches square, strongly arched with stone to a height of 6 feet 2 inches, and reached by a flight of eight stone steps. She repaired the chapel above the vault. She rebuilt the arches in the nave and the exterior buttresses. She recorded her work, though with some exaggeration, in an inscription on a

63. Sundial face on the Countess's Pillar, Brougham (Photo: the author)

64. Coats of arms of Lady Anne's parents, Countess's Pillar, Brougham (Photo: the author)

rafter in the south aisle, 'ANN CONNTESSE OF PEMBROKE IN ANO 1655 REPAIRED ALL THIS BVILDING'.[30]

The crucial year for Anne's Westmorland lawsuits, 1656, was a fallow one for building, but the £1,200 she received from fines between then and 1659 financed one of the peaks of her programme of reconstruction. She may have ordered the making of her own monument for St Lawrence's in 1656 but it was not completed and set up until the summer of 1657, over the vault she had made. It is a black and white marble standing monument, with a relief mural reredos and a broken segmental pediment (Pl. 76). Its family tree of twenty-four shields on the reredos and the inscription to herself below will be commented on further in Chapter 10. Anne's presence dominated the chancel for two decades before her eventual death.[31]

In the spring of 1658 Anne states that she pulled down St Michael's Church in Bongate, Appleby, and built it anew at her own expense. According to Holmes, it was most likely 'a matter of setting up what had fallen down rather than introducing anything fresh', though the outer archway of the porch may have been hers. An eighteenth-century view 'shows it as a barn-like building with a low-pitched roof and a small bell-cote at its western end'. Anne might have given it more attention had she known of the effigy (then mured up) of Elizabeth Roos, widow of Thomas, 6th Lord Clifford. Like Isabella de Vipont before her, Elizabeth had been granted in 1394 during her widowhood the office of Sheriffess of Westmorland. In the summer, Anne rebuilt St Wilfrid's Chapel at Brougham 'larger and stronger than it was before at my owne charge'. A year later, it was the turn of St Ninian's, the parish church of Kinekirks at Brougham. She received the sacrament there for the first time after its rebuilding on 30 March 1662.[32]

65. *Samuel Daniel's monument, with incised epitaph, erected by Lady Anne, St George's Church, Beckington, Somerset, c. 1654 (Photo: the author)*

Each of these three smaller churches is 'thick walled and buttressed, devoid of transept and tower and combines in one squat length nave and chancel'. All bear some evidence of Anne's refurbishing. At St Ninian's, her insertions included a rood screen, pulpit and box pew for the castle in 1660, a plain, octagonal font of local sandstone in 1662, and a poor-box of 1663. In its east wall is a plaster wreath with the initials 'A.P.' and the date 1660. St Wilfrid's, transformed since Anne's time, has a font which could be 1660 and on the west wall, high up, is a shield of Clifford impaling Vipont. In the chancel of St Michael's a carved and painted cartouche with Anne's initials set in strapwork commemorates her raising the church 'out of its ruins'. There is also a striking Clifford-Vipont shield in Kirkby Thore church, which might have been placed by Anne. The Cliffords had inherited the right of advowson there from the Viponts and Anne had claims on the property.[33]

Everything might have gone catastrophically wrong in 1659, as described in the previous chapter. With the threat from the Royalists' resurgence, the government sent garrisons on 4 August into Appleby and Brougham Castles as well as Skipton. At Appleby, they confined themselves to Caesar's Tower, were withdrawn and then returned. Happily the crisis passed without damage to either place. Yet, like Skipton, Anne's newly restored Westmorland castles were a potential threat to the regime. The Militia Commissioners of Cumberland raised the question with the Council of State on 7 September whether it would not be 'convenient' to demolish them as well as Greystoke and Cockermouth Castles. The council referred the matter to the Committee of Safety for its decision. Events then moved too fast for any action to be taken.[34]

Sensibly, Anne had kept to the last the rebuilding of her two long-decayed castles, Brough which Camden described as 'a little fortress,' and Pendragon, then 'a heap of stones'. It was during 1659, whilst at Appleby in April, that she directed in person the start of Brough's rebuilding. Its 'Roman' Tower, courthouse and thirteen or fourteen rooms were all erected on the old foundations. She is confusing over the timing of the reconstruction, because she later says that masons did the work in April and May 1660 and that 'it was soe well repaired by mee that the 16th of September in the next yeare I lay there for three nights together, which none of my Auncestors had done in 140 yeares till now'. Brough is the best surviving example of her castle restoration in Westmorland (Pl. 66).[35]

In 1660, also, Pendragon Castle, in ruins since the Scots burnt it in 1341, was rebuilt to her 'great costs and charges'. Like Barden, it may have been enlarged by her: its keep is exceeded in area only by Carlisle Castle in the north-west though, lacking height, it is squatter in shape (Pl. 67). Its principal room was a Great Chamber whose windows looked out to the south and west. She moved into the castle for three nights on 14 October 1661, 'which none of my Auncestors had done since Idonea, ye younger sister to Isabella de Viteripont lay in it, who dyed the 8th yeare of Edward the third, without issue'.[36]

What remained now was to add the necessary amenities and services already provided at Appleby to her other residences. In 1661 Brough Mill was restored, supplying ground corn and meal to her household and the local community, the profit from the mulcture also contributing to her revenues. In 1662, she knocked down the old brewhouse and bakehouse at Brougham Castle and

66. Brough Castle, Cumbria: Lady Anne's chamber was in the near round tower (Photo: the author)

erected new ones abutting the west inner wall, the only modern alterations she made to the medieval castle. Brough Castle was provided with a kitchen, bakehouse, brewhouse and stables within its courtyard, and Pendragon completed with a perimeter wall and arched gatehouse entrance, stable, coachhouse, brewhouse, bakehouse and washhouse.[37]

All her tenants by now were well served with refurbished churches except for the parishioners in Mallerstang around Pendragon. For them, Anne renovated Mallerstang Chapel (St Mary's, Outhgill). This was a chapel of ease within the parish of Kirkby Stephen and its living was a Clifford perquisite, the parish's being Lord Wharton's. Estimates were brought to her on 20 February 1663 by Mr Robert Branthwaite and the costs of the work, completed by the end of the year, were £46 15s 6d. The chapel is similar in construction to Ninekirks and the other more northerly chapels. Over the porch is an inscription recording her work.

The chapel's endowment of £6 13s 4d had been inadequate before the Parliament augmented it in 1646 with £50 a year from the parish tithes. This had ended with the Restoration. It was Anne who placed the chapel's revenues on a secure and permanent footing. Early in 1664 she endowed it with lands worth £11 a year bought at Cautley near Sedburgh for the maintenance of a parson and schoolmaster, Rowland Wright, who had started educating the local children three or four years earlier. On 22 November 1667 she confirmed her deed, in the presence of Branthwaite, Sedgewick and Edmund Foster, her chief butler. The income, she stated, was 'for a reader to read divine service, and to

67. Pendragon Castle, repaired by Lady Anne in 1660, drawn and engraved by Samuel and Nathaniel Buck, 1739 (Cumbria County Library)

teach and instruct the children of the dale of Mallerstang aforesaid to read and write'.[38]

Anne is one of two famous owners of the lordship of Mallerstang commemorated on Mallerstang Edge. The first was Hugh de Morville, remembered – infamous is perhaps the better term – for the part he played in the murder of St Thomas Becket in 1177. He gave his name to the high peak until recently known as Hugh's Seat Morville. Near there, on the Yorkshire border, he placed a boundary mark, Hugh's Pillar, which by Anne's time had fallen down. She rebuilt it in worked stone with the date, 1664, and an inscription to him. Since then it has been known as Lady Anne's Pillar. What would have appealed to her about Hugh's Pillar, apart from its delineation of the bounds of her properties, was that Morville's sister Maud married William de Vipont. The Morville arms are impaled on shields in Appleby Castle. Lady Anne's Pillar in time collapsed but is again a prominent landmark because of its restoration by John Breay and two helpers in 1953.[39]

After 1664, Anne's expenditure on buildings was mainly a matter of upkeep and making such improvements as good estate management dictated; none the less a heavy perennial call on her resources. In January 1665, four iron grates, each weighing over a hundredweight, were installed at a cost of £7 1*s* 7*d* in the Great Chamber, the Baron's Chamber, the Hall and the second chamber in the Tower of League at Brougham. In September, Caesar's Tower at Appleby and the watch-tower at Brough were leaded with over two tons, bought at £13 a ton from Sir Philip Musgrave. Next month, freestone was bought for the battlements on the four little turrets on each corner of Caesar's Tower and there was work on the four turrets at Brough. In 1668 she restored the old hunting lodge and its farm buildings at Julian Bower in Whinfell Forest, where

68. Mallerstang Chapel (St Mary's Outhgill), repaired by Lady Anne in 1663 (Photo: the author)

Roger, 2nd Lord Clifford, had kept his mistress. Here she accommodated her close friends the Gilmores who had come from Ramsbury to serve her. She kept the coachway beside the River Eden in good condition so that she could call on them on her way to Appleby.

There was much renovation from 1670/2 at Stainmore pits, which supplied Appleby, Brough and Pendragon Castles with coal. Fuel, because of its weight and bulk, came from whichever source was nearest, preferably Anne's own. Besides ling and chopwood and charcoal from Whinfell and Flakebridge, she bought coal in large quantities at 12*d* a load from Stainmore, some for Pendragon from Musgrave's mines in Cotterdale, and for Brougham from Caldbeck and Hartside in Cumberland. There was regular outlay on the corn mills, the biggest being at Brougham demesne mill in 1671/3, when a new weir was constructed and then had to be repaired after flood damage.[40]

The major work in Anne's later years was at Brougham Castle. A new garden wall was erected in 1671 and a new court wall in 1673, the former probably that standing today. Thomas Meason made a great gate for the bowling green in August 1674. Did Anne herself still indulge? A new coach house was put up in November 1675 and there was renewal of the slates of the chapel, kitchen and stables at the same time. A new garden was made and walled in January 1676 by workmen from Brough. Internal renovation included binding the hangings about the Great Chamber in November 1670. Inventories were made of all the castles in November 1671, which unfortunately have not survived.[41]

Anne was obviously proud at being able in 1661 to reside in Brough Castle, which had been denied her immediate forebears for 140 years, and even more in Pendragon, unused since Lady Idonea's time 320 years before. Now aged over seventy, she had achieved the twin objectives of mastering her tenants and restoring the fabric of her medieval and Tudor strongholds and churches throughout her Westmorland and Craven domains. She had a range of castle residences of varying sizes, all with quality chambers and newly renovated, indeed modern, fireplaces and toilets. The hearth tax returns show how many chambers and service rooms they had with heating, that is, fireplaces or furnaces. Appleby with its outhouses had forty; Brougham thirty; Brough twenty-four; Pendragon twelve; Skipton sixty-one (the same as before the slighting) and Barden Tower twenty-seven, again including outhouses.[42] Wainscot, decorated plasterwork, tapestry wall-hangings, paintings, and comfortable beds, like that surviving at Dalemain, gave a rich and welcoming setting not just for her officers and servants but also for her many relatives and other visitors who travelled north to pay court to her, as the *Diaries* show.

Pendragon's completion set the stage for her full-scale peregrinations. Remarkably, Anne did what no other Clifford could have done – stay in all six fortified houses, the four in Westmorland and two in Craven. Moreover, unlike her medieval predecessors, she did not vary the pattern with sojourns in monastic guest-houses (all gone), or with her relatives (too distant), or in any town or city. Occasionally she called on her officers and between Mallerstang and Skipton spent nights at inns or with friends like John Coleby near Bainbridge and John Symondson at Starbotton.[43] She behaved as if domestically self-sufficient. Relatives and others visited her, not vice versa.

This phase in her life lasted six years. Defeated in Craven by Currer, the Burlingtons and the Yorkshire establishment, she retired to Westmorland. She was now too frail to cross the rough, high Pennine passes in her horse litter. But she continued until near the end of her life the same pattern of removes, if now restricted to her Westmorland castles. Skipton and Barden were not redundant. They were kept in good repair by her Craven officers. Her relatives and other visitors frequently stayed there and the manorial courts were held in them as always. Skipton remained the often bustling administrative centre for all her Craven properties.

The appeal of what commentators on Lady Anne usually regard as her 'antique' and 'inconvenient' life-style, progressing periodically from one restored medieval stronghold to another, will be considered in the context of her whole outlook and activities as a grand old lady in the north in Chapter 11. But before that, two related facets of her achievements will be separately assessed. These will, incidentally, illuminate other features of her monuments, churches and castles not touched on so far and help explain the thrust of her mind during the years when she was absorbed in directing their construction.

CHAPTER 9

History and Legitimacy Proclaimed:
The Manuscript Records

Lady Anne stands alone in the conscious effort and manner by which she justified and publicized her right to her lands and titles. For her immediate family and descendants the medium was manuscript compilations – her Books of Record, summary histories, diaries and genealogies. For public as well as family viewing and consumption, she commissioned the triptychs and displayed heraldry on funerary monuments and her almshouses and also inside her castles, and placed plaques on her restored buildings which, besides commemorating her work, also stressed her rightful inheritance. The Books of Record and the triptychs were parallel enterprises which absorbed much of her attention from 1646 at Baynard's. The subject here is her manuscript legacy, the public proclamation of her legitimacy being considered in the next chapter.

The most remarkable of Anne's manuscript compilations, in both depth of treatment and detailed contents, are her three-volume 'Great' Books of Record. All three sets have been compared for this study, two of which are in the Hothfield MSS and the third in private ownership. The frontispiece of each Book states they are the Books of the Records of the Cliffords and Viponts, compiled in 1649 'by the Care & Industrie' of the Lady Anne Clifford, Countess of Dorset, Pembroke and Montgomery, 'Which Lady by Birthright from her Father and his Auncestors is Barones Clifford Westmorland and Vescy; and High Shreives of that County and Lady of the Honor of Skipton in Craven being lineally descended from both those Noble Familyes'.[1] By records she meant the historical documents, which will be assessed first. But she also inserted summaries in the Great Books in 1652 and added other writings afterwards, which will be discussed later in the chapter.

Anne's object was to compile in book form the incontrovertible proof of her right to the baronies of Westmorland and Skipton and the sheriffwick. The manner of presentation chosen was a documentary biography of each Vipont and Clifford holder of the titles and his wife or wives. As always, primacy was given to Westmorland. Book I starts with the first hereditary sheriff and baron of Westmorland, Robert, 1st Lord Vipont (d. 1228), and his wife Idonea de Builli. Idonea died in 1235 and left her body to be buried in Roche Abbey, Yorkshire, which had been founded in 1147 by Richard de Builli and Richard Fitzurgis. Anne set great store by the Builli lords and ladies and their names will recur in this and the following chapters.

The style of layout of this first section was followed for all the title-holders

THROUGH THE MERCIES OF THE HOLY TRINITY
GOD THE FATHER CREATOR OF THE WORLD
GOD THE SONN CHRIST IESVS REDEMER OF THE WORLD.
God the Holie Ghost Sanctifier and preserver of the world
DOTH PROCEED ALL BLESSINGS, BOTH TEMPORALL & ETERNALL

THIS IS THE FIRST BOOKE OF THE RECORDES,
CONCERNING THE TWO NOBLE FAMILIES OF THE
CLIFFORDS, WHICH WEARE LORDS CLIFFODS OF,
CLIFFOD CASTLE IN HEREFORDSHIRE, AND OF.
THE VETERIPONTS, WHO WERE LORDS BARONS
AND HIGH SHREIFS OF WESTMERLAND

which Booke was compiled Anno 1649

BY THE CARE & INDVSTRIE OF THE LADY ANN CLIFFORD,
Countes of Dorsett, Pembrooke & Montgomery, DAVGHTER
AND SOLE HEIRE OF GEORG CLIFFORD LATE EARLE OF CVM-
-BERLAND, WHICH LADY BY BIRTHRIGHT FROM HER FATHER
AND HIS AUNCESTORS, IS BARONES CLIFFORD WESTMERLAND,
AND VESCY, AND HIGH SHREIVES OF THAT COVNTY
AND LADY OF THE HONOR OF SKIPTON IN CRAVEN
BEING LINEALLY DESCENDED FROM BOTH
THOSE NOBLE FAMILYES.

The cheife of which Records in this Booke was by the Care and painfull industrie of that excellent Lady Margaret Russell Countess Dowager of Cumbreland, gotten out of seuerall offices and Courts of this Kingdome to prove the right title which her only childe the Lady Anne als Clifford, now Countess Dowager of Pembrooke, Dorsett & mongomery had to the inheritance of her ffather, and his Auncestors.

But the Sumaries were not written in, till the yeare 1652 :-

69. *The frontispiece to Lady Anne's First Great Book of Record, 1648 (Cumbria County Record Office, Kendal, WD/Hoth/A988/10/1)*

70. Illuminated family tree of Walter de Clifford and Margaret de Toeni, First Great Book of Record, 1648 (Cumbria County Record Office, Kendal, WD/Hoth/A988/10/1)

throughout the Books down to and including Anne herself. In colour on the first folio is a splendid genealogical tree of the Viponts spreading up from fine representations of Robert and his lady and with the appropriate coats of arms tricked out. Then, under a general heading, come the main entries, that is the transcriptions in their original Anglo-Norman French or Latin of the

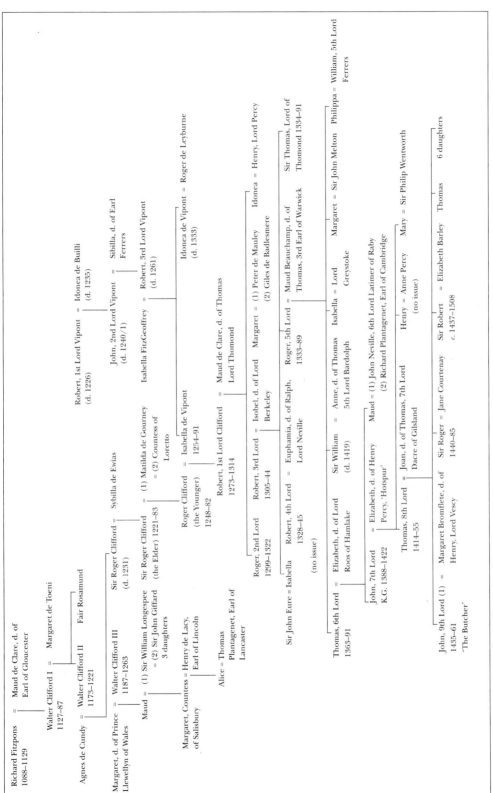

The medieval Clifford–Vipont descent

documents relating to Robert and Idonea, followed immediately by an English translation. Finally, a folio index lists all the records included in the section.

The far greater detail in the first two Books reflects the emphasis given to establishing Anne's title through her medieval predecessors. Book I, with about 200 folios covering one century, is devoted to the three Vipont lords and then the Clifford marcher lords from Walter (d. 1187), who took his name from Clifford Castle in Herefordshire, to Roger the Elder (d. 1283), whose son Roger the Younger married Isabella de Vipont. Book II, much the thickest with 536 folios, covers the 250 years from Roger the Younger (d. 1282) through his son Lord Robert, the first to combine the Vipont and Clifford titles, down to the death of Henry, the Shepherd Lord in 1523, who was the 'Fowerteenth Hereditary high shreif And Baron of Westmerland, & Tenth Lord of the honor of Skipton in Craven'. The beginning of Book III continues in the same vein, dealing with the first three earls of Cumberland in a further 95 folios. The cut-off point comes a little later with the Court of Wards pleadings of 1608, because the object had been achieved of proving Anne's case on the basis of the documentary evidence. Subsequent entries took the legal debate up to the 1615 judgment in the Common Pleas, but from 1608 the purpose of Book III alters, as will be explained below.

An outstanding, perhaps unique, feature of the Books, which impressed Sedgewick, is their scholarly apparatus, worthy of modern researchers' publications.[2] The origin and location of almost every document are given in marginal references. Sometimes, too, the person who helped make it available is named. Anne asserted at the bottom of the frontispiece that the chief of the 'Records in this Booke was by the Care and painfull industrie of that excellent Lady Margaret Russell Countess Dowager of Cumbreland gotten out of severall Offices and Courts of this kingdome'. Undoubtedly that is correct and the Books are a testimony to the countess's concentrated researches during 1607 and 1608 which brought the satisfaction of success in the Wards' hearings. Yet, the assertion needs qualification on two counts. The first is that the countess had professional help. The second is that Anne incorporated in the Books documents which she had herself obtained by various means from 1619 until as recently as 1648.

The countess and Anne were of the rank accustomed to hiring experts without feeling any obligation to acknowledge their help unless they were men of distinction or title or were regarded as friends. The skilled antiquary who guided the countess's researches was Mr St Loe Kniveton, as mentioned in Chapter 1. The entry on him by the eighteenth-century copyist of her diary for 17 March 1619 has been misread by the editors and Anne's biographers.[3] Anne herself does not help when naming him as a source of an entry in Book I: 'A Note of Mr Attoes an Excellent Antiquary sent to the Countess of Cumberland 1608 concerning the Particon between Isabella & Idonea 13 Ed. I'.[4] Not a great deal otherwise is known about Kniveton. However, he was distinguished enough to be one of seven antiquaries appointed by a House of Lords subcommittee on 6 February 1621 to search for the privileges of peers, the others including the great jurist John Selden, John Vincent and Henry Lassells.[5]

To be thoroughly conversant with the numerous and complex archives of the government departments, already massive by James I's reign, would be the stock-in-trade of an antiquary like Kniveton who, apart from being a collector, earned a living employed by nobility and gentry in legal and genealogical research. His collections out of the records for Nottinghamshire and Derbyshire were taken from the fines, charters, pleas, inquisitions, patent rolls, close rolls and Exchequer documents, all now part of the great national archive in the Public Record Office, London. The same depth of research applies to his work for the countess.[6]

The highest proportion of the records entered in the Books was discovered in the Tower of London, the great repository for Chancery. These would have been garnered by Countess Margaret with Kniveton's advice, if not actual help. The first record transcribed for her there, on 26 February 1606/7, was the great exemplification of the grants of Appleby and Brougham to the Viponts and Robert de Clifford. A marginal note in Anne's own hand about a plea of 41 Edward III concerning Roger, 5th Lord Clifford, transcribed about the same time, reads: 'This is the most Remarkable Plea amongst all the Recordes concerning the Cliffords.' An exemplification of letters patent from the patent rolls of 12 May, 21 Richard II, in the Tower was provided for the countess on 26 February 1608 by the Chancery clerks Matthew Carew and John Tindall. It looks as if it was Tindall who made the drawings of the large seals copied into the Books. Good use was also made of other Chancery records such as the fine rolls, the records of the clerk of the hanaper and the escheator's bundles.[7]

Later, for the Common Pleas hearings, Dorset acquired on his and Anne's behalf two important documents from the Chancery files. One, on 3 November 1613, was an exemplification; the other, on 6 May 1615, an extent of the castle and manor of Skipton, with its seal carefully drawn, again provided by John Tindall.[8] Several of the most vital records, especially those concerning Isabella and Idonea, were later found to have their counterparts in the Skipton Castle muniments.

Most of the departments of state were housed in Westminster and these, especially the great repositories of the Exchequer, yielded a number of vital records for the countess. The Court of Exchequer was located in one of the chambers off Westminster Hall and its records were in the custody of its senior official, the King's Remembrancer. Those transcribed included the Book of Knights' Fees for 6 Henry VI. The Great Rolls of the Pipe, from which the countess and Kniveton took extracts, were the responsibility, under the Remembrancer, of the clerk of the pipe and were kept in the gallery. Entries in the rolls revealed, for example, that Robert, 1st Lord Vipont, had been sheriff of various other counties apart from Westmorland. The Court of Receipt of the Exchequer had its own separate establishment. Arthur Agard and George Austin, clerks in the receipt, provided the countess with the copy of an important record on 28 November 1608 and also drew its fine seal.[9]

The Quo Warranto bags proved of great value, a combined one for Gloucester and Hereford and another for Westmorland, which were in the custody of the Treasurer and Chamberlain. The Westmorland quo warranto was that which required the Shepherd Lord to prove his title to Westmorland and the sheriffwick in 1505/6 when he ran foul of Henry VII. His success then was invaluable in arguing Anne's case.[10] Among other documents obtained was the act of attainder of John, 'the Butcher', 9th Lord Clifford, in 1461 which was transcribed by H. Elsynge in 1608 at Westminster from the parliament rolls of I Edward IV. John Greenwood, counsellor at law, collected notes for the countess's use about the shrievalty of Westmorland and other liberties and rights in the county.[11]

As a result of this labour, Anne inherited from her mother a considerable corpus of documents. These included the thorough and detailed submissions to the Wards and the Earl Marshal, some of which, as mentioned in Chapter 3, are still extant. A number of Kniveton's original transcriptions are in the Hothfield MSS and their endorsements show that Anne's lawyers, as well as the countess's, constantly made use of them.[12] The whole collection constituted for Anne proof of her title, no matter what King James might promulgate otherwise. It remained one of her psychological props, vindication of her adamant resolve to deny the validity of the King's Award. Probably for that reason, as well as a kind of homage to her mother's labours on her behalf, she employed Kniveton, most likely soon after the Award, to write them up in two volumes. She received them from him when at Knole on 18 March 1619 and, as she noted in her diary, she was able to compare them.[13] They do not appear to have survived. Although the extent of Kniveton's contribution is difficult to ascertain, he must share with the countess the credit for her painstaking research and, in particular, unearthing the evidence which wrecked Earl Francis's case at the Wards' pleadings in 1608. Moreover, his two volumes became the core and in a sense the framework of Anne's own Great Books of Record.

By the time Dorset died Anne, therefore, was the owner of a collection of which many an antiquary would have been proud. Besides the large archive of transcribed Chancery and other records and submissions, they had been duplicated in a much handier and presumably structured form in Kniveton's volumes. She would also possess copies of the submissions for her titles to the Earl Marshal which Kniveton had drawn up for the countess, several copies of which are known. Moreover, he had compiled and passed to the countess and so to Anne genealogies of the Viponts and Cliffords. In addition, she possessed both the manuscripts, notably Richard Robinson's, and a single-volume description of Earl George's voyages. Yet her collection was different in two respects from that of most contemporary antiquaries – first, in its cohesion and focus imposed by the inheritance issue and, second, in its writing up in vellum-bound book form. Too many antiquaries never reached the latter stage, their enthusiasms being assuaged by the pursuit and copying of sources and storing them in their libraries.

Anne may herself have added to the archive. She cites in Book I Camden's mention in *Britannia*, fol. 618, of the founding of Clifford Castle in Herefordshire, which she would have extracted from her own copy of the first English version of 1610.[14] However, what else she might have obtained is all but impossible to detect. The following discussion may well underestimate her contribution to the documents eventually written up in her Great Books. Her quandary, however, is plain. She was barred from access to the huge Clifford muniments at Skipton and Appleby Castles as long as her uncle and cousin lived. Not until 1646, when Skipton was in Parliamentarian hands, did the chance come for her to delve into her family's evidence by means of the antiquaries Charles Fairfax and Roger Dodsworth, as has been explained in Chapter 7.

In his reminiscences, Sedgewick emphasizes the 'extraordinary care she took' and 'the very great charge in the searching of ancient records' done by Dodsworth. The story is rather more complex than Sedgewick implies.[15] Certainly, in 1646/8 Anne employed Dodsworth to provide her with transcriptions of the Skipton documents but benefited as well from his many years of omniverous copying. What he provided was incorporated with the documents from Kniveton's volumes when they were all rewritten in large-folio format in her '3 Greatt Written hand Booke', as she called them.[16] From Dodsworth, too, came many of the smaller illustrations, mainly of monastic and other seals.

Dodsworth's reputation is that of an indefatigable antiquary whose merit is not as fully recognized as it should be because of his failure to publish any of his material. Two-thirds of the contents of Sir William Dugdale's great work on the monasteries, his *Monasticon*, which first made his reputation, he owed to Dodsworth. This he acknowledges. It ought to that extent to be known as Dodsworth's *Monasticon*, but Dugdale is rightly due the accolade because he had the drive and literary skill to complete the project. Dodsworth's industry in Anne's employ is evident from his transcriptions not just of the Skipton Castle muniments, but of those at Appleby and at Londesborough where he also worked during 1646, presumably with Lady Cork's approval. Of the 161-volume collection preserved in the Bodleian Library, Oxford, numbers 70, 74 and 83 are wholly or mainly Clifford evidences. Several others include extracts and there are more in the Yorkshire Archaeological Society's muniments. Dodsworth had access to Kniveton's transcriptions on the midland counties and his notes from them are to be found especially in the Bodleian volumes 134, 136 and 154.[17]

As with the *Monasticon*, Dodsworth's was a great though virtually anonymous contribution to the Books of Record in at least two ways. The Skipton documents he transcribed are second only to those from the Tower in number and are equally important in supporting Anne's title. Of the sixty-seven documents comprising the first section (on the 1st Lord Vipont), thirty-eight came from the Tower, twelve from Skipton and the other seventeen from various sources including the Exchequer.[18] The proportion from Skipton became greater in the later sections and the Books often note that documents identical to the Tower's had been located at the castle by Dodsworth. Mostly, however, the Skipton evidences extended the range of those Countess Margaret and Kniveton had obtained for the twenty generations of Vipont and Clifford lords. Dodsworth copied many into his own volumes. Good examples are the terms of the marriages negotiated for Countess Eleanor in 1535 and Lady Margaret in the 1550s; entered in Anne's Book II, fols 70–76, and his own Bodleian 88, fols 93–105.[19] The only disappointing aspect of his long visits to Skipton, Appleby and Londesborough is that he did not take the opportunity to record their heraldry, which he had already done for Yorkshire churches. This is particularly regrettable because Dugdale, who borrowed and copied from his records, laments the loss of the castle's wealth of heraldic glass in the 1648/9 slighting.[20]

Much of the new material Dodsworth provided from the Clifford evidences was of a piece with the documents Countess Margaret had obtained, that is grants, extents and exemplifications. But his own sources, including his notes from his fellow antiquaries' work, provided a different sort of information on Anne's forebears which gave the Books greater breadth, variety and, especially, personal interest. It has to be admitted that the extent of his contribution does raise slight doubts whether it was he, or even Anne herself, who obtained some of the documents which were attributed above to the countess and Kniveton. Dodsworth worked, for instance, on the Great Rolls of the Pipe in 1640/2 and the Books of Knights' Fees for Yorkshire.[21] It seems best, however, to allow that because the sheriffwick was a prime concern for the countess and Kniveton, as the submissions reveal, it was they who obtained all the transcriptions. Similarly, it was more likely Anne who obtained the plea concerning Roger Clifford the Elder which Scipio Squire, vice-chamberlain of the Court of Receipts of the Exchequer, examined and copied some time after 30 November 1620, when he was admitted to that office.[22]

A more intriguing question is whether it was Kniveton or Dodsworth who contributed the two extracts from documents from the famous library of the great antiquary Sir Robert Cotton (1571–1631). Cotton House in Westminster was a resort of scholars. Henry, Lord Clifford, it will be recalled, drew on Cotton's expertise over the barony of Clifford in 1628. The first extract is stated to be from the third book, 73 leaf 6 of the chronicle of Henry de Knighton, canon of Leicester Abbey, which Kniveton is known to have borrowed. It records that in 1265 Robert, 3rd Lord Vipont, joined Simon de Montfort, Earl of Leicester, siding with the barons to maintain the propositions for the benefit of Henry III and his kingdom. The second extract came from the cartulary of the abbey of Barlings, a house of the Praemonstratensian Canons east of Lincoln, concerning the lands of Sir Eubo Le Strange, second husband of Alice Lacy, Countess of Lancaster. On balance, Dodsworth was the likely source, though possibly making use of Kniveton's manuscripts.[23] Both extracts are examples of entries in the Great Books which do not directly sustain Anne's claim to the inheritance; rather, they fill out the historical content which would be of great interest to Anne herself and, she would suppose, to readers in times to come.

The entries on Godstow and Aconbury priories, both of which had emotional as well as historic appeal to Anne, would be from Dodsworth's own notes. The cartulary of Godstow, a house for ever associated with Fair Rosamund, was cited in Book I and in Dodsworth's volume LIX as in the custody of the King's Remembrancer in the Exchequer. The cartulary of Aconbury in Herefordshire was in the Court of Augmentations at Westminster, extracts from which Dodsworth included in his collections of religious foundations. Anne's interest in Aconbury would be twofold. First, the prioress and nuns benefited from an endowment with Clifford lands. Second, the heart of Margaret, widow of Walter Clifford III (d. 1263), was buried in Aconbury Church, her tomb bearing the Clifford arms with the red dragon of Wales, the origin of the Cliffords' crest.[24]

As the Bodleian volumes also show, it was Dodsworth who provided most of the entries in the Books attributed in the margins either to other antiquaries or to a number of owners of family archives. A more than usually convoluted route through Dodsworth is that of the notes Dugdale had made from the transcriptions of 'the learned Antiquarie' Monsieur de Chesne from the evidences of the abbey de Cerneio in France. This document entered in Book I concerned a grant by John de Vipont of tithes within the parish of Cerneio to the abbey, which was a member of the monastery of St John in the vale of Chartres. The charters of the abbey of Hepp (Shap) in Westmorland and the priory of St Constantine at Wetheral in Cumberland were in Lord William Howard's muniments at Naworth Castle, which Dodsworth examined in 1639. Again, the extracts concerned Vipont land-grants. When Hepp Abbey, founded in Preston in Lancashire, had moved to Shap, its possessions there had been confirmed by Robert de Vipont.[25]

The seal of Richard son of John and brother of the Abbot of Osney in Oxfordshire came from the book of seals of Dodsworth's antiquary friend Sir Christopher Hatton, Baron of Kirkby. Dodsworth had previously obtained excerpts from the register of the abbey, a house of Augustinian Canons, from Arthur Agard who had got them from Augustine Seward, its owner in 1596/9. But Hatton was both Anne's friend and her relation too. They and Lady Margaret were godparents in October 1668 of his granddaughter and Anne's great-granddaughter, Anne, who was born at Thanet House in London.[26]

The most numerous entries of this kind cite Sir Simonds D'Ewes (1602–50), the outstanding antiquary of Charles I's reign. A series of charters concerning the early Cliffords in Herefordshire and Abbey Dore were entered in Book I, fols 142–70, all from the originals in D'Ewes's possession. It was while at Skipton Castle, on 12 February 1646, that Dodsworth robustly answered a critical letter from D'Ewes about the collections he had made from the pipe rolls.[27] Dodsworth's colleague in sifting the castle's muniments, Charles Fairfax, provided him (rather than Anne) with notes from the records concerning Idonea, daughter of Robert, 1st Lord Clifford, by his wife Maud de Clare, who married Henry Percy, 2nd Lord Percy of Alnwick. The source, 'a certaine Register of the Evidences of the Noble Family of the Percyes lately remayning in Skipton Castle', was one of those Fairfax examined in 1646 and perhaps took for his own use, although he claimed he bought it. Subsequently it came into the hands of the earls of Northumberland and has been published.[28]

Among the most valuable inclusions in the Books were the records of the northern monasteries. These were in St Mary's Tower, York, and Dodsworth's notes taken from the chest of evidences of Roche Abbey and the charter rolls of the Benedictine priory of St Mary at Blyth, Nottinghamshire, were cited several times. They included the 1088 foundation charter of Blyth, by Roger de Builli and his wife Muriel, who endowed the monks with both the church and town. Idonea de Vipont granted to the priory the chapels of Bawtry and Austerley. However, her charter to her burgesses of Bawtry was discovered by Dodsworth in Skipton Castle, most likely because the 1st Earl Henry had been granted both those manors by Henry VIII.[29] Dodsworth and Fairfax were instrumental in helping rescue the monastic charters and other evidences from St Mary's Tower when it was blown up by the Parliament on Sunday 16 June 1644 during the great siege of the city. But, according to Dodsworth, it was Thomas Thompson, 'homo integerrimus', who at extreme hazard of his life carried most of them away to safety. They ended up in the archbishop's archives, where Thompson, a public notary, copied the 1st Earl of Cumberland's will, which was entered in Book III, fol. 9.

The last document Anne received before the Books were completed was the copy of a deed in French sent her in July 1648 by her 'worthy good frind', the lawyer Sir Thomas Widdrington, one of her counsel and brother-in-law of Charles Fairfax, who became Speaker of the House of Commons in the Interregnum. He, too, was a noted antiquary and wrote a history and topography of the city of York, *Analecta Eboracensia*. The deed concerned a dispute in 10 Edward III between Sir Henry FitzHugh, a great landowner in Richmondshire, and Robert, 3rd Lord Clifford, which Widdrington had taken from a law book entitled 'Anni Decem Prores Regis Edwardi Tertio 1596'.[30]

After the Great Books had been completed, Anne herself inserted two new documents. The first was the pardon granted the future 1st Earl for his livery and inquisition on 18 July 1523, a few weeks after the Shepherd Lord's death. This had not been found until the livery had been entered and so was added to the end of Book II. As late as October 1668 a deed of John, 7th Lord Clifford, came to her notice and she placed its translation also in Book II. The deed itself, which she remarked had a fine old seal of the Clifford arms, 'remains in the hands of Richard Marshall, a freeholder of Kirkby Stephen', the descendant of the original grantee.[31]

One separate manuscript survives which is proof not just of Anne's employment of Dodsworth but of her high regard for him. It comprises copies of charters of the late twelfth-century Walter and Richard de Clifford. Her marginal comment is worth quoting. 'Out of a greatefull Memory of her Pious Progenitors', it reads on the second folio , she 'hath caused this ensuing discourse to be Collected composed and dedicated A Dom 1648' (and interposed in her own hand) ' by her Goodfrind Mr Roger Dodesworth of Hutton Grange in Lancashire'. The question arises as to whether it could have been Dodsworth who oversaw the compiling of the Great Books. He worked for her in 1648 and is known to have spent 1649 in London delving in the Tower into the inquisitions and fine rolls, and so would have been at hand to advise.[32]

The case for Dodsworth or even Matthew Hale with his precise lawyer's mind is stronger than might at first appear. Anne's own annotations on Kniveton's original transcriptions show that the Books were begun much earlier than she says in the frontispiece. The documents concerning the Lords Clifford during Edward III's reign from 1327 were being entered in Book II from about fol. 128 in August and September 1648 so it must have been started perhaps in May. Widdrington's offering, received in July, was placed at fol. 177. Progress can be judged by the entries at folio 400 on 12 April 1649 of documents concerning John, 7th Lord, who died in 1422. Since the Books were not compiled in parallel, the first must have been finished in April or May 1648. The copy of this in the third set was sent to her at Appleby about April 1650. The copy of Book

II, 'the Bigest of them', had still not been completed then, although she expected it soon, and paper was being bought for Edward Langley to write the shorter Book III.[33] The proof that this was the third set is that Anne must have handled the first two sets at Baynard's to make her marginal comments in her own hand. When the scribe copied these in the third set, Anne was therefore in the north. She did insert some material in her own hand in the third set, but only in the third volume. Its foliation, too, is different.

Though Anne's household officers wrote the entries in the Books under the supervision of Dodsworth or someone like him, there is no doubt that it was she who masterminded the whole project. With Kniveton's two volumes as a guide, what was required in 1648 was to fit the old and the new documents into proper sequence. Anne would have required a skilled antiquary or lawyer to translate the medieval documents and understand them well enough to place them correctly. But, as was her wont, she checked everything and where misplacing had occurred her marginal annotations in the first two sets instructed the proper placing when the books were written out in the third set. It did not happen. The scribes merely copied her instructions.

However great the contribution of others, the Books of Record were incontrovertibly Anne's creation. True, her purpose kept faith with her mother's, to demonstrate her right title, but writing up all the transcriptions anew as a permanent record was her decision. The Books provided to Anne's satisfaction the complete documentary argument. Moreover, as Humphrey Hughes learnt, they were ready references and also quarries of information for her and her lawyers, a boon for them and their Thanet successors who also consulted them. The scholarly apparatus added enormously to their utility. One set was kept at Skipton Castle, another at Appleby and the third was provided for Hale's use at Lincoln's Inn while he acted as Anne's legal adviser.

Book III has to be considered separately because it differs in the respect that the record of past generations merges into the contemporary. Consequently, although it follows the same format as the first two Books it gives the impression of being more diffuse. The sections on the 1st and 2nd earls, ending at fol. 72, are as tightly presented as the first two Books devoted to the medieval lords. Then in the section on Earl George there is the first sign of Anne's straying because it includes, besides some of the relevant documents, Richard Robinson's description of his voyages, a filial tribute to ensure his maritime feats were not forgotten.

From fol. 95, where his section ends, Anne's approach does indeed change. She is dealing now, not with dead ancestors, but with her closest relatives whom she had known as an adult herself well able to make her own assessment of them and their activities. In effect, she offers essays about them, recollections in tranquillity which capture their essence. She devotes a great deal of space to her mother, in two separate entries, the fullest and most revealing of her pen-portraits which, through Williamson's and Gilson's publications, are well known and also have been drawn on in this study. The documents are fewer – the countess's 1593 jointure, the patent for founding Beamsley Hospital, the inquisitions taken in Westmorland and at York Castle in 1608 and the subsequent pleadings in the Court of Wards, the latter supplied by the Chancery clerks Carew and Tindall.

Anne even found room in Book III for Earls Francis and Henry, being prepared by 1648 to display magnanimity in victory. Though in a 'Summarie by way of digresion' she devoted only one folio to each of them, her comments are dispassionate. Her uncle Francis she recalls as an honourable gentleman of 'a good, noble, sweet and courteous nature'. Countess Grissell she describes as 'a prudent and a wise lady'. Her cousin Clifford (about whom previously she had hardly said a kind word) she commends as 'endowed with a good natural wit'. She would have noticed his similarity to her father, whose suits of armour he wore, because he was 'a tall and proper man, a good courtier, brave horseman, and an excellent huntsman, and had good skill in architecture and the mathematicks'.[34]

The rest of Book III is Anne's autobiography. It followed the same format as for her predecessors but as it burgeons it gives the impression of losing shape. She dealt first with her life before marriage as Lady Anne Clifford, but held to the basic purpose of the Great Books by including the two most apposite records of 1608, the patent to Earl Francis which is given in full and the Wards' documents emphasizing the debatable matter of the clause 'shuffled' into the Henry VI grant. Then follows the section covering her life as Countess of Dorset, the noteworthy records being the 1615 Common Pleas trial, the September 1616 pleas before the Lord President at York, and the King's Award. Her annotation on the latter lists in detail its defects which proved (in retrospect) to be to her advantage. In the succeeding section covering her life as Dowager Countess of Dorset, the documents included her 1628 petition to Charles I over her titles and her entries into the estates.

The final phase of her life falls under the heading 'The Course of her Life, while she was wife and widdow to Philip Herbert, Earl of Pembroke and Montgomery'. She maintained the format, following the pattern of previous owners who had two spouses. As has been seen, Anne was reticent about recording her activities during her twenty years' marriage to Pembroke, so that this study has had to tease them out from other sources. Its last phase, her journey north in July 1649 and Pembroke's death the following February, merge imperceptibly into the yearly 'memorial' or chronicle of her life as Dowager Countess of Pembroke, Dorset and Montgomery, with which she filled the remaining, spare folios of the Book.

This 'memorial' starting in early 1650 and ending in December 1675, three months before her decease, follows on from the 'Summaries' of the lives of her predecessors. As the first folios of the Books state, the summaries were not written in until 1652. There appears, likewise, to have been a long delay before the chronicle of her life was also begun; perhaps not until the summaries had been finished. There seems little doubt that Anne had decided in 1647/8 to follow up the compilation of the Great Books with a parallel history of her family. Spaces were deliberately left for the summaries to be written in near the end of each section, immediately after the records and before their listing. In theory, the summaries could have been composed while the Books were being written, but internal evidence makes clear that was not the case.

Anne stated that at the time the summaries were being drawn up her chief mansion house was the gallery and octagonal tower of Skipton Castle. She also commented on the execution of her relative, James Stanley, 7th Earl of Derby, who was beheaded at Bolton in Lancashire on 15 October 1651. She commented, also, that her Westmorland suits had started and were still depending, 'and God knows how long they may last', but her Craven disputes had mostly been reconciled. Anne resided a full year at Skipton from 14 February 1650 to 18 February 1651. She returned just over a year later, on 25 February 1652, and continued to live there until 29 November. For this and other reasons to be adduced later, the summaries would have been composed and entered in the Books during this second nine-months' stay in Skipton Castle. She was as busy and creative there as she had been at Baynard's.[35]

Anne's summary history of the generations of Viponts and Cliffords over the four centuries to Earl George's death is characterized by Dickens as 'diffuse, slow-moving and in detail repetitive'. It owed much to the records in the Books and to that extent was derived from them. Yet Anne, residing at Skipton and during 1651 also at Appleby, now had access to the castle's muniments, not just Dodsworth's notes. She was able, therefore, to flesh out the summaries with personal touches about her forebears drawn from letters, family traditions and also 'old Recordes and Chronicles'. One revealing comparison may be made. There are parallel comments on the Shepherd Lord's quarrels with his heir Sir Henry. In Book II, a document supplied by Dodsworth tells of the Shepherd's complaint against his son. Anne's marginal note explains it was set down so that 'Posterity maye avoyde the like sinne'. The summary repeated the story, but also cited letters from the Skipton evidences (most now lost) which underline and amplify that moral judgment.[36]

Anne's admittedly clumsy manner of presenting her material in the summaries reflects her tendency to compartmentalize the information rather than give a continuous narrative. Yet she displays more of an historian's sense of critical appraisal than she has been credited with. Her deep general knowledge of the past, the benefit of wide reading of Daniel, Camden and other authors, aided her assessment of, for instance, John the Butcher and the Shepherd Lord. How close she got to understanding the latter, even without access to modern published sources, may be judged from the present writer's study of him.[37] The intensity of feeling and involvement with all her forebears, the obsession with anniversaries, the moralizing and inimitable turns of phrase mark the summaries as Anne's own work.

The sections in Book III on her mother, her other relatives and herself continued the chronology of the summaries inserted into Books I and II up to 1650. Contrasting with them, the memorial of her life from 1650 to 1675 was very much a contemporary compilation. However, it was not a diary, though understandably it has been published as her *Diaries*. It did not record month by month or year by year, let alone from day to day, the happenings worthy of mention. Anne had it written up annually, mostly at the year's end, and later made additions and insertions. The effect of this is to appear to anticipate the outcome of events up to several years ahead. For instance, Anne frequently recorded the start of a long residence at a castle and in the same sentence when it ended. The dates of the death as well as the birth of grandchildren were mentioned together. At its most extreme, this practice can be disconcerting; for example, when she asserted in April 1656 that she made her first and last visit to the Dalston house at Melkinthorpe. Or in December 1660 when, dealing with the Dowager Queen Henrietta and the Thanets, she looked ahead to 1663 and even 1665. Furthermore, the paragraphs describing events in any one year were often out of chronological sequence. They are in as many as six different hands – 1663 is a case in point – because they were written by whichever household officer was available for Anne to dictate to, but this the published editions cannot show.[38]

The memorial, therefore, has to be approached with caution as an historical source because so much of it is retrospective. It has other shortcomings. There are long gaps during the deep winter months which suggest that little happened of note in her northern residences. Certainly there were fewer visits to her, not surprising in view of the difficulties of travel, especially to Westmorland. Yet from her household accounts the picture is of life continuing as normal and to that extent they supplement and correct the impression the memorial gives. Anne also padded out the year's events by describing what the Thanets, Corks and other relatives were doing. This was a natural human concern for and curiosity about their affairs, yet there was so much more she might have written about herself instead. She may consciously have been recording their lives for the benefit of their descendants. But the entries on them were the product of an external source of information, that is, the letters from her daughter Thanet and other members of her family which arrived by the weekly post and to which she replied in the same way. Even less satisfying is her inclusion of national and international news in the memorial. Certainly, it is proof that she did not lead an introspective, even cloistered life in the north. She regularly received the *London Gazette*. Other newsletters were brought to her by Edmond Sandford, 'the deafe Gentleman', author of the invaluable 'Relation' about the north-west. Near the end of her life, on 4 June 1674, she got tired of reading them and rewarded him with £1 on condition he brought her no more 'papers of newes'.[39]

However, quite the biggest defect of the memorial, as Chapters 7 and 8 have made clear, is the omission of the controversial issues. These Anne probably considered would reflect ill on her in her descendants' eyes. She did not subscribe to Cromwell's notion of depicting herself 'warts and all'. Even so, the memorial is an invaluable insight into her life-style and her attitudes, contrasting sharply with the meagre offerings about her first widowhood and then as Countess of Pembroke. The qualification to be borne in mind is that what Anne chose to reveal in her writings was guarded, the self-projection of an image as implicit in them as it was explicit in her pictorial displays for private as well as public and popular consumption.

Near the end of her life, it seems, Anne decided to have the summaries and memorial written out to provide a single, continuous manuscript record of her family's history from King John's reign until just three months before her own death. This original manuscript has not survived and is known only from eighteenth-century copies, of which the most accessible is British Library Harley MS. 6177. Its long general heading suggests the original, 'A Summary of the lives of the Veteriponts, Cliffords, and Earls of Cumberland, and of the Lady

Anne, Countess Dowager of Pembroke, Dorsett and Montgomery etc. daughter and heir to George Clifford, Earl of Cumberland, in whom the name of the said Cliffords determined. Copied from the original manuscript the 29th of December 1737 by Henry Fisher.'

Harley MS. 6177 has been published in parts, but not in its entirety; the early sections covering the two and a half centuries of the Vipont and Clifford lords up to John, the Butcher, 9th Lord, have not yet appeared in print. Dickens included the next sections – from the Shepherd Lord to Henry, 2nd Earl of Cumberland – with the Clifford letters he edited, illuminating both with meticulous scholarship. Gilson published the remainder in his *Lives*, and Clifford the last part, from Anne's arrival in the north in 1650 to 1675, in his *Diaries*. Other authors such as Williamson and Hugh Clifford drew on both the Harley MS. and Gilson for details of individual members or generations of the Clifford family. Whether there are grounds for an edited publication of the entire Harley MS. or the summaries themselves, the latter being the original material, will be considered below.

Anne left two other principal writings which have both now been published, the 'Knole Diary' and her 'day-book' for January to March 1676 up to her death. Of the two editions of the Knole Diary, by Vita Sackville-West in 1923 and Clifford in 1990, reference will mainly be made to the latter. Only four years of the 'diary' survive, for 1603 and then for 1616, 1617 and 1619. However, internal evidence indicates that its starting-date was before 1603 and it continued at least to 1620. In its surviving form, the diary was probably the product of Anne's sedentary and introspective years at Knole when she was out of countenance with Dorset at the height of the inheritance dispute and immediately afterwards. Indeed, the urge to record events in diary form may have been sparked by the death of her mother.

It looks, from Anne's own comments, as if she and Edward Marsh were jointly or individually noting down monthly, even daily, her activities during 1617 while at the same time writing up her 'diary' of a decade earlier. On 14 February 1617, Anne mentions that Marsh 'did write the Chroonicles of 1607', which is taken to mean the diary for that year, now missing. Again, on 1 April 1619 she records 'in the morning I wrote in the Chronicles' and on 27 December 'I spent the time as before in looking at the Chronicles'. The form of the diary for 1603 gives substance to the image of Anne recollecting the events of that year and dictating them to Marsh. It is continuous, lacking the divisions into months which characterize the 1616/19 diary. Some events described are out of place. One comment is clearly the product of the inheritance dispute. The resolving in her father's favour of the contention over carrying the king's sword in the city of York in 1603 elicits Anne's assertion that because it was an office by inheritance, it was 'lineally descended to me'. The language, expression and understanding are not girlish; indeed, there is a maturity in the words employed and in the comprehension of the political realities of the Jacobean Court well beyond that of a thirteen-year-old. Anne had a sharp memory, but in the 1603 diary she is not frightened to state that she does not remember certain details. Her marginal additions look to have been remembrances triggered by reading through Marsh's text.

The 1616/19 diary is much more a monthly and daily record, possibly kept in rough which Marsh wrote up for her afterwards and she then read, again adding marginal notes. However, the latter were very close to the events, unlike the 1603 additions. For example, Lord Chancellor Ellesmere was created Viscount Brackley (Anne writes Brakely) in November 1616 and her marginal comment must have been made before his death a few months later in 1617. In only one place did she look ahead to events. On 29 October 1619 she recorded that she did not stir out of her own bedchamber until 23 March 1620. This is the only clue that she continued the diary after 1619 and, granted her indisposition then, it is far from conclusive. She did, however, much later add the birthday of her future son-in-law Thanet, 11 December 1616.[40] The lack of notes from 1620 to July 1623 may suggest more lost years of the diary, although the fuller court life and her changed mood described in Chapter 4 could equally be the explanation. The twenty-six years from 1623 to 1649 Anne covered in the summary of her life, even if superficially and unsatisfactorily. There is no indication that she had at hand either a diary or even rough notes to consult in writing that account.

Anne's 'day-book' covering the eleven weeks of 1676 until her death on 22 March was appositely appended by Clifford to his edition of the *Diaries*. It has affinities with both the memorial of her life, which it continues and completes, and the 1616/19 Knole Diary. Yet it comes far closer than the latter to being a true diary, being dictated regularly at various times in the day, as the different hands reveal (Pl. 71). It is an intimate record of how she lived, albeit in advanced old age and confined to Brougham Castle and latterly to her chamber; a poignant picture of her slowly subsiding towards the grave. Nothing else reveals her private feelings, her attitudes, her relations with her friends and servants and her habits in quite the same way as the day-book. There are no inhibitions nor any disposition to hoodwink the reader about her condition or what she is doing.

Her mind was absorbed by the past almost as much as the present, anniversaries of events of fifty and sixty years before bringing memories flooding back which, duly described, happily make up for their omission from her Knole Diary. The existence of this single and quite brief day-book arouses a suspicion that Anne might have been a diarist in some form or other throughout her adult life, at least from her mother's death. Sedgewick asserts she 'kept in a large folio paper book a diary or journal, wherein she caused to be entered the occurences of the day, and all strangers that came to her house, whether upon visits or business'.[41] However, a record as detailed as the day-book throughout her life can be discounted. In old age there was abundant time and officers at hand for dictation. At court or at Wilton with Pembroke she would have lacked both time and privacy. At Baynard's Castle she would have had the time but until 1646 little worth the setting down by her criteria of self-justification. Much more likely would be a continuation of the Knole-type diary, though the argument against that happening remains as strong as when it was posited earlier in the chapter.

Besides the corpus of writings discussed above, numerous other documents which relate to some aspects of Anne's affairs survive in various repositories around the country, including genealogies and submissions to the courts for her titles and lands. The Queen's College, Oxford, submission looks as if it is a Kniveton original annotated by Langley. Hale's copy in Lincoln's Inn Library has attached to it the countess's submission to James I for her daughter's titles, which Anne must have given him. The countess's letters, notably those directed to Privy Councillors and others over the suits, were written up for Anne in a letter-book and sections of her Diaries bound with them.[42]

71. Front cover of Lady Anne's day book, 1676, with superimposed her silver gilt medal, obverse (Private collection. Photo: the author)

The two 'Hale' documents in the Hothfield MSS are of inestimable value. They are histories of the Viponts and Cliffords which Anne commissioned. Hale, apart from being her legal adviser and a judge of distinction, was a considerable antiquary. One extract he made from a Close Roll of Edward III's reign in the Tower of London was copied by Dodsworth and included in Book II, fol. 221.[43] The shorter history is 62 folios in length and is restricted to the Viponts from Robert, 1st Lord, to Isabella and her husband Roger Clifford the Younger. The other is a full history of 105 folios which incorporates much greater detail and continues up to Anne herself, though excluding Earls Francis and Henry. The heading of the shorter history is ambiguous:

THIS COPPY WAS TRANSCRIBED FOR MEE, IN JANUARY 1655,

OUT OF THE PAPERS OF COLLECTIONS OUT OF MY GREATE BOOKES

OF RECORDS OF MY AUNCESTORS COMPOSED BY MR MATTHEW HALE,

NOW ONE OF THE JUDGES OF YE COMMON PLEAS ATT WESTMINSTER

and added is the comment:

WHICH PAPERS WERE SENT MEE DOWNE BY MR HALE IN NOVEMBER 1651

72. *Chief Justice Sir Matthew Hale (1609–76), attrib. to J.M. Wright (The Treasurer and the Masters of the Bench of Lincoln's Inn)*

The most straightforward interpretation is that after the first set of Books had been completed at Baynard's Castle, Anne lent Hale her 'collections' of original papers. He 'composed' a manuscript history from them and in November 1651 returned them to Anne, who was then residing at Appleby Castle. In 1655 Anne had a transcription made, the shorter history, direct from the papers. A second, though less likely, view is that Hale masterminded the compilation of the Great Books, and having completed them by November 1651 returned the documents to her at Appleby. Both Bishop Nicholson and Whitaker correctly assumed that Hale had written the longer history and quoted from it, recognizing that it was the product of a very knowledgeable and incisive legal mind.[44]

Hale's history, it is clear, was derived from the same documentary material as the Books and he probably had the third set by him for reference. Indeed, the London-based Yorkshire antiquary Dr Nathaniel Johnston, whom Anne allowed to use it at Skipton Castle soon after its completion, believed that Hale had abstracted the details from 'the Countesse of Pembroke's great booke of Records'.[45] It is a cool, detached and factual work, tightly organized and argued, as would be expected. Its approach to the lives of the Viponts and Cliffords is legal and historical, judicious and balanced, if in a dry style. It can hardly be deemed superior to Anne's rather disjointed and committed story in her summaries because the same ground is covered and the sources were identical. Rather, Hale's history complements Anne's by concentrating on the legal evidence, especially land ownership, grants, transactions, jointures and wardship and livery.

Two particular aspects may be picked out for comment. First, Hale's original contribution is that he devoted the first fifth of his history to the Viponts from pre-Conquest times to the first Westmorland lord, which none of Anne's works had done and which Johnston latched on to. Second, he dealt succinctly with their successors. He picked out the salient facts of the lives of the Lords and their spouses, rearranged them to suit his narrative summaries and left out what he judged to be extraneous material. His section on Thomas, 6th Lord, is drawn from Book II, fols 297, 300/301, 299, 319/25, in that order. Whitaker, attracted by Hale's precision, preferred to print extracts from him instead of Harley MS. 6177 when relating the lives of the Cliffords from Roger the Elder's time to Thomas, 8th Lord. For this reason, any editing of the Harley history without incorporating Hale and the other extant manuscripts would be incomplete. In any case, Hugh Clifford's *The House of Clifford* covers the same ground.[46]

Hale's history would particularly appeal to Anne because it was directed to justifying her title to the inheritance. Hale understood better than anyone else the issues in the dispute. In his discussion, he lucidly presented the arguments and explained the course of the litigation, the Common Pleas' judgment of 1615 and the King's Award, which Whitaker again drew on for his description.[47] By ignoring Earls Francis and Henry (which not even Anne had done) Hale pointed to the direct line of succession from her father to herself. His heading for the section on her reiterated the historic rights and titles she most coveted, 'Anne Lady Clifford, 15th hereditary shreife, Baroness of Westmerland, 14th owner of ye Honor of Skipton, Baroness of Vescy'.

Anne's various manuscript books were one of her absorbing interests until the very end of her life. Her accounts mention which servants she paid for copying them. In May 1669, William Watkinson, then 'the chief writer of my books', was given 10s for his pencils for writing 'for mee out of ye ancient recordes of the Cliffords'. In June 1671, he was paid £1 10s 'for copying out of ye Great Booke of the Summary of my life containing four sheets of paper which is to be inserted into my Great Book at London'; a clue as to how the latter was kept up to date. Thomas Strickland gent. of Sizergh Castle, another officer, received £1 in October 1670 for writing in the 'Great bookes of ye Summary of my life'.[48] The extract he took for her on 27 August 1675 about her life in 1655 was bound into Book III of the third set at fols 58/9.

In these latter years, Anne frequently commissioned pedigrees and other works, enough to suggest a considerable output after she settled in the north. Strickland received £1 10s on 30 April 1669 for 'drawing over a coppy of an antient pedigree of the Cliffords & others of my Ancestors for mee'; how ancient may only be guessed. Watkinson was paid the same for a large pedigree of the Cliffords on 20 August. They repeated this work the next year, Watkinson between 25 July and 1 August, Strickland in October. It is just possible that these pedigrees were of the large-scale type for exhibition within her chambers, as in some noble establishments. Two copies were made of the book of Earl George's sea voyages. The first, in 1669, was probably written by Edward Guy of Appleby on Dutch horn paper he had bought for Anne at York. The second was done by Edward Fawcett, clerk of Kirkby Stephen, who was paid £1 10s for it on 28 March 1675. This volume was bound on 1 April at a cost of 6s by Michael Reynoldson, also of Kirkby.[49]

It is worth assessing Anne's literary achievement. She bequeathed to her Thanet successors four parallel histories of her forebears – the documents, the summary in the Great Books, the copied-out version, and Hale's work. In addition, they inherited the genealogies, submissions, other related manuscripts and the big collection of transcriptions from all manner of evidences on which the books were based, at least three copies – one illustrated – of Earl George's voyages and a volume of her mother's letters. It is possible to quibble at the use of such a term as 'histories' for Anne's compilations. They are not strictly history in the critical, objective sense which had appeared a little earlier in Camden's publications. But, equally, they are not antiquarian, because there was a purpose beyond the mere collection of records of the past for its own sake or out of curiosity. Anne's manuscript books blend elements of the two, chronology, family history and the presentation of documentary sources which, even if narrowly focused in intent, are wide-ranging both in origin and in their pointers to the national events which shaped the lives of her forebears. Few, if any, noble families could at that time boast so comprehensive a delineation of their history and it is even harder to identify one today. Moreover, in the Books of Record Anne collated the raw material for a comprehensive study of her family, impeccable in scholarship, which leaves modern researchers heavily in her debt. Her objective, the vindication of her rights, is present in the 'histories', yet it is not so obtrusive as to distort the picture because the interpretation, as Hale showed, was soundly based. Yet with the summary and memorial of her own life, caution has to be employed.

The Books of Record and their derivatives were the product of the driving imperative to attain justice and the admirable industry of Countess Margaret and her daughter, two intelligent, highly educated noble ladies whose achievement owed much to professional antiquaries, notably Kniveton and Dodsworth. For Anne, Samuel Daniel would be the first stimulant with his poem on Fair Rosamund. Deeper awareness would come from the lawsuits. Then followed a long drawn-out, self-educatory exercise starting with her commissioning of Kniveton's volumes. They provided substance and depth, placing in comprehensible sequence the documents which would have introduced her to her ancestors and their possessions. Thirty years later, Dodsworth opened her eyes further by taking her roots deeper into the Buillis and Viponts and their pre-Conquest origins and Clifford connections around Aconbury, Abbey Dore and Blyth. When Anne received Hale's work in 1655 she had an understanding of her family's past unmatched by anyone else before or since.

The generous format of the Great Books, the clear penmanship of the officers Anne instructed to do the writing and the colourful genealogical tables and drawings add greatly to the pleasure of studying them and understanding their *dramatis personae*. Moreover, interest is constantly sustained by Anne's additions, corrections and interpolations, which show that she meticulously examined all the entries not just when they were being written but for many years to come. The most endearing feature of these as of all Anne's histories is that she treats the whole family, the wives and children as well as lords, though the latter as title-holders and chief grantees require and are given the greater attention. The same principles apply and the identical material was presented in Anne's great pictorial achievement, the triptychs, which were also the product of her last years at Baynard's Castle and will be examined in detail in the following chapter.

CHAPTER 10

History and Legitimacy Proclaimed: The Visual Displays

No one in the Stuart era appreciated better than Lady Anne the power of publicity in projecting an image and propounding a cause. She had been reared in an atmosphere of royal pageantry, witnessing herself the progresses of Astraea, the Virgin Queen, Elizabeth I, and the artificial yet convincing aura which surrounded that monarch during a long reign. At the Caroline Court she had lived within the favoured circle enveloped by the apotheosis of majesty created for their royal patrons by the genius of Inigo Jones, Rubens and Van Dyck. She had indulged to a degree in self-publicity in Westmorland in 1616 and with her formal entries into her estates, and had learnt the adverse effects of anonymity when humiliated over the King's Award and during her years of separation from Pembroke.

Until Earl Henry's death any thoughts of self-projection by her would have been meaningless. New vistas opened up after the fall of Skipton Castle. She could then anticipate travelling north to take over her patrimony. Her northern neighbours and dependants would mostly be ignorant about her, though they would quickly learn from her journeyings and assertion of her seigneurial authority. But to inculcate in them her own perception of her high noble lineage and unique status she would need to resort to forms of public display which would project her as baroness and sheriffess and proclaim her Clifford and Vipont origins and inherited rights. Once begun, she never ceased this campaign of self-justification. By the end, she had re-created features of the Cliffords' visual heritage destroyed during the Civil Wars; or, rather, her version of it, because her personality and her interpretation of their history were as indelibly stamped as in her Books of Record.

The triptychs begun at Baynard's Castle in 1646 were the first as well as the most ambitious and complex of Anne's pictorial and written displays of her rank and titles. They are also the most difficult to interpret; yet, once done, this provides the key to her other forms of self-publicity. There were two versions of the triptych, one kept at Appleby and intended for Lady Margaret, her Westmorland heiress, and a second at Skipton Castle for Lady Isabella. The Skipton version eventually deteriorated and was destroyed. Nevertheless, much is known about it. Because it was more accessible, scholars tended to study it rather than the Appleby version. The Leeds antiquarian Ralph Thoresby spent eight hours copying the Clifford pedigrees from it on 9 June 1684. An unidentified chronicler of the Clifford family saw it in the middle of the eighteenth century. So did Pocock, the historian of the Tufton family, before the close of that century. Whitaker examined it when compiling his History of Craven. George Perfect Harding made a careful, small-scale water-colour of it in 1835, with the precise attention to detail required for an intended engraving, which he never executed. His painting reveals that in certain respects the versions differed, a matter which will be discussed as these visitors' impressions are considered below.

Pocock described the Skipton triptych as 'a curious picture in form of an altar-piece or three-leaved screen'. Anne herself called each wing a 'leaf or door case'. The medieval religious triptych form proved admirably adaptable to her purposes, for a variety of reasons. Altarpieces were intended to fold shut, only being opened at specific times. The hinged wings of the Appleby triptych (though not the centre panel) have heavy wooden backs which, when closed, give protection. Anne's triptychs could be permanently fixed to a wall, as Pocock noted, and kept closed when she was absent, being opened out to reveal their full glory for public admiration when she was in residence. The religious connotation of altarpieces was not misplaced. Secular features in their themes were common and there is an element of exaltation and worship in Anne's depiction of her family.

Even with its wings folded, the Appleby triptych (on which much of the following description is based) would require a large wall on which to hang it, far greater when opened. Including the wooden frame, it stands 9 feet high, its centre panel is 10 feet wide and each side-leaf 4 feet wide, giving overall dimensions of 10 x 9 feet shut, 18 x 9 (549 x 274 cm) open. Though lower in height than the Great Picture of the Pembroke family at Wilton, it opens out wider and challenges it in area. So huge a composition matched the ambition of Anne's project. The 'Pembroke Family' was not necessarily the inspiration. Another very large painting, the 'Table of Ceres' done by a great master, hung in Wilton's great hall, as Aubrey relates. Most likely there were triptychs in the collection. Anne's Cork relations owned a triptych which she might have known about though would not have seen. This was the 'Donne Triptych', by Memlinc, now in the National Gallery, London, which had been brought to Londesborough by Countess Grissell. On the other hand, Anne would have viewed the splendid St John triptych with its family grouping and heraldic genealogies in St Mary's church, Lydiard Tregoze, Wiltshire, on her visits to her relatives there. Quite possibly, too, she would have seen the big Courtenay triptych at Powderham Castle in Devon, near the Russell house at Exeter. Moreover, she was conversant through the Arundel and royal collections with other composite paintings. She rigorously directed the Anglo-Flemish painter she employed. He did not enjoy the inspirational licence Pembroke had allowed Van Dyck. Anne's outlay on her two large paintings may be surmised by comparison with her husband's great picture which cost him at least £500 in 1636 and was valued at his death at £1,000.[1]

The Appleby triptych is often, though mistakenly, called the 'Great Picture'. Anne is explicit that the Great Picture is the centre panel (see Frontispiece). By contemporary English standards even that was a large canvas. Its purpose was commemorative. Anne states that the four standing figures of her parents and brothers and the four smaller portraits in gilt frames of her four aunts, Derby, Wharton, Warwick and Bath, were copied from paintings made about the beginning of June 1589 and completed in 1646 'in memoriall of them'.[2] The scene is not an instance frozen in time like the 'Pembroke Family' because it does not record a particular or historical episode. The Cliffords are a composite creation, bound together by relationship, supposedly at the family gathering on the eve of Earl George's departure for the Azores, but mainly because Anne had been conceived on 1 May and she was present in the tableau *in utero*, the unseen focus of the group as her inscription makes clear.

The Great Picture, therefore, is Anne's memorial of her family and a construct of their relationships. She may have considered that in 1646 a painting was the only practicable memorial available to her. Church monuments and stained glass, the traditional forms of commemoration, were ruled out because of their widespread destruction by religious extremists and not just because she had as yet no access to her northern castles and churches. Pictures fared better, except for the royal collection, and what Anne planned could be completed in the privacy of her own home which, appositely, was safe because of Pembroke's standing as a Parliamentarian grandee. Through the medium of painting, Anne could pay her respects to all her family including its head, her father. In 1646 there was no certainty that she would have the chance to erect a monument to him as she had to her mother. Commissioning and composing the Great Picture would have been for her a welcome distraction from the worrying collapse of royalism and the Anglican Church. Yet overseeing the creation of the triptychs was emotionally a highly charged experience and that has to be borne in mind in considering her purpose.

At one level the Great Picture comprises in its depictions of the eight figures and in their highly detailed, related inscriptions a biography of Anne's immediate family. They and the spans of their lives were re-created, though all were now dead and either she had never known or she barely could have remembered her brothers and her aunts Wharton and Derby. Brought to life before her eyes, they would recall her younger days and give companionship and a sense of pride. Her extended family, interlinking in the portraits and coats of arms six noble houses, sparkles with quality, riches and status, through dress, demeanour, pearls, jewels, furnishings, medallions, Garter knighthoods and armour. No viewer could be left in doubt as to the status of Anne's parents and their relatives. For Anne's descendants, the Great Picture would be a colourful, pictorial instruction about their roots in the rarified ranks of the high Elizabethan nobility. One point worth noting here is that, even if the ladies predominate, matriarchalism is not intended, as will be explained below.

The portraits of Anne's brothers are the most pleasing in the tableau and are good likenesses of the surviving originals, made it is thought by a pupil of Robert Peake the Elder, though they are identically dressed. For all the other portraits, there are problems in accepting Anne's statement that the originals were made in early June 1589. Lady Derby, then nearing fifty, and Lady Warwick, well into her forties, are flattered, though the depiction of the latter is recognizably her at a much younger age. By mistake the inscription for Warwick was transposed with that of her sister Bath. According to Strong, there is only one authentic portrait of Countess Margaret, by the Yorkshireman George Gower, with several copies mostly dated 1585. No full-length portrait is known. That in the Great Picture, Slowe has pointed out, was worked up from the same prototype, 'which poses an intriguing dichotomy of dates'.[3] In life the countess was probably more petite in build, like her daughter, the earl being tall for an Elizabethan. Yet the overall impression is of a good likeness of her in authentic dress, though at a younger age than in 1589.

The real difficulty is with Earl George. As Holmes has noted, the painter was not familiar with Elizabethan armour. The earl could not have put on the velvet tunic when he was already harnessed and, in fact, it was intended to be worn beneath the armour. Moreover, the Earl's position, in front his wife but with his right arm interlinked with hers, 'is awkward, and indeed practically impossible'. Unwittingly a pose which was intended to demonstrate their unity implies some distance between them. However, what is crucial is that the painter took liberties with the armour, suggesting he had no full-length portrait of the earl to copy. It is closest to the famous Hilliard miniature of the earl as Queen's Champion and he makes the same mistake at the collar. In 1646 the armour itself was inaccessible in Skipton Castle whereas the miniature should have been in Anne's possession. However, that was not executed until 1590/1, so either a portrait unknown today was at hand or Anne's dating is questionable.

There are other chronological dissonances. The earl did not receive the honour of the Garter until 1592, yet the painter shows him wearing its blue riband across his chest, the St George badge at his left hip and the Garter itself buckled over his armour at the left knee. His coat of arms above his head, likewise, is encircled with the Garter. These are acceptable embellishments considering the honour of the award and, Holmes suggests, were later additions, perhaps at Anne's request. However, they widen the chronological latitudes around the supposed dating. To draw attention to these discrepancies is not to carp at Anne's lapses from strict accuracy but to put the record straight. Directing the painter to his sources would not have been easy. Nearly sixty years after the event, her understanding of an occasion she knew about only at second hand could not have been secure.

In any case, the significance of early June 1589 was as the countess's confirmation that she had conceived Anne and only she could have been the source of that information. Anne's presence *in utero* makes her the central feature of the Great Picture because her prime object was to demonstrate the legitimacy of her inheritance. There are affinities with 'The Family of Henry VIII: An Allegory of the Tudor Succession' (attrib. to Lucas de Heere *c.* 1572) which Anne could well have seen in the Walsingham house at Scadbury, near Chislehurst in Kent. The artist depicts the Tudor inheritance as being directed by Henry VIII to his heir Edward VI and from him, after a divisive tenure by Mary I and Philip II, it devolved on Queen Elizabeth, 'to England's joy'. Elizabeth ushers in peace and prosperity. In the Great Picture, Countess Margaret gestures to her sons, after whose deaths Anne was the lawful successor but her uncle and cousin intervened, 'detayning' the inheritance from her. Significantly, it is her mother who makes explicit the chain of succession, not her father who appears to stand apart. Herein might lie the reason for the conspicuous absence of male relatives. Francis Clifford and Lord Wharton supported Earl George in excluding Anne, whilst in 1605 the earls of Warwick and Derby were dead and the earl of Bath seems to have been a bystander in Clifford matters.[4]

The most testing problem is the difference between the two versions of the triptych. What is crucial is the reliability of Harding's water-colour copy of the Skipton triptych, which is at Woburn Abbey. Williamson compared the central panel, the Great Picture, of the Skipton version when it was still in good condition at Hothfield Place with Harding's painting and also with a photograph of the Appleby version. He affirmed that Harding was correct in omitting four inscriptions because, although they appeared in the Appleby triptych, they did not in the Skipton version. 'Furthermore', he continued, 'the detail, notably in the column of the archway of the Hothfield picture, is more elaborate than in the Appleby one, and this fact Harding sets forth clearly.'

Williamson could have been more explicit. Harding, in fact, shows that behind the archway is an alcove or corridor, perhaps a room, and that the curtain behind Earl George is partly drawn across it from the right. The framed portraits of the Russell sisters and the shelf of books below them are within the alcove, well set back therefore from the tableau of the earl's family. Although it is visible in the Appleby triptych, there is a far greater three-dimensional feeling about the alcove in the Harding painting and, by inference, in the Skipton version.[5]

There is so much variation in the visitors' description of the triptych's colouring, made even more confusing by Harding's Woburn copy being blue, slate and sand in its tones, that any detailed discussion here would be sterile. For his 1878 edition of *Craven*, Morant examined the Appleby triptych to amplify Whitaker's description based on the Skipton version. He denotes its overall shading as subdued brown, reddish brown, and gold. The earl wears a 'brown tunic', the countess a 'rich brown brocaded gown' with a 'white satin brocaded petticoat' and 'light white brocaded' sleeves. The child Francis wears 'a blue frock, brocaded with gold and having tight yellow sleeves'.[6] Well over a century has passed since Morant scrutinized the Appleby triptych and the colours can have changed little. In fact, the countess's gown is a very dull purple, easily mistaken for brown. The background on the left wing is a greenish grey, with the pillar darker; on the right wing, grey. The curtains are russet-brown. New techniques of analysing pigmentation would help settle issues about the original colouring.

There is no lack of richness in the Appleby costumes, but Countess Margaret's raises more uncertainty. All her portraits, after Gower, show her in black, the standard Elizabethan colour for women which showed off pearls and lace to great effect, as in the four inset portraits. The purple or brown of the Great Picture may have been to match the earl who is known to have purchased tawny attire, both velvet cloaks and satin doublets.[7] If so, then the painter again took liberties which Anne must have found acceptable. What does need stressing is that the painting is of very high quality.

It has been suggested that Anne commissioned either Jan Van Belcamp or Remigius Van Lemput, both first-rate copyists and good painters in their own right. Yet Belcamp's known work at Knole and Van Lemput's hardly seem good enough. Moreover, there are variations, Anne's head in the right wing being noticeably more luminous. A painter of the calibre of Peter Lely, who at about the same time did the prototype head-and-shoulders portrait of Anne, is a possibility. The employment of more than one painter was customary in studios. Without documentary proof this is an open question. An appealing element is the touch of whimsy by the painter, seen at the tip of Lord Francis's scroll, the elf on the tendril, droll human and animal faces, one a lion, on the drapes, which lightens the severity of the tableau's composition.

The wings of the triptych belong to Anne, encapsulating her life. When half-opened, they appear in one sense mirror images of the same person four decades apart, though there is an element of chronological continuity. The left wing pinpoints in its portrait Anne as a girl of fifteen, yet the inscription in the scroll near her head describes the events of her first forty years up to her marriage with Pembroke in 1630, its detail amazing considering how little space was available. The right posits Anne still as Countess of Pembroke, although now she holds noble titles and properties in her own right. The wings, indeed, indicate Anne at the age when she expected to and should have inherited from her father and forty years later when she had done so. The inscription in the right wing, placed on the table under her hand, ends with Isabella's marriage in July 1647. It is necessarily shorter than the other, but she left space for its completion after her death, which her successors failed to carry out. There is more than elapsed time in the facing images; the freshness of youth has given way to the careworn look of a woman who has experienced the buffeting of life.

In obvious ways the scenes on the wings balance each other – the pose of the figure, the table covers, bookshelves and the double portraits on the walls of persons who had greatly inflenced different phases of Anne's life. The painter has cleverly picked out the dress colours in the table covers. In one important respect, however, they are different. There is the same chronological latitude surrounding the fifteen-year-old girl on the left as noted previously. Her features are based on a head-and-shoulders miniature at that age which only survives in David des Granges's later copy. The hour-glass, music and embroidery were hers then, as mentioned in Chapter 1, though there could be symbolism in the first with its connotation of the passage of time. The lozenge coat of arms hanging from the scroll denotes Anne's single status. Her dress, however, would be the oldest still in her possession, its green-tinged sheen suggesting the seawater-green satin costume Anne ordered in 1617 when coming out of mourning. She had learned to play the bass lute in 1603 but the instrument leaning against the table is a lute of post-1630 date. The framed portraits of her tutor Daniel and governess Mrs Taylor are testimony to Anne's appreciative remembrance of them. Daniel's resembles the engraving in his *Works*.

To Anne's eyes, she was 'lively depicted' at the age of fifteen. Yet, the portrait on the right wing is the only one in the triptych which could have been taken from life. Anne wears a matronly rich black satin dress set off with lace and pearls and a matching head-dress. In Holmes's words, 'the firmness and muscular tension' of her face have gone, 'the cheeks are beginning to sag with a

73. *Portrait of Samuel Daniel, with books displayed, inset, left-hand panel, the Appleby Triptych (Reproduced by courtesy of Abbot Hall Art Gallery, Kendal. Photo: the author)*

74. Portrait of Mrs Anne Taylor, with books displayed, inset, left-hand panel, the Appleby Triptych (Reproduced by courtesy of Abbot Hall Art Gallery, Kendal. Photo: the author)

suggestion of puffiness and flabbiness'. After several years mewed up in Baynard's Castle this is not surprising. On the wall hang portraits of her two husbands, both good copies. She would have owned the originals and the painter would have seen Pembroke in the flesh. Their coronets and Garters shed honour on Anne too.

After Isabella's marriage, Anne was left alone and a cat and a dog are shown as her companions. She owned cats and this one is alertly watchful with a resemblance to an owl, the ancient symbol of wisdom, which is regarded as appropriate to a book-strewn room. A dog symbolizes loyalty, fidelity and constancy, all qualities admired by Anne. This Italian greyhound or whippet was a fashionable dog, popular at court. The pattern of the Turkey carpet is of mid-seventeenth-century date and would denote richness. The high-quality table carpet is suitably dark, matching the sombre hues of Anne's dress and the pillar.[8]

The display of books in the triptych (Table 5) has attracted scholarly comment with suggestions that they are a clue to Anne's youthful education under Daniel's guidance and also demonstrate her closet library.[9] However, her object in displaying, to use her words, 'those books hereafter ensuing depicted and Titled', was to illustrate further the memorial of her family. They were, it will be argued, her parents' books as much as her own, representing a part of her own collection which had been garnered by inheritance, purchase and probably also donation. If there is symbolism in how they were placed, then it implies the ordered life of the countess in the centre panel, Anne's own structured childhood in the left, and a sense of her casual, if regular, use of literature in later life. In either case, they are a metaphor for the course of her family's as well as her own affairs between 1589 and 1649.

Giving and receiving books was a friendly and often ritualistic act. Moreover, books in themselves were friends, a familiar and reassuring presence offering instant access to, and interplay with, learned and imaginative minds and polemical engagement. Most of the English authors shown were, indeed, friends or acquaintances of either Anne's parents or herself and were now all dead. Earl George had been at Elizabeth's Court with Sidney, Spenser (who had dedicated a volume to him), Greville and Camden. George Sandys was his godson. Countess Margaret, likewise, would have met them, and knew Greville well.[10] Anne was godmother to the present Fulke Greville, who was descended from Sir Fulke's cousin and, more appositely, was grandson of Francis, 4th Earl of Bedford.[11] The countess's and Anne's closeness to Daniel and Florio, and Anne's also to Donne, Herbert and Wotton, need not be laboured.

The intellectual scope of Anne's library is not surprising. The Cliffords were a highly educated and literate family, the 2nd Earl, for instance having an excellent library, as Anne had affirmed in her summary of him in Book III.[12] Anne found solace in reading, would have relished in her happier moments wrestling with the more abstruse and disputatious of the authors and looked fondly on the works of Daniel, Herbert and others who had been part of her life. Sedgewick affirms that 'she was an indefatigable reader, and had a library stored with very choice books, which she read over, not cursorily, but with judgment and observation'. She could give a good account, he tells us, of most

TABLE 5 *Books displayed in the Appleby Triptych*

LEFT WING

1 *On the Floor* (from top to bottom)
W. Camden, *Britannia* (tr. Philemon Holland, 1610)
A. Ortelius, *Theatre of the Whole World* (tr. M. Coignet, 1603)
C. Agrippa, *The Vanity of the Arts and Sciences* (tr. J. Sandford, 1575)
M. Cervantes, *Don Quixote* (tr. Thomas Shelton, 1612)

2 *On the Lower Shelf*
(i) *Standing* (left to right)
P. De La Primaudaye, *The French Academy* (3 vols, tr. 1586)
B. Castiglione, *The Courtier* (tr. Thos. Hoby, 1561)
(ii) *Lying* (top to bottom)
Tasso, *Godfrey of Bulloigne* (tr. Edward Fairfax, 1600)
L. Le Roy, *The Variety of Things* (tr. R. Ashley, 1594)
S. Daniel, *Chronicles of England* (1612), tutor to the young Lady
Lord Michel de Montaigne, *Essays* (tr. John Florio, 1603)
John Gerard, *Herbal* (1597)

3 *On the Upper Shelf*
(i) *Lying left* (top to bottom)
P. Sidney, *Arcadia* (1593)*
E. Spenser, *Works* (1609)
Ovid, *Metamorphoses* (tr. Golding, 1565)
(ii) *Standing*
The Holy Bible
St Augustine, *City of God* (tr. J. Healy, 1610)
Eusebius, *History of the Church* (1577)
Joseph Hall, *Works* (1621)
(iii) *Lying above*
The Manuel of Epictetus (tr. 1567)
Boethius, *Book of Philosophical Comfort* (tr. 1556)*
S. Daniel, *All the Works in Verse*, tutor to the young Lady
(iv) *Lying right* (top to bottom)
J. Downham, *The Christian Warfare* (1604)
S. Du Bartas, *Divine Weeks and Works* (tr. J. Sylvester, 1620)*
Chaucer, *Works* (1561)

GREAT PICTURE

1 *In Countess Margaret's hand*
The Book of Psalms

2 *On the shelf* (top to bottom)
Ms of Alchemical Extractions*
Seneca
The Holy Bible

RIGHT WING

1 *Under Lady Anne's Hand*
The Holy Bible
P. Charron, *Book of Wisdom* (tr. out of French into English 1612)

2 *On the lower shelf above* (left to right)
G. Strode, *Anatomy of Mortality* (1618)
Plutarch, *Lives*, in French
F. Guicciardini, *History* (in French, tr. from Italian 1568)
Plutarch, *Morals*, in French
Sir Francis [Fulke] Greville, Lord Brooke, *Works* (1633)
G. Hakewill, *Apologie of the Power and Providence of God* (1618)
Sir Henry Wotton, *The Elements of Architecture* (1624)

3 *Upper Shelf*
(i) *Tumbled* (left)
G. Sandys, *Paraphrase upon the Psalms of David* (1636)
P. de Commines, *History* (tr. 1596)
John Moore, *A Mappe of Mans Mortalitie* (1617)
Ben Jonson, *Works* (1616)
John Donne, *Poems* (1633)
(ii) *Standing* (left to right)
Henry Cuffe, *The Difference in the Ages of Mans Life* (1603, 1633, 1640)
George Herbert, *Poems* (1633)
John Barclay, *Argenis* (tr. 1625)
M.A. Antoninus, *Meditations* (tr. 1557, Casaubon, 1635)
John King, *Sermons* (1606)
(iii) *Lying right* (top to bottom)
William Austin, *Meditations* (1635)
John Donne, *Sermons* (1640)
A. Marcellinus, *Roman Historie* (tr. Philemon Holland, 1609)

* See Appendix II
Source: the Appleby Castle Triptych. For the titles actually inscribed on the triptych, see Williamson, pp. 498–500, and for the difficulties in ascribing editions, pp. 339–44.

---

histories then extant in the English tongue. One example of the deep impression they could make on her will suffice. Her famous comment that 'the marble pillars of Knole and Wilton were to mee oftentimes but the gay Arbours of Anguish' was a phrase remembered from *Arcadia*, 'Come from marble bowers, many times the gay harbour of anguish'.[13]

Attributing original ownership of the books in the triptych is not straightforward. Some allowance has to be made for the replacement of earlier editions. Earl George would have owned, and his countess almost as likely, the three indispensable instruction books of Elizabethan courtesy and manners – Castiglione's *The Courtier* (1561), Spenser's *Faerie Queene* (1590) and Sidney's *Arcadia* (1593). The early published histories – Ovid's *Metamorphoses* (1565), the two volumes of Plutarch's works and Guicciardini's history (1579), all three in French, and Commine's memoirs (1596) – were more likely the earl's, because the countess knew no foreign tongue. But, equally, they may have been Dorset's, obtained during his stay in France. Maps were Earl George's province, as an expert navigator and oceanic privateer. Ortelius's work of 1603 with dividers nearby suggests a gift to his daughter to further her awareness of the outside world; if not, then it is a memorial to him. The later published histories, Tasso's romance of the First Crusade *Godfrey of Bulloigne* (1600), Marcellinus on Rome (1609), Camden (1610) and Daniel (1612) have more of Anne's stamp on them than her mother's. With them she could fruitfully have passed her time during Dorset's absence abroad. Her historical phase continued with reading a history of the Low Countries from her mother's library at Brougham in September 1616, Sandys's history of the Turks borrowed from her husband's closet in January 1617 and her mother's copy of the Book of Josephus in December 1619.[14]

The centre panel unequivocally belongs to Countess Margaret as owner of not only the Book of Psalms in her left hand but the Bible, the stoic Seneca's *Works* in translation and the manuscript volume of alchemical extractions and distillations which had come from Brougham. These, as Parry has remarked, were her 'defences against the world'.[15] If the archway was meant as leading into an alcove, then that could have represented her closet study and the books she shared with her sisters whose portraits look down on her. Yet the countess, renowned for her stoicism, religious devotions and Puritanism, must also have owned all the Elizabethan publications on those subjects (her sisters, too, independently) and perhaps some of those of later date. They comprise the books of religious instruction, Eusebius (1577), the Puritan John Downham (1604), Bishop King's *Sermons* (1606) and possibly St Augustine (1610). Healy's translation of the latter was dedicated to Pembroke, his elder brother Earl William and the earl of Arundel. Besides Seneca, there are three standard works by stoic authors, Boethius (1556), Epictetus (1567) and Antoninus (1577), and the modern French neo-stoicism of Pierre Charron's *Book of Wisdom* (1612). To judge by Anne's pose in the right-hand panel, that copy of Charron and her Bible had become the mainstays of her existence when the triptych was composed. In 1651, it will be recalled, it was the uplift Chaucer gave her that she wanted John Selden to know about.[16]

Countess Margaret, with her searching mind, would have been continually exercised with the questions of the state of nature and decline examined by Cornelius Agrippa (1575), the three-volumed *French Academie* (1586), Louis Le Roy (1594) and Henry Cuffe (1603). Gerard's *Herbal* (1597) was an essential source for her medical distillations, which she noted in a manuscript volume of her own. Two more of her books, not shown here, were mentioned in Chapter 4, Harrington's 'In Praise of a Solitary Life' and 'Leicester's Commonwealth'.[17]

These inherited volumes, over half those displayed, were the core of Anne's library shown in the triptych. To her favourite reading, Ovid, Chaucer, Spenser, Sidney and possibly Tasso, only *Don Quixote* (1612) was added. The more demanding of her mother's books which Anne added to her own library rehearsed arguments and viewpoints which had exercised her parents' generation. She would have studied them while at Knole and may have turned back to them periodically in her maturer and more reflective years. Kniveton's volumes of family records, though avid reading about the same time as 'Leicester's Commonwealth', were it must be remembered also a kind of lawyer's brief to equip her to continue fighting her cause.

Throughout her life Anne regularly added new authors to her library, those in vogue and with novelty and dealing with the topics currently under debate. Daniel's *Chronicles* (1612) and Florio's translation of Montaigne's *Essays* (1603) could well have been presentation copies, the latter perhaps in September 1616 when Dorset's officers read them to her.[18] Ben Jonson's *Works* (1616) would have been unalloyed pleasure, bringing back memories of her participation in his court masques. Anne's moods of despair over the next two years are captured by Moore's *A Mappe of Mans Mortalitie* (1617) and Strode's *Anatomy of Mortality* (1618). Knowing how best to approach death and die well were attributes of titled men and women. Anne still obviously valued them in 1649 and her death, often anticipated, when it eventually came about upheld convention.

There are two clear strands in Anne's acquisitions after she recovered from the worst of her trauma. The first gives the impression of an intelligent, concerned woman keeping abreast of current political and religious issues and controversies, the very stuff of informed debate. The second is recognition of the dues of friendship. Hakewill's *Apologie* (1618) continued the debate on the state of nature posited in the earlier volumes which had come into Anne's possession. Joseph Hall's moderate Calvinistic writing of 1621 reflects the growing concern among Anglicans of Anne's bent which came to the fore as James I's Parliament met after an interval of seven years. The Roman Catholic John Barclay's *Argenis* was a work she much commended to Bishop Rainbow because he criticized Cardinal Bellarmine for allowing too much authority, including temporal, to the Pope. It is particularly interesting to witness Anne informing herself about the more high church tenets of Austin (1635) when Laudianism, with Charles I's blessing, was in full spate.

With all the other authors Anne had personal connections, whatever the religious or metaphysical slant of their writings. First, in 1620, came Joshua Sylvester's dedication to Anne of his translation of Salluste Du Bartas's *Divine Weeks and Works*, which Parry calls 'a delightful encyclopaedia of natural history' not overburdened with doctrine. In 1624 her relative Sir Henry Wotton published his study of architecture with, as has been mentioned, his views of hospitality subsumed. There were three publications dating from 1633, when Anne was at the hub of cultural life at court, the poems of Pembroke's relative and chaplain, her friend George Herbert, John Donne's and also Greville's collected writings which included his 'Letter to a Countess', intended most likely for her mother. Donne's poems she would have found a feast of the erotic and the sacred. The emotional and escapist appeal of her reading deserves special study; but this is not the place.[19] By 1636 Anne was again in need of the spiritual uplift of George Sandys's *Paraphrase upon the Psalms of David* and in the same vein would be Donne's *Sermons* of 1640. Then, it would appear, her outlay on literature temporarily ended.

On the eve of the Civil Wars her library comprised (or at least she chose to exhibit) almost fifty volumes. The qualification is important. Apart from those which remained at Appleby, many, annotated in her own hand, were in the evidence room at Skipton Castle when Whitaker examined the family papers. Happily, they were listed in 1739, altogether sixty-three, comprising twenty-two in manuscript and forty-one printed books, most of which had belonged to Anne's parents and all to herself (App. II). They were her family's books, which she had requested in her will should remain as heirlooms in the castle. Combined with those displayed in the triptych, they give a far better notion of the range of writings garnered by a noble family with wide political and religious involvements. Among them were early manuscript extracts from Sylvester's translation of Du Bartas, which would explain the dedication to Anne; Plutarch on education, Roger Bacon on alchemy, and Isaac Casaubon; a manuscript copy of part of Daniel's 'Civil Wars'; foreign publications; and the lives of the ill-fated Earl of Essex and the recusant Lady Magdalen Dacre, Earl George's aunt who had helped bring him up at Battle Abbey.[20] But Anne also owned two 'Great Books of Mercator' which she lent Sir John Lowther in September 1668 and which almost certainly were her father's.[21] Precise attribution of ownership is muddied by the knowledge that several books and manuscripts from the 1739 list and possibly also on view in the triptych had originated with the Sackville family.

It is worth considering the lacunae in the triptych display. The towering giants by today's criteria, Shakespeare and Milton, are absent, likewise Raleigh, Sir Francis Bacon and James I. In view of the Pembrokes' patronage, Shakespeare's absence is a little surprising, especially as the Lords Clifford figured in his histories and, by an understandable slip, Earl George as 'Clifford of Cumberland'.[22] She may have had political and personal reservations about the others. Milton was a Parliamentarian apologist, Bacon a Cecilian who opposed her mother and herself and was hostile to the Westmorland tenants who stood up to her uncle, and King James had proved too partial to Dorset and her uncle Francis. Anne was aware of her father's privateering associations with Raleigh and had visited Lady Raleigh just before they were freed from the Tower in January 1616. By the time his *History of the World* was published in 1634, her own historical attention had long veered towards her family's past.

Anne found no room for Michael Drayton, whom Fair Rosamund had entranced and who included Earl George's successful 1589 attack on the Azores in his verse-history *Poly-Olbion*. But Drayton was beyond the pale perhaps because Earl Edward was his patron.[23] Most surprising is that she exhibited no woman author on the triptych's shelves, not even Aemilia Lanyer who, as described in Chapter 1, had been so close to her and her mother. Maybe their style or content was not to her taste. However, to comment on missing authors is in a sense quibbling, whatever reasons may be adduced. Anne's library had admirable scholarly breadth and depth and its pictorial representation is unique. What needs bearing in mind is that the books were a memorial to her family and in their accumulation over two generations declaim her mother's literary interests even more than her own. It is evident that both ladies actually read the books portrayed. They were not shown in the triptych just to impress, although that function was served. Most of the authors and titles would be familiar to visiting nobility, gentry and clergy and appraised approvingly.

On the vertical borders of the Great Picture, Anne backed up and extended her pictorial claim of legitimate inheritance by an astonishing genealogical display of shields and potted biographies, their shapes and colour enhancing the whole composition. In one sense they can be taken as an amplification of the memorial to her family, a glorification through its origins and the constellation of great houses with whom the Cliffords had intermarried. The chronological context is enormous, six centuries from before the Norman Conquest until Lady Isabella's wedding in 1647. Thirty-six shields were planned, but those for the two earliest, Richard and William Fitzpons, were left blank for lack of certainty about them; commendable scholarship, although modern research shows Anne missed a generation or two.

The shields with their inscriptions were placed so that a viewer could read them from the bottom upwards. The right-hand sequence proclaims Anne's unbroken Westmorland title – the seventeen shields up to her father's, who was the seventeenth hereditary sheriff and baron of Westmorland, a recurrent theme in the discussion that follows. The sequence starts, like the Books of Record, with Robert, 1st Lord Vipont, who was endowed with the sheriffwick and barony in 1203/4 by King John. His Vipont arms impale his wife's Builli coat, which would remind Anne of the priories of Blyth and Roche and the Honour of Tickhill. Next above, John, 2nd Lord's Vipont arms are joined with the Ferrers', who were thought to have held the title of earls of Derby, the kind of historical link over which she enthused. Robert, 3rd Lord Vipont, had married Isabella FitzPiers (who brought that Christian name into the Vipont and Clifford families), one of the four coheiresses of John, Baron of Berkhamsted, chief justice of England.

The fourth shield was the most important in the series, marking Roger Clifford the Younger's marriage with Isabella de Vipont. A small parchment scroll near Earl George's scabbard makes clear to the uninitiated that this match brought Roger 'and consequently his posterity by the blessing of God to inhabit in Westmerland and in the northern parts, for many generations'. From this, too, stemmed 336 years of unbroken inheritance of the barony and sheriffwick down to Anne herself, except that the 'lands and honors were wrongfully detayned from her for many yeares by hir Unkle the earle of Cumberland and his sonne' until the latter's death 'her Inheritance cam back to her agayne'.[24]

Above Roger's shield, the sequence continued, as will be seen. But a viewer glancing left to the parallel series of shields at the other edge of the Great Picture would be enlightened about Roger's forebears and thus Anne's Clifford and Fitzpons antecedents back to the Norman Conquest. After Richard and William Fitzpons came Walter who by marrying Margaret de Toeni (his inscription tells) obtained Clifford Castle in Herefordshire and changed his name to Clifford. They were notable too, Anne remarks, as the parents of Fair Rosamund. Two more Walters followed. The first married Agnes de Cundy, the second Margaret de Breuse but, with only a daughter, Maud, to succeed him and no male heir, he was the last of the line of Clifford marcher lords.

At this point, Anne digressed in the inscription, following the female line from Walter. Maud married Sir William Longespee (possibly also descended from Fair Rosamund) who died before he could inherit the earldom of Salisbury. Their daughter and heiress Margaret, *de jure* countess of Salisbury, inherited the Clifford and Salisbury estates and married Henry de Lacy, Earl of Lincoln. Their daughter and heiress Alice married (at the age of thirteen) Thomas, 2nd Earl of Lancaster (d. 1322) and died without issue. It was Countess Alice whose Lincolnshire properties Dodsworth told Anne about, witness that entry in the Book of Records. Continuity of female inheritance and marriages into the greatest families appealed to Anne, hence her comment that from Maud's daughter by her second husband descended, again through the female line, many noble families including the Talbots, Earls of Shrewsbury, from whom, via her grandmother Anne Dacre, Anne herself was descended. By this somewhat circuitous route, Anne traced her descent from Walter, the last Clifford marcher lord, albeit by the female line. Her father, of course, shared the same descent, though for him the female line did not count, his title coming via Walter's younger brother Roger, through whom the Clifford male line had continued.[25]

Walter's son (mistakenly called Roger Clifford the Elder) was the first to bear the fess gules on his shield which distinguished him and his successors from the marcher lords. Although Anne may have been unaware of the exceptional lineage of Roger's first wife, Sibilla de Ewias, she would have known of their connection with Abbey Dore and his tomb effigy in its church, as the entries in the Book of Record indicate.[26] Their emblazon, the sixth of the left-hand series, ends Anne's sequence of the early Cliffords, who now merge into the right-hand series underneath Roger the Younger and Isabella, as she states in the inscription to them. This sequence continues with the long succession of thirteen Clifford lords, the last three also Earls of Cumberland. Earl George's inscription reiterates that Anne was his sole heir. Understandably, she omitted Earls Francis and Henry from this sequence. Finally, she topped the right-hand column with herself. Her husbands' Sackville and Herbert coats successively impale her own and she tells of her marriages with them in their inscriptions. However, there was no room above for her daughters, so she had to spill over on to the top of the left-hand column. The Compton-Sackville and Tufton-Sackville shields there complete the direct succession from Robert, 1st Lord Vipont, on the one hand and Richard Fitzpons on the other down to Margaret, Countess of Thanet, and Isabella, Countess of Northampton.

One theme running through their inscriptions is worth stressing. The emphasis is on Westmorland. The 1st Lord Robert is called 'Robert Lord Clifford of Westmorland'. His elder son Roger, 2nd Lord, is given the title used in a document entered in Book I, 'Lord Shevaler of Appleby'. Apart from Anne, only the legally trained might have appreciated why she stressed that title.

Everyone called by writ to Parliament was termed 'Chevalier', so this was an explicit buttress to her claims. Earl George is called the '14th Baron Clifford of Westmerland, and Sheriff of that county by inheritance, and in the same discent the 13th Lord of the Honor of Skipton in Craven, and also Lord Vipont, and Baron Vessey'. The conclusion reached by a viewer of the shields and Anne's inscriptions is that the Cliffords moved from Herefordshire and Worcestershire into their pre-ordained role in the north as barons and sheriffs of Westmorland, with the Skipton title and lands being tacked on later. This, of course, is how she interpreted the inheritance and in strict historical terms she was correct. Sir Matthew Hale endorsed this view by his choice of heading in his manuscript history, as was seen in the previous chapter.[27]

After completing her Vipont and Clifford sequences of shields, Anne had nine places empty in the middle of the left-hand column. How should she fill them? First, the Londesborough line had to be given their due. The top three places she gave to her uncle Francis, cousin Henry and his heiress Elizabeth, Countess of Cork, and their respective spouses. They were, after all, her closest Clifford relatives and the Clifford coat is all they were given – no other titles or honours even implied. Still, the Corks would have been appreciative when they visited Skipton Castle in 1664. In the remaining six places she redressed the gender balance, finding room for ladies whose coats could not be accommodated in the main sequences. In doing so, she achieved more than that. The bottom coupling was Maud, daughter of John, 7th Lord, and her husband Richard Plantagenet, Earl of Cambridge, whose royal blood added the distinction of the arms of France and England to the heraldic display. Above Maud comes the Shepherd Lord's daughter Mabel (by Lady Anne) who achieved the standing of a countess through her husband William Fitzwilliam, Earl of Southampton. A touch of snobbery here.

Then follows, not the Shepherd's second wife Lady Florence, who was only of lesser gentry stock, but their daughter Dorothy who married Sir Hugh Lowther. Their shield and entry would please her senior officer and friend Sir John Lowther and his family. The same criterion applied to the shield above, that of Sir Richard Cholmley of Whitby and his wife Katherine, the 1st Earl's 'pious and beautiful' daughter. As Anne noted in their inscription, Sir Henry and Sir Hugh Cholmley, then living, were descended from them. The eleventh and twelfth shields had special meaning for Anne. The Clifford–Talbot pairing marked the 1st Earl's first marriage to the 4th Earl of Shrewsbury's daughter Margaret. No children were born, but her sister Elizabeth was Anne's ancestor through the Dacre connection which, as has been seen, reached back to the marcher lord Walter. Finally, the shield of the 2nd Earl and his first wife Countess Eleanor would evoke for Anne her godmother, her aunt Derby and the Tudor royal blood in the veins of her cousin James, Earl of Derby.

Anne's choices were shrewdly calculated. She had gratified not just her daughters and their spouses but families who were close to her and to whom she was already beholden. As in the Books of Record, Anne had brought her uncle and cousin and her nearest surviving Clifford kin into the fold. Viewers would have noted that all the shields in the main sequences were of Anne's male ancestors and relatives. Patriarchalism was upheld. Anne's legitimacy was through male inheritance and then, after two generations, herself and her daughters, it would again continue. That was not just legitimate; in her eyes it was quite proper. Anne achieved another objective in the triptychs. Just as in asserting her mastery over her properties and restoring her buildings, she did not just revivify the Clifford heritage, which should have come to her as heir general through the male line, but created a new heritage for her male Tufton and Compton successors.

A word must be said about the collaboration over the completion of the triptych. Anne was indubitably the author of the text in the inscriptions. No one but she had the breadth of understanding of her family's history, the intimate personal knowledge and the judgment it reveals. Historians are at the mercy of their sources and the triptych, derived largely from the Books of Record, owed most to Countess Margaret, Kniveton and Dodsworth. The first Book had been completed in 1648 before the triptych inscriptions were inserted because it is given as the authority for details about Walter de Clifford and Margaret de Toeni. The strengths and limitations of the inscriptions, as of the Books, reflect the priorities of Countess Margaret's object and also the bounds of antiquarian research in the Stuart era. However, in their phraseology Anne's personality rings through; for instance, twice asserting that her lands and honours were wrongfully detained from her by her uncle and his son and also that she had many enemies in the time of her widowhood 'from whose evell and crafty devises it pleased God to deliver hir'.[28]

Whoever was responsible for painting the inscriptions showed admirable mastery. This was most likely her officer Edward Langley whose distinctive cursive script can also be identified in volumes 2 and 3 of the Great Books. After he had finished the inscriptions he was free to help with the Books and, in particular, write most of the entire third set. The coats of arms would probably have required the skills, or at least the advice, of an experienced painter of escutcheons as well as the careful authentication of the shields, which Anne implied in explaining 'wee cannot find by record' either the marriages or coat armour of Richard and William Fitzpons. There was a later contribution, its extent not easy to ascertain. John Bracken, the noted painter of Kirkby Stephen whom Anne frequently employed, spent two to three days at Appleby in January 1673 'mending my great Picture in ye Hall'. A careful scrutiny may well discern his handiwork.[29] What strikes most about the triptych is the audacity and grandness of the concept which leaves a certain awe at the power of mind and thrust of purpose which infused the whole composition. It is perhaps all to the good that the men Anne employed are hard to identify, leaving her undiminished as the sole begetter of this enormous and unique pictorial family history and its vindication of her rightful inheritance.

Anne's own book of coats of arms post-dates the triptychs, being drawn for her by Thomas Webster soon after Pembroke's death and 'butt a little befor his' own. It follows the same lines as in the triptych and her other commissions (as will be seen) but it was an even more personal document. Earl George was given the place of honour, with a double-page coat as Knight of the Garter, the first of the twenty-three shields. Second came that of Sir Simon Musgrave of Hartley Castle impaling Jane, fourth daughter of Thomas, 8th Lord. Their descendant, the Royalist Colonel Sir Philip, was to be a trustee of her Appleby almshouses. The prominence of the third, Sir Hugh Lowther and Dorothy, has been commented on above. Then followed the Viponts and their successors down to Anne and her daughters, her claim as sole heir repeated. The final shield upheld her other baronial title, 'The Clifford Armes Quartered with the Armes of Bromflett, who was Lord Vescy'.[30]

Striking as her triptychs were, Anne needed to reinforce their visual impact at Appleby and Skipton and restore to the rest of her castles the heraldry almost totally lost during the Civil Wars or in earlier destruction. The only stained glass known to have survived was at Appleby, in the Great Hall, the Great Chamber and the chapel built by Thomas, 8th Lord Clifford, in 1454, the year before he was slain. The Hall windows bore his parents' arms, his own and his wife's Dacre arms, and the Viponts'. In the chapel, eight windows in two sets of four depicted the Vipont-FitzPiers shield and Clifford coats impaled with Clare, Vipont, Berkeley, Beauchamp, Neville, and Roos, Lord Thomas's with Dacre and his son John's with Bromflete. Over them in the ninth pane was St George. The whole window, therefore, was in honour of Lord Thomas's father John, 7th Lord, and his Garter knighthood. It was the latter who had built the great gatehouse on the north side of the castle which, though demolished as a result of the 1648 Royalist uprising, Anne had seen and remembered as 'all arched with stone and decorated with the arms of the Veteripontes, Cliffords, and Percies'.[31]

She supplied the want at Brougham and Appleby castles with two sets of shields, forty-two coats in all of 'my Ancesters the Cliffords', for which she paid 7s each, total £14 14s, to John Bracken on 11 October 1670. This commission was late in her life. Had her early accounts survived, most likely they would have shown payments for shields for her other residences. A set of twenty-one suggests a full series as displayed on the triptych. Large in size, they would be decorative and educative, and for Anne would enhance her sense of pride and place of living in the great houses of her famed ancestors.[32] Her Thanet successors were to keep up the practice at Appleby. At Skipton, there is heraldic interest in the Shepherd Lord's shields and the Clifford crests on the rain-water heads in the Conduit Court, the full emblazon of the 1st Earl's Clifford and Percy coats over the entrance to the inner gatehouse and the 5th Earl's shield on the outer gatehouse. Anne's contribution was the 'Desormais' which catches the eye on the upper stonework of the outer gatehouse.

The triptychs' blend of pictorial images with the written word was a powerful medium for getting across the complexity of both Anne's argument of legitimacy and her family relationships over its 600-year span. Yet the numbers who might view them were restricted, however open Appleby and Skipton Castles were while the assizes, quarter sessions and manorial courts were held. For much wider public projection that medium would have to be simplified. A weakness of the triptych formula was that coats of arms were less immediately comprehensible to townsfolk and husbandmen than to the gentle ranks in society. In buildings more public than her castles, the written word would need to be given separate and special emphasis. The Civil War conflicts had inspired an avalanche of illustrated texts in pamphlets, chapbooks and newsletters, which pointed one direction to take.

Anne's best opportunities to proclaim her status and legitimacy to the public at large were the monuments in Skipton and Appleby churches, St Anne's Hospital and the plaques she placed on the ecclesiastical and secular buildings she reconstructed. Location influenced her choice of shields. On her father's monument in Skipton parish church the Vipont and Clifford sequence of seventeen shields is the same as on the triptych. However, she put the earls' shields prominently together at the top of a much taller marble upright slab than the present one, with the 2nd Earl Henry's in the centre and above those of his father and his son. That arrangement was aesthetic. His shield is broader because his Clifford coat is accompanied by his Brandon wife's on the left side, Dacre's on the right. The appearance and the balance were improved because the two flanking shields have the embellishment of their Garter knighthoods (Pl. 75). But, as noted above, the prominence of the Brandon and Dacre coats would give Anne pleasure, even if the general public missed the meaning.

The written word was served admirably by her lengthy composition (really an epitaph) on the tablet she erected just below those shields, so in a commanding and readable position, as the illustration in Whitaker shows. Its obscure place now, on the wall behind, was a result of the nineteenth-century restoration which may also have transposed the 1st and 3rd Earls' shields. She praised her father's Garter knighthood, his sea-voyages undertaken 'for the Good and Honor of the Government' and his 'Blessed and Virtuous Lady', her mother, who was buried at Appleby. He was (as his shields implied) the seventeenth of his blood to be hereditary high sheriff of Westmorland and the thirteenth to be lord of the Honour of Skipton. But the greatest weight in the inscription she gave to herself, because she was Earl George's only legitimate child and followed him,

WHO BY RIGHT OF INHERITANCE FROM A LONG CONTINUED DESCENT OF ANCESTORS WAS LORD VETERIPONT, BARON CLIFFORD, WESTMERLAND, AND VESCIE, LORD OF THE HONOUR OF SKIPTON IN CRAVEN, & HEREDITARY HIGH SHERIFFE OF WESTMERLAND; AND WAS THE LAST HEYRE MALE OF THE CLIFFORDS, THAT RIGHTFULLY ENIOYED THOSE ANCIENT LANDS OF INHERITANCE IN WESTMERLAND AND IN CRAVEN, WITH THE BARONIES AND HONOURS APPERTAYNINGE TO THEM.

As Anne pointed out to Humphrey Hughes, she did much to beautify the church. This included the refurbishment of the earlier monuments which had suffered during the Civil Wars when the soldiers stole the brass plates with their inscriptions, in particular that to Margaret Percy, the 1st Earl's Countess, and the brass of the 2nd Earl and his family on the marble upright slab of his father's monument. Happily, Dodsworth had recorded them in 1620 so what was lost is known.[33] Anne replaced them with her own inscriptions on new tablets, the wording more in keeping with current ecclesiastical taste. In affixing the new tablet on the 1st Earl's upright slab to match Earl George's, she covered up the matrices of the stolen brasses to the 2nd Earl's family, which was not realized until the nineteenth-century restoration.

75. *Alabaster coats of arms of the first three Earls of Cumberland, made by John Ellis, stonecutter of Skipton, 1654/5, Earl George's monument, Holy Trinity Church, Skipton-in-Craven (Photo: the author)*

In this joint inscription to the Earls Henry, Anne took the chance to duplicate the details of her father's (and of course their) titles and inheritance. More surprising is that she again went out of her way to highlight Sir Henry and Sir Hugh Cholmleys' descent from Lady Katherine; her aunt Derby's (and so the current earl's) from 'Lady Eleanor Brandon's Grace'; and Philip, Lord Wharton's from Lady Frances Clifford. By apparently commemorating her forebears, she was projecting her own concerns, with the result that the monuments henceforth were as much about her as the three earls. With her extensive restoration and the monuments' heraldry and inscriptions, it was Anne who now dominated the chancel of Holy Trinity, 'the Countesses quire'.[34]

Even though Appleby was the smaller place, Anne had as great a scope for publicity there as at Skipton. It was the county town often thronged when the assizes, quarter sessions, elections and market days occurred and, though not her borough, she treated it as such and it was dominated by her castle. St Anne's Hospital was her only entire construction and in a favoured position off the main street. Its drawback in terms of self-publicity was the limited space to fill with shields. She found room on the walls between the individual houses for nine coats; the three Vipont lords' impaling Builli, Ferrers and FitzPiers; four Cliffords – the Butcher, the Shepherd Lord and the two Earls Henry – and her own two Sackville and Herbert coats. Over the archway she placed, prominently, her parents' joint shield. In this display of shields both her legitimate inheritance and all her titles and honours were implied, except for her Skipton barony and that was hardly relevant in Appleby.

St Lawrence's was the borough church. Already for two generations the full Clifford emblazon had been familiar to the congregations there, complementing the Russell arms at the other end of her mother's monument. Anne, with a completely free hand, planned her own standing monument as the showpiece for the Clifford family as well as herself. Its reredos, a large, vertical black marble slab, was an ideal background on which to chronicle her descent (Pl. 76). Its pictorial presentation was a family tree, reminiscent of the St John monument at Lydiard, of twenty-four shields with engraved over them the names of the lords and their ladies. From the top downwards, three shields abreast, she followed the full Vipont-Clifford sequence to Thomas, 8th Lord. Then, side by side, came Lord John's with Vescy and the Shepherd's with St John.

At this point, the width of the slab allowed the earls' coats, under their coronets, to be placed in one row, with the 2nd Earl Henry's triple shield – Brandon, Clifford-Vipont quarterly, Dacre – in the centre, as on her father's Skipton monument, though more elaborate. The bottom and most visible row was for herself and her daughters, laid out in the same way and all under coronets. On the left, she placed the Tufton-Sackville shield for Lady Margaret; on the right, the Compton-Sackville coat for Lady Isabella; and in the centre another triplet of shields denoted herself flanked by her husbands, her own shield being a replica of the 2nd Earl Henry's, with Clifford and Vipont quarterly. The prime position in this comprehensive grouping was strikingly that of Anne herself, proudly asserting that she now embodied the full inheritance. Under her Clifford shield is engraved 'SHE WAS BARRONESSE CLIFFORD'. To make doubly sure her message was not missed, her long inscription on the lower face of the monument spelled out the familiar litany of her inheritance and titles. A simpler assertion of her status and descent can be

76. *Lady Anne's monument, St Lawrence's Church, Appleby-in-Westmorland, 1657 (Photo: the author)*

77. Lady Anne's commemorative plaque, Barden Tower, 1659 (Photo: the author)

found as far afield as Beckington where, in the short epitaph to Daniel, she found room to assert that she was the Dowager Countess of Pembroke, Dorset & Montgomery and 'sole Daughter and Heire to George Clifford Earl of Cumberland' (Pl. 65).[35]

Anne's memorials impressed her contemporaries and satisfied her own urge to make known to everybody her rights and her family's honoured past. Yet in the long term her greatest impact, amounting to a public relations coup, came from the written word alone, in the plaques she erected to mark her restorations of buildings in Craven and Westmorland. Clear in style and expression and still hardly touched by weathering, they put her signature on castles and churches where it would best catch the eye. No one reading the plaques is left in doubt about who she was, what titles and honours had fallen to her and her legitimacy as Earl George's sole heiress. Her medium of finely incised script backed by the authority of her titles has proved irresistible. The simplicity of her message has dulled critical faculties about the condition of the buildings before she repaired them. As noted in this study, every plaque has to be treated with reserve. Some are positively misleading. The interlopers, Earls Francis and Henry, are by inference denigrated. Quite rightly, though, a modern viewer can blame, not Anne, but her Thanet successors for the current ruined state of all but Skipton and Appleby Castles. With these plaques, Anne sloughed off the medieval world of heraldic pomp and pre-empted the modern with its obeisance to the authenticity of the oft-repeated, stately written word.

CHAPTER 11

Authority and Piety: Lady Anne's Westmorland Regime

1665–76

The enduring picture of Lady Anne has been of an elderly, dominating noblewoman processing in stately fashion from castle to castle and holding court attended by dutiful relatives, neighbours and tenants. Even more than that, she is held to have stepped back in time, adopting an antique pattern of living more in keeping with her obsolete medieval strongholds than the ostentation and flamboyance of Restoration England. There is substance to this view and it will be explored in the course of this chapter. It will be postulated that she deliberately re-created, though within sensible limits, a late medieval baronial context in which to spend her remaining years. As the last of her line, she made a conscious decision to live in a manner enjoyed by her Clifford forebears.

Yet, as always with Anne, there are qualifications to any assertions about her. If this was a kind of regression, it was neither an act of fantasy, nor romantic in its notion. No one was more practical and down-to-earth than she, as episodes described in this study have demonstrated. Never in her later years did she lose her grip on realities. In her choice of the kind of environment to live in and the tastes to indulge she was eclectic, picking out what suited her from the past as well as the present. There were patent advantages, too. Enacting the role of surrogate northern royalty left no one in doubt who was the mistress not just on her estates but wherever her interests reached. Indeed, she was prepared to overstep the bounds, as has already been pointed out in examining her policies in Craven and will be commented on further in the concluding chapter.

The contrast between Anne's years in the north and the earlier periods in her life is stark. She had known the splendours and comforts of royal palaces, Knole, de Caus's Wilton and Smythson's glass extravaganza at Hardwick, and the intimacy of Bolebrooke and Ramsbury. Instead of following the fashion of erecting modern mansions, she repaired her ruined castles and their associated churches. Just the thought of experiencing a near-medieval life-style as she approached sixty would have been novel and stimulating. That, it may be argued, would be reason enough for deciding to adopt it and to her it would seem fitting in view of her titles and the sheriffwick which, as the previous chapter showed, meant so much to her.

In making the decision, as in everything else, Anne's impulses were modulated by shrewd intelligence and reason; witness her choice of architectural styles for her constructions after she came north. The mixture of

Gothic, Classical and the vernacular has puzzled commentators.[1] Anne's own explanation would have been straightforward, because she chose appropriately on social and historical grounds. The vernacular of her almshouses was appropriate for women of lowish rank, minor gentry families at best and mostly of yeoman stock; in keeping with her sense of hierarchy and of charity to inferiors. Between the almshouses and Anne's other creations was a chasm of style and quality. Her father's monument had a provincial look and was, indeed, the work of a local craftsman. But its tomb-chest shape was designed to give symmetry with the 1st Earl's and its marble top, alabaster shields and epitaph would leave no one in doubt about its noble pretensions. In her other constructions, the castles and churches long associated with her family, she faithfully kept to their Gothic origins, with a rare Gothic Revival feature in Ninekirks. She therefore spent most of her waking and sleeping hours and worshipped in Gothic settings, though with modern amenities.

In all her other creations, she was up-to-date. The monuments for Bourchier, Countess Margaret, Spenser and Daniel were in the current idiom, or close enough to it, with classical components. Anne's own monument, the Brougham pillar and the lettering on her stone plaques were classical and so was the quotation from Horace lauding her father on Skipton Castle's gatehouse. The floor tablet (as his rank required) for her steward Gabriel Vincent, buried in St Michael's Church, Brough, in February 1666, has incised classical script with a touch of runic (Pl. 83). She gave the keeps of her Westmorland castles names which suited their historical siting, Caesar's at Appleby, Clifford's and Roman at Brough (where the Roman town was known), Pagan at Brougham. In these various ways she showed the influences on her of Inigo Jones and the Stuarts' rediscovery of an older European past, that of ancient Greece and Rome. Arthurianism, which had infused her father's pageantry as Champion, was minimal; just the name 'Guinevere' for her companion bitch in her last years.

The antiqueness of her castle-dwelling has been rather exaggerated. Other nobility still lived in castles and their richness and comfort can be attested today by such as Sizergh, Berkeley and Sudeley. In amenities and interior furnishings, there would have been little to choose between Appleby and Hardwick Hall. The stairs would be the most inconvenient feature, especially for an elderly woman. What obviously gratified her was the luxury of six medieval and Tudor residences, all attractively located and each with its unique appeal, from which she derived great pleasure. They had in common a rural aspect, with fine views of the surrounding countryside. The big halls she inserted into both Barden and Pendragon looked out south on to valleys and fells, the Wharfe, with its arboreal deer parks, and Mallerstang. The Octagonal Tower and Long Gallery at Skipton can hardly be matched for their intimate atmosphere and views of the Aire Valley and heather moors. From Anne's chamber and the upper storeys at Brougham there was a panorama encompassing the Eamont, Lowther and Eden Valleys, the Pennine fells and the mountains of the Lake District. Brougham had exterior gardens and Skipton within its walls both a garden and a walk, first laid out for Countess Eleanor and called today 'Lady Anne's Walk'. In the small towns of Appleby, Brough and Skipton, she could play to the full her role as the great living-in noble lady.

78. Lady Anne's chamber, top storey, north-west corner of the Inner Gatehouse, Brougham Castle, Cumbria (Photo: the author)

Her wish to confer those pleasures on her posterity so that they would 'make their owne houses the place of Selfe fruition' is perhaps another reason for adopting her distinctive way of life. With the psalms to prompt her, she wrote 'The Lott is fallen unto mee in a pleasant place. I have a fair Heritage.' And 'I may truly say', she added in words redolent of Samuel Daniel, 'From many Noble Progenitors I hold Transmitted Lands, Castles, and Honours, which they swayd of old.'[2]

Nevertheless, Anne's inclination towards castle-dwelling in the north must have long pre-dated the actuality. What inspired her outlook is a complex matter. Most likely several influences fused together. First, during her most impressionable years, came Daniel's teaching about her historical roots and then her mother's fervent pursuit of her rights in the vibrant atmosphere of Westminster Hall. This in time aroused her burgeoning interest in the deeds, charters, properties and attainments of generations of Viponts and Cliffords and, primed by Sir John Taylor, her father's achievements. The long wait for her titles and lands may have stoked up an obsessive fascination with the lost baronial world of her forebears. There are, also, echoes in her own journeyings of the progresses of Queens Elizabeth and Anne of Denmark and the respect they commanded, which would have impressed itself on her sense of status.

The self-contained element may have had different origins. More than once in the past Anne had withdrawn into herself, largely shunning the outside world. The best-recorded occasion was 1616/17 when, as has been described, she jibbed against what was expected of an earl's consort in dress and comportment. Two years later, she took to her chamber for five months, never leaving it from late October 1619 to late March 1620, ostensibly ill, but the symptoms unstated; pregnancy or miscarriage perhaps. Most introverted of all were her six years and more in Baynard's Castle before she rode north. What she did there is worth pondering. Her activities were self-regarding. She corresponded with her officers about her properties in Craven and Westmorland. She married off Lady Isabella, which left her even more on her own. She planned and supervised the execution of the triptychs and Books of Record. Instructing the painters and liaising with Dodsworth and other helpers would have been for her a safari into the past, a personal odyssey into her youth and a painstaking exploration of the actions and relationships of her ancestors through documentary and heraldic sources. Absorption in her baronial antecedents, combined with her Old Testament sense of destiny and the precepts of patriarchalism, could well have helped develop in her an exalted if narrow vision of her future role. From 1649, the year of Charles I's execution, distaste for the Parliamentarian and Cromwellian regimes would have discouraged her from embracing current norms. She rejoiced at the Restoration, yet shunned its excesses and moral laxity.

In the sea-change which, by the middle 1640s at least, had come over Anne, two ancestors above all caught her imagination, Isabella de Vipont and the Shepherd Lord. Isabella appealed to her in two respects, one particular, the other general. The particular was that in her widowhood Isabella exercised the office of sheriff in person, sitting on the bench herself, judging even matters of life and death. How this may have affected Anne's own attitude will be explained in the concluding chapter. More generally, in Anne's opinion Isabella deserved to be remembered by her posterity with honour and reverence in that 'she brought soe faire and noble an Inheritance unto them which by Gods blessinge hath continewed to her Successors for soe manie generations as the parallel is hardly to be found in the Kingdome'.[3] For Anne, Isabella was an even more compelling example than Maud de Clifford of what could follow from inheritance through a female. Not only had Anne herself benefited eventually but she was conscious of being in a similar situation.

Anne seems to have studied and understood the Shepherd Lord better than any of her remoter forebears. He was of special interest to her because they shared a comparable experience and faced problems of a like nature. When she writes of what he accomplished one senses a bond of respect and fellow-feeling. The Shepherd had been denied his estates for twenty-four years by the Yorkist kings. When he was restored in 1485 by Henry VII he found his properties badly neglected. His castles were partly ruined and his tenants obstreperous. With toughness of mind and action he made himself master. He renovated his castles, built modern apartments for his lady, Anne St John, within the Conduit Court at Skipton Castle and converted the forest lodge at Barden into a stone tower with laid-out gardens and deer parks. His lady brought to Skipton the great series of fifteenth-century tapestries which Anne herself hung in the best chambers in the restored drum towers. Furthermore, the Shepherd was the last Clifford before Anne to maintain a fully itinerant household.

79. Lady Anne, aged 'about 60', by John Bracken, 1670 (H.T. Fattorini Esq.)

She would have approved of his robust treatment of his neighbours and rivals. She appreciated that he deserved some censure by his Tudor monarchs but noted that he did not shrink from their bullying. His rumbustious living and illegitimate offspring she would have taken, as she did Dorset's, as the way of the world. Most of all, perhaps, she would have admired the Shepherd's

208

outstanding patronage of ecclesiastical building, a preoccupation which she shared with him above all other Cliffords. One other facet of efficient lordship they had in common, a desire to get in all the moneys due to them and carefully record and audit how these were disbursed.[4]

This was the key not only to Anne's management of her landed properties and household economy but to her entire life-style. She may always have been careful with money, having shared her mother's difficulties and flinching from her father's and husband Dorset's wastrel ways. From 1650 it became vital. She then had two jointure holdings far away in Sussex and Kent and big estates in Craven and Westmorland so that she was an absentee landlord always from her southern lands and from one or other of her northern estates. The following discussion of how she dealt with her finances is based on her accounts for the last ten years of her life when she peregrinated in Westmorland, but there is no reason to suppose that her methods had changed at all since 1650, or even earlier.

The cash Anne received from Craven, Kent and Sussex was net income, despatched by her officers Robert Collings from Skipton and William Edge from the south after they and her other estate officers had met the necessary upkeep of her properties and other administrative expenses. She treated the moneys which came from them and her Westmorland receivers in exactly the same way. Usually there were three or four despatches of cash from each area annually, following the collection of revenues on specified rent days. In 1665, for example, Collings sent just over £1,036 (to Allen Strickland) on four occasions – £263; £290; £330, and £153. Anne noted where each sum originated, checked it and kept it in a separate bag with a note of the date it was delivered to her. She put the bags from each source together in their particular place in the strong box which always stood, under her eye, in her own chamber. She would know at any time of day precisely how much cash was in each bag and altogether in the strong box.[5]

Anne recorded the cash which came into her hands in her annual Books of Receipts,[6] naming the four sources Westmorland; Craven; Returned Moneys (that is, her jointure rents); and Borrowed Moneys. This last was Returned Moneys treated in a different way, because she borrowed in Westmorland on the security of her jointure revenues. For this, she gave bills of exchange which her local creditors presented to Edge in London and he would honour them from the revenues he had received. In the table of Anne's income and expenditure, Borrowed Moneys counts as jointure revenues (Table 6). She kept a separate running account for not just each source but each bag in that source. This made for a multiplicity of small accounts subsumed within the Book of Receipts. In 1671, for example, she received seven deliveries from Westmorland, three from Craven and two from the south, that is, Borrowed Moneys with Returned Moneys.

Anne recorded in Books of Disbursements[7] how she spent this cash, all of it in the north and mainly in Westmorland. She would take money from one bag and record what it was spent on, subsuming that account within the main category, say Returned Moneys. One instance will suffice. In April 1669, she borrowed £400 from Mr William Williamson of Greystoke, Cumberland, for

TABLE 6 *Lady Anne's net receipts and expenditure, 1669–75*

	1669	1670	1671	1672	1673	1674	1675
Cash remaining at close of previous account.	£1,126 5s 11d	716 4s 11d	808 7s 3d	552 4s 6d	882 14s 8d	683 8s 10d	351 11s 2d [sic]
Of which*	C– 663 19s 8d	400 0s 0d	577 16s 10d	457 0s 0d	423 0s 0d	313 0s 0d	351 11s 2d
	W– 438 9s 11d	216 4s 11d	228 14s 1d	92 8s 2d	336 1s 5d	320 8s 10d	—
	RM– 22 0s 0d	100 0s 0d	—	—	123 13s 3d	50 0s 0d	—
	Br–1 16s 4d	—	1 16s 4d	1 16s 4d	—	—	—
Jointure lands in Kent and Sussex	711 0s 0d	496 0s 0d	250 0s 0d	402 0s 0d	252 0s 0d	230 0s 0d	600 0s 0d
Westmorland	928 19s 1d	845 13s 10d	894 12s 3d	932 12s 2d	879 18s 4d	740 16s 0d	855 11s 5d
Brougham town revenues	—	1 16s 4d	1 16s 4d	—	1 16s 4d	1 16s 4d	1 16s 4d
		1 16s 4d					
Craven	1036 0s 0d	1295 16s 10d	1420 4s 9d	1456 12s 2d	1267 0s 0d	1253 0s 0d	1312 12s 7d
Borrowed moneys	300 0s 0d	—	—	—	—	—	—
SUM TOTAL	4102 5s 0d	3357 8s 3d	3375 0s 7d	3343 8s 10d	3283 9s 4d	2909 11s 0d	3121 11s 6d
Disbursements	3386 0s 1d	2549 1s 0d	2822 16s 1d	2460 14s 2d	2600 0s 6d	2557 9s 7d	2434 7s 9d
Remaining in cash to carry over	716 4s 11d	808 7s 3d	552 4s 6d	882 14s 8d	683 8s 10d	357 10s 10d	687 4s 6d
Net income	2675 19s 11d	2641 3s 4d	2566 13s 4d	2791 4s 4d	2400 14s 8d	2226 2s 2d	2770 0s 4d

*C– Craven rents; W– Westmorland rents; RM– Returned Moneys (jointure rents); Br– Brougham town rents

Sources: **KRO.JAC 495/7**

which she gave him a bill of exchange to Edge. She began to spend that £400 in June and it was used up by the end of July. She then noted, 'So all this Four Hundred Powndes is disbursed by me.' However, she did not empty one bag and then start another. She would take from as many as three concurrently over a period of two or three months, so that she was keeping parallel accounts for them during that period. For a researcher to follow what she spent on one of her projects, such as repairs to a corn mill, is not straightforward; but that was not her object.

This practice of accounting for her receipts and expenditure is one aspect of Anne's idiosyncratic system of managing her finances. It enabled her to know precisely when and what cash she received and when and for what purpose and by which officer it was disbursed. She knew how every activity was financed. Moreover, she could and did cross-check from the Books of Receipts to the Books of Disbursements. She checked every item and made marginal notes in the Books of Disbursements in her own hand of where each sum had originated. When at the close of the year the accounts were audited, her chief officers signed in witness in her presence and the auditor, Thomas Gabetis, approved them. Then Anne formally acknowledged that the account had been read to her and gave her own approval (Table 8).

Anne's accounting was based on the old-established premise that a landowner should closely supervise his income and expenditure. Fortunes have been made and gentry and noble dynasties risen because a steward or receiver siphoned off his master's revenues. Earl George had been defrauded like that in Westmorland.[8] Anne, like her mother, was determined not to suffer in the same way. Although the mercantile community was adopting new, Italian-style, accounting methods, Anne's bailiffs and receivers followed the old 'charge' and 'discharge' system. By this, an officer 'charged' himself with the receipt of moneys and 'discharged' himself of that spent or passed on to other officers or Anne herself. This made deception more difficult. Anne's accounts were kept on the same basis, but with the greater complexity and security of her multiple cross-checking. Moreover, she had an extra means of oversight, as is explained in the following paragraph.

Two other kinds of accounts were kept and audited in the same way as the others. Anne's clerk of the kitchen, Allan Strickland, kept Books of Weekly Household Expenditure.[9] In these, he recorded his daily and weekly expenditure on the foodstuffs and drink consumed by the household and a few other items. But his entries as well as those in the Books of Disbursements were duplicated in a quite separate series of accounts, the Books of Household Expenses.[10] These were Anne's personal record of payments. At the front she entered the sums of cash she gave to Strickland for his purchases. At the reverse end she noted the payments from her Private Purse, which included lawsuits. From her Books of Household Expenses Anne could quickly tell the amounts which had been disbursed and for what purposes. She made marginal comments. All the recipients of the cash she doled out signed their name or made their mark. Both the individual entries and the summaries at the close of the accounts allowed cross-checking with the other Books described above.

Anne's convoluted method of financial management reveals a facet of her

TABLE 7 *Rental of Lady Anne's jointure lands in Sussex and Essex, reversion to Richard, 5th Earl of Dorset, c. 1673*

Sussex[1]

	£	s	d
The manor of Hangleton	280	0	0
The manor of Swanborough	279	1	8
The manor of Milton	207	3	8
The manor of Lullington	93	15	6
The manor of Michelham	252	2	0
Fourth part of the manor of Houndean	108	5	2
The manor of Chiddingley	64	2	2
The manor of Blackham	191	2	0
The manor house and demesnes of Collinghurst	40	3	0
The manor of Broome	82	5	10
Sum total	1,598	1	0

Essex

	£	s	d
A rent charge of £60 per annum out of the manors of Bergholt Sackville alias Sackfield and Mountburies	60	0	0
Total	1,658	1	0

NOTE

1. She also held the moiety of the manor of Meeching.

Source: CKS, U269/E483

---

personality which hitherto has only been glimpsed. It has to be viewed in the context of the attitude of nobility to cash. Noblemen rarely handled coins except when gambling. A pursebearer would disburse cash at his master's behest and keep a running account which was audited. Noblewomen had far more direct control of the spending of their allowances, although it is rare for one of their accounts to survive. Anne would have become used to dealing with her own finances after marrying Dorset, as her 1616/19 diary shows. From 1624 she had a big jointure income to manage (Tables 2, 7) and then, after a quarter of a century's experience during which her ideas matured, became a major landowner. The fulfilment of her creative energies depended on close financial control, ensuring that all moneys due to her came into her hands and that they were spent entirely on what she wanted. This was the corollary of her estate management and tenurial policies. Finance was at the core of her regime. She devoted a great deal of her time – and her officers did likewise – to an elaborate system of accounting and checking all the details. For her, it must have been a highly satisfying pastime. But its ultimate objective was to enable her to indulge in all the activities she thought fitting for the noble Clifford she was. The Shepherd Lord had done it; so could she.

From her disposable income, it is clear that as a dowager countess (and well before that) Anne was far wealthier than has hitherto been supposed (Table 6). What she received, as noted above, was the net income from her estates, not their gross revenues which would have been larger. Collings's Craven outlay in 1665 was £716 from gross receipts of £1,752, leaving £1,036 surplus for Anne's coffers. A gross income of up to £8,000 would have placed Anne in the middle rank of noble landowners in the Stuart century. Being more careful than her male counterparts and not obliged to attend court, she would enjoy greater disposable resources than most. Sedgewick, having studied her accounts, asserted credibly that in her lifetime she spent over £40,000 on her buildings.[11] Moreover, Anne turned money-lender – £6,400 on bonds at the time of death including £3,400 to city merchants for their own credit transactions.[12] Wealth could be translated into power. It commanded loyalty, respect and service. It gave independence and security. It allowed the best lawyers to be hired to fight causes in the Westminster courts, as Countess Margaret had done. Anne's riches did all this and much more, enabling her to follow her chosen way of life which exalted her own standing and, conversely, imposed an element of subservience on her associates.

Two of the constants which infused Anne's outlook were her Anglican faith and noble beneficence. They are so interwoven it would be hard to describe her daily activities in Westmorland without reference to one or the other and often both. Their manifestation in piety, charity and hospitality was the essence of her relations with the dual communities of her household and the localities where she resided. Anne is a shining exception to what contemporary writers discerned and lamented as the decline of hospitality compared with the Middle Ages. They included Sir Henry Wotton and William Camden, for whom Elizabethan mansions were 'the great ornament of the kingdom', but to the 'great decay of the glorious hospitality of the nation'.[13] Anne had turned her back on these mansions and, in Sedgewick's words, 'A great estate God had blessed her with, and given her withal a noble heart and an open and liberal hand, to do good generally to all'.[14]

To be open-handed meant consciously curbing two areas of the chronic over-consumption which was the ruin of many of her fellow nobility. First, her household establishment was modest in numbers, male-orientated as was the custom and with surprisingly few female attendants for a noblewoman (Table 9). She did buy in some labour, employing outsiders, which suggests caution in drawing conclusions about the size of the household and its expenditure. Second, in these later years she took almost to excess her preference for plainness in her own chamber, its furniture and her apparel which, in Bishop Rainbow's well-chosen phrases, clothed her in humility all over, her dress, 'not disliked by any', being 'imitated by none'.[15]

Anne's accounts confirm Sedgewick's precise and critical comment about her 'very plain and mean apparel, indeed far too mean for her quality'. A petticoat and waistcoat of black serge, he added, were her constant wear and nobody

TABLE 8 *Lady Anne's household expenditure, Westmorland, 1673*

	£	s	d
In weekly expenses as per Book	355	8	10
In malt for the howse as per Book	96	10	0
In wine for the howse as per Book	146	11	6
In coales	160	8	6
In oats & straw, sadlers work smiths work & ffarrier work	101	11	3
In Lead for the houses	58	15	10
For Plumber work	20	19	2
Repairs of mills & dams, the Court wall at Brougham Castle & the walls & fences at Flakebridge and stooping & railing & fencing of the demesnes & for millstones	130	15	7
For mowing, making, leading & stacking hay this year	25	10	8
Removing charges	18	9	0
In sheep & oxen for the house use	120	19	10
In Servants wages	254	15	0
In Board wages	11	6	0
In Extraordinaries	296	7	3

Your Honours Private Purse			
Given in clear mony as per Book	413	15	6
In Plate & Scarlett bought of Mr Sedgewick & for silk ducape, books, sessments, travelling charges, Law charges & other extraordinaries as per Book	307	16	7
Summa Totalis disbursed	2600	0	6

Remaining in Cash at first of January 1673/4 £683 8 10
which goes forward to Account for 1674 from New
Years day last.

[Margin]   3 Feb 1673/4
        Exd by Thomas Gabetis Auditor
        at Appleby Castle
        Witness hereto
            Henry Machell
            George Goodgion
            Edmond Foster
            Allan Strickland

                    Examined at Appleby Castle
                    3 February 1674 A P

Source: KRO, JAC 495/7, 50

TABLE 9 *Lady Anne's officers and servants, 1669*

Wages		Bequests, 1676
£		£
20	Mr George Sedgewick	240
	John Jackson his man	
20	Mr Thomas Strickland, Receiver in Westmorland	30
	John Gilpin his man	
20	Mr Edward Hasell, Secretary	20
4	Thomas Cornell his man	
20	Mr Henry Machell, Steward of the House and	
	Gentleman of the Horse	20
?20	Mr Thomas Gabetis, Auditor and Deputy Sheriff	two silver
	Rowland Dent his man	fruit dishes
8	George Goodgion, slaughterer and Caterer of	
	the Kitchen	30
8	Edmond Foster, chief Butler	10
8	Allan Strickland, Groom of the Chamber and	
	clerk of the Kitchen	15
7	Edward Smith, coachman	
4	John Hall, groom of the Stables	6
4	Abraham Fitton, postillion	6
4	Isaac Walker, groom of the Stables	4
10	William Watkinson 'who writes for me'	
6	John Taylor 'who sometimes reads to me'	
10	Thomas Millner, chief Cook	
4	Thomas Wilson, second Cook	
3	William Dargue, scullery man	8 (dead)
4	Arthur Swinden, under Butler and firemaker	6
4	George Padgett, Baker and Porter	
4	John Harrison, Brewer	
	Gaven Scott, gardener	
10	Mrs Frances Pate, chief Gentlewoman	50
10	Mrs Elizabeth Shaw, other Gentlewoman	
4	Dorothy Demaine, Laundry Maid	40
4	Elizabeth Demain, " "	
4	Margaret Dargue, " "	10 (married)
2 12s	Isabell Dargue, " " (her sister)	
	Widow Margaret Ling, washerwoman (1669 almswoman)	
	Housekeepers and keepers	
4	William Johnson, at Appleby Castle	£3

Housekeepers and keepers

4	Richard Lewis, at Brougham Castle	3
8	Robert Harrison, at Brough Castle	3
	Mr Robert Branthwaite, at Pendragon Castle	
	Widow Wright, at Skipton Castle	
	George Demaine of Percivells, at Barden Tower (afterwards, his wife)	
	Mr John Gilmore, Keeper at Julian Bower	
	Henry Law, underkeeper	
	William Law, underkeeper	
6	Francis Mason, warrener of Whinfell	
	John Taylor, miller of Bongate mills	

Receivers

Mr Robert Collings, Craven	4 oxen to his son Peter
Mr William Edge, Sussex and Kent	40

Source: KRO, JAC 495/7, 1

---

could persuade her to change. Emanuell Jackson, the tailor of Penrith, made her dimity waistcoats in April 1671 and a black cloth serge gown for 8*s* in December 1675. Robert Harrison, her housekeeper at Brough, in June 1674 made her six linen waistcoats and two knee cloths at 6*d* apiece, the full cost with the thread being only 5*s* 6*d*. In August, he made a flannel petticoat for her. The material of her bed linen was no finer. In September 1670, at the age of eighty and obviously feeling the cold, she paid 13*s* 4*d* for ten yards of linen cloth to cover her feet at night. The day after, she bought 8*s* worth of red worsted and inkle for her bed. More unusually, Thomas Atkinson of Barden supplied for her own use eight ready-made fox skins at 2*s* 5*d* each.[16] All this contrasts, as will be seen, with the quality of the material she obtained to give away.

Anne's room at Brougham would have appeared unusual to most visitors. Bishop Rainbow wrote that 'although she had not many Books in her Chamber, yet it was dressed up with the flowers of a Library'. This is because she decorated its walls, her bed, hangings and furniture with sayings or remarks from authors she had read or learned, which her servants wrote out for her, pinned up so that she or they when dressing 'might remember, and make their discants on them'. However, her books were up-to-date, because she kept adding to her stock mostly with publications akin to those in the triptych, a matter which calls for separate analysis. One of these has survived, Sir Anthony Weldon's *The Court of King James* which she annotated, agreeing with the author on the king's speech – she had, after all, been kissed by him! Sedgewick purchased for her on 3 April 1669 a copy of the first edition of *Angliae Notitia* by

80. Edward Rainbow, Bishop of Carlisle (1608–84), attrib. to C. Netsher (Private collection)

Edward Chamberlain, FRS; on 19 May, George Herbert's various writings entitled *Remaines*, and on 18 August, *The Lord Hatton's Psalter* published at Michaelmas 1668. William Watkinson copied for her Aristotle on affection from his 'Rhetoricks' on 16 November 1669. On 29 September 1670 Sedgewick paid four shillings for a newly printed book by Izaak Walton on the lives of her friends Donne, Wootton, Herbert and the Anglican theologian Dr Richard Hooker, which had been licensed as recently as 21 June. Rainbow did not mention that Anne's chamber and nearby were cluttered up not only with her strong box but six or seven trunks of her mother's old belongings which she kept there and in an adjoining room.[17]

The almost nunnish aura of Anne's 'study-bedroom' stopped at its door. The public rooms would be ostentatious, with rich tapestries, ornamental plasterwork, oak wainscoting and many family portraits not just to proclaim her own standing but to make her high-ranking visitors feel at home. Anne possessed all the gold and silver tableware to lift formal meals into sumptuous occasions, some inherited, some bequeathed by her husbands, the rest purchased by her (Table 11).[18] Nor did she stint on good quality food and drink. Wine was regularly bought from Mr William Webster of Stockden, Barnard Castle. Mr Francis Catterson dispatched from Skipton runlets of sack and white wine with other things in 1669. Gabetis bought wine for her in York and Mr Peachall, steward to the bishop, in Carlisle. Much of the choicer food was obtained at Newcastle; for instance, the judges' fare at Appleby assizes in 1673 which included raisins, currants, nutmeg, anchovies, capers, sturgeon, pickled oysters and Westphalia hams. Bucks were driven from her own Haw Park and Barden for her table in Westmorland. Horseloads of tench in barrels of water were sent from Skipton. The many gifts of food from her neighbours included twelve turkeys for Christmas 1673 from

81. Lady Anne's chair, Appleby Castle, 1660, ornately carved and displaying Clifford, Albemarle (Bolton Priory) and Isle of Man (earls of Derby) arms. This was probably one of a set decorated with shields of families historically connected with the Cliffords (Photo: the author)

the Laytons of Dalemain and thirteen from the now widowed Mrs Layton for Christmas 1675. Mr Richard Graham of the Nunnery sent salmon in April 1675.[19] One of Anne's interests was preserving and her accounts show how much this activity contributed to her household's domestic economy (Table 10). Her guests, casual visitors, officers and other servants could not have complained about the fare offered at her table.

With the massive over-provision of quality chambers in her major castles, it is not surprising Anne could welcome her relatives and their servants for longish visits. Her *Diaries*, and especially her daily record in 1676, show how many people called on her, most to be rewarded with a gift as well as her blessing. Her daughters and her grandchildren tended to stay for several weeks. Visits by them and other relatives and friends are detailed in her *Diaries* and the gaps in the latter are filled by entries in her accounts. For instance, Lady Margaret Coventry and her two children stayed from 1 September 1669. Anne's son-in-law Northampton with Colonel Francis Carr of Stackhouse, Giggleswick, also came that month and another Civil War stalwart, her 'cousin' Colonel William Middleton, in October, shortly before his death. The Lascelles family were with her in March 1671; Mr Robert Clifford of Southwark, son of the Sir Conyers killed in Ireland late in Elizabeth I's reign, her godson Fulke Greville and Middleton's sons in August 1674.[20] She granted Sir John Lowther a lodging for himself and his servants for life in the Green Chamber of Appleby Castle, 'as a testimonie', he wrote, 'of her love and affection'. In return for this, at the assizes he sent her a buck; his deer, herded, being better than hers which ran free.[21]

Various hitherto unknown members of Clifford branches called on her. Thomas Clifford of Warrington's wife and their young son William came on 2 November 1668, and were given £1 and 10s respectively. Mr Richard Clifford, a Devonshire man, received only 2s in August 1669. How Anne could react to these distant relatives, all in hope of gifts or preferment, was described by Abraham Clifford gent. of Frampton, a physician. He arrived at Appleby at the end of July 1664 with a glowing recommendation from his master, Lord Wharton, whose sons he had looked after during their Continental stay. Reporting to Wharton from Hartley Castle, he wrote that Anne had readily acknowledged his relationship to the family of Cliffords of Cumberland and complimented him accordingly. Yet he came away disappointed. Several friends 'who pretended to know her humor' had encouraged him to expect to reap great advantage by his addresses to her, but there was nothing, least of all 'such golden mountaines' as might persuade him to leave Wharton's service for hers. Anne quickly wearied of frequent importuning. She gave Robert Clifford £2 in May 1674 provided he did not pester her in future.[22]

One of her most welcome visitors would be Sir William Dugdale, the distinguished herald and antiquary, who stayed at Brougham on 24 March 1665 on his visitation of the north-west. He had stopped at the King's Arms in Appleby to authenticate and record altogether seven pedigrees of local gentry such as the Birkbecks of Hornby and Dalstons of Acorn Bank. He would have had the chance to see both the church and castle with their coats of arms and the famous triptych. While at Brougham he rode to Lowther to take Sir John's

TABLE 10 *Lady Anne's preserving, 1673–5*

Book	Date	
	1673	
30	July	Currants and cherries (done by Arthur Swinden and Mrs Pate)
	Aug.	Raspberries
31	Oct.	Quinces and apples, and makes lemon purée
	1674	
32	28 April	Oranges
34	25 May	Makes conserve of cowslips
33	19 June	Makes syrup of lemons and oranges
	19 June	Gets strawberries from her Brougham garden, and artichokes, cherries, gooseberries, lavender and other herbs
34	21 July	Makes conserve of roses
	6 July	Makes syrup of oranges
	6 Aug.	Apricots and Cherries. Aniseed water bought to make Scone Cakes, withall called Manus Christy
	11 Aug.	Raspberries
	14 Aug.	Lemons
	2 Sept.	Plums and apricots
	30 Sept.	Apricots sent by Mr Layton of Dalemain
	1675	
38	22 May	Oranges and cowslips
37	2 July	Makes jelly of currants and conserve of raspberries
38	18 Aug.	A large quantity of several fruits sent by John Paulet, 5th Marquis of Winchester

Source: KRO, JAC 495/7

pedigree. Anne would have been for Dugdale a rarity, a learned conversationalist with a deep understanding of her family's records and pedigrees. She had her Great Books and other manuscript collections to display to him. His diminutive young assistant Gregory King, who was to achieve fame in his own right, had made his first drawing, of Lancaster Castle, just over a week before. He must have quickly collected a portfolio of his work or even drawn for Anne because she described him as 'so ingenious in taking ye forme of Castles & townes with a Led penne' and rewarded him with £1 10s. When Dugdale reached Skipton on his visitation he recorded the Clifford coats of arms and borrowed Dodsworth's collections from Lord Fairfax at Denton.[23]

Anne's depth of reading on theological issues has been commented on in Chapter 10. Her understanding and command of scriptural language were attested by Bishop Rainbow relating how deftly and courteously she dealt with the 'godly men' sent by the county committee to interrogate her at Appleby Castle in June 1651. They subsequently left her in peace. She did not, during the Interregnum, challenge religious policy publicly in the parish churches, but she did maintain the Church of England worship in private.

All Anne's visitors, titled or otherwise, encountered in her castles a pious and dutiful establishment and, eagerly or not, would be expected to conform. 'The psalms of David', writes Sedgewick, 'appointed for the day she constantly read, and had three or four chapters read to her by some of her women daily.' She and her family received the sacrament at least four times a year and after every remove with a sermon also. Her resident clergymen at Brougham and Appleby were constantly with her and others who visited included Robert Sutton, vicar of Skipton, and Anthony Proctor, minister of Rossendale, who preached in her private chapel. Edward Guy, her officer and son of one of her almswomen, preached a good sermon before her in Appleby Church on 14 December 1673.[24]

Some of Anne's benevolence, therefore, was overtly religious and designed to aid if not foster observance. William Smith of Appleby provided the twenty-four books for £4 2s which she gave her servants when they received the sacrament with her at Easter 1670. She purchased the thirty-five books of divinity on 22 June 1670 from Smith for £6 4s 7d to give to Lady Alethea Compton's servants as well as her own.[25] Smith's provision of them hints at a flourishing literary culture spreading from the castle, school and church. To her officers, or perhaps her ladies or almswomen, she gave a silver medal to wear like the lesser George at the chest. On the obverse it showed her portrait, inscribed around with her titles (Pl. 71). On the reverse was 'Religion', crowned, standing profile to the right, leaning against a cross, the gospels held under her arm, and inscribed around with

SOLE. DAUGHTER & HEIRE. TO GEORGE. EARLE OF. CUMBERLAND.

However, most of Anne's lavish munificence was secular. To her family she was generous to a fault. Some of the sums were large. For instance, she paid the £89 costs of Lady Margaret Coventry's stay with her in September 1670. Her cousin Sir Thomas Wharton received £50 on 24 April 1674 to buy himself a piece of plate.[26] Her grandchildren could expect regular gifts. George Coventry wrote from Croome to his 'grandmother-in-law' on 11 December 1658 to thank her for the two crystal cups she had sent him. Her son-in-law Mr James Herbert expressed his gratitude on 7 December 1664 that she had agreed to be godmother to his son Philip and for sending 'soe noble a piece of plate' to the new-born child. At the time of her death she had lent – effectively given – Countess Margaret £3,000 and £200 to John Tufton.[27]

Even granted her wealth, the range and quality of Anne's munificence to all and sundry is still surprising. Jonathan Jackman paid £1 4s at Kendal in May 1669 for five plain silk scarves and three black silk hoods for her to give away.

Edward Guy bought in York for her to bestow thirteen mourning rings for £6 14s in July 1669; twelve gold rings for £4 4s on 26 September; six silver French porringers at £1 7s apiece in August, and another six of the 'newest fashion' for £7 19s in March 1670. Sedgewick purchased four silver French porringers in August 1675 which, with box and carriage, came to £5 10s. The recipients are not named. Other gifts were equally practical if not always so expensive. Sedgewick paid 4s for twelve pairs of spectacles in September 1671 and eight pairs of tweezers which must have been silver because six cost 12s each and the others 6s each. A grey Scottish Galloway horse bought at Brough Fair in August 1674 for £2 13s 4d was another gift to some fortunate fellow. At Brougham Castle in May 1673 her servants received livery cloth and baize from Wakefield, cost 14s.[28]

Sedgewick made the point well that Anne's mainly local purchasing with ready money of farm produce, groceries and other goods for household use, especially avoiding so far as possible buying in London, was intended to benefit her Westmorland communities. Bishop Rainbow, likewise, praised her building as a work of piety and her charity as a benefaction since they set people to work; and Westmorland was one of the poorest counties in the kingdom.[29] Far more than that, Anne was near-unique in spending in the north her estate revenues garnered in Sussex and Kent, reversing the normal tide, in however minor a way, of capital flowing to the London region. Her father had been one of the worst culprits in that respect, with her uncle and cousin compelled to follow suit. This outflow from the north strangled local purchasing power and depressed local enterprise while stimulating the capital's booming economy. The impact of Anne's practices was different, that of local redistribution, collecting estate income which she spent as the whim took her; a question which has been raised elsewhere but whose consequences deserve further consideration.[30]

For Anne's officers, employment in her household could escalate them to affluence and higher social rank, as was often the case in great establishments. Besides their salaries, they got extra cash rewards from her and generous tips also from her titled guests. In return, she expected loyalty and probity and the employment of all their varied skills. Sedgewick had special treatment from her. He describes how, when he took charge of her young grandson John Tufton on their long visit to the Low Countries in 1656/7, her 'good allowance' of £400 a year for John, his man and footman and himself, with £50 more annually for John's clothes and £20 for his own, arrived punctually by bills of exchange from London. She had given Sedgewick a £21 rent-charge and £50 in gold before he left and on his return £100 in money and another £20 rent-charge. Moreover, Anne was instrumental in settling him in his estate at Collinfield and in 1676 bequeathed him £200, much her largest cash legacy.[31] Edward Hasell carefully noted in a book all the various monetary rewards which came to him; Anne's being confirmed by her accounts, like writing her final will at Pendragon Castle for which he got £5 on 1 May 1674. He saved them and, eventually reaching £1,200, they helped him purchase the Dalemain mansion and its lands for £2,710 in 1679, which remains his family's home.[32] To the lucrative leases Collings, Vincent and fellow officers held in Craven, described in Chapter 7, she would have added others in Westmorland.

Entries in Anne's accounts prove that she took equally good care of the more lowly household servants, as she had at Knole during Dorset's absence in 1612. Mrs Shaw received medical attention when she suffered from bleeding. Anne sent her own litter to fetch back little Thomas Rudd when he was accidentally shot in the foot. She paid for her servant John Taylor's coffin, funeral and burial in Kirkby Stephen church on 16 April 1672 and for the arvel dinner afterwards for three score and twelve men, as his age required. She may have done the same for Gabriel Vincent in Brough. She was keen on helping with the education of the young. She gave 5*s* on 27 April 1671 to Isaac Bonaster, a poor scholar at the university who wanted maintenance there. William Layburn, an under-keeper at Whinfell and son of

82. Sir Edward Hasell (1642–1707), by Sir Peter Lely (Private collection)

one of Sir John Lowther's keepers, received 10*s* to pay for 'his learninge at Scoole' to enable him to write, a practical aid for his job, and 10*s* more for himself. The scholar Mr Thomas Machell of Queen's College, Oxford, called on her on 4 March 1675 and was given 10*s* for his return south.[33] Anne's gifts and solicitude reveal kindness and affection towards her closest intimates, such as her old servant from Ramsbury Mrs Gilmore.

Bishop Rainbow attests that her conversation, drawing on wide-ranging knowledge, was not only 'useful and grave, but also pleasant and delightful'. Whether she could really relax and joke the records do not reveal. Only two, modest instances hint that she might have done. On 6 June 1671 her entry reads, 'given the 6 day to poeticall Ambrose my old fisherman' 5*s*. On 12 October 1675 she described the chief keeper of her kitchen and haircutter in alliterative, even grandmotherly words, 'young Mr Goodgion who is my bold brave battering Beefbraining Butcher'.[34]

Anne's was a beneficent and thoughtful regime, religious and also baronial in what may be judged the most creditable sense of the term. Yet those who paid court to her would have known how best to compose themselves. Bishop Rainbow's coded phrases in his funeral sermon would not be lost on anyone who had experienced being ushered into her presence. They are worth repeating. The 'Sober and Wise', he pointed out,

83. Gabriel Vincent's tablet monument, placed by Lady Anne, St Michael's Church, Brough, Cumbria, 1666 (Photo: the author)

might look at her Chamber, as a Temple, a Court, a Tribunal, an Almonary; a place where God was daily, nay, thrice a day, worshipped; where almost every day some addresses were made from some of the chief of these parts, and strangers of the best Quality; a Tribunal where all submitted to the Doom of her Judgment, even to the sentence of her lips, as to an Oracle; and it were not insignificant if I should call it a Royal Burse, or Exchequer, where variety of presents and money flowed, and was issued out daily to some or other Objects of her Charity, Kindness, or Bounty.[35]

Outside her chamber, indeed beyond her castles' massive walls, Anne's local dominance equally prevailed. Her household removes were renowned ceremonial occasions, in which local gentry and other people often attended her in a great train, almost a royal progress. The practical side was the hiring of carts to transport the bulky furniture, hangings, linen and kitches utensils. It took forty-eight double carts at 2s 6d each to carry her goods from Appleby to Brough in September 1675. At every remove there was munificence. When, for example, she left Appleby for Pendragon on 24 March 1674 she gave 5s to the prisoners in Appleby gaol, the same to the poor, and to the ringers and waits who gave her a musical send-off. The poor on the way got 7s, those at Pendragon Castle 2s 6d, two men who helped with the trunks 4s and two men who walked beside her litter 10s; no small boost to their incomes. Interestingly, she travelled not on the highways but her own route over the fields. She disbursed to 'severall persons for pulling downe Gapps, and going, through theire Grounds at many places, by the way in compensation amounting to £1 7s 6d'.[36]

Anne's progresses were a noted feature in the life of the Eden Valley communities. Until she was approaching her eightieth birthday she also gave the lead in local celebrations. She was at Appleby at the Restoration but because of a gap her *Diaries* do not mention how she helped welcome it. Thomas Machell tells of the great rejoicing in the royalist borough and Anne's participation. On Charles II's coronation day, he writes:

there were almost as many bonfires as houses, and two stately high scaffolds at each end of the town, hung with cloth of arras and gold; whither after service done at the church, the Countess of Pembroke with the Mayor, Aldermen, and all other gentry of the country ascended, with I know not how many trumpets, and an imperial crown carried before them, where they proclaimed, prayed for, and drank, the health of the King upon their knees; the aged Countess seeming young again to grace the solemnity. The expenses of that day were very considerable. For throughout the town was kept open house, after the example of that noble Countess who thought not her gates were then wide enough to receive her guests, which had before been too wide to receive armies of soldiers.[37]

Thereafter, Anne celebrated Charles II's birthday and restoration on 29 May every year in great style. In 1668 she paid the 14s 6d costs of 'ye bone fire made on the greene by ye water side before this Brougham Castle, (vizt) for Gunpowder, Ale, the poore, Ringers and ffidlers'. At Pendragon in 1670 her 8s outlay reflects a smaller-scale but no less fervent expression of relief at the Stuart monarchy's return.[38]

Anne's charity towards the local communities was praised by Sedgewick. Every Monday morning she had 10s distributed among twenty poor householders near the castle where she was then staying, besides the daily alms disbursed to all who came to its gate. Moreover, she continued – in Westmorland perhaps resurrected – an old Clifford tradition of feasting many of her neighbours and tenants at Christmas and the New Year. For those of Bongate and Scattergate invited to Appleby Castle in 1668 the estimated cost was £14. They would have numbered dozens, all partaking of a richer fare than they normally enjoyed and perhaps with presents to boot.[39]

Appleby borough benefited most from her benevolence. With a house and lands called Kittegarth near Temple Sowerby, purchased from Edward Nevison gent. of Newby Stones in 1653 and worth in rent about £7 per annum, she established a trust for yearly repairs of the church, bridge, the school and court-house. Her relations with the school remained close. She helped secure its finances with a fund set up in 1656. On 23 October 1665 she records giving dinner to its master and scholars, all gentry's sons, probably a regular event when she stayed in the castle. In 1668 she rewarded at a cost of 3s 6d twenty-three boys of Scattergate and Appleby who came for their New Year's gifts.[40]

Anne was not at the forefront of musical patronage. Yet music obviously gave her enjoyment. The schoolboys played their part. Those at Brough sang for her at the castle on 30 December 1665 'as they usually doe at Christmas'. Rewards totalling 18s 6d were given to players and New Year's Boys at Brougham on 16 January 1671. The players, New Year's Boys, the Lights and Torch Boys and the waits of Brough received £1 1s on 12 January 1674. Anne had a harpsichord at Brougham and virginals at Appleby which were regularly repaired and must have been used during her stays. John Shaw, the fiddler of Mallerstang, frequently played for her in her chamber and visiting pipers too, so it was not quite so austere as the bishop implies. John Corbett, the Appleby wait, sang under her window at the castle every morning in the winter of 1674. He would have earned his mulled ale in the kitchen afterwards.[41]

Lady Anne's most intimate relations outside the castle were with her Appleby almswomen. Rainbow tells how she frequently visited them, sat chatting with them and shared their dinner. In return, several came to the castle weekly to eat and talk with her, all of them once a month. She insisted her relatives called on the Sisters whenever they came to see her, before reaching her if possible.[42] Her deigning to be in their company was not so humbling as Rainbow implies because, as mentioned in Chapter 8, the almswomen were old servants, some from minor local gentry families who were also her friends, so that at St Anne's Hospital they really remained within her household.

Like Beamsley, St Anne's was a strict religious establishment, as a glance at the biblical sayings painted on its walls reminds visitors today (Pl. 84). The parson of Appleby, as Reader, received £2 a quarter for saying daily prayers. The Mother got £2 a quarter, with £3 yearly for repairs to the building. Each Sister received £1 10s quarterly. Anne gave them the coal to heat their chambers, such as thirteen loads for which she paid 11d a load on 17 April 1669 to Mr Henry

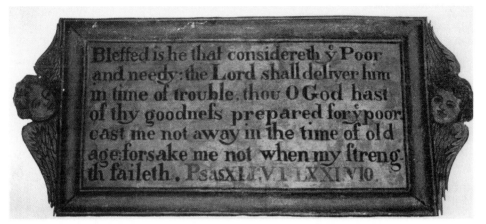

84. *Biblical wall text, St Anne's Hospital chapel, Appleby-in-Westmorland, eighteenth-century replacement of the original (Photo: the author)*

Machell. With their endowment the inmates, therefore, were well catered for and their free coal kept their chambers and common room cosy. Moreover, Anne always employed one or two of the more nimble sisters, which would keep them alert in body and mind. Jane Dargue was one; in November 1671 she obtained for Anne 80 yards of coarse linen cloth at 1*s* 6*d* a yard to make seven pairs of sheets for use in the house.[43]

With her gentry neighbours and friends, Anne's donations created a kind of client relationship, though there is no reason to doubt that, as with the gifts of food from the Laytons and other presents, there was reciprocation. The difficulty posed in interpreting whether for Anne there was any special meaning is, first, that there was nothing unusual about noble–gentry connections, indeed it was part of the bonding which held society together. Nor, second, is there any telling whether the symbolism of Anne's gifts carried for the parties the weight that is assumed today. It is, perhaps, best to allow that friendship, practicality and gratification of Anne's love of munificence were the reasons for her choice of such gifts, as they were for the presents described above.

The beds Anne bestowed on her officers were, it is believed, to ensure that she got a good night's sleep when she visited them. Yet beds were symbolic of close marital relations, at the heart of the family, in which Anne set great store. The surviving beds are proof that they were constructed sturdily and with style. Anne's penchant for George Dent's locks is well known, for her castles, churches and bestowing them on friends; not so the hyperbole with which she described their purchase; for '3 Huge, great, mighty large Stock-locks to give away at 20*s* a Locke', £3.[44] Mighty they remain, as serviceable as when they were affixed and, engraved with the initials 'AP', lasting memorials to their noble donor (Pl. 85).

For all the multiplicity of paintings produced in the workshops of the great court artists like Van Dyck and Lely, nothing matches the proliferation of the copies of her own portrait Anne commissioned from the Kirkby Stephen painter Mr John Bracken. Donated to her family, gentry officers and neighbours they would bring the immediacy of the great lady to the mind's eye,

85. *Stock-lock, made for Lady Anne by George Dent, whitesmith of Appleby, and incised with her initials and date, Dacre Church, Cumbria, 1671 (Photo: the author)*

whether the recipients had met her or not, and give dignity to their picture galleries, at no cost to themselves. The twenty or more known copies have been analysed and Bracken's career outlined by Mary Burkett.[45] But under Anne's patronage his work was far more varied, because he also copied for her portraits of members of her extended family and coats of arms, as new details from her accounts show (App. III). It is one of the oddities of Anne's later years that she employed Bracken, not to paint new depictions of her, but to repeat Lely's when she was 'aged about 60', even when she had reached her eightieth birthday, a form of self-flattery. The copies project a certain sourness in her looks, yet that is how she preferred to be known. By contrast, Bracken's portrait of her in extreme old age as a veritable mother superior is a sensitive and finely executed study (Pl. 86).

Lady Anne's eminence as a great landowner and sheriff in Westmorland would have been incomplete without the reality of political influence. In fact, she stands alone as a Clifford lady in her exercise of political patronage in the county. During the Interregnum there was little she could do but wait for more favoured times, ushered in by the dissolution of the Long Parliament in March 1660. In her *Diaries* she writes that at the ensuing elections for the Convention Parliament there were chosen for the 'most part by my means' her cousins Sir Thomas Wharton (Lord Philip's brother) and Sir John Lowther as knights of the shire for Westmorland and her cousins and officers Sir Henry Cholmley and Christopher Clapham Esq. as burgesses for Appleby. Both the latter were Yorkshiremen and supporters of the Cromwellian regime, and Clapham was a close friend of the former member, Captain Adam Baynes. Anne had never hesitated to employ adherents of the Parliament or Cromwell, placing her interests and friendship above politics, witness Widdrington, Hale, the Cholmleys and Claphams.

It was hollow boasting for her to claim credit for the election of the Westmorland members. She could not influence 3,000 electors, the bulk of them in Kendal barony, though her support would help. Lowther's own egotistical assertion that his popularity and outlay on expenses carried the day for himself, with Wharton tagging on, carries more conviction. Anne would have been equally supportive and gratified by the election of her cousin Sir Philip Musgrave and Sir Thomas

86. *Lady Anne in extreme old age, by John Bracken (Reproduced by courtesy of Abbot Hall Art Gallery, Kendal)*

Strickland, another former Royalist colonel, as knights of the shire for the 'Cavalier Parliament' in 1661.[46]

The Appleby burgesses, however, were very much her nominees. A small borough in the shadow of a great castle, it had always been politically as well as economically dominated by the Cliffords. The earl of Cork had sat for it in 1640 as Earl Francis's nominee. For the 'Cavalier Parliament' of 1661, Anne not only returned the writ as High Sheriff but again patently chose as burgesses John Lowther Esq., son of Sir John, and John Dalston Esq. of Dalston in Cumberland, another Royalist officer of note. The corporation would have approved. How absolute her influence was became apparent to court as well as county on Lowther's death, when there was great competition to replace him. The gentry aspirants included Christopher Clapham again; two more Yorkshiremen, Humphrey Wharton and Anthony Lowther, a relation of Sir John; two local men, Sir Richard Sandford and Richard Brathwaite, and Henry Sidney, who appealed to the townsmen because of the patronage he could offer. Most formidably, Joseph Williamson, another Cumbrian, enjoyed powerful advocacy as private secretary to the Secretary of State Sir Henry Bennet, Earl of Arlington.

The efforts of Arlington and other influential lobbyists to persuade Anne to yield the seat to their man have been described by Dr Williamson. In an exchange of courteous letters, Anne (then at Brougham) explained her prior commitment to see that one of her four Tufton grandsons, now all of age, was elected. Various correspondents made plain that only she could decide. Daniel

Fleming Esq. of Rydal told Williamson that the electors of Appleby 'dare not go any way but that which is chalked them out by my Lady, she is (I believe) as absolute in that borough as any are in any other'. Williamson's brother George was even more forthright. He told Joseph that Appleby town was for him and so were most of the gentry and persons of quality in the barony and they had 'left no stone unturned with the old woman . . . but to no purpose for she is resolved wholly to stand for her grandchildren'. Sir Philip Musgrave likewise could not prevail with her. Her under-sheriff Gabetis tended to favour Williamson and so did Sedgewick but he confessed that with Anne so strongly for her relations 'I am forced to acquiesce and submit to that, above all interests whatsoever.'

With his brothers out of town, it was Thomas Tufton who accepted his grandmother's offer of a burgess-ship and efforts to persuade him to stand aside failed. He was duly elected in 1668 and again at the next election, with Dalston as his fellow. Anne was filled with pride and pleasure at having her first-ever grandson member in parliament and representing her borough. To argue, as some of the writers did, that local issues would not be addressed and the people would be undone if Tufton was elected was specious, because so many members of parliament were nominees and Tufton's worthy behaviour when he became earl (as will be seen in Chapter 12) suggests he was in sentiment no outsider. As a nobleman's younger son he would covet a seat and dare not offend his grandmother. She, it was averred, had promised Sir John Lowther that Anthony would get the place if Tufton withdrew, but also was heard to say that if all her grandsons refused 'she will stand for it herself'; as well she might have, considering her views on the efficacy of noblewomen in tendering advice to the Crown.

What the voluminous correspondence reveals is how Anne was viewed by her contemporaries. Those who called her 'the old woman' did so more from frustration than disparagement. Those who understood her best were realistic. Dalston of Acorn Bank affirmed that to 'move the countess in anything that is averse to her own resolutions (as Sir Philip Musgrave can tell you) would not only be labour in vain, but even a prejudice to those who press it to her'. Anyone with even an inkling of Anne's experiences of courtier machinations would have known that she could match Arlington's blandishments, marshalling telling counter-arguments of sentiment and proven loyalty which he must have wryly appreciated. 'I know very well how powerful a man a Secretary of State is, throughout all our King's dominions', she confessed to him, so she was confident he would quickly help Joseph Williamson to a burgess-ship 'without doing wrong or discourtesy to a widow that wants but 2 of fourscore years old, and to her grandchildren, whose father and mother suffered as much in their worldly fortunes for the King as most of his Majesty's subjects did'.[47]

If there is a touch of a born-again medieval suzerain in Anne's manipulations of the Appleby elections, just as in her exercise of seigneurial authority within her barony of Westmorland, it was subsumed within a world-view enriched by knowledge from the inside of the workings of royal administration and politickings in Westminster. Fending off a mere secretary of state from far-away Appleby where she held all the cards was easily managed when she had already achieved the like against the overweening authority of the Westminster lawcourts, which will be the opening theme of the final chapter of this study.

CHAPTER 12

The Grand Matriarch

For the last of the four 'ages' of her life, almost a third in terms of years, Lady Anne was the matriarchal head of an extended family of two daughters and their husbands, many grandchildren and great-grandchildren, her Burlington cousins, and her Dorset and Pembroke stepchildren and grandchildren. Her relationship with, and behaviour towards, them is crucial to any interpretation of her character and attitudes. The munificence and expressed affection described in the previous chapter were one side of the coin. The other, as uncompromising and litigious as against her tenants, was touched on when explaining her subtle campaign against the Corks in Craven. This element in her attitude, which will now be more broadly treated, was redolent of medieval baronialism. Although Isabella de Vipont had lived almost four hundred years before, Anne donned her mantle, assuming the posture of a Plantagenet suzerain in Westmorland.

This mode surfaced during tense legal battles in the Westminster lawcourts concerning, not her own northern properties, but her Sussex jointure manors. She upset her Dorset and Thanet relatives and seriously offended royal administration by acting as if the barony of Westmorland were an independent fiefdom and her shrievalty set her apart from, even above, the law of the realm. She was not obliged, as her baronial forebears would have been, to man her castles and stand defiant in her Westmorland fastnesses; she managed to remain inviolate by other means.

Anne's penchant for litigation has been amply illustrated in the course of this study. It was while in the throes of the suits she inflicted on Currer, Cork and her Westmorland tenants that she had forced on her, as defendant, two even more tortuous issues. The first was a new phase in the recurrent squabbles over Sackville College's income. The other, which has not been noticed until now, was the renewal after forty years of the great inheritance dispute just when Sir Matthew Hale was asserting in his 'History' that the matter was long finished.[1] During the 1660s these separate issues merged to create the most intense wrangling within the various branches of Anne's extended family which she or they ever experienced. Anne was the chief instigator of the worst troubles yet it was her close relatives, not she, who suffered as a result.

The Civil Wars had exacerbated the financial privations of the almspeople of Sackville College. In 1648 they again resorted to law, initially against the earl of Thanet. Then, in a series of Chancery suits during the 1650s, Anne joined with Thanet and her other son-in-law Northampton against Earl Edward's successor, Richard Sackville, 5th Earl of Dorset, and Lord William Howard's successor, Charles, Earl of Carlisle. The warden and poor were involved with both sides,

87. John Tufton, 2nd Earl of Thanet (1609–64) and Margaret Sackville, Countess of Thanet (1614–76), artist unknown, 1640 (H.T. Fattorini Esq.)

sometimes as complainants, at other times as defendants, according to which party best helped their cause or against which they had to defend their interests. Anne's case against the college, printed as was now the fashion in 1655, conceded that the lands in dispute were her jointure lands yet forcefully maintained that what she had paid the college had been to her own disadvantage because her tenants, having been served with attachments following a decree in Chancery, had appealed and were acquitted.[2]

Nevertheless, early in 1660 Dorset and Howard won the argument, with a 'final' decree in favour of themselves and the warden and poor. Samuel Pepys was an observer in Westminster Hall on 9 February and recorded in his diary that he heard the action 'very finely pleaded between my Lord Dorset and some other noble persons, his lady and other ladies of quality being there'.[3] Anne and her sons-in-law, all three occupying parts of her Sussex jointure estates, were now faced with paying large cash sums to the college, the arrears of their rents due over many years. There were indignities for both Thanet, who was arrested in January 1660/1, and Dorset who was threatened with the Fleet prison if he did not attend the sittings.

The decree, as so often happened, did not end the dispute because of the problems of enforcing it. Anne did her best to circumvent it by taking the extreme but understandable action in 1662 of presenting a bill to the House of Commons which, if enacted, would have protected the full value of her jointure revenues. It was objected to and proceeded no further.[4] Instead, she and, quite separately, Dorset resorted to more Chancery suits against the college and in 1667 Countess Dowager Margaret and Lady Alethea Compton (Countess Isabella having died) instituted proceedings against Dorset and the college jointly.

The central issue, however, remained that of enforcing the 1660 court order. Anne defied the court with the result that her co-defendant Thanet became the scapegoat. He was imprisoned in the Fleet for a month between 21 December 1663 and 21 January 1664, thus spending both Christmas and the New Year in the unfestive discomfort of gaol, as Anne rather casually notes in her *Diaries*.[5] The stance Anne had taken was the burden of Dorset's complaint to the court at the hearings on 24 May 1667 in a new suit he brought against her. It is a striking insight into how she regarded herself now, safely insulated within her Westmorland domains.

She had, Dorset reminded the court, deliberately caused long delays, 'she being sherriff of the County of Westmorland by Inheritance'. To be specific, she had refused to answer Dorset's bill, which prevented any progress in the suit, and when the court issued an attachment against her to persuade her to bow to its will she had by implication browbeaten one of the coroners into not returning an answer, which made the other coroner's return null and void. Earl Francis, it will be recalled, did not abuse his position as sheriff in this manner when in dispute with Anne's mother. He allowed the coroners to substitute for him impartially. Not so Anne. Dorset now asked the court to issue another attachment against her, to extract from her a proper answer to his bill and to send a messenger to enforce the attendance of the miscreant coroner, which would allow the earlier return from Westmorland to be completed to the court's satisfaction.[6]

Patently, Anne had rejected her lawyer Howell's correct interpretation of her powers as sheriff, learnt from her Stainmore tenants during the 1650s how impotent the Westminster courts were to enforce compliance in the far north and shamelessly exploited the weakness of county administration if the sheriff, herself, refused to co-operate with the courts. In short, all she need do was over-awe one of the two coroners and that would make returns from the shire to Westminster null and void. In 1650 she had wanted to obstruct the Corks' resort to what she termed 'my County Court' in Westmorland. Later, she had been guilty of packing the juries at Appleby assizes, though they had not proved amenable to her cause. Now she was deploying other underhand methods in order to get her own way. She well understood how vital the sheriff was in serving writs for the Westminster lawcourts. In every other shire an incompetent or non-cooperative sheriff could be dismissed; but not Anne. Exploiting her hereditary authority for private advantage was reprehensible. Sheriffs had got away with it in the high Middle Ages with a weak king on the throne. John 'the Butcher', 9th Lord Clifford, was probably the last to do so and escape censure. All his successors had eschewed it, well aware of how Yorkist and then Tudor wrath would make them suffer. Anne all but arrogated to herself the powers Fulke Greville ascribed to Scottish sheriffs in his poem 'A Treatise of Monarchy':

In *Scotland* their hereditarie sheriffes,
Each as a viceroy in his natyve shere.[7]

Anne was both fortunate and deeply perceptive. Times had changed. Her anachronistic behaviour nonplussed the Westminster courts. Charles II would have looked absurd as a latter-day Henry VII demanding the submission of an elderly dowager countess. Moreover, she was impervious to the usual Stuart bribes of office, land, titles and pliant mistresses. Best therefore to take a relaxed attitude and, as Oliver Cromwell is reputed to have concluded over her castle rebuilding, leave her be. After all, even though she went scotfree, Thanet and her other relatives could be, and were, made to bear the brunt of Chancery decrees in support of the almspeople. All this would have been well known to Arlington when he and his friends crossed swords with Anne over the 1668 Appleby election and learnt at first hand how absolute 'the old woman' was in that domain.

The second and greater issue embraced the whole of Anne's extended family, the Thanets, Northamptons, Dorsets and Burlingtons. Anne provoked it with her studied campaign to overthrow the King's Award. Then it developed an impetus of its own in a direction none of the parties could have predicted. As mentioned in Chapter 7, Burlington in the early 1650s became annoyed and then exasperated at Anne's ejectments of tenants in Craven and Westmorland on the grounds that their grants had been sanctioned by the King's Award. He was not a man to be trifled with once he had cleared himself of the stigma of royalism. Although he was handicapped throughout that decade by having to remain in Ireland to manage his affairs there, he fired warning shots across Anne's bows which she would have done well to heed.

Burlington made up his mind in 1652. His intention was to force Anne to stop claiming his Skipton and Cumberland properties, to halt her suits against the tenants and, in general, make her comply with the award. If she did not do so, his plan was to take possession of the six Sussex manors assigned in 1617 to John Ecton and Thomas Pickering as security against Anne's failing to abide by the award and recover from them the £17,000 paid by Earl Francis, which he regarded now as forfeit. Because these were also Anne's jointure manors, which she had in part granted to her daughters, neither she nor they and their husbands could remain aloof.

Burlington scrupulously followed the correct legal procedures. He located the heirs of Ecton and Pickering, that is Richard Ellis and Shadrack Dunning and his wife Elizabeth. When Anne ejected the Jennings family from Silsden in 1654 and George Shaw of Stainmore in 1656 Burlington got Ellis and Dunning to leave notes at Dorset House detailing the ejectments and requiring repayment of the £17,000 by Dorset's successor, the present Earl Richard. The latter, not best pleased, defended himself by introducing a bill in Chancery against Burlington and Countess Elizabeth conjoined with Lady Anne, requesting that the former should enter Anne's jointure manors to indemnify themselves against her breach of the award. This would, he hoped, safeguard himself and the £17,000. His worry was that if Anne, 'being a person of great years', died he would be held accountable for her misdemeanours.

Anne was served with a subpoena to attend the court and the Burlingtons, again in Ireland, with similar processes. All failed to answer. They still had not done so in 1662 when Burlington, back in Craven, stepped up his pressure on Anne. In an indenture tripartite of 12 April he got Ellis and Dunning to assign the Sussex manors in trust to his wife's cousin Sir Clifford Clifton of Clifton, Nottinghamshire, and Anthony Eyre Esq. Then, on 12 May, Clifton and Eyre levied a fine on the manors in Lady Cork's name, she being the right heir to Earls Francis and Henry. This action would have alarmed not just Dorset but Thanet, Northampton and Anne herself, because all three enjoyed income from Anne's jointure and Dorset had the reversionary interest on her death. They had difficulties enough already because of Chancery's orders on behalf of Sackville College, for which the court was still levying part of the manorial revenues. It appears to have been Burlington's threat which persuaded Anne to limit her Craven claims to just Eshton, Grassington, Nesfield, Malham and the Skipton properties, as commented on in Chapter 7. If so, then he had largely achieved his object.

The denouement, when it came two years later, took an unexpected turn. All hinged on Nicholas, Lord Tufton. He was independent-minded, possibly too much for his own good because he had ended up in the Tower more than once for plotting against the Cromwellian regime. His father Thanet, having refused in 1650 to give him an allowance unless he married, had since endowed him with a sizeable estate, so that he had ample means of his own. Thanet approved of Burlington's daughter Lady Elizabeth Boyle and had told his heir he could marry her whenever he chose. But Tufton (now thirty-four) pursued the 48-year-old, thrice-widowed Annabel, Dowager Countess of Kent, until she finally rejected him and only then did he turn to Lady Elizabeth. He agreed terms with Burlington, but did not tell his parents. In the marriage settlement drawn up on 3 February 1664 and the agreement of 9 April 1664, Burlington gave his daughter a portion of £10,000 and Tufton assigned all his own lands as her jointure estate and assured her a yearly income of £1,500. On Easter Monday, 11 April, Burlington bound himself in a £20,000 recognizance to pay the portion to Tufton. The wedding took place that same day in Countess Elizabeth's chamber in Clifford's Inn. It was very private. Their son Richard, Sir Henry Jones and 'honest Graham our Sollicitor' were the only others present.[8]

Tufton's parents were kept in the dark about the wedding. Countess Margaret complained to her mother on 5 May that they suspected he had married and had asked him about it but he had denied it. Lady Anne probably learnt of it before them. The Tufton–Boyle match completely overturned the alignments within her extended family. On the one hand, Burlington, Lord Nicholas and his bride and Anne were drawn closer together because Anne's grandson had married her goddaughter, which touched her sentiments. On the other hand, Northampton veered towards Dorset with whom he was on excellent terms and who was godfather to one of his sons. By contrast, Thanet and Countess Margaret seemed out on a limb. Then the whole family situation was subverted by Thanet's death on 7 May. With Nicholas now earl and Elizabeth his countess, his mother was relegated to a back seat as dowager countess. On 29 July Earl Nicholas and his bride and his brother John rode to Appleby to pay court to their formidable grandmother who, as her diary tells us, made much of them.[9]

At precisely this moment Anne's officer in the south, William Edge, was informing the Dorsets of the fine Burlington had levied in 1662 – or possibly a new fine – on all Anne's jointure estate. This uncompromising action, which ostensibly was directed against Anne over her breach of the award, in practice proved far more to the Dorsets' discomfort. Earl Richard and his Countess Frances wrote separately on 1 August from Dorset House imploring Anne to think of the consequences for them of the fine on their reversion of the manors and the future burden it would impose on them. They appealed to her sense of honour, reminded her of her honourable late husband Dorset and besought her to make the case her own. They prayed that she, who had the 'ffame of doing good to all the world', would not be the occasion of their ruin and destruction. The countess appended: 'All mine humbly kisse your Ladyship's hands and your Godsonne beggs your blessing.'[10]

Earl Richard was so distraught over the possible financial consequences that he petitioned Charles II to intervene. He rehearsed for the merry monarch's benefit the history of the disputes from the time of the King's Award, Anne's litigation to eject her tenants and Burlington's counter-actions from 1652/3 when he first deposited notes at Dorset House. He stressed the great damage Burlington's levying the fine would do to him. He closed with an appeal to Charles (because it had been his grandfather King James who made the original award) to hear the differences between Burlington and himself and, in his princely wisdom, make a further award or decree.[11]

The suspicion is that Burlington was less concerned with Anne, the tenant issues and the King's Award than with the welfare of his daughter and her husband who had now entered the big Thanet inheritance in the south and were heirs to Anne's Westmorland estates. Earl Nicholas was constrained to come to terms with his numerous brothers about the succession to the Thanet inheritance and Burlington was a party to the settlement drawn up on 6 February 1665. As for Anne, her contentment with the Tufton–Boyle match seems to have doused much of her former fire. Now that she and the Burlingtons were doubly related and her lawsuits were petering out the issues between them were allowed to subside, at least in an active sense.[12] The exasperated Dorsets could make no headway against her. She would have been quietly satisfied with her success in arrogating shrievalty powers which even the brashest of medieval lords would have hesitated to use and which horrified her legal advisers.

This is the context in which to consider and interpret the 'Portrait of a Lady' (Pl. 88).[13] It is an imposing painting, unframed 44 x 36 inches (111.9 x 91.5 cm), which has only recently come to light. The subject is a widow, three-quarter length, half-turned right, seated in a chair in front of a pillar and draped curtain, and in the background left a country scene with a castle. The costume and lace date it to the 1660s, with 1665 as perhaps the closest. That, it may be argued, rules out Lady Anne as the sitter, because in 1665 she would have been seventy-five and the features and arms of the subject are clearly those of a much younger woman. If that major obstacle is set aside for the time being, all the other elements coalesce into supporting a conjecture that it could indeed be she.

88. 'Portrait of a Lady', supposedly Lady Anne, artist unknown, c. 1664/8 (Private collection)

The sitter is patently a lady of the highest social standing. Her attire, though sober and restrained, is nevertheless material of the finest quality, black silk and satin with a black silk hood and, what was then extremely costly and worn only by the wealthiest, black-silk lace, often hard to see but in this painting delicately visible. The tight-boned bodice slopes to a deep point at the front, with tabs

237

flaring out at the hips, their white, curvilinear decoration just discernible under the diaphanous silk overskirt. The ruffled sleeves leave the lower arms bare but for black strings. Over the high forehead is a tipmut, or pointed hat, and three diaphanous scarves cover her head and are tied under the chin. The whisk, or collar, of heavyish Flemish lace, its intricate pattern containing oak leaves and strawberries, falls deep over her shoulders and breast, part-covered by the overskirt. The painter has gone to pains to etch in the fine mesh and patterns of the white-laced whisk.

The chair is English, richly upholstered in green leather, with fringes and tassels of gold thread and matching studs; a rich item appropriate to the wealthy. The sitter's left hand rests easily on the curve of the arm, positioned to show off the two rings on her third finger, one with and one without a gemstone. The plain heavy gold wedding ring symbolized an indissoluble bond and so lifted a widow's standing. The jewel of the other is an emerald, its symbolism venereal, betokening love. In her gracefully cocked right hand, the sitter holds an ostrich feather fan, another status symbol enhanced in this case by its gold mount, similar to that shown by Wenceslaus Hollar in his 1647 engraving, *Fashion Accessories*.

Pillars in portraits emphasize position and authority, for women as for men. In this 'Portrait of a Lady' it stands solid and large, the chair all but touching its broad base. Three colours dominate the foreground: the black of the costume, wrist-strings, ribbons and fan; the green of drapes, chair and emerald; and the gold of the rings, chair fringes and fan mount with, not too dissimilar, the dark sand of the pillar. All these point up the paler flesh texture of face and arms and the white of the whisk. The country scene adds to the depth and perspective, the sombre shades of the landscape brightened by clouds streaked with blue sky and silvered by the glow of a late evening, seemingly late summer sun.

The seated figure has a commanding presence, with a calm, self-assured posture and dignity of demeanour. Full-eyed to the viewer, she is strikingly no ordinary lady. Her widow's weeds are unusually rich and the symbols of affluence and status are discreet but explicit. Some elements in the composition, such as the strings, chair and drapes, date to the eras of Mytens and Van Dyck or even earlier. But others, notably her dress and whisk and, it may be argued, the shape of the pillar, place the painting firmly in the era of Lely and his contemporaries. Since Lady Anne is not known to have commissioned an original portrait between Lely's in 1649 and Bracken's near the end of her life (both of them head and shoulders only) postulating her as the subject of this quite distinctive painting may be considered all the harder to sustain.

Nevertheless, the case has substance. The equally restrained richness of Anne's black attire in the right hand wing of the triptych readily comes to mind. But here there are neither pearls to denote affluence nor coats of arms to point to subordination to a husband; only the rings hint at that. What is most telling is that as a psychological study of Anne the portrait could hardly be bettered. Here enthroned almost is the triple baroness in her own right; the triple countess displaying the gold rings which brought her those titles; and the High

Sheriffess of Westmorland, who had asserted her suzeraignty over her tenants and defied the judges in Westminster. The marble pillars of Knole and Wilton had brought her anguish; her own pillar here is a massive symbol of her standing in her own countryside. The scene in the background clinches the argument (Pl. 89). The castle depicted is her treasured Brougham, set within Whinfell Forest, the River Eden (or perhaps Eamont) flowing below, and receding towards the skyline the range of hills she would have viewed from her own chamber in this most historic and nostalgic of her properties.

However, three particular difficulties remain, notably the age discrepancy, the occasion, and the attribution to a known painter of the Restoration era.

89. Inset, showing country scene with Brougham Castle, 'Portrait of a Lady', artist unknown, c. 1664/8 (Private collection)

Severest is the matter of age. Flattery has always been a feature of the art of accomplished portraitists and Anne indulged herself by her gifts of Bracken's copies of her near-sixty portrait until she was over eighty. She might have recovered some of her youthful looks after Lely painted her, her country life restoring the vitality lost by her six-year-long incarceration in Baynard's. She was certainly more sprightly at the Restoration festivities in Appleby. Yet in 1667 she wrote that she was suffering the infirmities of old age.[14] That would require the painter to imagine Anne's looks in her younger days, a problematical matter when the musculature of the features indicates they were most likely painted from life, not copied as in the triptych. That said, the eyes, nose, mouth, dimple on the chin, line of jaw and the deep line between nose and cheek are all too reminiscent of Anne; not least, the hint of sourness of the triptych likeness and Bracken's copies.

An apposite occasion would be the sixtieth anniversary of Anne's rightful inheritance in 1605, properly 30 October when she lay at Appleby. However, her *Diaries* ignore that event. Indeed, what she makes most of, as described above, was Earl Nicholas's wedding a year earlier. During the following July and August 1664 a succession of Tuftons visited Anne at Appleby. Her favourite grandson John came and went; Earl Nicholas and his countess stayed with her for eleven days from 29 July, and the Dowager Countess Margaret with her three youngest daughters from 16 August. What makes 1664 special was that Anne

90. Thanet fireplace, Langdale Chase Hotel, Windermere, Cumbria, with Thanet and Boyle arms and inscription, 1664 (Photo: the author)

commemorated Nicholas's marriage with a highly ornate fireplace-surround custom-built for one of the Appleby chambers, perhaps the Baron's in Caesar's Tower which is where he and his bride slept (Pl. 90).

Nothing like this fireplace has survived from any of the Clifford residences. It is large, ornate and finely crafted in oak. The Tufton and Boyle coats are prominently and repeatedly incised in the decorated panels; respectively, 'Sable, an eagle displayed ermine within a bordure argent', and 'Per bend embattled, argent and gules'. Naked antique or primitive male and female figures, a popular feature of carvers of this era, symbolize sexual unity and harmony. The rows of capital letters, large at the top of the upper section and decreasing further down, read:

GODS PROVIDENCE IS MINE INHERITANCE

ANO 1664

CAROLVS 2nd DEI GRATIA

NICHOLAS TVFTON EARL OF THANET AND ELIZABETH COVNTESSE OF THANET

ALES VOLAT PROPRIIS HONOR VIRTVIS PRAEMIVM

This bottom line is, first, the Tufton motto, translated as 'A Bird flies on its own wings' (their eagle) qualified by 'Honour flies by the rewards of valour'.

The Christian message of the top line is strikingly reinforced by the two large panels which Dr Gladstone has identified as depicting lauded incidents in the reign of King Canute (Pl. 91). The left-hand scene is the famous occasion recorded by the chronicler Henry of Huntingdon which Camden described at length. Canute, seated in his chair on the shore, commanded the sea not to come upon his land. As it still flowed, forcing him to retire, he proclaimed 'that vaine and frivolous is the power of Kings, and that none is worthy the name of King, but hee to whose command the heaven earth and sea by bond of everlasting law are subject and obedient'. The historic scene of the right-hand panel is Canute's grand convention with his nobles at Oxford when he made good laws, especially those regarding religion. Sir Richard Baker highlighted both episodes in his history of the kings of England, first published during the political crisis of 1641 and frequently reissued after the Restoration.[15]

If this splendid fireplace was the welcome which greeted Earl Nicholas and his bride on 29 July, then the 'Portrait of a Lady' could well be their reciprocal gift. Perhaps not then, but on 31 July 1668 when Earl Nicholas arrived at Appleby after a long journey with his company from Hothfield House in Kent, but without his wife who had stayed with Anne at Barden Tower a year earlier. After Elizabeth's visit, Anne had written to her cousin complimenting her on her daughter whom she had found very acceptable and a good conversationalist. She accounted her grandson 'very happie in soe good, soe vertuous & soe discreete a Wife' and closed 'Your La[dyshipps] Affectnatt

91. *Detail showing panels depicting incidents in King Canute's reign, Thanet fireplace, Langdale Chase Hotel, 1664 (Photo: the author)*

Cossen and Humble Sarvant Anne Pembrooke'. Nicholas was entertained at Appleby for a week and, unusually, Anne gave him £100.[16] There is no entry in Anne's accounts of payment for any painting between 1665 and 1668, albeit they are incomplete for those years. So the best guess is that she received the portrait as a present from her grandson and goddaughter. Despite its English style, Netherlandish influences, and hints of similarity in the pillar to those in pictures by Lely's circle, the painter cannot be identified. One of the portrait's more intriguing features is its lack of mannerism, notably in the sitter's hands. For the time being, precise attribution of both sitter and painter remains speculative. Yet it is hard to envisage any other widowed lady but Anne, aptly seated in baronial style before her beloved Brougham Castle.

Lady Anne died on Wednesday 22 March 1676 about six o'clock in the afternoon, having endured all her pains with Christian fortitude, in the Brougham chamber where she wanted to end her life, as her mother had done. Her express wish was for a quiet family funeral but she left the door open for relatives and friends to attend. It was not to be missed and a huge assembly heard Bishop Rainbow's three-hour-long panegyric. Anne's unopened body, wrapped in lead and in a lead coffin, was buried in the vault she had built for herself. The coffin is just over 6 feet long, tapering from its greatest width of 17 inches (43 cm) at the shoulder. It bears an engraved figure of face and body ending at the chest and below is a brass plate with her own inscription:

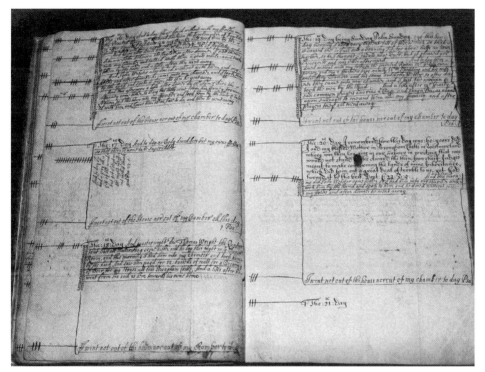

92. The final folios of Lady Anne's day book, 16–21 March 1676 (Private collection. Photo: the author)

> Ye body of ye most noble, virtuous, and religious Lady
> Anne, Countess Dowager of Pembroke, Dorset, and Montgomery,
> daughter and sole heir to ye Right Honourable
> George Clifford, Earl of Cumberland, and Baroness
> Clifford, Westmerland and Vescey, Lady of ye Honour
> of Skipton in Craven, and High Sheriff by inheritance
> of Westmerland, who departed this life at her castle
> at Brougham, in ye county, ye 22nd March, 1675, having
> attained ye age of 86 years ye 30th of January before.[17]

For two of her relatives, Richard, 5th Earl of Dorset, and Philip, 7th Earl of Pembroke, there were no regrets at the death of the 'old Countess'. From the early 1660s, Dorset had been eagerly awaiting his aunt's demise. He regularly checked the rental value of her jointure manors which he stood to inherit, the income by this time said to be about £2,000 (Table 7). From 1660 he had been entering into bonds to pay debts and agreements with his children, promising to honour them as soon as Anne's manors fell to him.[18] His hopes were prematurely raised in 1668 when incorrect reports of her decease reached him from several informants. He would have been distressed had he known then that the estates would be detained from him for another eight years. It has to be

TABLE 11 *Miniatures, jewels and plate bequeathed by Lady Anne, 1676*

1 *Miniatures of*:

Lady Anne, aged about twenty, set in a tablet case of gold with
   black enamelling
Earl George; Countess Margaret; set together in a tablet of gold
   and enamelled in blue
Philip, 4th Earl of Pembroke, by Hilliard 'the famous limner', set
   in a gold case and enamelled in blue
Philip, 4th Earl of Pembroke, in her pamicie picture case with a
   diamond on one side and a ruby on the other which had been her
   aunt the Countess of Bath's
Countess Isabella, set in blue stone
Lady Margaret Coventry (her granddaughter), set in gold

2 *Jewels*

Best ring, set with a great oriental amethyst, which had been her
   aunt the Countess of Warwick's
Bracelet of 57 little pomander beads set in gold and enamelling,
   given by King Philip to her great-grandmother Anne, Countess
   of Bedford, usually worn under her stomacher
Silver medal, and a case for it, engraved with William, 1st Earl of
   Pembroke on one side, the Temple of Virtue guarded by a dragon
   on the other, inscribed round in Latin (d. 1562)

3 *Plate*

Gold cup with cover, eng'ed with the arms of James, Earl of Northampton,
   Countess Isabella and Lady Anne
Gold cup with cover, engraved with the arms of John, Earl of Thanet,
   Countess Margaret and Lady Anne
Silver basin and ewer, engraved with Scripture history and some of
   the kings of England, which had been the Earl of Pembroke's
Twelve silver plates of the same workmanship, previously Pembroke's
Terra-Lemnia jug with cover, set with gold and enamelling, bought from
   Pembroke's executors
A little heliotropan cup, set in silver and gilt, previously Earl
   George's
Agate jug, formed with gold and with a gold cover, bought from Pembroke's
   executors
Twenty silver plates, engraved with Pembroke's and Lady Anne's arms
Large silver standish, legacy from her uncle William, Lord Russell
Crystal cup, cut in flowers and made in the fashion of a boat
Crystal cane, bought from Pembroke's executors
Four of her best silver fruit dishes

Source: Clay, pp. 408–10

said that Anne administered the manors considerately, with an eye to the Dorsets' reversion, ensuring that the terms of leases made and other decisions taken would be in their interests as well as her own. That was little consolation for being denied them for so long.[19]

Dorset was overjoyed at Anne's demise. Her manors helped restore his parlous finances. A bonus was their half-yearly revenues which her timely death brought him. All the other arrears went to Countess Margaret. No wonder there was competition to let him know the welcome news. The winner of the race to bring word could hope for 20 guineas in reward. Pembroke reacted in similar fashion, the Kent lands reverting to him after Anne had outlived his three predecessors. Because her interest in Ramsbury (her designated jointure house perhaps) was extinguished, he sold it in December for £32,000.[20]

No other residual issues were settled so swiftly. Characteristically Anne, emulating her father though far more intrusively, tried to rule her inheritance from the grave. She claimed in her will that her uncle's action in breaking the entail in 1607, which she had never recognized, gave her the power as the last heir general to leave her lands as she wished. She bequeathed all her Westmorland properties and rights to Countess Margaret and all those in Craven with the Honour of Skipton to her granddaughter Lady Alethea Compton, as direct heir of Countess Isabella. She tied her daughter's hands over use of the Westmorland woods, taking her cue from the court orders Earl Francis had won restricting her mother's felling. Ignoring the King's Award, she included in Lady Alethea's inheritance both Barden and the holdings she still disputed with her cousins, Skipton, Nesfield, Langbar, Eshton, Malham and Grassington with their valuable lead- and coal-mines 'though they be now and have been for some yeares last past in the tenure of the earle and Countesse of Burlington'. These manors she claimed as rightly hers because they had been part of her father's possessions, even though the Cliffords had only obtained them (and mostly by marriage) during the Tudor century.

Controversial and wilful to the last and again following in her father's footsteps, Anne burdened her Tufton successors with an inheritance squabble over the Westmorland properties by favouring John at the expense of the legitimate heir, Earl Nicholas. Her excuse was that Nicholas was sufficiently endowed with great estates in the south. She willed that, after Countess Margaret died, John and his heirs male would inherit all the Westmorland lands and if Lady Alethea had no heirs the Craven lands also would fall to him. John, lacking estates, would have eagerly acceded to Anne's desire for successors who would appreciate the attractions of her northern residences. Countess Margaret obviously concurred because she made similar dispositions before her death on 14 August 1676, only five months after Anne, neither it seems wedded to the principle of primogeniture if Earl Nicholas were to be the gainer.[21]

John took over the Craven estate as Anne intended when Lady Alethea died in 1678. However, Earl Nicholas rightly objected to the interference with his legitimate succession in Westmorland. He instituted proceedings against John and won back the estates. He did not enjoy his victory for long, because he died without heirs on 24 November 1679. The Craven and Westmorland properties were now reunited in a single inheritance under John, 4th Earl, but his tenure

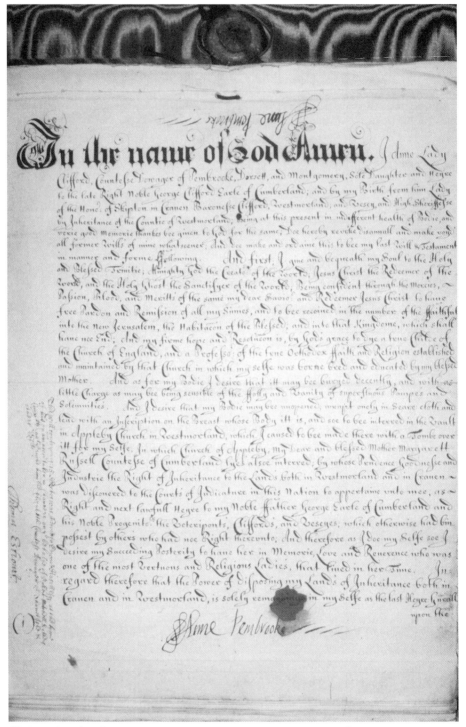

93. Lady Anne's will, written out for her by Edward Hasell on 1 May 1674 and proved on 3 April 1676 (Cumbria County Record Office, Kendal, WD/Hoth/A988/8/2)

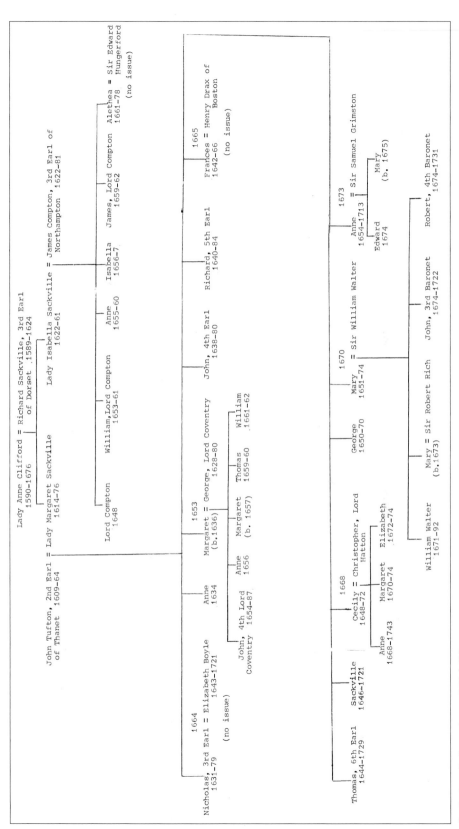

Lady Anne's descendants, 1614–76

lasted only five months before he died unmarried at Skipton Castle on 27 April 1680. His successor, Richard, 5th Earl, also died unmarried four years later. Thomas, 6th Earl, noted for his beneficence to his tenants, held the estates for forty-five years but in 1729 he died without male heirs. Consequently, the inheritance descended to his nephew Sackville, 7th Earl, whose father Sackville, the youngest of Lady Anne's grandsons, had predeceased Thomas. The male line continued through him.[22]

Under these successive Tufton earls, the Craven and Westmorland tenants had contrasting experiences. Seven of the Silsden men who held by long leases granted in 1618/19 were persuaded to surrender them between 1680 and 1686 and another in 1706. Otherwise the Craven people enjoyed relative tranquillity and for almost half a century the philanthropy of Earl Thomas.[23] In Westmorland, the see-sawing tussles with their Clifford landlords were renewed by Earl Richard after thirty years of settled relations. He demanded an arbitrary fine on entering the estates, caused writs of ejectments to be served and commenced suit in the King's Bench. His early death intervened and under Earl Thomas fines reverted to the fixed rates established by Anne's litigation.

It was under Earl Sackville that the long saga of tenurial issues was finally concluded. The fixed fines had brought the tenants greater affluence, evidenced in the improvements on their estates and the great rebuilding. Sackville, with an eye on this untapped wealth, imposed arbitrary fines, huge gressums indeed, and allowed little leeway for payment. Although it was eighty years since Anne had won her suits, the collective as well as legal memory locally was strong. The earl was vehemently opposed in a ten-year struggle as bitter as that experienced by Countess Margaret or her daughter.

Eventually, in 1739, a jury in Middlesex found for the tenants. Their verdict of a maximum ten-years' general fine and a seventeen-years' dropping fine was incorporated in a decree by Lord Chancellor Hardwick. A separate award restored tenure by tenant-right and customary estates of inheritance and confirmed the tenants' customary rights to wood, peat and stones and other traditional liberties enjoyed on the old Clifford lordships. These decisions were embodied in manorial laws which lasted until the 1920s.[24] After 130 years of recurrent disputes, the clock had been put back beyond Lady Anne and her mother to Earl George's time, but now cemented with the authority not just of custom but legal judgment. At every stage in those disputes, the courts' decisions had been a touchstone for the prevailing climate of legal opinion and, indeed, in the van of the changing landlord–tenant relationships in the north of England.

It took almost as long to resolve the competition between the earls of Thanet and Burlington over ownership of Barden, the right to the Clifford titles and the independence of Clifford Fee. Burlington brought an action of ejectment over Barden and eventually won his case. But his occupation and that of his successors was uneasy, because the Thanets did not relinquish their claims. In 1686 Burlington, learning of Earl Thomas's presence in Craven, wrote to his agent 'since my L[ord] Thanet goes this silent way, I must desire that you will, without noyse, putt into Barden Tower a trusty person that may secure the place'; just as Earl Francis had done in 1607 when Countess Margaret and Anne were expected from Westmorland. Much later still, in 1729, the architect Richard, 3rd Earl of Burlington, was edgy about the new Earl Sackville's arrival at Skipton. Writing from London on 14 August, he instructed his agent to 'keep ye Gates and doors in Barden Tower all Lockt and Secure' during Sackville's stay.[25]

Lady Anne's Great Books were the invaluable source on which Earl Thomas based his claim for the title of Lord Clifford (1299). He employed Gregory King to draw up his petition. It was referred by the House of Lords on 27 November 1690 to the Commission for Privileges, who decided in his favour.[26] On his death, however, the Clifford barony fell into abeyance between his daughters. Burlington had to be content with the two recent baronies, Clifford (1628) and Clifford of Lanesborough (1644), and also yielded precedence with his English earldom. His countess tried to lift him above the Thanets by having the Cumberland title revived for him after Prince Rupert's death, which would also have prevented its adding distinction to another family. She failed, and its eventual bestowal by the Hanoverians on 'Butcher' Cumberland made the tainting of the original Clifford barony by 'the Butcher' pale into insignificance. The later history of the baronies and the sheriffdom has been treated in detail by Dr Williamson.[27]

By 1740, therefore, all the issues which had racked Earl George's successors had been resolved. Of the principal protagonists, only Lady Anne was accorded an honoured place in the pantheon of memorable personalities of the Stuart era. In her own lifetime, as the Dorsets' letters make clear, she was known for 'the fame of doing good to all the world'. As Countess of Pembroke, she was the only woman commemorated in heraldic glass by the Dean and Chapter of Ripon in 1664 when the Civil War damage to the cathedral was repaired. Hers was one of the many shields commissioned from the virtuoso York glass-painter, Henry Gyles, and was placed in the upper window of the south side of the church. She shared the limelight there with James I, the Yorkshire peer Conyers, Lord Darcy, and the descendants of Lord Chancellor Ellesmere and Lord Bruce of Kinloss.[28]

The printing of Bishop Rainbow's funeral sermon with 'some Remarks On the Life of that Eminent Lady' in London as early as 1677 reinforced her reputation among the literary and social elite. The eighteenth-century Clifford chronicler deemed her 'celebrated' and the 'hero daughter of an heroic father'. To Horace Walpole, she was 'the famous Countess Anne'; no need to specify which.[29] Anne's creations had attracted the interest of men of scholarly bent during her own lifetime and soon after, such as Dugdale, Johnston and Thoresby, as has been seen. For those touring Britain, her visible legacies were not to be missed. Bishop Pococke in 1751 admired Skipton Castle, whose grand appearance on the outside reminded him of Windsor. He was misled by hazy local memories into believing that the Skipton triptych showed Earl George about to set off on embassy to Spain. Even worse, he was told the earl had been tried for deviating from Queen Elizabeth's instructions after peace had been made and his estates forfeited for being too great a subject. At Brougham, he examined the countess's pillar and recorded its inscription.[30]

Much the most interesting and fullest account by an early eighteenth-century

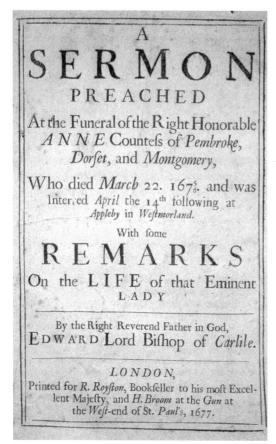

A

SERMON

PREACHED

At the Funeral of the Right Honorable
A N N E Counteſs of *Pembroke,*
Dorſet, and *Montgomery,*

Who died *March* 22. 167⅚. and was
Interred *April* the 14th following at
Appleby in *Weſtmorland.*

With ſome

REMARKS

On the L I F E of that Eminent
L A D Y

By the Right Reverend Father in God,
E D W A R D Lord Biſhop of *Carlile.*

L O N D O N,
Printed for *R. Royſton,* Bookſeller to his moſt Excellent Majeſty, and *H. Broom* at the *Gun* at
the *Weſt-*end of St. *Paul's,* 1677.

94. The title page of Bishop Rainbow's funeral sermon, 1677 (Private collection)

visitor to Westmorland is that of Robert Harley, Earl of Oxford, returning in 1725 from Edinburgh where he had been elected a burgess. Entering the county, Oxford stopped at Brougham to admire and record accurately the detail of 'the Lady's Pillar' as he calls it and the charity Anne had established there. At Appleby Castle he studied in the hall 'a notable picture representing George Earl of Cumberland, together with several members of his family, an account of each person being wrote over the picture which represents him'. He was shown the earl's Greenwich armour, 'of very curious workmanship', which was then kept in a strong box in one of the lower rooms. He was favoured by being allowed to examine

three large folio MSS. giving a very particular account and history of the family, and drawn up from authentic papers by the direction of Ann, Countess of Pembroke, &c., whose own life is likewise at the end of one of the volumes, and a great deal of it is of her own handwriting.

In the Baron's Tower, he continues, he saw Lady Anne's wedding bed, being all of 'curious needlework', as was the whole furniture belonging to that apartment where the judges used to repose when they came there. While at Appleby, he bought one of Anne's silver medals, that which later came into Horace Walpole's hands and is now in the British Museum's collection.[31]

It was the great regional historians, Nicolson and Burn on Westmorland and Cumberland in 1777 and Whitaker on Craven in 1805, who affirmed Anne's merit to the literate public at large and placed her in the context of her family and the localities of her northern estates. They drew heavily on her Great Books of Record, Harley MS 6177, Hale's history, Rainbow and Sedgewick for their interpretation of her character and activities, all sources tending towards the adulatory. A new edition of Rainbow's funeral sermon in 1839 reinforced their views. How universal her appeal became is shown by Professor Heywood who has postulated that Anne, her portraits and her circumstances were an inspiration to Emily Brontë in *Wuthering Heights*. The literary sources Emily particularly drew on were the 1812 edition of Whitaker and Hartley Coleridge's essay on Anne in his *Worthies of Yorkshire and Lancashire* (1839).[32]

Modern writers have veered towards exalting Anne at the expense of her husbands and rivals for the Clifford inheritance. Some have descended to the absurd. The first critical, almost damning, estimate of her was penned by Vita Sackville-West in her study of Knole and the Sackvilles, published in 1923, the year she edited the 'Knole' diary. She wrote that Anne, once entrenched in her numerous castles in the north, 'was free to turn tyrant' over her undisputed realm, ruling autocratically over her servants, tenants, neighbours and the generations and ramifications of her family. She noted her idiosyncrasies and praised, among other attributes, Anne's 'amazing memory', yet concluded:

95. *Lady Anne's communion jug, c. 1570, pearl necklace with a pendant baroque pearl and matching ear-rings which feature in her portraits. The pearls may have been booty from Earl George's privateering. (Private collection)*

This vigorous mind was not, perhaps, planned on a very broad scale. It was self-centred and self-sufficient; severe but not reckless; no fine carelessness endears her to us, or surprises, even her acts of generosity, and they are numerous, are recorded with the same scrupulous accuracy.[33]

Terms such as 'tyrant' and 'autocratic' – Vita's own verbal extravagance – are today inadmissible, but she has come closest to understanding Anne's mind. The present writer's 'Reappraisal', a lecture given to mark the tercentenary of Anne's death in 1676 and subsequently published, was a critical assessment of her character and actions with a far wider spectrum and phrased so as to provoke discussion about them which until then had been conspicuously absent.

This study has aimed at taking that appreciation a stage further and on an even broader canvas. It has considered her known concerns in greater depth, examined areas previously ignored, and drawn on documentary sources neglected until now, including the accounts for her later years which were not thought to have survived. This enlarged perspective has made possible a more comprehensive and balanced understanding of her personality and activities. The flaws have been aired as well as her virtuous traits, about which so much has been written in the past. The valid viewpoints of her 'enemies' have been propounded as well as her own moral and legalistic stances. The menfolk in her life, who have deserved to be heard, have been accorded their due. The issues of right and wrong, which appeared to her so clear-cut, have been shown as no different from other divisive questions of the time, murky, muddled and troublesome to resolve with any permanency.

The picture of Lady Anne as she appeared to her 'opponents', including the Burlingtons whose goodwill towards her is undoubted, helps redress the self-image she projected in her diaries and pictorial and other creations. It is no longer enough now to praise her as 'indomitable' and 'long-suffering' in her private affairs, hitherto favourite terms used by writers about her. To these must be added adjectives such as shrewd, subtle, calculating, tough and tenacious; much closer to Vita's insight but supported now by accessible documentary evidence. Anne emerges from this examination a far more rounded, credible person, with human frailties as well as strengths.

96. Lady Anne's jewels and pendant (Private collection)

Furthermore, she has gained in stature. It has been shown that she was far more prominent at the Stuart Court than had been supposed, especially as Pembroke's consort. In her role as landlord in the north (skated over by her biographers), she proved a disturbing as well as a dominating presence in Craven and Westmorland from 1649, not just recurrently litigious but politically challenging to Burlington and the entrenched upper gentry faction in Restoration Yorkshire. But her landed concerns were not confined to the north. By marriage and inheritance she entered the ranks of the greater landed proprietors of the later Stuart era, holding widespread manors and advowsons in

Sussex, Kent and Essex, as well as in Westmorland and Yorkshire. She carefully directed and controlled the expenditure of estate revenues to her chosen ends. Pouring massive resources into castles, churches, funerary monuments, almshouses and other philanthropic purposes no longer appears eccentric; indeed, she wins plaudits today for her commitment to conservation, the environment and social awareness. Her impact on the local economy was considerable, though it awaits a proper assessment.

Anne's innate ability and learning have never been doubted. What this study has affirmed is that, with her intellectual interests and scholarly connections, she must be placed alongside the leading antiquaries, indeed historians, of the Stuart era. She lays claim to being a trailblazer in family history and, in current usage, a medievalist to boot. True, as Vita asserted, Anne's mind in this respect was narrowly focused. But the understanding she gained was immense, cohesive (not always a strong point of antiquaries) and its product a documentary and pictorial legacy of a high order. Reflected in it is the Stuart cultural milieu which she shared, the court artists such as Van Somer, Honthorst and Lely; writers like Daniel, Lanyer, Donne and Herbert; and the circle of antiquaries whom she employed in one or more capacities but in whose researches she revelled, such as Kniveton, Dodsworth, Fairfax, Widdrington and Dugdale.

What must not be lost sight of, in interpreting Anne's attitudes and actions, is that first and foremost she was a lady of the highest rank, proud descendant of some of the great noble dynasties in the realm, and a Christian secure in her faith and deeply versed in Biblical texts. These constants infused and justified all her thoughts and actions. Her belief in her right as a female to inherit her father's estates and baronial titles never wavered, her notions moulded by her mother's arguments laid out in the 1606/8 submissions to the Earl Marshal and the Court of Wards. She did not – and might plausibly claim she was not allowed to – employ her landed wealth in the service of the realm as her forebears had done. Yet in her own way she was as profligate as her father and her husband Dorset in expending her riches; the surplus income, however, and sensibly not the capital. Moreover, unlike Dorset, the end may be deemed worthwhile, poles apart from his wasting the Sackville fortunes. Nevertheless, her choice was very personal and she ignored other possibilities, such as enlarging her properties which was the priority of many of her ambitious contemporaries. Her father's estates were all she coveted, provided she could get them.

Not until she was nearing thirty did Anne free herself from her mother's and her first husband's dominance. Thereafter, for over twenty years she manipulated her circumstances as best she could to the benefit of herself and her daughters. Then from 1643, in control of her destiny on inheriting her northern estates, she made her unique and enduring mark on the Stuart age. After her death it took two generations for the reverberations of her impact on her family concerns to subside, during which her reputation soared. If Bishop Rainbow went too far eulogizing her in his funeral oration, yet in one judgment he cannot be faulted. As this study has contrived to demonstrate, the story of Lady Anne's long life, spanning over eighty-six years, satisfyingly complete in the eventual triumph of right, virtue and fortitude over adversity, is 'fitter for a History than a Sermon'.

Lady Anne's Accounts

1668–76

BOOKS OF DISBURSEMENTS

Reference	Year	Months	Source of Money
1	1669	January to June	All
2		June to December	RM
3		June to December	W
4		July to November	C
5		September	B/JR
6	1670	January to May	All
7		2 April	Brougham Rents
8		May to December	W
9		June to December	C
10		August to October	B/JR
11		August to September	B/JR
12	1671	January to May	W
13		May to June	B/JR
14		June	W
15		June to August	C
16		August	W
17		August	W
18		August	C
19		September	C
20		September	B/JR
21		October	W
22		October	C
23		November	W
24		December	W
25	1672	January to April	W
26		April to December	B/JR
27		April to December	W
28		May to November	C
29	1673	January to May	All

Reference	Year	Months	Source of Money
30		May to December	W
31		June to December	C
32	1674	January to April	W
33		April to December	W
34		May to December	C
35		June to August	RM
36	1675	January to March	C
37		March to December	W
38		May to December	C
39		May to October	RM

Key: B – Borrowed; C – Craven; JR – jointure rents; RM – Returned Moneys, i.e. jointure rents; W – Westmorland

BOOKS OF HOUSEHOLD EXPENSES (FRONT) *AND LADY ANNE'S PRIVATE PURSE* (REAR)

Reference	Year
40	1669
41	1670
42	1671
43	1672
44	1673
45	1674

BOOKS OF RECEIPTS (CRAVEN, WESTMORLAND, AND JOINTURE LANDS RENTS, BORROWED MONEYS)

Reference	Year
46	1669
47	1670
48	1671
49	1672
50	1673
51	1674
52	1675

BOOKS OF WEEKLY HOUSEHOLD EXPENDITURE

Reference	Year
53	1668–70
54	1670
55	1674–6

Source: KRO, JAC 495/7

'A Catalogue of the Books in the Closset in the Passage Room next the Pantry in Skipton Castle 28th August 1739'[1]

1 MANUSCRIPTS

A folio Manuscript being a Translation of Boetius dedicated to the Countess of Cumberland[2]

The Praise of Private Life, a folio Manuscript[3]

A Brief Commemoration of the Voyage of the Right Honorable the Lord Buckhurst in his Embassage to the States of Holland and Zealand[4]

My Lord of Cumberlands Sea Voyages 1586 & 1587*[5]

The Case of Anne Glemham presented to the Lords of the Counsell, no date[6]

The Doctrine of the Sabboath etc. taught in certain Sermons upon 95th psalm[7]

Arnoldus de Nova Villa his book called the New Light[8]

A Treatise entituled Woemens Work and Childrens playe

A Book entituled the Ladder of the philosophers

The practise of the great Work etc. by the Monk of Berye

An old Book of Chemistry and Alchimy, no title, unbound[9]

Another Book of Alchimy entituled a Dialogue between Nature and a Disciple of Philosophie, a stiched folio[9]

Part of a very old imperfect Manuscript of Alchimy[9]

A brief and true Report of the honorable Voyage unto Cadiz etc. 1596*[10]

A very old poem in folio stichd, of Alchymy[9]

A very old Abstract of some Book of Alchimy[9]

Part of a very ancient Book writ on parchment[9]

An Epistle upon the Life and death of the Brothers of Suffolk by T.W. pind together

The High Way to Heaven, a poem[11]

Certain Notes etc. for the better Understanding of the two Books of Aristotles –
Rhetoricks concerning Affections[12]

Plutarch of the Education of Children [from the translations of T. Eliot or
E. Grant, 20056–7]

The Civil Wars between the Houses of York and Lancaster, a poem only
2 Cantos ending with the death of Richard 2nd[13]

2 PRINTED BOOKS

The Compound of Alchymy etc. first written by [Sir] George Ripley and
dedicated to King Edward 4th [in 1471] set forth by Ralph Rabbards Gent. A
Poem. London 1591 [21057][14]

Another of the same[14]

The Raising of them that are fallen, a Discourse etc. by Thomas Savile Gent.
London 1606 [21787]

A Discovery of certain Errors in the much commended Britannia 1594, by Yorke
Herault[15]

The History of the Great and mighty Kingdom of China [by Juan Gonzalez de
Mendoza, 1588] translated out of Spanish by R[alph] Parke. London 1608
[12003]

The Relation of a Voyage to Guiana performed by Robert Harcourt Esqr. 1609
London 1626 [enlarged edn 12755]

Fior Angelico de Musica: nuovamentes dal R. P. frate Angelo da Pintono,
Conventuale dell' Ordine Minores, Organista preclarissimo, composto. 1547

The Mirror of Honor etc. London 1597*[16]

The Overthrow of Stage plays by the way of Controversie betwixt D. Gager and
D. Rainolder. [John Rainolds] Middleburgh 1600 [20616]

A true Narration of the strange and grievous Vexation by the Devil of seven
persons in Lancashire etc. by John Darrell Minister of the Gospel. 1600
[6288][17]

An Apologie for the Oath of Alegiance by King James. London 1609 [14401–2]

Academiarum quae aliquando fueres & hodie sunt in Europa Catalogus etc.
Londini 1590 [by Miles Windsor. 25841]

God and the King, a Dialogue etc. upon the Oath of Alegiance London 1615
[14418.5]

A Discoverie of the true Causes why Ireland was never entirely subdued etc. till
the beginning of his Majesties happy Reign. London 1612 [by Sir John Davies.
6348]

Solon his Folly or a politique Discourse touching the Reformation of
Commonweales etc. by Richard Beacon Gent. Oxford 1594 [1653]

A Treatise Paranetical, that is to say, an Exhortation wherein is shewed the right
way etc. to resist the Violence of the Castalian King etc. London 1598*[18]

The Answer of Mr Isaac Casaubon to the Epistle of Cardinal Peron, London
1612 [4741]

A Monument of Remembrance, a Poem on the Departure etc. of Frederick and
Elizabeth Prince and Princess Palatine, by James Maxwell 1613 [17703]

A New Years Guift, a Poem, by Richard Vennard. London 1612

The Use of the Celestial Globe in plano etc. by Tho. Hood. London 1590*
[13694]

The Mirror of Alchymy by Fryer Roger Bachon. London 1597 [1182]

The Life of the Lady Magdalen Viscountess Montague. 1627 [by Richard Smith.
22811]

An Apology for Religion by Edward Bulkley D.D. London 1602 [4025]

Directorium Chori ad usum omnium Ecclesiarum etc. Roma 1589

[Guillaume de Salusto] Du Bartas first days Work of the Creation by F.B.
Minister. 1598[19]

Bartas forenoon of the fourth day of his second Week, by John Sylvester.
London 1607 [21665][19]

Solomons Song translated into English Meeter etc Middleburgh 1594

Nova Disquisitio de Helia Artista Theophrasteo, inqua de Metallorium
transformatione adversus Hagelii & Pererii Jesuitarum Opiniones etc.
disseritur, Auctore Heliophilo a percis philochemico. Marpurgi 1606[20]

The Humble Petition of the Communalties to Queen Elizabeth etc. 1588*

Lingua, or the Combat of the Tongue and the five Senses for Superiority, a
Comedy. London 1622 [by Thomas Tomkin, 1607. 24104]

A Conference between father Gentier and Dr Du Moulin etc. London 1615
[7319]

A Manifestation of the Motives whereupon the Archbishop of Spalato [Marco
Antonio de Dominis] undertook his Departure thence. London 1616 [6998]

News from Parnassus, the political Touchstone etc. printed at Helicon 1622

An Antiquodlibet or an Advertisement to beware of Secular priests.
Middleburgh 1602

A true Discourse concerning the certain possession etc. of 7 persons in one
family in Lancashire, by George More, Minister etc. 1600 [18070]

Dichiaratione della Caggioni che Hanno Mosso la Serenissima Reina
d'Inghilterra etc. London 1585

Honours Fame in Triumph riding or the Life and death of the late Honorable
Earl of Essex. London 1604*[21]

The Description of a Voyage by certain Ships from Holland into the East Indies
from 1595 to 1597. London 1598* [by Bernardt Langenes. 15193]

Sir Philip Sidneys Arcadia

A parcel of old pamphlets etc.

The Shepherds Calendar a poem containing 12 Aeglogues. London 1597 [by
Edmund Spenser. 23093]

NOTES:

* Probably Earl George's books
1. YAS, DD121/111. Details in brackets are from *STC*.
2. YAS, DD121/118/12. It was presented to Countess Margaret on 1 January
1585 and had been borrowed and read by her brother Lord Francis Russell
before his murder on the Borders on 27 July.

3. KRO, WD/Hoth/A988/21.

4. Embassy of either 1586 or 1589 (*DNB*, XVII, 587–8).

5. John Saracold's or Thomas Hood's description (Spence, pp. 66–7, 71–2).

6. Anne, daughter of Cicely Baker, 2nd Countess of Dorset, who married Sir Henry Glemham knt. of Glenham, Suffolk.

7. Probably by George Walker, Amsterdam, 1638 [24957].

8. KRO, WD/Hoth/A988/3, dated 10 July 1590. On Villa Nova, see H.S. Redgrove, *Alchemy: Ancient and Modern*, 2nd rev. edn (London, Rider, 1922), p. 47.

9. These were probably the MSS described by Whitaker (pp. 473–8) and now in KRO, WD/Hoth/A988/1, 2. Of these, A988/1 has a commentary on the *Liber Dictorum Universalis* by Ishak ibn Sulaiman Al Israel (known as Isaac) and the *Liber Dictorum Particularum*, with fragments of other works, in different hands of the late thirteenth and fourteenth centuries. On fol. 117v of the latter work in a later hand is 'John Wyaninggum alias baldocke'. A988/2 is a much damaged late medieval document, a kind of Index Rerum with references to a work of 153 chapters. On the final folio is written 'Isaac Holland booke'; he being the father of Dutch alchemy (Redgrove, *Alchemy*, p. 53). The canons of Bolton Priory, the Shepherd Lord, Henry, 2nd Earl, and Countess Margaret are known to have been serious students of alchemy. All these manuscripts were found in the castle's muniment room by Williamson.

10. By Sir William Slingsby, printed in *The Naval Tracts of Sir William Monson*, ed. M. Oppenheim, vol. 1, Navy Records Soc. XXII (1902), 344–95.

11. Thomas Sparke, *The high way to Heaven by the cleare light of the gospel*, 1597 [23021]. He preached at the burial at Chenies on 14 September 1585 of Francis, 2nd Earl of Bedford [23021.5].

12. Written out for Anne by William Watkinson, 16 November 1669 [KRO, JAC 495/7, 4].

13. The parts of Samuel Daniel's work seen at the castle by Whitaker (p. 385).

14. One copy is in YAS, DD121/109.

15. I.e. Camden's *Britannia*. By Ralph Brooke, 1599 [3834].

16. John Norden, *The mirror of honor: wherein everie professor of armes, may see the necessitie of the feare of God* [18614].

17. This book was ordered burnt 29 October 1600.

18. Cf. 'a treatise exhortatory . . . of the Castilian' (A *Transcript of the Registers of the Company of Stationers at London, 1554–1640 AD*, ed. Edward Arber, vol. III (1876), p. 31b.

19. *The First Day* was first published in 1595 with an unknown translator. For the whole work, see *The Divine Weeks and Works of Guillaume de Saluste, Sieur du Bartas. Translated by Joshua Sylvester*, ed. Susan Snyder (2 vols, Oxford, Clarendon Press, 1979).

20. Probably Theophrastus Paracelsus, the famous alchemist.

21. By John Pricket, and apparently suppressed [20339].

APPENDIX III

Lady Anne's patronage of the painter Mr John Bracken of Kirkby Stephen

1670–4[1]

Book	Date	
	1670	
41	4 June	Paid £12 for seven copies 'of my own picture which was formerly taken of me when I was about 60 years old and which I now caused him to draw for me (I being now over 80 years old . . .) which I intend to give away amongst my friends'.
10	11 Oct.	Paid £14 14s for making forty-two coats of arms of 'my Ancessters the Cliffords' at 7s apiece, one set to be set up in Brougham Castle and the other in Appleby
	1671	
12	1 March	Paid £7 10s for drawing over five copies of her own picture, at £1 10s apiece
	1672	
27	11 May	Paid for drawing over three copies of 'my father George Cumberlands picture out of the original in Pendragon Castle', at £1 15s apiece, to give away
	1673	
30	26 July	Paid £1 13s for drawing over the Countess of Warwick's picture
31	23 Aug.	Paid for drawing over four copies of Lord Treasurer Dorset's picture at £1 10s apiece, with 2s 6d to his man Lancelot Musgrave

	28 Nov.	Draws over a copy of Lord Treasurer's Dorset's wife Cicely Baker's picture
	1674	
45	7 Jan	Paid £3 5s for copies of pictures of the Countess of Warwick and Dorset's wife
32	5 May	Paid £7 for drawing over four copies of the picture of her cousin-german, Francis, 4th Earl of Bedford, at £1 15s each
	1675	
36	22 Jan.	Paid £7 for drawing over four copies of the four ages of her life, which will hang at Brough Castle
37	24 April	John Beck of Kendal is paid £2 10s for the materials and making of 'four large Oval Picture Cases in one fframe for my four Pictures of the 4: severall ages of myself'.
38	1 Dec.	Paid £1 10s for a picture of her first lord the Earl of Dorset

Source: KRO, JAC 495/7

NOTE:

1. For other known work by Bracken, see M.E. Burkett, *John Bracken* (Kendal, Abbot Hall, 1980).

Notes

1 Lady Anne Clifford: Upbringing and Maternal Influences, 1590–1609

1. G.C. Williamson, *George, Third Earl of Cumberland (1558–1605) His Life and Voyages* (Cambridge University Press, 1920), pp. 288–9; Clay, pp. 400–1; Spence, pp. 90, 148–9, 216–18.

2. Gilson, pp. 18–19; *Diaries*, p. 26.

3. Whitaker, p. 354; Williamson, pp. 72, 74–5.

4. Spence, pp. 27–9; J. Parker, *Books to Build an Empire: A Bibliographical History of English Overseas Interests to 1620* (Amsterdam, N. Israel, 1965), p. 144.

5. Lambeth Palace Library, Talbot MS 3203, fol. 308; HMC, *Twelfth Report: Manuscripts of Earl Cowper (Coke MSS)* (London, HMSO, 1888), App. I, 47; Williamson, p. 76. For the descent of Bolton, see Whitaker, pp. 496–7.

6. Spence, p. 33; Williamson, *Third Earl*, p. 270; *Diaries*, pp. 29, 80.

7. *Diaries*, p. 74, n. 61.

8. Spence, pp. 212, 216–18; Gilson, pp. 36–7.

9. Gilson, pp. 19–20.

10. Williamson, *Third Earl*, pp. 285–8, 291–4; Spence, pp. 213–14; Gilson, p. 24.

11. Williamson, pp. 446–7. On Kniveton, see below, chap. 9.

12. Williamson, p. 38; *The Private Diary of Dr. John Dee*, ed. J.O. Halliwell, Camden Society, 19 (1842), pp. 47, 53.

13. R.T. Spence, 'Mining and Smelting in Yorkshire by the Cliffords, Earls of Cumberland, in the Tudor and Early Stuart Period', *YAJ*, 64 (1992), pp. 162–3, 167–8; T.K. Rabb, *Enterprise and Empire* (Cambridge, Mass., Harvard University Press, 1967), p. 266; Gilson, p. 26.

14. Williamson, pp. 339, 490; G. Parry, 'The Great Picture of Lady Anne Clifford', *Art and Patronage in the Caroline Courts (Essays in honour of Sir Oliver Millar)*, ed. D. Howarth (Cambridge University Press, 1993), p. 208.

15. Williamson, *Third Earl*, pp. 291–5; *The Works of William Perkins*, ed. Ian Breward (Appleford, Berks, Sutton Courtenay Press, 1970), pp. 13, 389–91. Ryther's translation is now YAS, DD121/118/12. Dedications are indexed in *STC* and F.B. Williams Jr, *Index of Dedications and Commendatory Verses in English Books Before 1641* (London, Bibliographical Society, 1962).

16. W. J. Craig, 'James Ryther of Harewood and his Letters to William Cecil, Lord Burghley', Part I, *YAJ*, 56 (1984), p. 117.

17. Spence, pp. 25–6, 34–5; Whitaker, pp. 444–5; YAS, DD139, 240 (Beamsley Hospital Papers); R.M. Butler, 'Further Information on James Ryther of Harewood', *YAJ*, 59 (1987), pp. 179–82; PRO, Chancery, Close Rolls, C54/2076; *Feet of Fines*, ed. W. Brigg, *Tudor Period*, vol. IV, YAS Record Series, 8 (1890), p. 145; *Stuart Period*, vol. I, YASRS, 53 (1915), p. 34; Clay, p. 393. On coverture, see A.L. Erickson, *Women and Property in Early Modern England* (London, Routledge, 1993), pp. 1–5.

18. PRO, Signet Office, SO3/1; W.H. Dawson, *Loose Leaves of Craven History*, Series I (Skipton, Craven Herald, 1891), pp. 163–4.

19. Aemilia Lanyer, *Salve Deus Rex Judaeorum* (1611); G. Blakiston, *Woburn and the Russells* (London, Constable,

1980), pp. 40–3; A.L. Rowse, *Simon Forman, Sex and Society in Shakespeare's Age* (London, Weidenfeld & Nicolson, 1974), pp. 99–117; Gilson, p. 26.

20. Whitaker, p. 351; Williamson, Pl. 43; Spence, pp. 39, 91, 97–8.

21. Spence, pp. 25, 213–14; A.L. Rowse, *The Elizabethan Renaissance. The Cultural Achievement* (London, Macmillan, 1972), pp. 63–5, 304–5; Parry, 'The Great Picture', pp. 210–14.

22. Diaries, pp. 41, 48, 54; *Sir Philip Sidney The Countess of Pembroke's Arcadia*, ed. V. Skretkowicz (Oxford University Press, 1987), p. xxxix. For Clifford connections with the manuscript 'Arcadia', see Jean Robertson's edition, same title (Oxford University Press, 1973), pp. xliii–xliv. For authors who inspired Sidney and are also shown in the Appleby Triptych see Robertson's introduction and below, chap. 10.

23. Sedgewick, p. 299; *Diaries*, pp. 21–7.

24. Holmes, p. 98.

25. *The Complete Works in Verse and Prose of Samuel Daniel*, ed. A.B. Grosart (4 vols, privately printed, 1885), I, 213–14; J. Rees, *Samuel Daniel* (Liverpool University Press, 1964), pp. 81–2.

26. Whitaker, pp. 387–8; *Diaries*, p. 27.

27. Williamson, p. 61; Grosart, *Daniel's Works*, I, 215–16; J. Pitcher, *Samuel Daniel: The Brotherton Manuscript*, Leeds Texts and Monographs, New Series, 7 (University of Leeds School of English, 1981), pp. 189–90.

28. *Diaries*, pp. 21–7; Spence, pp. 214–15; Clay, p. 393.

29. *The Correspondence of Dr. Matthew Hutton*, ed. J. Raine, Surtees Society, 17 (1843), pp. 282–5; *Diaries*, p. 27

30. Williamson, p. 78; Gilson, p. 39; YAS, MD240, Box 4/4.

31. Spence, p. 216.

32. Gilson, pp. 37–8; L. Stone, *The Crisis of the Aristocracy 1558–1641* (Oxford University Press, 1965), pp. 597, 626; PRO, State Papers, SP14/19, no. 9; J. Nichols, *The Progresses of King James The First* (4 vols, London, Nichols, 1828), II, 193–5.

33. Holmes, p. 17; Lanyer, *Salve Deus*.

34. Nichols, *Progresses*, II, 214, 484–5, n. 2; Holmes, pp. 19, 33–4; *The Letters of John Chamberlain*, ed. N.E. McClure (2 vols, Philadelphia, American Philosophical Society Memoirs, XII, pts I–II, 1939), I, 280.

35. Holmes, p. 23; Catalogue, pp. 32, 44. For the masques, see Nichols, *Progresses*, II, 164–74, 214–45.

36. Williamson, p. 81; CKS, U269/Q18/1; C. J. Phillips, *History of the Sackville Family* (2 vols, London, Cassell, 1930), I, 257; McClure, *Chamberlain Letters*, I, 287.

37. *Diaries*, p. 5; BL, Harley MS 6177, fol. 53r; Spence, pp. 127, 214–18; Spence, 'Earls', pp. 287–8 (Bolton redemption).

38. Spence, pp. 73, 185, 211.

2 COUNTESS MARGARET AND HER WESTMORLAND JOINTURE ESTATES

1. Chatsworth, Hardwick Papers, A670/5.

2. R.T. Spence, 'The Pacification of the Cumberland Borders, 1593–1628', *Northern History*, XIII (1977), pp. 107–9.

3. Spence, pp. 2–3, 51, 202–6; KRO, WD/Hoth/34.

4. M.H. and R. Dodds, *The Pilgrimage of Grace, 1536–37, and the Exeter Conspiracy, 1538*, (2 vols, London, Cass, 1915), I, 225, 370–1; *Letters and Papers of Henry VIII*, xii (1), p. 235; J.F. Curwen, *The Later Records relating to North Westmorland or the Barony of Appleby*, Cumberland and Westmorland Antiquarian and Archaeological Society, Record Series, viii (Kendal, 1932), pp. 50–2, 97–9, 128–9; M. Holdgate, *A History of Appleby* (Clapham, Dalesman Books, 1982), pp. 35–6. For the musters taken by Earl Francis, see Bolton MSS, Book 268.

5. KRO, WD/Hoth/35, 'Remembrance', fols 1–2; Spence, pp. 204–5; C.R. Hudleston and R.S. Boumphrey, *Cumberland Families and Heraldry*, CWAAS, Extra Series, XXII (Kendal, 1978), pp. 97, 315.

6. *The History of Parliament: The House of Commons, 1558–1603*, ed. P.W. Hasler, (3 vols, London, HMSO, 1981), II, 160; III, 442–3; Williamson, *Third Earl*, p. 114; J.T. Cliffe, *The Yorkshire Gentry from the Reformation to the Civil War* (London, The Athlone Press, 1969), p. 257.

7. Craig, 'James Ryther', p. 117.

8. PRO, SP14/19/9; Alnwick, Syon MSS, XII.III, 7,h,5; KRO, WD/Hoth/34.

9. Spence, pp. 205–6; Alnwick, Syon MSS, XII.III. 7,h,4; III, 1,4,d; PRO, Chancery, Decrees and Orders, C78/153/4; Revd John Breay, *Light in the Dales*, vols II and III (Norwich, the Canterbury Press, 1996), II, chap. 9. Breay's work includes much detail about the Cliffords and Westmorland, but its traditional interpretation is outmoded by this study.

10. KRO, WD/Hoth/44.

11. PRO, C78/153/4, 5; PRO, Chancery, Entry Books of Decrees and Orders, C33/119, fols 43, 656–7; /121, fol. 395. For the precedents, see A.B. Appleby, 'Agrarian Capitalism or Seigneurial Reaction? the Northwest of England, 1500–1700', *The American History Review*, 80 (1975), pp. 581–6.

12. PRO, Star Chamber, 8/89/11; KRO, WD/Hoth/34, fol. 123v.

13. Appleby, 'Agrarian Capitalism', pp. 587–8.

14. Breay, *Light in the Dales*, II, 28–9.

15. HMC, *Tenth Report, App. IV, Manuscripts of Lord Muncaster* (Eyre & Spottiswoode, 1885) p. 270; *Salisbury*, XIX, 217, 277; PRO, C33/117, fols 947, 991; /119, fol. 366v; /121, fol. 575; /123, fols 498, 762, 841. For the custom, see the Preston Patrick custumal (PRO, SP/23/258), printed in Breay, *Light in the Dales*, II, 76.

16. Whitaker, p. 362; PRO, SP14/63/2; *The Reports of Judge Sir Henry Hobart in the Common Pleas* (3rd edn, 1671), pp. 37, 85.

17. PRO, St. Ch. 8/392/17, 18.

18. CRO, DX/99/3; Alnwick, Syon MSS, X.II,3,7,h,13; KRO, WD/Hoth/33; Clay, pp. 393–6.

19. Gilson, p. 25.

20. Clay, pp. 393–6; *Diaries*, p. 36.

21. Holmes, pp. 117–18; N. Pevsner, *The Buildings of England. Cumberland and Westmorland* (Harmondsworth, Penguin Books, 1980), pp. 30, 217.

3 THE GREAT INHERITANCE DISPUTE, 1606–17

1. Stone, *Crisis*, p. 276.

2. Williamson, p. 49; GEC, i, 35; *DNB*, XIV, 249–50.

3. Lincoln's Inn, Hale MS 104; Queen's College, Oxford, MS 105.

4. J.H. Round, *Peerage and Pedigree* (2 vols, London, James Nisbet, 1910), I, 93–4; *The Life, Diary and Correspondence of Sir William Dugdale*, ed. W. Hamper (London, Harding, Lepard, 1827), p. 368.

5. Clay, pp. 370–87; Spence, pp. 2–6, 17–18, 96–8; Currey, 33/138, fols 125–7. Barry Coward succinctly explains the legal aspects of disputes between collateral heirs male and heirs general in relation to the Derby disputes in *The Stanleys Lords Stanley and Earls of Derby 1385–1672*, Chetham Society, 3rd series, XXX (1983), pp. 41–53.

6. HMC, *Salisbury*, XVII, 586.

7. PRO, SP14/17/85.

8. PRO, SP14/19/9; Pitcher, *The Brotherton Manuscript*, p. 169.

9. HMC, *Salisbury*, XIX, 74–5.

10. Clifford, pp. 51, 53; Clay, pp. 356–8; R. Houlbrooke, *The English Family, 1450–1700* (London, Longman, 1984), p. 237.

11. William West, *Symboleography* (2 parts, 1618, 1622), I, sect. 1; *Statutes of the Realm*, iii, 790, 919.

12. Whitaker, p. 358.

13. HMC, *Salisbury*, XIX, 277.

14. HMC, *Salisbury*, XIX, 217.

15. James Ley, *Reports of Divers Resolutions in Law* (1659), fols 3–4; *The English Reports*, LXXVII (1907), pp. 1459–60; LXXX (1907), pp. 587–8; Spence, p. 62.

16. Book III, 180; Clay, pp. 391–2.

17. *The English Reports*, LXXVII, 726–7; CXLV (1914), pp. 291–4; Sir Edward Coke, *Reports* (1658), VIII, 806–7; Whitaker, p. 358; Book III, 108, 143.

18. Erickson, *Women and Property*, pp. 3, 5, 33.

19. Williamson, pp. 151–3; McClure, *Chamberlain Letters*, i, 287; GEC, iv, 423.

20. *Wentworth Papers 1597–1628*, ed. J.P. Cooper, Camden Soc., 4th ser., 12 (1973), pp. 53, 56.

21. BL, Althorp, B.1; Williamson, p. 147.

22. Whitaker, pp. 358, 367; BL, Additional MSS 25463, fols 73–4.

23. Whitaker, pp. 367–8.

24. KRO, WD/Hoth, Box 44.

25. Bolton MSS, Sundry Letters, 125.

26. Williamson, pp. 151–3.

27. Whitaker, p. 367.

28. *Diaries*, pp. 30–2; Williamson, p. 154.

29. Williamson, pp. 93–4.

30. YAS, DD121/36A/3, fols 74–6; *Diaries*, p. 37; BL, Althorp, B.1; Whitaker, pp. 368–9. For the uncompleted assurances, see Currey, 28/138/68.

31. HMC, *Twelfth Report*, App. VII, 14.

32. *Diaries*, pp. 36–8.

33. BL, Add. MSS 25463, fols 74–5.

34. *Diaries*, p. 39; Book III, 253.

35. HMC, *Twelfth Report*, App. VII, 14.

36. Book III, 254.

37. *Diaries*, p. 40.

38. YAS, DD121/36A/3, fols 79–82; Bolton MSS, Bk 96, fol. 156.

39. Bolton MSS, Sundry, III, 45.

40. *Diaries*, p. 42; McClure, *Chamberlain Letters*, II, 35.

41. *Diaries*, pp. 45–7; R.T. Spence, 'A Royal Progress in the North: James I at Carlisle Castle and the Feast of Brougham, August 1617', *Northern History*, XXVII (1991), pp. 41–89.

42. KRO, WD/Hoth, Box 5. Williamson's summary (App. V) is incomplete, Breay's far preferable (*Light in the Dales*, II, chap. 18).

43. PRO, C54/2348; Lord Chamberlain's Office, Recognizances, LC4/198/385.

44. *Diaries*, p. 56. Anne Compton, the dowager countess, died on 22 September 1618 (GEC, iv, 423).

45. *Commons Debates 1621*, eds W. Notestein, F.H. Relf, and H. Simpson (7 vols, Yale University Press, 1935), iv, 349–50; v, 376.

46. Spence, 'Earls', chap. X.

4 ANNE, COUNTESS OF DORSET, 1609–24

1. Williamson, pp. 126, 152, 154; Lanyer, *Salve Deus Rex Judaeorum*; John Aubrey's *'Brief Lives'*, ed. A. Clark (2 vols, Oxford, Clarendon Press, 1898), I, 127, 229–30; *John Aubrey, The Natural History of Wiltshire*, ed. K.G. Ponting (Newton Abbot, David & Charles, 1969), Introduction. Arthur Collins relied almost entirely on Anne for his comments on Dorset in *Memorials of the Antient and Noble Family of Sackville* (1742), pp. 553–9.

2. Holmes, p. 23; Nichols, *Progresses*, II,

361. The theme and Anne's role are discussed in J. Pitcher, '"In those figures which they seeme": Samuel Daniel's *Tethys' Festival*,' in *The Court Masque*, ed. D. Lindley (Manchester University Press, 1984), pp. 33–46.

3. CKS, U269, A2/2.

4. *Diaries*, p. 252; Nichols, *Progresses*, II, 499–501, 527–8, 609.

5. KRO, WD/Hoth, Box 44.

6. Nichols, *Progresses*, II, 628–67; McClure, *Chamberlain Letters*, I, 446, 450.

7. PRO, Exchequer, Accounts Various, E101/437/8. Richard Hutton was one of the Queen's counsel.

8. Nichols, *Progresses*, II, 707–29, 759; Williamson, p. 86.

9. *Diaries*, p. 274; Williamson, pp. 146–9.

10. PRO, E101/437/8.

11. Williamson, pp. 150–2, 154; *Diaries*, pp. 28–9, 253.

12. C.J. Phillips, *History of the Sackville Family*, I, 240.

13. *Diaries*, pp. 30, 255–67; M.R. Holmes, 'A Tudor Organ-Case at Appleby-in-Westmorland', *Antiquaries Journal*, LVII (1979), pp. 320–32.

14. Pitcher, *The Brotherton Manuscript*, pp. 168–9.

15. *Diaries*, pp. 37–45, 239–40; Catalogue, pp. 32–3.

16. *Diaries*, pp. 45, 47–8, 50–65.

17. *Diaries*, pp. 29, 43, 71, 75, 257.

18. Williamson, *Third Earl*, p. 293.

19. W. Camden, *Reges, Reginae, Nobilii et Alii in ecclesia . . . Westmonsterii . . . sepulti . . . 1600* (Huntington Library, 97069, University Microfilms, Ann Arbor, Michigan, 1799/200); W. Camden, *Remaines Concerning Britain* (London, John Russell Smith, 1870); *A Transcript of the Registers of the Company of Stationers at London, 1554–1640 AD*, ed. E. Arber (5 vols, London, priv. printed, 1875–91), III, 56; *The Workes of Mr. Edmund Spenser in Six Volumes*, ed. John Hughes (London, Jacob Tonson, 1715), I, xvii–xix. Cf. Williamson, pp. 63–4, and T. Cocke, 'Classical or Gothic? Lady Anne Clifford Reconsidered', *Country Life*, 31 January 1980, p. 325.

20. *Diaries*, pp. 40–1, 47, 60.

21. *Diaries*, pp. 56–7; Williamson, p. 148.

22. *Diaries*, pp. 60, 64, 79 n.67, 43, 66.

23. *Diaries*, pp. 29, 43, 80.

24. *Diaries*, pp. 82, 64, 75–6, 78 n.65, 79, 81 n.74.

25. PRO, Wards, 9/98, fols 36, 138.

26. *Diaries*, pp. 68, 70, 76 note, 81; Williamson, p. 111; Spence, pp. 14–15; KRO, WD/Hoth/A988/21; *Leicester's Commonwealth*, ed. D.C. Peck (London, Ohio University Press, 1985), pp. 2–5; *DNB*, XV, 417.

27. *Diaries*, p. 64.

28. KRO, WD/Hoth, Box 44, letter of 22 September 1615.

29. *Diaries*, pp. 65, 81. On Slingsby's maritime career, see Spence, pp. 114, 154.

30. *Diaries*, pp. 73, 75 note, 81; *Lowther Family Estate Books 1617–1675*, ed. C.B. Phillips, Surtees Soc. CXCI (1979), pp. 223–7; PRO, Chancery, Proceedings, C2/JACI/C4/37.

31. Spence, 'Royal Progress', p. 89.

32. *Diaries*, p. 66; Catalogue, p. 36; Vita Sackville-West, *Knole and the Sackvilles* (London, Heinemann, 1923) p. 73.

33. Catalogue, pp. 33–5.

34. Nichols, *Progresses*, IV, 632–47,

35. Spence, 'Royal Progress', pp. 69, 89; Nichols, *Progresses*, III, 443, 450, 455, 472, 494, 500–43.

36. CKS, U269, E66/3; Phillips, *History of the Sackvilles*, I, 268–70; East Sussex Record Office, Radford Deeds, SPK (Radford) PT1, A.3405. I am very grateful to D.J.H. Clifford for drawing my attention to this deed.

37. Nichols, *Progresses*, III, 654–5; R. Lockyer, *Buckingham* (London, Longman, 1981), p. 96.

38. KRO, WD/Hoth, Box 44; *Diaries*, p. 246; Williamson, p. 142.

39. *Diaries*, pp. 241–2. Anne was also godmother to Lord Howard de Walden's 'child' on 16 February 1623 (CKS, U269/A3, fol. 131).

40. *Diaries*, p. 250; Williamson, pp. 142–3, 156.

41. *DNB*, IV, 423–4.

5 Dowager Countess of Dorset, 1624–30

1. Clay, p. 400; Williamson, p. 147; *Diaries*, p. 78; Cooper, *Wentworth Papers*, pp. 184, 150–1.

2. Williamson, p. 142; CKS, U269, T70/10; W.D. Scull, 'Bolebroke House', *Sussex Archaeological Collections*, LII (1909), pp. 32–7; J. Stow, *A Survey of London, 1603* (London, Dent, Everyman edn, 1970), p. 353. I am very grateful to D.J.H. Clifford for drawing my attention to the Meeching draft lease in East Sussex Record Office, AMS 4878.

3. Phillips, *History of the Sackvilles*, I, 257; Williamson, chap. XXIX; PRO, C78/279/9.

4. Williamson, pp. 460–2; PRO, Prerogative Court of Canterbury, PCC, PROB, 11/351.

5. Williamson, pp. 413–14; *Diaries*, p. 246.

6. YAS MD240, Box 4/5; PRO, Wards 9/417, fols 31r, 84v, 143r; /418, fols 100v, 169r, 212v, 232v, 278r, 307v; Castle Ashby Papers, Compton Family Documents, 833. Anne averred in 1650 that she had paid every penny due to the court (Williamson, p. 219).

7. Sedgewick, pp. 301–2; W.C. Renshaw, 'Some Clergy of the Archdeaconry of Lewes and South Malling Deanery', *Sussex Arch. Coll.* LV (1912), p. 224.

8. *Diaries*, pp. 87–8; Whitaker, p. 350.

9. Cooper, *Wentworth Papers*, pp. 323–4; Spence, p. 31.

10. *CSPD*, 1628–1629, pp. 95, 432; *Lords Proceedings 1628*, eds M.F. Keeler, M.J. Cole, and W.B. Bidwell (New Haven, Yale University Press, 1983), V, 86–91, 103–8; BL, Cotton, Julius C. III, 60.95.

11. Book III, 213–14.

12. Spence, p. 52.

13. CKS, U455, T287/1.

14. PRO, Wards 9/88, fols 36, 138.

15. *Diaries*, pp. 88, 245.

16. *Acts of the Privy Council of England*, 1630–1631, ed. J.R. Dasent (HMSO, 1964), no. 92.

17. *CSPD*, 1628–1629, p. 535.

18. Catalogue, pp. 37–8.

19. Buckinghamshire County Record Office, Aylesbury, Chenies Parish Register.

20. KRO, WD/Hoth, Box 47; *Diaries*, p. 91.

21. *Diaries*, pp. 105–6; Williamson, pp. 170–1; Spence, 'Royal Progress', p. 43.

22. *Ceremonies of Charles I. The Note Books of John Finet 1628–1641*, ed. A.J. Loomie (New York, Fordham University Press,

1987), pp. 61, 83, 92, 116, 156; G.E. Aylmer, *The King's Servants. The Civil Service of Charles I, 1625–1642* (London, Routledge, 1961), pp. 206, 349; Ponting, *Aubrey's Wiltshire*, pp. 88, 91.

6 COUNTESS OF PEMBROKE, DORSET AND MONTGOMERY, 1630–50

1. Sedgewick, p. 296; Loomie, *Finet Notebooks*, pp. 88–9, 97, 121, 144–5, 148–50; T. Birch, *The Court and Times of Charles I* (2 vols, London, 1848), vol. II, 128.
2. C. Platt, *The Great Rebuildings of Tudor and Stuart England* (London, UCL Press, 1994), pp. 84–7, 90; Williamson, pp. 172–7; Rainbow, p. 43.
3. Book III, 212, 217–18.
4. YAS, DD139, Box I, Box 4/2; Williamson, p. 372; Wiltshire County Record Office, Wilton House Records, 2057/E1/1.
5. KRO, WD/Hoth/A988/9; Lismore, 18, fol. 20.
6. *CSPD*, 1633–1634, p. 237; Sedgewick, p. 297; Whitaker, p. 389.
7. Loomie, *Finet Notebooks*, pp. 174, 255.
8. KRO, WD/Hoth Boxes, 46, 47; Book III, 276; *Diaries*, p. 92. For Danvers, see *DNB*, V, 490–1; Finch, VII, 14–18 ; and Pye, XVI, 514.
9. C. Brown, 'Van Dyck's Pembroke Family Portrait: An Inquiry into its Italian Sources', *Van Dyck's Paintings*, eds A.K. Wheelock, S.J. Barnes, and J.S. Held (London, Thames & Hudson, 1991), pp. 37–44.
10. *The Diary of John Evelyn*, ed. E.S. de Beer (6 vols, Oxford University Press, 1955), vol. III, 100.
11. Williamson, p. 177; Book III, 221; *Diaries*, pp. 94, 178.
12. *The Private Journals of the Long Parliament 3 January to 5 March 1642*, eds W.H. Coates, A.S. Young and V.F. Snow (Yale University Press, 1982), p. 1; Williamson, p. 179; Book III, 221.
13. Williamson, pp. 180–1; Wiltshire CRO, Wilton House Records, 2057/E1; Scull, 'Bolebroke House', p. 36.
14. Stow, *Survey*, p. 61; J.H. MacMichael, 'Baynard Castle, and Excavations on its Site', *Journal of the British Archaeological Society*, XLVI (1890), pp. 173–85; *CSPD*, 1633–1634, p. 237; *Diaries*, p. 95.
15. Lismore, 28.
16. R.T. Spence, 'A Noble Funeral in the Great Civil War', *YAJ*, 65 (1993), pp. 115–17.
17. Trinity College, Dublin, MS 689/1–8; BL, Stowe, 592.
18. *Diaries*, p. 95; R.T. Spence, *Skipton Castle in the Great Civil War, 1642–1645* (Skipton Castle, 1991), pp. 53–4, 90–1; YAS, DD121/5/2; /23/3.
19. Currey, 43/39; KRO, WD/Hoth, Box 44; Spence, *Skipton Castle*, pp. 89–90.
20. Spence, *Skipton Castle*, pp. 100, 107–8; *Memorials of the Civil War. The Fairfax Correspondence*, ed. R. Bell (2 vols, London, Richard Bentley, 1849), I, 312–13; Whitaker, p. 416. Anne supported Charles Fairfax's son at Queen's College, Oxford. He later became a Fellow of Magdalen College (Sedgewick, p. 302). There was a Clifford–Fitzhugh coat of arms in Fairfax's house at Steeton (YAS, MS 338, fol. 266).
21. Dawson, *Loose Leaves*, I, 130–2; YAS, DD121/3/12.
22. KRO, WD/Hoth, Box 47; Spence, *Skipton Castle*, pp. 103–5; Whitaker, p. 416.
23. BL, Althorp, B7; PRO, Chancery, Depositions, Bridges Division, C5/405/174; Depositions, C22/214/43.
24. *Diaries*, p. 96; Whitaker, p. 384, n.; GEC, x, 415–17; *CSPD*, 1625–1649, p. 717.
25. Castle Ashby Papers, 833.
26. P.R. Newman, *Royalist Officers in England and Wales, 1642–1660. A Biographical Dictionary* (New York, Garland, 1981), pp. 79–80; *Diaries*, p. 96; Castle Ashby, 833. John Howell and Christopher Marsh were witnesses.
27. *Diaries*, p. 100; Williamson, p. 196.
28. Sedgewick, pp. 296–7; E. Hasted, *The History and Topographical Survey of the County of Kent* (12 vols, Canterbury, W. Bristow, 1797–1801), VI, 168, 175, 226, 237, 246, 252.
29. Williamson, pp. 210–11; *Diaries*, p. 112.

7 BARONESS OF SKIPTON, 1643–76

1. Whitaker, pp. 11–13; Spence, p. 5.
2. *Yorkshire Royalist Composition Papers*,

ed. J.W. Clay (3 vols, YAS, Record Ser.), II (1895), pp. 122–3; Lismore, 29; Chatsworth, BAS2, Box B/3.

3. Whitaker, p. 310; Williamson, pp. 193, 210.

4. YAS, DD121/32/18, 22, 40, 42; Dawson, *Loose Leaves*, I, 17–22.

5. *Diaries*, p. 106; Williamson, p. 215; Clay, *Royalist Composition Papers*, II, no. 83.

6. KRO, WD/Hoth, Box 44.

7. YAS, DD121/36A/2, 3; Dawson, *Loose Leaves*, I, 199–200. On the Claphams of Beamsley, see Barbara Clapham, *The Clapham Family* (Hurst Village Publishing, 1993), chap. II.

8. YAS, DD121/25/44; /32/13, 40, 43, 48; Spence, 'Earls', pp. 330, 334–5, 349–51; Williamson, pp. 223–4; KRO, WD/Hoth, Box 44; East Sussex Record Office, AMS 4878.

9. YAS, DD121/32/3, 48; W.H. Dawson, *History of Skipton* (Skipton, Edmondson, 1882), p. 245.

10. Bolton MSS, Sundry, Letters, II, 37; B.D. Henning, *The House of Commons 1660–1690* (3 vols, London, Secker & Warburg, 1983), II, 647–8. There are surveys of Jennings's Silsden holdings in YAS, DD121/32/ 9, 47, 54.

11. Bolton MSS, Sundry, II, 36.

12. Whitaker, p. 448; YAS, MS 1325 *passim*; YAS, DD121/76. Leases in the Estate Ledger confirm the changes (YAS, DD121/110). The windmill was in existence by 1579/80, Arthur Mawde gent. being the previous tenant at a rent of 8s 4d a year (YAS, DD121/24/8).

13. PRO, SP19/351.

14. Bolton MSS, Book 265, Carleton, fol. 7r; Dawson, *Loose Leaves*, I, 164–6.

15. *Diaries*, p. 120; PRO, Exchequer, Depositions, E134, 12 Charles II, Mich. 27; 19 Ch. II, East. 18, 19, 25; YAS, MS 1325, p. 46.

16. Lismore, 75A; YAS, MS 1325, p. 46.

17. Accounts, 1668. The 1667 depositions are in YAS, DD121/100/40.

18. Lismore, 29; YAS, DD121/109/1 (printed in Dawson, *Loose Leaves*, I, 128–9).

19. Lismore, 29; *Diaries*, p. 108.

20. YAS, DD121/32/34; /109/1; Dawson, *Loose Leaves*, I, 129.

21. Bolton MSS, Sundry II, 17.

22. Chatsworth, BAS2, Skipton Folder; DD121/109/1. See below, chap. 12.

23. Bolton MSS, Sundry, II, 35.

24. Currey, 24/38; Bolton MSS, Sundry II, 35.

25. Bolton MSS, Sundry, II, 36, 38; Book 274, fol. 17; *Diaries*, p. 125; *The Parish Register of Skipton-in-Craven 1592–1680*, ed. W.J. Stavert (Skipton, 1894), p. 292. Walker's gravestone with its brass plate was placed in the north aisle (YAS, MS 338, fol. 422).

26. *Diaries*, p. 125; YAS, DD121/109. Thoresby wrote that there were large deposits of alabaster at Fairburn, near Ledsham, east of Leeds, which were used for funerary monuments (Ralph Thoresby, *Ducatis Leodiensis*, ed. T.D. Whitaker (2nd edn, Leeds, 1816), App. p. 130).

27. W. Camden, *Britannia* (1610), p. 694; Spence, *Skipton Castle*, pp. 1–2; *Diaries*, p. 125; Bolton MSS, Sundry II, 36.

28. Bolton MSS, Sundry, II, 35; Chatsworth, BAS1, 3/1, fol. 5r.

29. *Diaries*, p. 121; Bolton MSS, Sundry, II, 37.

30. *Diaries*, pp. 133, 137–8; *CSPD*, 1657–1658, p. 59.

31. Whitaker, pp. 409–11; J. Ward, *Skipton Castle*, 2nd edn, (Skipton, Edmundson, 1877), p. 83.

32. *Diaries*, p. 142; R. Pocock, *Memorials of the Family of Tufton, Earls of Thanet* (London, R. Pocock, 1800), p. 114; *CSPD*, 1659–1660, p. 73; Spence, *Skipton Castle*, p. 105. Anne continued to buy lead for the castle, e.g. two tons on 17 September 1660 (Chatsworth, BAS1, 3/1, fol. 5r).

33. *Diaries*, pp. 138, 142–3, 147; Spence, *Skipton Castle*, p. 98; Whitaker, pp. 309, 311; Accounts, 39; Camden, *Britannia*, p. 697.

34. Lismore, 75A; Bolton MSS, Sundry, II, 37; YAS, MD240, Box 2, 19; *Diaries*, p. 148; Chatsworth, BAS2, 'Notes of Business at Bolton 1667–69'.

35. Whitaker, pp. 11–13; Chatsworth, BAS2, box, Wapentake of Staincliffe.

36. BL, Althorp, Burlington Papers, Box IV; PRO, Exchequer, Parliamentary Surveys, E317, Yorks. no. 14.

37. YAS, DD121/109; Chatsworth, Londesborough Papers, I (i), 65; *Diaries*, p. 127.

38. Chatsworth, BAS II, box, Wapentake of Staincliffe; Lismore, 75A, 28.

39. *Memoirs of Sir John Reresby*, ed. A. Browning, 2nd edn (London, Royal Historical Soc., 1991), pp. 67, n.4, 156. On Burlington, see T.C. Barnard, 'Land and the Limits of Loyalty: The Second Earl of Cork and First Earl of Burlington (1612–1698)', *Lord Burlington Architecture, Art and Life*, eds Toby Barnard and Jane Clark (London, the Hambledon Press, 1995), pp. 167–99.

40. *Diaries*, pp. 171, 184–5; Lismore, 28.

8 BARONESS OF WESTMORLAND, 1643–76

1. PRO, *Lists and Indexes*, IX (1898), p. 151.

2. Spence, *Skipton Castle*, pp. 50, 66, 81; PRO, SP28/215, fol. 135.

3. Williamson, pp. 190–2; KRO, WD/Hoth, Box 44; Curwen, *Later Records*, p. 288. On Lowther, see H. Owen, *The Lowther Family* (Chichester, Phillimore, 1990), chap. 14.

4. F.H. Sunderland, *Marmaduke Lord Langdale* (London, Jenkins, 1926), p. 126; Holdgate, *Appleby*, pp. 41–2.

5. *Diaries*, p. 100; Williamson, pp. 192–4; R.T. Spence, 'Mining and Smelting by the Cliffords, Earls of Cumberland, in Westmorland in the early seventeenth century', *Trans. CWAAS*, XCI (1991), p. 116.

6. *Diaries*, pp. 106, 112; Chatsworth, Londesborough Papers, F/21–6.

7. *Diaries*, p. 110; *Calendar of the Committee for Compounding, 1643–1660* (HMSO, 1887–92), I, 257. Anne later quarrelled with Mrs Bowes of Barnard Castle over the bounds of Stainmore, which led to another protracted lawsuit (Accounts, 1).

8. KRO, WD/Hoth, Box 44.

9. PRO, C78/632/10; Williamson, pp. 267–8. Transcripts of the depositions are in CRO, DX/99, no. 3.

10. BL, Harl. 7001, fol. 212. For Selden, see *DNB*, XVII, 1150.

11. YAS, DD121/110 (Skipton Rentroll, 1650, end papers); Williamson, p. 217.

12. *Calendar of the Committee for Compounding, 1643–1660*, I, 195–6.

13. Williamson, pp. 216–17; *Diaries*, p. 110.

14. *Diaries*, pp. 113, 115; *CSPD*, 1651–1652, p. 29.

15. *Diaries*, p. 116.

16. *Diaries*, p. 120; Bolton MSS, Sundry, II, 21.

17. *Diaries*, p. 122; YAS, DD121/109.

18. *Diaries*, pp. 127, 130.

19. *Diaries*, pp. 130, 132; Williamson, p. 106.

20. *Diaries* p. 133. See above, chap. 6, p. 106.

21. *Diaries*, p. 132; Williamson, p. 212.

22. CRO, Lowther Papers, D/LONS/6/3; R.W. Brunskill, 'The Development of the Small House in the Eden Valley from 1650–1840', *Trans. CWAAS*, LIII (1953), pp. 160–89.

23. *Diaries*, p. 174; M.M. Thompson, *Mallerstang* (Appleby, Whitehead, 1965), pp. 40–2; Breay, *Light in the Dales*, III, *passim*.

24. *Fleming–Senhouse Papers*, ed. E. Hughes, Cumberland Record Series, II (Carlisle, 1961), pp. 10, 28; *Diaries*, pp. 110, 120; J. Charlton, *Brougham Castle* (London, English Heritage, 1988), *passim*.

25. *Diaries*, pp. 110, 116; Williamson, pp. 379–83; KRO, WD/Hoth, Box 12; YAS, MD240, Box 4.

26. Diaries, pp. 110, 118–19; J. Charlton, 'The Lady Anne Clifford (1590–1676)', *Ancient Monuments and their Interpretation. Essays presented to A.J. Taylor*, eds M.R. Apted, R. Gilyard-Beer and A.D. Saunders (Chichester, Phillimore, 1977), pp. 305–6.

27. Williamson, pp. 388–91; Blake Tyson, 'Who Built the Countess's Pillar at Brougham?', *Trans. CWAAS*, LXXXVIII (1988), pp. 243–6; Accounts, 15.

28. PRO, C5/623/132.

29. Pevsner, *The Buildings of England. North Somerset and Bristol*, p. 142.

30. *Diaries*, p. 124; M.R. Holmes, *The Parish Churches of Appleby* (Parochial Church Council, 1994), *passim*; Holdgate, *Appleby*, pp. 43, 46.

31. *Diaries*, p. 133; Williamson, pp. 410–12.

32. Holmes, *Parish Churches*; *Diaries*, pp. 138, 141, 156.

33. Williamson, pp. 307–9, 471; T. Cocke, 'Repairer of the Breach', *Country Life*, 25 October 1990, pp. 85–6; T.W.H. Rutherford, *The History of the Parish of*

Brougham (1980); Holmes, *Parish Churches*.

34. *Diaries*, pp. 141–2; *CSPD*, 1659–1660, pp. 192–3.

35. Camden, *Britannia*, p. 760; *Diaries*, pp. 141, 146; Charlton, 'Lady Anne Clifford', pp. 308–9.

36. *Diaries*, pp. 146, 154, 159.

37. *Diaries*, pp. 150, 157–8.

38. *Diaries*, p. 169; KRO, Dalston/Ewbank Records, WD/DE, Box 46/T/1; Thompson, *Mallerstang*, pp. 29–31.

39. Thompson, *Mallerstang*, p. 9; *DNB*, XIII, 1065–6; R.S. Boumphrey, C.R. Hudleston and J. Hughes, *An Armorial for Westmorland and Lonsdale*, CWAAS, Extra Ser., XXI (1975), p. 210.

40. *Diaries*, p. 246; Accounts, 1665–1668, 6, 8, 12, 14, 21, 24, 25, 28, 31; R.T. Spence, 'Clifford Houses: Julian Bower, Westmorland', *Clifford Association Newsletter* (vol. 2, no. 4, June, 1991).

41. Accounts, 9, 15, 22, 30, 38; *Diaries*, p. 246.

42. Curwen, *Later Records*, pp. 62–4, 290; *The Hearth Tax List for Staincliffe and Ewcross Wapentakes West Riding of Yorkshire Lady Day 1672*, ed. J. Hebden (Ripon Historical Soc., 1992), pp. 11, 47.

43. *Diaries*, pp. 181, 185.

9 HISTORY AND LEGITIMACY PROCLAIMED: THE MANUSCRIPT RECORDS

1. KRO, WD/Hoth/A988/10/1, 2, 3. Thomas, 6th Earl of Thanet, implies a fourth set at the end of Book III (cf. Gilson, p. xxxiv).

2. Sedgewick, p. 302.

3. *The Diary of the Lady Anne Clifford*, ed. V. Sackville-West (London, Heinemann, 1923), p. 91; *Diaries*, p. 70; Williamson, p. 446.

4. Book I, 124.

5. HMC, *Hastings IV: Manuscripts of Mr R.R. Hastings, 1543–1750* (London, HMSO, 1947) p. 286.

6. *Three Catalogues*, ed. Joseph Hunter (London, Pickering, 1838), p. 222.

7. Books II, 354, 255; III, 120; II, 68, 73, 165, 37. On the repositories, see S.R. Scargill-Bird, *A Guide to the Various Classes of Document preserved in the Public Record Office*, 3rd edn (London, HMSO, 1908).

8. Book II, 91, 74–85.

9. Books II, 402; I, 14–16, 187; II, 27, 30.

10. Book I, 189, 128; R.T. Spence, *The Shepherd Lord of Skipton Castle* (Skipton Castle, 1994), esp. pp. 9–10.

11. Books II, 441; I, 126.

12. Lincoln's Inn Library, Hale MS 104; KRO, WD/Hoth, Box 45.

13. *Diaries*, p. 70.

14. Book I, 140; Accounts, 1668. For Edward Fairfax of Fewston, translator of Tasso and an illegitimate half–brother of Col. Charles Fairfax, see *Godfrey of Bulloigne*, ed. K.M. Lea and T.M. Gang (Oxford, Clarendon Press, 1981), p. 4.

15. Sedgewick, p. 302.

16. KRO, WD/Hoth, Box 44, letter to Marsh, 19 April, 1650.

17. Hunter, *Catalogues*, pp. 62–3, 150–2, 154–6, 165, 222–4, 242 and, for Dodsworth's life, pp. 59–82.

18. Book I, 1–25.

19. Hunter, *Catalogues*, pp. 170–1.

20. YAS, MS 338, fol. 423. This comment was written 31 March 1666 during his visitation.

21. Hunter, *Catalogues*, pp. 100–3, 109–10.

22. Book I, 188; '"A Book of All the Severall Officers of the Court of Exchequer . . ." by Lawrence Squibb', ed. W.H. Bryson, *Camden Miscellany*, XXVI, Camden Soc., 4th Ser., 14 (1975), p. 128.

23. See above, chap. 5, p. ; Book I, 65–6, 175; *VCH, Lincs*, II, ed. W. Page (1906), pp. 202–5, where Dugdale and Cotton are the cited sources. I am most grateful to Dr Colin Tite and Prof. Geoffrey Martin for elucidating Kniveton's and Dodsworth's use of Cotton's collection.

24. Book I, 140, 161; Hunter, *Catalogues*, pp. 137, 144; Clifford, pp. 24–5.

25. Book I, 12–14, 51–2; Hunter, *Catalogues*, pp. 132–3, 126, 146; Sir William Dugdale, *Monasticon* (3 vols, London, Sam. Keble, 1693), II, 295 (Hepp).

26. Book I, 73; Hunter, *Catalogues*, pp. 149, 172, 183; YAS, MS 283, fols. 166–9; *Cartulary of Oseney Abbey*, ed. Revd. H.E. Salter (3 vols, Oxford, Oxford Historical Soc., 1929), pp. ix–x; *Diaries*, pp. 191–2.

27. Hunter, *Catalogues*, p. 101, note.

28. Book II, 133; Hunter, *Catalogues*, pp. 154–5; *The Percy Chartulary*, ed. M.T. Martin, Surtees Soc. 117 (1911); Spence, *Shepherd Lord*, pp. 54–5.

29. Book I, 28, 33–5, 69. The Blyth Cartulary was owned at the time by the family of Anne's cousin, Sir Gervase Clifton (*The Cartulary of Blyth Priory*, ed. R.T. Timson (2 vols, London, HMSO, 1973), I, vii).

30. Hunter, *Catalogues*, pp. 94–5. For Widdrington, see *DNB*, XVI, 182–4. A book on the reign of Edward III by Cuthbert Burby was published 1 December 1595 (*STC*, 7501).

31. Book II, 177, 543–6, 375.

32. KRO, WD/Hoth/A988/9, fol. 2r; Hunter, *Catalogues*, p. 75.

33. KRO, WD/Hoth, Boxes 44, 45/27–8.

34. Gilson, p. 16. It is to be noted that he gives, and corrects, in his footnotes Anne's biblical references in their Harley MS 6177 version.

35. *Clifford Letters of the Sixteenth Century*, ed. A.G. Dickens, Surtees Soc. CLXXXII (1962), pp. 142, 145; Williamson, p. 358.

36. Dickens, *Letters*, pp. 127, 135–6; *Diaries*, p. 154; Book II, 523.

37. Spence, *Shepherd Lord*, passim.

38. *Diaries*, pp. 126, 149.

39. *Diaries*, p. 231; Accounts, 33.

40. *Diaries*, pp. 49, 71, 82, 22, 41, 80, 85, 42 n.28.

41. Sedgewick, p. 303.

42. Hunter, *Catalogues*, pp. 316, 318, 340–1; Pitcher, *The Brotherton Manuscript*, p. 169.

43. *DNB*, VIII, 902–8; Hunter, *Catalogues*, p. 234.

44. KRO, WD/Hoth/A988/9, nos 5, 6; N&B, I, 268–9; Whitaker, pp. 312, 317.

45. Bodleian, MS. Top. Gen. C49. Anne records on 24 February 1676 that Johnston had sent her 'by my Lord Marshall's directions severall of my Ancestors letters' (*Diaries*, p. 257).

46. Whitaker, pp. 311–17. Clifford, however, omits the Vipont lords.

47. Whitaker, pp. 357–8.

48. Accounts, 1, 8, 14, 8, 9.

49. Accounts, 2, 1, 3, 10, 8, 37.

10 HISTORY AND LEGITIMACY PROCLAIMED: THE VISUAL DISPLAYS

1. Whitaker, p. 339; Beverley County Record Office, Chichester–Constable Papers, DDCC/144; Williamson, pp. 334–5, n.1, 499; Pocock, *Memorials*, p. 114; Ponting, *Aubrey's Wiltshire*, pp. 84–5.

2. Williamson, pp. 498, 493–4.

3. Catalogue, pp. 28–9; 26.

4. Holmes, pp. 133–6; *Dynasties. Painting in Tudor and Jacobean England 1530–1630*, ed. Karen Hearn (London, Tate Gallery Publishing, 1995), p. 81.

5. Williamson, pp. 334–5, n.1.

6. Whitaker, p. 342.

7. Lambeth Palace Library, Shrewsbury MSS, 700, fol. 109.

8. Holmes, pp. 136–7; Catalogue, pp. 31, 39–40.

9. E.g. Parry, 'The Great Picture'.

10. Spence, pp. 28, 94.

11. *The Visitation of the County of Warwickshire, 1682–1683*, ed. W.H. Rylands, Harleian Soc. LXII (1911), p. 9.

12. Dickens, *Letters*, p. 149.

13. Sedgewick, p. 302; *Diaries*, p. 94; Robertson, *Arcadia*, pp. 85, 435.

14. *Diaries*, pp. 45, 166, 81.

15. Parry, 'The Great Picture', p. 208.

16. *Diaries*, p. 68. See above, chap. 7, p. 141.

17. See above, chap. 4, p. 71.

18. *Diaries*, p. 41.

19. Spence, pp. 213–14.

20. Whitaker, p. 335; Spence, p. 17.

21. Clay, p. 407; Accounts, 1668.

22. R.C. Wilton, 'Historic Londesborough', *Transactions of the East Riding Antiquarian Society*, III (1905), p. 2.

23. *Diaries*, p. 28; *The Works of Michael Drayton*, ed. J.W. Hebel (5 vols, Oxford, Blackwell, 1932–41), II, 140–5, IV, 406, 447.

24. Williamson, p. 504.

25. Book I, 164, 169; Williamson, p. 501; *DNB*, VII, 395–6; Clifford, pp. 36–7.

26. Book I, 156.

27. Lincoln's Inn Library, Hale MS 104. See above, chaps 3, p. 41; 9, p. 179.

28. Williamson, pp. 497, 500, 504.

29. Williamson, p. 500; Accounts, 29.

30. KRO, WD/Hoth/A988/14.

31. Book II, 434.
32. See Append. IV.
33. Williamson, p. 489; YAS, MS 338, fols 420–2; Whitaker, illustration facing p. 431.
34. Whitaker, p. 433.
35. Williamson, pp. 62–3.

11 AUTHORITY AND PIETY: LADY ANNE'S WESTMORLAND REGIME, 1665–76

1. E.g. Cocke, 'Classic or Gothic?'
2. *Diaries*, pp. 112, 252.
3. Book I, 131.
4. Spence, *Shepherd Lord, passim.*
5. Accounts, *passim*: YAS, DD121/25/44.
6. Accounts, 46–52. Cf. *Diaries*, pp. 234, 254, 259.
7. Accounts, 1–59.
8. Spence, pp. 203–5.
9. Accounts, 53–5.
10. Accounts, 40–5.
11. YAS, DD121/25/44; Sedgewick, pp. 300, 303.
12. Clay, p. 411.
13. Felicity Heal, 'The Idea of Hospitality in Early Modern England', *Past and Present*, 102 (February 1984), pp. 71–3, 81, 90.
14. Sedgewick, p. 301.
15. Rainbow, pp. 41–2; Williamson, p. 326.
16. Sedgewick, p. 303; Accounts, 12, 37, 31, 34, 9.
17. Rainbow, p. 40; *Diaries*, p. 64, n.46; KRO, WD/Hoth/A988/2; Accounts, 1, 4, 9; E. Arber, *The Term Catalogue 1668–1709*, (3 vols, London, priv. printed, 1903–6), I, 3, 43, 50, 51.
18. Clay, pp. 408–10.
19. Accounts, 38, 2, 3, 25, 11, 31, 33, 37.
20. Accounts, 2, 12, 13, 17, 35.
21. Phillips, *Lowther Estate Books*, p. 185.
22. Accounts, 1668, 33; Bodleian, MS Rawlinson, Letters, 53, no. 55; PRO, PCC, PROB 11/349 (I owe this reference to the kindness of Dick Clifford).
23. Hamper, *Life of Dugdale*, p. 124; Accounts, 1665. On King's drawings, see Sir William Dugdale, *Heraldic Miscellanies* (London, Cadell, 1800), p. 29.
24. Rainbow, p. 56; Sedgewick, p. 302; Accounts, 10, 38, 44; *Diaries*, p. 242. See also, P. Crawford, *Women and Religion in England, 1500–1720* (London, Routledge, 1993), pp. 76–91.
25. Accounts, 6, 9.
26. Accounts, 2, 33.
27. KRO, WD/Hoth, Box 44; Clay, p. 411.
28. Accounts, 1, 37, 4, 2, 6, 37, 42, 30, 35, 30.
29. Sedgewick, p. 302; Rainbow, p. 27.
30. Spence, 'Lady Anne Clifford, Countess of Dorset, Pembroke and Montgomery (1590–1676): A Reappraisal', *Northern History*, XV (1979), pp. 59–60.
31. Sedgewick, pp. 298–9; Clay, p. 401.
32. Accounts, 33; Dalemain MSS, notebook.
33. Accounts, 28, 26, 12, 17, 36.
34. Rainbow, p. 40; Accounts, 12, 39.
35. Rainbow, p. 43.
36. Accounts, 37, 32.
37. Holdgate, *Appleby*, p. 45.
38. Accounts, 1668, 8.
39. Sedgewick, p. 302; Accounts, 1668. Sandford's *A Cursory Relation of all the Antiquities & Familyes in Cumberland circa 1675*, ed. R.S. Ferguson, CWAAS Tract Series, IV (Kendal, 1890), is invaluable for understanding the regional context of Anne's activities.
40. Clay, p. 407; Holdgate, *Appleby*, p. 47; Accounts, 1665, 1668.
41. Accounts, 1665, 12, 36, 8, 38, 42, 32.
42. Rainbow, p. 42.
43. Accounts, 1, 2, 3, 1, 22.
44. Williamson, pp. 311–12; Accounts, 12.
45. M.E. Burkett, *John Bracken* (Kendal, Abbot Hall, 1980).
46. *Diaries*, p. 144; Phillips, *Lowther Estate Books*, pp. 164–5.
47. Williamson, pp. 288–302; *Diaries*, p. 188; Henning, *House of Commons 1660–1690*, I, 433–5, where the members during the Interregnum are also discussed.

12 THE GRAND MATRIARCH

1. KRO, WD/Hoth/A988/9/6.
2. Castle Ashby, 833/7; Williamson, p. 452.

3. *The Diary of Samuel Pepys M.A. F.R.S*, ed. H.B. Wheatley (10 vols, London, Bell, 1920), I, 50–1.

4. CKS, U269, L23/1.

5. *Diaries*, p. 168; PRO, C78/650/4; C33/211, 213, 215, 225, 229 *passim*.

6. PRO, C33/277, fol. 494.

7. *Fulke Greville, Lord Brooke. The Remaines being poems of Monarchy and Religion*, ed. G.A. Wilkes (Oxford University Press, 1965). This was first published in 1670.

8. Currey, 28/138, fols 67–8; *DNB*, VII, 176; Lismore, 28, 75A; CKS, U991/T282.

9. KRO, WD/Hoth, Box 44; *Diaries*, p. 172.

10. KRO, WD/Hoth, Boxes 44, 4.

11. CKS, U269/E73/3; Dawson, *Loose Leaves*, I, 125–8.

12. CKS, U991/T282.

13. I am grateful to Ms Santina Levey, Sir Oliver Millar, Miss Vicky Slowe and Dr Helen Gladstone for their comments on this painting. The conclusions are my own.

14. KRO, WD/CAT/MUS/A 2113.

15. Sir Richard Baker, *A Chronicle of the Kings of England* (London, 1641).

16. *Diaries*, p. 190; BL, Althorp, B.6; Accounts, 1668.

17. *Diaries*, p. 269; Holdgate, *Appleby*, p. 46.

18. PRO, C78/650/4; CKS, U269/E483; /E72/4, 5.

19. CKS, U269/C14/2, 24, 82, 93/9; /C22/56/3.

20. HMC, *Fourth Report, Manuscripts of Earl De La Warr (Knole MSS)* (London, Eyre & Spottiswoode, 1874), App. p. 310; *Seventh Report, Manuscripts of Lord Sackville (Knole MSS)* (London, HMSO, 1879), App. p. 467.

21. Clay, pp. 401–11; PRO, PCC, PROB, 11/351.

22. Williamson, pp. 283–4.

23. YAS, DD121/32/5, 6; *Lord Thanet's Benefaction to the Poor of Craven*, ed. R. Hoyle (Friends of Giggleswick Parish Records, 1978).

24. N&B, pp. 306–8; CRO, D/LONS/6/3; W. Nicholls, *The History and Traditions of Mallerstang Forest and Pendragon Castle* (Manchester, John Heywood, 1883), pp. 49–53.

25. Whitaker, p. 311; YAS, DD121/36A/2, fol. 264; Chatsworth, BAS2, A1/6.

26. Book III, end folios; Boumphrey et al, *Armorial*, p. 302.

27. Barnard, 'Land and the Limits of Loyalty', p. 193; Williamson, chaps XVIV, XXVIII.

28. KRO, WD/Hoth, Box 44; J.T. Brighton, *Henry Gyles Virtuoso and Glass Painter of York, 1645–1709*, York Historian, 4 (Yorkshire Architectural and York Archaeological Society, 1984), pp. 27–9.

29. Beverley Record Office, DDCC/144/4; *Vertue Note Books* (6 vols, Oxford, Walpole Society, 1930–55), II, 73.

30. *The Travels through England of Dr. Richard Pococke*, ed. J.J. Cartwright (2 vols, Camden Soc., New Series, 42, 44, 1888–9), I, 33–4, 48, 194–5.

31. HMC, *Thirteenth Report: Manuscripts of the Duke of Portland, VI (Harley MSS)* (London, HMSO, 1901), p. 132; *DNB*, X, 266–8.

32. C. Heywood, 'Portraits of a Lady: Lady Anne Clifford and *Wuthering Heights*', Quarto, XXX, no. 4 (Kendal, Abbot Hall Art Gallery, 1993), pp. 10–14.

33. Sackville-West, *Knole and the Sackvilles*, pp. 73–5.

Bibliography

Except where otherwise stated, the place of publication is London.

PRIMARY SOURCES

1. Manuscript

British Library
Althorp Papers
Additional MSS, 25463
Cotton, Julius C. III
Harleian MSS, 6177, 7001
Stowe MSS, 592

Public Record Office
C2 Chancery, Proceedings
C5 Chancery, Bridges Division
C22 Chancery, Depositions
C33 Chancery, Entry Books of Decrees and Orders
C54 Chancery, Close Rolls
C78 Chancery, Decrees and Orders
E101 Exchequer, Accounts Various
E134 Exchequer, Depositions
E317 Exchequer, Parliamentary Surveys
LC4 Lord Chamberlain's Office, Recognizances
PCC Prerogative Court of Canterbury, Wills
SO3 Signet Office Docquet Books
SP14 State Papers, Domestic, James I
SP19 Committee for the Advance of Money
SP28 State Papers
St.Ch.8 Star Chamber Proceedings, James I
Wards 9 Court of Wards, Miscellaneous Books

Alnwick Castle
Syon MSS

Beverley County Record Office
DDCC Chichester–Constable Papers

Bodleian Library, Oxford
MS Dodsworth 88, 118
MS Rawlinson
MS Top. Gen.

Buckinghamshire County Record Office
Chenies Parish Register

Castle Ashby
Compton Family Documents

Chatsworth
Bolton MSS
Bolton Additional Series, BAS1, 2
Currey Papers
Hardwick Papers
Lismore Papers
Londesborough Papers

Cumbria County Archives
Carlisle D/Lons/L, Earl of Lonsdale, Lowther MSS
DX, Carlisle, Miscellaneous
Kendal WD/Hoth, Hothfield MSS
WD/D–E, Dalston–Ewbank Records
JAC 495/7, Lady Anne's Accounts, 1668–75

Dalemain
Lady Anne's Day-Book, 1676
Sir Edward Hasell's Notebook

East Sussex Record Office
AMS 4878
SPK, Radford Deeds, Miscellaneous

Hatfield House
Hatfield MSS

Kent County Record Office, Centre for Kentish Studies
Sackville MSS
Tufton MSS

Lambeth Palace Library
Shrewsbury Papers 700
Talbot MSS

Lincoln's Inn Library
Hale MS 104

Queen's College, Oxford
MS 105

Trinity College, Dublin
TCD, MS 689/1–8

Wiltshire County Record Office
Wilton House Records

Yorkshire Archaeological Society
DD121 Skipton MSS
DD139 Beamsley Hospital Records
MD240 Beamsley Hospital Records
MS 338 Dodsworth's Book of Arms and Monuments
MS 784 Notes for a history of Appleby by C.B. Norcliffe, 1875
MS 1325 'Holden Park: a study', by T.M. Steel, 1979

2. Printed
Acts of the Privy Council, 1613–31, 13 vols, HMSO, 1921–64
Arber, E. *The Term Catalogues 1668–1709*, 3 vols, London, priv. printed, 1903–6
—— (ed.). *A Transcript of the Registers of the Company of Stationers at London, 1554–1640 AD*, 5 vols, London, priv. printed, 1875–91
Beer, E.S. de (ed.). *The Diary of John Evelyn*, 6 vols, Oxford University Press, 1955
Bell, R. (ed.). *Memorials of the Civil War*. The Fairfax Correspondence, 2 vols, Richard Bentley, 1849
Breward, I. (ed.). *The Works of William Perkins*, Appleford, Berks, Sutton Courtenay Press, 1970
Brigg, W. (ed.). *Feet of Fines of the Tudor Period, 1486–1603*, 4 vols, Yorkshire Archaeological Society, Record Series, II, V, VII, VIII (1887–90)
—— . *Yorkshire Fines for the Stuart Period, 1603–1625*, 2 vols, YASRS, LIII, LVIII (1915, 1917)
Browning, A. (ed.). *Memoirs of Sir John Reresby*, 2nd edn, Royal Historical Society, 1991
Bryson, W.H. (ed.). 'A Book of All the Severall Officers of the Court of Exchequer . . . by Lawrence Squibb', *Camden Miscellany,* vol. xxvi, Camden Society, 4th Series, 14, 1975
Calendar of the Committee for Compounding, 1643–60, 5 parts, HMSO, 1887–92
Calendar of State Papers, Domestic Series, 1603–60, 39 vols, Longmans, 1857–85
Camden, W. *Reges, Reginae, Nobilii et Alii in ecclesia ... Westmonsterii sepulti . . . 1600*, 1600, Huntington Library 97069, University Microfilms, Ann Arbor, Michigan, 1799/200
——*Remaines Concerning Britain*, London, John Russell Smith, 1870
Cartwright, J.J. (ed.), *The Travels through England of Dr. Richard Pococke*, 2 vols, Camden Society, New Series, 42, 44, 1888–9

Cholmley, Sir Hugh. *The Memoirs of Sir Hugh Cholmley Knt. and Bart,* 1777

Clark, A. (ed.). *John Aubrey's 'Brief Lives',* 2 vols, Oxford, Clarendon Press, 1895

Clay, J.W. (ed.). *Yorkshire Royalist Composition Papers,* 3 vols, YASRS, XV, XVII, XX, 1893–6

Clifford, D.J.H. (ed.). *The Diaries of Lady Anne Clifford,* Stroud, Alan Sutton Publishing, 1990

Coates, W.H., Young, A.S. and Snow, V.F. (eds) *The Private Journals of the Long Parliament 3 January to 5 March 1642,* Yale University Press, 1982

Cokayne, G.E. (ed.). *The Complete Peerage,* 13 vols, 1910–59

Coke, Sir Edward. *Reports,* 1658

Cooper, J.P. (ed.). *Wentworth Papers 1597–1628,* Camden Society, 4th Series., 12, 1973

Daniel, S. *The Whole Workes of Samuel Daniel Esquire in Poetrie,* 1623

Dickens, A.G. (ed.). *Clifford Letters of the Sixteenth Century,* Surtees Society, CLXXXII (1962)

Dictionary of National Biography

English Reports, LXXVII, LXXX, CXLV

Ferguson, R.S. (ed.). Edmund Sandford, *A Cursory Relation of all the Antiquities & Familyes in Cumberland circa 1675,* Cumberland and Westmorland Antiquarian and Archaeological Society, Tract Series, IV, Kendal, 1890

Grosart, A.B. (ed.). *The Complete Works in Verse and Prose of Samuel Daniel,* 4 vols, privately printed, 1885

Halliwell, J.O. (ed.). *The Private Diary of Dr. John Dee,* Camden Society, 19, 1842

Hasler, P.W. (ed.). *The History of Parliament: The House of Commons, 1558–1603,* 3 vols, HMSO, 1981

Hearn, K. (ed.). *Dynasties. Painting in Tudor and Jacobean England 1530–1630,* Tate Gallery, 1995

Hebden, J. (ed.). *The Hearth Tax List for Staincliffe and Ewcross Wapontakes West Riding of Yorkshire Lady Day 1672,* Ripon Historical Society, 1992

Hebel, J.W. (ed.). *The Works of Michael Drayton,* 5 vols, Oxford, Blackwell, 1932–41

Henning, B.D. *The House of Commons 1660–1690,* 3 vols, London, Secker & Warburg, 1983

Historical Manuscripts Commission: *Fourth Report: Manuscripts of Earl De La Warr (Knole MSS)* Eyre & Spottiswoode, 1874

Seventh Report: Manuscripts of Lord Sackville (Knole MSS) HMSO, 1879

Tenth Report: Appendix IV, Manuscripts of Lord Muncaster, Eyre & Spottiswoode, 1885

Twelfth Report: Manuscripts of Earl Cowper (Coke MSS), HMSO, 1888

——. *Manuscripts of Le Fleming, 1340–1849,* HMSO, 1890

Thirteenth Report: Manuscripts of the Duke of Portland VI (Harley MSS), HMSO, 1901

Hastings IV: Manuscripts of Mr R.R. Hastings, 1543–1750, HMSO, 1947

Salisbury MSS: Manuscripts of the Marquess of Salisbury at Hatfield House, 24 vols, HMSO, 1883–1976

Hoyle, R. (ed.). *Lord Thanet's Benefaction to the Poor of Craven,* Friends of Giggleswick Parish Records, 1978

Hughes, E. (ed.). *Fleming–Senhouse Papers,* Cumberland Record Series, II, Carlisle, 1961

Hughes, J. (ed.). *The Workes of Mr Edmund Spenser in Six Volumes*, London, Jacob Towson, 1715

Hunter, J. (ed.). *Three Catalogues*, Pickering, 1838

Keeler, M.F., Cole, M.J. and Bidwell, W.B. (eds). *Proceedings in Parliament 1628*, 6 vols, V, *Lords Proceedings 1628*, New Haven, Yale University Press, 1983

Lanyer, Aemilia. *Salve Deus Rex Judaeorum*, 1611

Lea, K.M. and Gang, T.M. (eds). *Godfrey of Bulloigne*, Oxford, Clarendon Press, 1981

Letters and Papers . . . of Henry VIII, vol. XII, HMSO, 1887

Ley, J. *Reports of Divers Resolutions in Law*, 1659

Loomie, A.J. (ed.). *Ceremonies of Charles I. The Note Books of John Finet 1628–1641*, New York, Fordham University Press, 1987

McClure, N.E. (ed.). *The Letters of John Chamberlain*, 2 vols, Philadelphia, American Philosophical Society Memoirs, XII, pts I–II, 1939

Martin, M.T. (ed.). *The Percy Chartulary*, Surtees Society, 117, 1911

Notestein, W., Relf, F.H., and Simpson, H. (eds). *Commons Debates 1621*, 7 vols, New Haven, Yale University Press, 1935

Oppenheim, M.M. (ed.). *The Naval Tracts of Sir William Monson*, vol. 1, Navy Records Society, XXII, 1902

Parsons, D. (ed.). *The Diary of Sir Henry Slingsby, of Scriven*, Bart, Longman, 1836

Peck, D.C. (ed.). *Leicester's Commonwealth*, Ohio State University Press, 1985

Phillips, C.B. (ed.). *Lowther Family Estate Books 1617–1675*, Surtees Society, CXCI, 1979

Pollard, A.W. and Redgrave, G.R. (eds). *A Short–Title Catalogue 1475–1646*, 2nd edn, 3 vols, The Bibliographical Society, 1976–91

Ponting, K.G. (ed.). *John Aubrey, The Natural History of Wiltshire*, Newton Abbot, David & Charles, 1969

Rainbow, E. *A Sermon preached at Appleby, April 14, 1676, at the Funeral of the Rt Hon Anne Clifford, Countess of Pembroke, Dorset & Montgomery, by Edward Rainbow, Bishop of Carlisle*, 1839

Raine, J. (ed.). *The Correspondence of Dr Matthew Hutton Archbishop of York*, Surtees Society, XVII, 1843

Robertson, J. (ed.). *Sir Philip Sidney The Countess of Pembroke's Arcadia*, Oxford University Press, 1973

Rylands, W.H. (ed.). *The Visitations of the County of Warwickshire, 1682–1683*, Harleian Society, LXII, 1911

Sackville–West, V. (ed.). *The Diary of the Lady Anne Clifford*, Heinemann, 1923

Salter, H.E. (ed.). *Cartulary of Oseney Abbey*, 3 vols, Oxford Historical Society, 1929

Skretkowicz, V. (ed.). *Sir Philip Sidney The Countess of Pembroke's Arcadia*, Oxford University Press, 1987

Snyder, S. (ed.). *The Divine Weeks and Works of Guillaume de Saluste, Sieur du Bartas. Translated by Joshua Sylvester*, 2 vols, Oxford, Clarendon Press, 1979

Southern, A.C. (ed.). *An Elizabethan Recusant House*, Richard Smith's 'The Life of the Lady Magdalen Viscountess Montague (1538–1605)', Sands & Co., 1954

Statutes of the Realm

Stavert, W.J. (ed.). *The Parish Register of Skipton-in-Craven 1592–1680*, Skipton, 1894

The Reports of Judge Sir Henry Hobart in the Common Pleas, 3rd edn, 1671

The Victoria History of the Counties of England: Lincoln, 1906

Timson, R.T. (ed.). *The Cartulary of Blyth Priory*, 2 vols, HMSO, 1973

Vertue Notebooks, 6 vols, Oxford, Walpole Society, 1930–55

Wheatley, H.B. (ed.). *The Diary of Samuel Pepys M.A. F.R.S.*, 10 vols, Bell, 1920

Whitaker, T.D. (ed.). *Ralph Thoresby, Ducatus Leodiensis*, 2nd edn, Leeds, 1816

Wilkes, G.A. (ed.). *Fulke Greville, Lord Brooke. The Remaines being poems of Monarchy and Religion*, Oxford University Press, 1965

Wood, J.C. (ed.). Gervase Holles, *Memorials of the Holles Family 1493–1656*, Camden Society, 3rd Series, 55, 1937

SECONDARY WORKS

Appleby, A.B. 'Agrarian Capitalism or Seigneurial Reaction? the Northwest of England, 1500–1700', *The American History Review*, 80 (1975), 574–94

Aylmer, G.E. *The King's Servants. The Civil Service of Charles I, 1625–1642*, Routledge, 1961

Baker, Sir Richard. *A Chronicle of the Kings of England*, London, 1641

Barnard, T.C. 'Land and the Limits of Loyalty: The Second Earl of Cork and First Earl of Burlington (1612–1698)', in Toby Barnard and Jane Clark (eds), *Lord Burlington Architecture, Art and Life*, The Hambledon Press, 1995, pp. 167–99

Birch, T. *The Court and Times of Charles I*, 2 vols, 1848

Blakiston, G. *Woburn and the Russells*, Constable, 1980

Boumphrey, R.S., Hudleston, C.R. and Hughes, J. *An Armorial for Westmorland and Lonsdale*, Cumberland and Westmorland Antiquarian and Archaeological Society, Extra ser., XXI, 1975

Breay, Revd J. *Light in the Dales*, Vols II and III, *The Agrarian Background to the Rise of Political and Religious Dissent in the Northern Dales in the sixteenth and seventeenth Centuries*, Norwich, the Canterbury Press, 1996

Brighton, J.T. *Henry Gyles Virtuoso and Glass Painter of York, 1645–1709*, York Historian, 4, Yorkshire Architectural Society and York Archaeological Society, 1984

Brown, C. 'Van Dyck's Pembroke Family Portrait: An Inquiry into its Italian Sources', in A.K. Wheelock, S.J. Barnes, and J.S. Held, (eds), *Van Dyck's Paintings*, Thames & Hudson, 1991, pp. 37–44.

Brunskill, R.W. The Development of the Small House in the Eden Valley from 1650–1840', *Transactions of the Cumberland and Westmorland Antiquarian and Archaeological Society*, new series, LIII (1953), 160–89

Burkett, M.E. *John Bracken*, Kendal, Abbot Hall, 1980

Butler, R.M. 'Further Information on James Ryther of Harewood', *Yorkshire Archaeological Journal*, 59 (1987), 179–82

Camden, W. *Britannia*, 1610

Charlton, J. *Brougham Castle*, English Heritage, 1988

——. 'The Lady Anne Clifford (1590–1676)', in M.R. Apted, R. Gilyard-Beer and A.D. Saunders (eds), *Ancient Monuments and their Interpretation. Essays presented to A.J. Taylor*, Chichester, Phillimore, 1977, pp. 303–14

Clapham, B. *The Clapham Family*, Hurst Village Publishing, 1993

Clay, J.W. 'The Clifford Family', *Yorkshire Archaeological Journal*, xviii (1905), 355–411

Cliffe, J.T. *The Yorkshire Gentry from the Reformation to the Civil War*, The Athlone Press, 1969

Clifford, H. *The House of Clifford*, Chichester, Phillimore, 1987

Cocke, T. 'Classical or Gothic? Lady Anne Clifford Reconsidered', *Country Life*, 31 Jan. 1980, pp. 324–6

——. 'Repairer of the Breach', *Country Life*, 25 Oct. 1990, pp. 84–6

Collins, A. *Memorials of the Antient and Noble Family of Sackville*, 1742

Coward, B. *The Stanleys Lords Stanley and Earls of Derby 1385–1672*, Chetham Society, 3rd Series, XXX, 1983

Craig, W.J. 'James Ryther of Harewood and his Letters to William Cecil, Lord Burghley', Part I, *Yorkshire Archaeological Journal*, 56, (1984), 95–118

Crawford, P. *Women and Religion in England, 1500–1720*, London, Routledge, 1993

Curwen, J.F. *The Later Records relating to North Westmorland or the Barony of Appleby*, Cumberland and Westmorland Antiquarian and Archaeological Society, Record Series, viii, Kendal, 1932

Dawson, W.H. *History of Skipton*, Skipton, Edmonson, 1882

——. *Loose Leaves of Craven History*, 1st Series, Skipton, Craven Herald, 1891

Dodds, M.H. and R. *The Pilgrimage of Grace, 1536–37, and the Exeter Conspiracy, 1538*, 2 vols, Cass, 1915

Dugdale, Sir W. *Heraldic Miscellanies*, Cadell, 1800

——. *Monasticon*, 3 vols, Sam. Keble, 1693

Erickson, A.L. *Women and Property in Early Modern England*, Routledge, 1993

Gent, T. *History of Ripon*, 1733

Gilson, J.P. *Lives of Lady Anne Clifford Countess of Dorset, Pembroke and Montgomery (1590–1676) and of Her Parents*, Roxburghe Club, 1916

Hamper, W. *The Life, Diary and Correspondence of Sir William Dugdale*, Harding, Lepard, 1827

Hasted, E. *The History and Topographical Survey of the County of Kent*, 12 vols, Canterbury, W. Bristow, 1797–1801

Heal, F. 'The Idea of Hospitality in Early Modern England', *Past and Present*, 102 (1984), 66–93

Heywood, C. 'Portraits of a Lady: Lady Anne Clifford and *Wuthering Heights*', Quarto, XXX, no. 4, Kendal, Abbot Hall Art Gallery, 1993, 10–14

Holdgate, M. *A History of Appleby*, Clapham, Dalesman Books, 1982

Holmes, M.A. 'A Tudor Organ-Case at Appleby-in-Westmorland', *The Antiquaries Journal*, LVII (1979), 320–32

——. *The Parish Churches of Appleby*, Appleby, Parochial Church Council, 1994

——. *Proud Northern Lady. Lady Anne Clifford 1590–1676*, Chichester, Phillimore, reprint, 1984

Houlbrooke, R. *The English Family, 1450–1700*, Longman, 1984

Hudlestone, C.R. and Boumphrey, R.S. *Cumberland Families and Heraldry*, Cumberland and Westmorland Antiquarian and Archaeological Society, Extra Series, XXII, Kendal, 1978

Lockyer, R. *Buckingham*, Longman, 1981

MacMichael, J.H. 'Baynard Castle, and Excavations on its Site', *Journal of the British Archaeological Society*, XLVI (1890), 173–85

MacPherson, S.J. and Slowe, V.A.J. *'Proud Northern Lady'* Lady Anne Clifford 1590–1676, exhibition catalogue, Kendal, Abbot Hall Art Gallery, 1990

Newman, P.R. *Royalist Officers in England and Wales, 1642–1660. A Biographical Dictionary*, New York, Garland, 1981

Nicholls, Revd W. *The History and Traditions of Mallerstang Forest and Pendragon Castle*, Manchester, John Heywood, 1883

Nichols, J. *The Progresses and Public Processions of Queen Elizabeth*, 3 vols, Nichols, 1823

——. *The Progresses of King James The First*, 4 vols, Nichols, 1828

Nicolson, J. and Burn, R. *The History and Antiquities of the Counties of Westmorland and Cumberland*, 2 vols, 1777

Owen, H. *The Lowther Family*, Chichester, Phillimore, 1990

Parker, J. *Books to Build an Empire: A Bibliographical History of English Overseas Interests to 1620*, Amsterdam, N. Israel, 1965

Parry, G. 'The Great Picture of Lady Anne Clifford', in D. Howarth (ed.), *Art and Patronage in the Caroline Court (Essays in honour of Sir Oliver Millar)*, Cambridge University Press, 1993, pp. 202–19

Pevsner, N. *The Buildings of England. Cumberland and Westmorland*, Harmondsworth, Penguin Books, 1980

——. *North Somerset and Bristol*, 1958

Phillips, C.J. *History of the Sackville Family*, 2 vols, Cassell, 1930

Pitcher, J. *Samuel Daniel: The Brotherton Manuscript*, Leeds Texts and Monographs, New Series, 7, University of Leeds School of English, 1981

——. '"In those figures which they seeme": Samuel Daniel's *Tethys' Festival'*, in D. Lindley (ed.), *The Court Masque*, Manchester University Press, 1984, pp. 33–46

Platt, C. *The Great Rebuildings of Tudor and Stuart England*, UCL Press, 1994

Pocock, R. *Memorials of the Family of Tufton, Earls of Thanet*, London, R. Pocock, 1800

Public Record Office, *Lists and Indexes*, IX, 1898

Rabb, T.K. *Enterprise and Empire*, Cambridge, Massachusetts, Harvard University Press, 1967

Redgrave, H.S. *Alchemy: Ancient and Modern*, London, Rider, 1922

Rees, J. *Samuel Daniel*, Liverpool University Press, 1964

Renshaw, W.C. 'Some Clergy of the Archdeaconry of Lewes and South Malling Deanery', *Sussex Archaeological Collections*, LV (1912), 220–77

Round, J.H. *Peerage and Pedigree*, 2 vols, James Nisbet, 1910

Rowse, A.L. *The Elizabethan Renaissance. The Cultural Achievement*, Macmillan, 1972

——. *Simon Forman, Sex and Society in Shakespeare's Age*, Weidenfeld & Nicolson, 1974

Rutherford, T.W.H. *The History of the Parish of Brougham*, 1980

Sackville-West, V. *Knole and the Sackvilles*, Heinemann, 1923

Scargill-Bird, S.R. *A Guide to the Various Classes of Document preserved in the Public Record Office*, 3rd edn, HMSO, 1908

Scull, W.D. 'Bolebroke House', *Sussex Archaeological Collections*, LII (1909), 32–7

Spence, R.T. 'The Cliffords, Earls of Cumberland, 1579–1646: a study of their fortunes based on their household and estate accounts' (unpublished Ph.D. thesis, London University, 1959)

——. 'Clifford Houses: Julian Bower, Westmorland', *The Clifford Association Newsletter*, vol. 2, no. 4 (June, 1991)

——. 'A Noble Funeral in the Great Civil War', *Yorkshire Archaeological Journal*, 65 (1993), 115–23

——. 'Lady Anne Clifford, Countess of Dorset, Pembroke and Montgomery (1590–1676): A Reappraisal', *Northern History*, XV (1979), 44–65

——. 'Mining and Smelting by the Cliffords, Earls of Cumberland, in Westmorland in the early seventeenth century', *Trans. CWAAS*, XCI (1991), 101–17

——. 'Mining and Smelting in Yorkshire by the Cliffords, Earls of Cumberland, in the Tudor and early Stuart Period', *Yorkshire Archaeological Journal*, 64 (1992), 157–83

——. 'The Pacification of the Cumberland Borders, 1593–1628', *Northern History*, XIII (1977), 59–160

——. *The Privateering Earl George Clifford, 3rd Earl of Cumberland, 1558–1605*, Stroud, Alan Sutton Publishing, 1995

——. 'A Royal Progress in the North: James I at Carlisle Castle and the Feast of Brougham, August 1617', *Northern History*, XXVII (1991), 41–89

——. *The Shepherd Lord of Skipton Castle*, Skipton Castle, 1994

——. *Skipton Castle in the Great Civil War, 1642–1645*, Skipton Castle, 1991

Stone, L. *The Crisis of the Aristocracy 1558–1641*, Oxford University Press, 1965

Stow, J. *A Survey of London, 1603*, Dent, Everyman edn, 1970

Sunderland, F.H. *Marmaduke, Lord Langdale*, London, Jenkins, 1926

Thompson, M.M. *Mallerstang*, Appleby, Whitehead, 1965

Tyson, B. 'Who Built the Countess's Pillar at Brougham?', *Trans. CWAAS*, New Series, LXXXVIII (1988), 243–6

Ward J. *Skipton Castle*, 2nd edn, Skipton, Edmundson, 1897

West, W. *Symboleography*, 2 parts, 1618, 1622

Wiffen, J.H. *Historical Memoirs of the House of Russell*, 2 vols, 1833

Whitaker, T.D. *The History and Antiquities of the Deanery of Craven in the County of York*, 3rd edn, ed. Morant, A.W., Leeds, Joseph Dodgson, 1878; reprinted Skipton, 1973.

Williams, F.B. Jr. *Index of Dedications and Commendatory Verses in English Books Before 1641*, Bibliographical Society, 1962

Williamson, G.C. George, *Third Earl of Cumberland (1558–1605) His Life and Voyages*, Cambridge University Press, 1920

——. *Lady Anne Clifford, Countess of Dorset, Pembroke & Montgomery. 1590–1676. Her Life, Letters and Work*, Kendal, Titus Wilson and Son, 1922

Wilton, R.C. 'Historic Londesborough', *Transactions of the East Riding Antiquarian Society*, III (1905), 1–12

Index

Page numbers in italics denote illustrations.